MIND
HACKS™

Other resources from O'Reilly

MIND
HACKS™

Tom Stafford and Matt Webb

Foreword by Steven Johnson

O'REILLY®

Beijing · Cambridge · Farnham · Köln · Sebastopol · Taipei · Tokyo

Mind Hacks™
by Tom Stafford and Matt Webb

Copyright © 2005 O'Reilly Media, Inc. All rights reserved.
Printed in the United States of America.

Published by O'Reilly Media, Inc., 1005 Gravenstein Highway North,
Sebastopol, CA 95472.

O'Reilly books may be purchased for educational, business, or sales promotional use. Online
editions are also available for most titles (*safari.oreilly.com*). For more information, contact our
corporate/institutional sales department: (800) 998-9938 or *corporate@oreilly.com*.

Editor:	Rael Dornfest	**Production Editor:**	Sarah Sherman
Series Editor:	Rael Dornfest	**Cover Designer:**	Hanna Dyer
Executive Editor:	Dale Dougherty	**Interior Designer:**	David Futato

Printing History:

November 2004:   First Edition.

 This book uses Otabind™, a durable and flexible lay-flat binding.

ISBN: 978-0-596-00779-9

[M]   [7/08]

"What to do with too much information
is the great riddle of our time."

—Theodore Zeldin,

An Intimate History of Humanity

Contents

Foreword

Few developments in the brain sciences over the past 20 years have been as crucial as the steady eradication of the brain-as-computer metaphor that dominated so much of our thinking about thinking in the '60s and '70s. Partly the metaphor declined because artificial intelligence turned out to be a vastly more complicated affair than we imagined; partly it declined because we developed new tools for understanding and visualizing the biology of the brain, which didn't look like a microprocessor after all; partly it declined because an influential group of scientists began exploring the vital role of emotion in brain function. It's true the brain contains elements that resemble logic gates of digital computing, and some influential researchers continue to describe the activity of mind as a kind of computation. But for the most part, we now accept the premise that computers and brains are two very different things that happen to share some aptitudes: playing chess, say, or correcting spelling.

At first glance, the book you're holding in your hand might be accused of reviving the old brain-as-computer conceit: "hacks" is a software term, after all, and the previous books in the series have all revolved around digital computing in one form or another. But I think this book belongs instead to a distinctly 21st-century way of thinking about the brain, one we might call—in the language of software design—*user-centric*. The wonders of brain science are no longer something we contemplate exclusively in the lab or the lecture hall; we now explore how the brain works by doing experiments on our own heads. You can explore the architecture and design of your brain just by sampling the many exercises included in the following pages. Consciousness exploration is an old story, of course—one of the oldest—but consciousness exploration with empirical science as your guide is a new one. We've had the age of Freud, of psychedelics, of meditation. This book suggests that a new form of introspection is on the rise, what I've called, in another context, "recreational neuroscience."

I think the idea of a brain hack is a wonderful one, and Matt Webb and Tom Stafford have assembled here a collection of tricks-of-the-mind that will astound you, and give you a new appreciation for the way your brain shapes the reality you perceive. But it's worth pointing out a subtle distinction between the software use of the word "hack" and the way Matt and Tom use it here. In programming, a hack is something we do to an existing tool that gives it some new aptitude that was not part of its original feature set. When we hack a piece of code, we are bending the software to fit our will; we're making it do something its original creators never dreamed of.

The mind hacks that will delight and puzzle you in the coming pages largely work in the opposite direction. When you undergo these experiments, what you're sensing is not your brain's subservience to your will, but rather its weird autonomy. These hacks amaze because they reveal the brain's hidden logic; they shed light on the cheats and shortcuts and latent assumptions our brains make about the world. Most of the time, these mechanisms are invisible to us—or so ubiquitous we no longer notice their existence. A brain hack is a way of pulling back the curtain of consciousness to glimpse—however fleetingly—the machinery on the other side.

This can be a profoundly unsettling experience, precisely because it reveals the way the brain is not always subservient to your will, which very quickly leads you down an existential slide. (Whose will is it anyway?) But it's a journey that anyone interested in the mind cannot afford to miss. Our brains have a kind of life of their own, quite apart from what we think we know about ourselves. That's a scary thought, but being scary doesn't make it any less true. As you read through the coming pages, you'll no doubt find yourself alarmed at the strange cognitive behavior you can trigger just by following a simple set of instructions. But I suspect you'll also find yourself with a new sense of wonder about the mystery of consciousness—along with some killer cocktail party tricks.

So that is the inward adventure that lies before you. May it mess with your head in all the right ways.

—Steven Johnson
Brooklyn, New York

Steven Johnson is the author of *Mind Wide Open: Your Brain and the Neuroscience of Everyday Life* (Scribner).

Credits

About the Authors

Tom Stafford likes finding things out and writing things down. Several years of doing this in the Department of Psychology at the University of Sheffield resulted in a Ph.D. Now sometimes he tells people he's a computational cognitive neuroscientist and then talks excitedly about neural networks. Lately he's begun talking excitedly about social networks too. As well as doing academic research, he has worked freelance, writing and working at the BBC as a documentary researcher. Things he finds interesting he puts on his web site at *http://www.idiolect.org.uk*.

Matt Webb is an engineer and designer, splitting his working life between R&D with BBC Radio & Music Interactive and freelance projects in the social software world. In the past, he's made collaborative online toys, written IM bots, and run a fiction web site (archived at *http://iam.upsideclown.com*); now he's content with hacky web scripts and his weblog, Interconnected, at *http://interconnected.org/home*. Matt reads a little too much, likes the word "cyberspace," lives in London, and tells his mother he's "in computers."

Contributors

The following people contributed to this book:

- Adrian Hon (*http://mssv.net*) graduated from the University of Cambridge with a degree in natural sciences, specialising in neuroscience. He has also researched synaesthesia with Prof. V. S. Ramachandran at the University of California, San Diego, and spent a year at the University of Oxford researching integrative physiology. In the past few years, Adrian has been the cocreator of the NASA award-winning web site Astrobiology: The Living Universe and has spent 2 weeks in the Utah desert in a simulation of a manned mission to Mars (during which time he realised a long-held ambition of wearing a spacesuit). More recently, Adrian has developed a serious interest in alternate reality games and is currently working on Perplex City.

- Alex Fradera (*http://farmerversusfox.blogspot.com*) is a psychology grad student at University College London. He likes to make science seem like fun, but all too often fun seems like science. No matter. When not testing patients or writing programs, he may be found fronting his band, reading comics, or playing capoeira.

- Andy Brown is currently reading for a Ph.D. in developmental cognitive neuropsychology at the University of Sheffield. He has an M.Phil. in psychology (looking at cognitive impairment following stroke) and has also spent 2 years as a research assistant at University College London looking at computer-based interventions within primary care clinical psychology. He is also a photographer (*http://www.envioustime.co.uk*).

- Chris Bird (*http://www.icn.ucl.ac.uk/members/Bird448/*) is a researcher at the Institute of Cognitive Neuroscience in London. He investigates the effects of brain damage on cognition.

- Dr. Christian Beresford Jarrett (*http://www.christianjarrett.btinternet.co.uk*) is writer/editor of the British Psychological Society's *Research Digest* (*http://www.bps.org.uk/publications/rd.cfm*), research associate with the sensorimotor neuroscience group at the University of Manchester, and freelance editor for *Trends in Cognitive Sciences*. He lives in West Yorkshire.

- Disa Sauter (*http://www.psychol.ucl.ac.uk/people/profiles/sauter_disa.htm*) is a Ph.D. student at University College London. She passionately researches emotional sounds, the way in which we laugh, cry, cheer, and grunt. When not in the office, Disa likes to practice yoga and travel.

- Dylan Evans (*http://www.dylan.org.uk*) is the author of several popular science books, including *Emotion: The Science of Sentiment* (Oxford University Press) and *Placebo: The Belief Effect* (HarperCollins). After receiving his Ph.D. in philosophy from the London School of Economics, he did postdoctoral research in philosophy at Kings College London and in robotics at the University of Bath before moving to the University of the West of England, where he is currently senior lecturer in intelligent autonomous systems.

- Ellen Poliakoff (*http://www.psych-sci.manchester.ac.uk/staff/EllenPoliakoff*) is a lecturer in psychology at the University of Manchester and enjoys working somewhere between psychology and neuroscience. In her free time, she enjoys, among other things, visiting stone circles and playing in a band (*http://www.stray-light.co.uk*).

- Iain Price (*http://www.iain-price.com*) studied the neurosciences for his bachelor and doctorate degrees at Cardiff University. He is now pursuing science communication projects in conjunction with his continued fascination with the philosophies of the human mind. Recently he has helped to develop and present the BBC's community outreach events to accompany *The Human Mind* TV series (*http://www.open2.net/humanmind*).

- Karen Bunday (*k.bunday@imperial.ac.uk*) is studying for a Ph.D. in movement and balance at Imperial College London, having already graduated with a B.Sc. in psychology from Royal Holloway, University of London. She has been published as a coauthor in the journal *Current Biology* and is currently writing two papers based on her own Ph.D. research for future publication.

- Michael Bach, Ph.D. (*http://www.michaelbach.de*), holds a professorship in neurobiophysics, running the section functional vision research in ophthalmology, at the Medical School of the University of Freiburg, Germany. He is happily married and has three children. Professionally, he provides electrodiagnostic services for patients with eye diseases, and is interested in basic and applied vision research, thus covering both physiology and pathophysiology of visual perception. His hobbies include reading, swimming, programming optical illusions, riding his recumbent bike, and in winter snowboarding or skiing. His web site demonstrates and explains many interesting optical illusions and visual phenomena (*http://www.michaelbach.de/ot/index.html*).

- Mike Bywaters

- Myles Jones is a lecturer in psychology at the University of Sheffield (*http://www.shef.ac.uk.spinsn/*). His main research interest is understanding the relationship between neuroimaging signals and the underlying neural activity.

- Nicol Spencer Harper is a CoMPLEX Ph.D. student in the physiology department of University College London. His main interest is neural coding in the auditory system—how the electrochemical impulses in our brain represent sounds in the world. His other interests include eating and sleeping.

- Dr Sarah-Jayne Blakemore is a Royal Society Research Fellow at the Institute of Cognitive Neuroscience at University College London. Her current research focuses on the brain mechanisms underlying social interaction in autism and the development of social understanding during adolescence. She read experimental psychology at Oxford and then went on to complete a Ph.D. in neuroscience at UCL in 2000. She frequently gives talks about the brain in schools, writes articles about her research in newspapers, and gives interviews on the television and radio.

- Suparna Choudhury is studying cognitive development during adolescence for her Ph.D. research at the Institute of Child Health, University College London, having completed a B.Sc. in neuroscience. Her research focuses on the development of perspective-taking and motor imagery. She is also interested in phenomenology and philosophy of mind and is involved in public understanding of science.
- Vaughan Bell (*http://www.cf.ac.uk/psych/home/bellv1*) is a researcher and visiting lecturer at Cardiff University, where he is involved in teaching and studying psychology, mostly in an attempt to better understand mental illness and brain injury. Particularly, he works with members of the public and with staff and patients at local hospitals, as part of an ongoing research project investigating the neuropsychology of belief, anomalous experience, psychosis, and delusions. He is not without a few delusions of his own, so generally feels quite at home.
- William Bardel (*http://www.bardel.info*) is an information designer living in the United States, specializing in information graphics, mapping/wayfinding, and design strategy. His work involves making complex ideas simple and accessible through structure. Will holds a master of design degree in the fields of communication planning and information design from Carnegie Mellon University, and a B.A. in English from Kenyon College; he has studied information design at the Rhode Island School of Design SIGDS.

Acknowledgments

We would like to thank all those who contributed their ideas, hacks, expertise, and time to this book. To all those who share their research and demonstrations online: you're doing a wonderful thing.

Rael Dornfest has been our editor and guide. We've traveled a long way, and we wouldn't have come even close to this point without him or, indeed, without the rest of the O'Reilly team. Thanks all.

Our technical editors and advisors have been absolute stars. Thanks for watching out for us. And of course, James Cronin, who, in Helsinki, provided both the wine and conversation necessary to conceive this book.

Many thanks to the BBC for being flexible and employing us both (in different capacities) part-time over the past few months. Thanks also to our colleagues and friends there and for Radio 4.

Amongst the many applications we've used, throughout planning, researching, and writing, the MoinMoin Python WikiClone (*http://moin.sourceforge.net*) has been the most valuable.

Oh, we must acknowledge the role of tea. So much tea. Possibly too much, it has to be said.

Tom

Matt was the best coauthor I could imagine having—thanks for getting me on board and for seeing us through. It's been both an education and great fun.

I'd like to thank all my lecturers, friends, and colleagues in the department of psychology at the University of Sheffield. It was there that I acquired an appreciation of just what a good account of mind might be, and how exciting the endeavor to provide it is.

I couldn't have made it without my family and friends—old, new, nearby, and far away. I am astoundingly grateful to everyone who took me out, shared time with me, fed and watered me, sheltered me, and was kind enough to indulge my occasionally overexcited blather. I have too much gratitude to be able to list names individually, but I'm sure you all know who you are.

Special thanks to my brother Jon, to Nicol who was always there and who always understood, and to Dan and Gemma who have been taking me out to play while I've been in London and who are both inspirational in their own way.

Matt

When I've read the effusive thanks and apologies authors give to their loved ones, I must admit I've thought it a little overdone. It turns out it's not. Thank you, Ehsan.

Second, if you get a chance to go for a drink with Tom, don't turn it down. Our weekly breakfast meetings over the summer have been mind-blowing.

For the record, my last point, the surface of my light cone is enveloping the star system *p Eridani* in the hours I write these words. *p Eridani*, hello!

What would these people reccomend I pursue in college?

Preface

Think for a moment about all that's happening while you read this text: how your eyes move to center themselves on the words, how you idly scratch your arm while you're thinking, the attention-grabbing movements, noises, and other distractions you're filtering out. How does all this work? As one brain speaking to another, here's a secret: it isn't easy.

The brain is a fearsomely complex information-processing environment. Take the processing involved in seeing, for instance. One of the tasks involved in seeing is detecting the motion in every tiny portion of vision, in such and such a direction and at such and such a speed, and representing that in the brain. But another task is seeing a face in the light that falls on the retina, figuring out what emotion it's showing, and representing that concept in the brain, somehow, too.

To an extent, the brain is modular, so that should give us a way in, but it's not that clean-cut. The processing subsystems of the brain are layered on top of one another, but their functionality mingles rather than being organized in a distinct progression. Often the same task is performed in many different places, in many different ways. It's not a clear mechanical system like clock-work or like a computer program; giving the same input won't always give the same output. Automatic and voluntary actions are highly meshed, often inextricable. Parts of vision that appear fully isolated from conscious experience suddenly report different results if conscious expectations change.

The information transforms [*mations*] in the brain are made yet more complicated by the constraints of history, computation, and architecture. Development over evolutionary time has made it hard for the brain to backtrack; the structure of the brain must reflect its growth and repurposing. Computation has to occur as fast as possible—we're talking subsecond responses—but there are limits on the speed at which information can travel between physical parts of the brain. These are all constraints to be worked with.

All of which leaves us with one question: how can we possibly start to understand what's going on?

Cognitive neuroscience is the study of the brain biology behind our mental functions. It is a collection of methods (like brain scanning and computational modeling) combined with a way of looking at psychological phenomena and discovering where, why, and how the brain makes them happen. It is neither classic neuroscience—a low-level tour of the biology of the brain—nor is it what many people think of as psychology—a metaphorical exploration of human inner life; rather, it's a view of the mind that looks at the fundamental elements and rules, acting moment by moment, that makes up conscious experience and action.

By focusing both on the biological substrate and on the high-level phenomenon of consciousness, we can pick apart the knot of the brain. This picking apart is why you don't need to be a cognitive neuroscientist to reap the fruit of the field.

This book is a collection of probes into the moment-by-moment works of the brain. It's not a textbook—more of a buffet, really. Each hack is one probe into the operation of the brain, one small demonstration. By seeing how the brain responds, we pick up traces of the structures present and the design decision made, learning a little bit more about how the brain is put together.

Simultaneously we've tried to show how there isn't a separation between the voluntary "me" feeling of the mind and the automatic nature of the brain—the division between voluntary and automatic behavior is more of an ebb and flow, and we wield our cognitive abilities with unconscious flourishes and deliberate movements much as we wield, say, our hands, or a pen, or a lathe.

In a sense, we're trying to understand the capabilities that underpin the mind. Say we understand to what extent the holes in our vision are continually covered up or what sounds and lights will—without a doubt—grab our attention (and also what won't): we'll be able to design better tools, and create better interfaces that work with the grain of our mental architecture and not against it. We'll be able to understand ourselves a little better; know a little more, in a very real sense, about what makes us tick.

Plus it's fun. That's the key. Cognitive neuroscience is a fairly new discipline. The journey into the brain is newly available and an enjoyable ride. The effects we'll see are real enough, but the explanations of why they occur are still being debated. We're taking part in the mapping of this new territory just by playing along. Over the course of writing this book, we've spent time noticing our own attention systems darting about the room, seen ourselves catching gestures from people we've been talking to, and played games with the color of traffic and peripheral vision. That's the fun bit. But we've also been gripped by the arguments in the scientific literature and have had new insights into facets of our everyday lives, such as why some web sites are annoying and certain others are particularly well-made. If, through this book, we've managed to make that world a little more accessible too, then we've succeeded. And when you've had a look around and found new ways to apply these ideas and, yes, new topics we've not touched on, please do let us know. We're here for the ride too.

Why Mind Hacks?

The term *"hacking"* has a bad reputation in the media. They use it to refer to those who break into systems or wreak havoc with computers as their weapons. Among people who write code, though, the term *"hack"* refers to a "quick-and-dirty" solution to a problem, or a clever way to get something done. And the term *"hacker"* is taken very much as a compliment, referring to someone as being *"creative,"* having the technical chops to get things done. The Hacks series is an attempt to reclaim the word, document the good ways people are hacking, and pass the hacker ethic of creative participation on to the uninitiated. Seeing how others approach systems and problems is often the quickest way to learn about a new technology.

The brain, like all hidden systems, is prime territory for curious hackers. Thanks to relatively recent developments in cognitive neuroscience, we're able to satisfy a little of that curiosity, making educated explanations for psychological effects rather than just pointing those effects out, throwing light on the internal workings of the brain.

Some of the hacks in this collection document the neat tricks the brain has used to get the job done. Looking at the brain from the outside like this, it's hard not to be impressed at the way it works. Other hacks point to quirks of our own minds that we can exploit in unexpected ways, and that's all part of learning our way round the wrinkles in this newly exposed technology.

Mind Hacks is for people who want to know a bit more about what's going on inside their own heads and for people who are going to assemble the hacks in new ways, playing with the interface between ourselves and the world. It's wonderfully easy to get involved. We've all got brains, after all.

How to Use This Book

You can read this book from cover to cover if you like, but each hack stands on its own, so feel free to browse and jump to the different sections that interest you most. If there's a prerequisite you need to know, a cross-reference will guide you to the right hack.

We've tried out all the demonstrations in this book, so we know that for most people they work just as we say they do; these are real phenomena. Indeed, some are surprising, and we didn't believe they'd work until we tried them ourselves. The explanations are summaries of the current state of knowledge—often snapshots of debates in progress. Keep an open mind about these. There's always the chance future research will cause us to revise our understanding.

Often, because there is so much research on each topic, we have linked to web sites, books, and academic papers to find out more. Follow these up. They're fantastic places to explore the wider story behind each hack, and will take you to interesting places and appear interesting connections.

With regard to academic papers, these are bedrock of scientific knowledge. They can be hard to get and hard to understand, but we included references to them because they are the place to go if you really need to get to the bottom of a story (and to find the cutting edge). What's more, for many scientists, evidence doesn't really exist until it has been published in a scientific journal. For this to happen, the study has to be reviewed by other scientists working in the field, in a system called peer review. Although this system has biases, and mistakes are made, it is this that makes science a collective endeavor and provides a certain guarantee of quality.

The way journal articles are cited is quite precise, and in this book we've followed the American Psychological Association reference style (*http://www.apastyle.org*). Each looks something like this:

- Lettvin, J., Maturana, H., McCulloch, W., & Pitts, W. (1959). What the frog's eye tells the frog's brain. *Proceedings of the IRE, 47*(11), 1940–1951.

Before the year of publication (which is in parentheses), the authors are listed. After the year is the title of the paper, followed by the journal in which you'll find it, in italics. The volume (in italics) and then the issue number (in parentheses) follow. Page numbers come last. (There's a crib sheet online: *http://www.liu.edu/cwis/cwp/library/workshop/citapa.htm*.) One convention you'll often see in the text is "et al." after the main author of a paper. This is shorthand for "and others."

Many, but not all, journals have an electronic edition, and some you can access for free. Most are subscription-based, although some publishers will let you pay per paper. If you go to a library, generally a university library, make sure it not only subscribes to the journal you want, but also has the year in which the paper you're after was published.

If you're lucky, the paper will also be reprinted online. This is often the case with classic papers and with recent papers, which the authors may have put on their publications page. A good query to use at Google (*http://www.google.com*) for papers online in PDF format using a query like:

```
"What the Frog's Eye Tells the Frog's Brain" filetype:pdf
```

Alternately, search for a researcher's name followed by the word "publications" for papers, demonstrations, and as-yet-unpublished research, a gold mine if you're learning more about a particular topic.

Recommended Reading

If you're interested in getting a general overview, rather than chasing the details of a particular story, you might like to start by reading a book on the subject. Here are some of our favorite books on our own pet topics, all of which make specialist material accessible for the rest of us:

- *Descartes' Baby: How the Science of Child Development Explains What Makes Us Human* by Paul Bloom (2004). Lively speculation from a leading researcher.

- *Natural-Born Cyborgs: Minds, Technologies, and the Future of Human Intelligence* by Andy Clark (2003). Clark asks whether intelligence is bounded by our skulls or is part of the tools and technologies we use.

- *Symbolic Species: The Co-Evolution of Language and the Brain* by Terrence Deacon (1997). A dizzying, provocative integration of information across different disciplines.

- *Consciousness Explained* by Daniel Dennett (1991). Psychologically informed philosophy. Consciousness isn't explained by the end, but it's a fun ride along the way.

- *Eye and Brain: The Psychology of Seeing* by Richard Gregory (1966). Erudite and good-humored—a classic introduction to vision.

- *The Nurture Assumption: Why Children Turn Out the Way They Do* by Judith Rich Harris (1998). The Evolutionary Psychology of child development, a great read that challenges the assumption that parents are the most important influence in a child's life. See also the web site at: *http://home.att.net/~xchar/tna.*

- *Mind Wide Open: Your Brain and the Neuroscience of Everyday Life* by Steven Johnson (2004). How the latest developments in brain science and technology inform our individual self-understanding.

- *The Language Instinct: How the Mind Creates Language* by Steven Pinker (1995). Compelling argument for our innate language ability and brain structure being reflected in each other.

- *Phantoms in the Brain: Probing the Mysteries of the Human Mind* by V. S. Ramachandran & Sandra Blakeslee (1998). Tales of what brain injury can tell us about the way the brain works.
- *The Man Who Mistook His Wife for a Hat and Other Clinical Tales* by Oliver Sacks (1995). Informative and humane anecdotes about patients with different kinds of brain damage.

If you're looking for something a little deeper, we recommend you try:

- *The Oxford Companion to the Mind*, edited by Richard Gregory (1999). Authoritative and entertaining collection of essays on all aspects of the brain.
- *Godel, Escher, Bach: an Eternal Golden Braid* by Douglas Hofstadter (1979). The classic exploration of minds, machines, and the mathematics of self-reference. The back of my copy rightly says "a workout in the finest mental gymnasium in town."
- *How to Think Straight About Psychology* by Keith Stanovich (1997). How to apply critical thinking to psychological topics.

How This Book Is Organized

The book is divided into 10 chapters, organized by subject:

Chapter 1, *Inside the Brain*

The question is not just "How do we look inside the brain?" but "How do we talk about what's there once we can see it?" There are a number of ways to get an idea about how your brain is structured (from measuring responses on the outside to taking pictures of the inside)—that's half of this chapter. The other half speaks to the second question: we'll take in some of the sights, check out the landmarks, and explore the geography of the brain.

Chapter 2, *Seeing*

The visual system runs all the way from the way we move our eyes to how we reconstruct and see movement from raw images. Sight's an important sense to us; it's high bandwidth and works over long distances (unlike, say, touch), and that's reflected in the size of this chapter.

Chapter 3, *Attention*

One of the mechanisms we use to filter information before it reaches conscious awareness is attention. Attention is sometimes voluntary (you can pay attention) and sometimes automatic (things can be attention-grabbing)—here we're looking at what it does and some of its limitations.

Chapter 4, *Hearing and Language*

Sounds usually correspond to events; a noise usually means something's just happened. We'll have a look at what our ears are good for, then move on to language and some of the ways we find meaning in words and sentences.

Chapter 5, *Integrating*

It's rare we operate using just a single sense; we make full use of as much information as we can find, integrating sight, touch, our propensity for language, and other inputs. When senses agree, our perception of the world is sharper. We'll look at how we mix up modes of operating (and how we can't help doing so, even when we don't mean to) and what happens when senses disagree.

Chapter 6, *Moving*

This chapter covers the body—how the image the brain has of our body is easy to confuse and also how we use our body to interact with the world. There's an illusion you can walk around, and we'll have a little look at handedness too.

Chapter 7, *Reasoning*

We're not built to be perfect logic machines; we're shaped to get on as well as possible in the world. Sometimes that shows up in the kind of puzzles we're good at and the sort of things we're duped by.

Chapter 8, *Togetherness*

The senses give us much to go by, to reconstruct what's going on in the universe. We can't perceive cause and effect directly, only that two things happen at roughly the same time in roughly the same place. The same goes for complex objects: why see a whole person instead of a torso, head, and collection of limbs? Our reconstruction of objects and causality follow simple principles, which we use in this chapter.

Chapter 9, *Remembering*

We wouldn't be human if we weren't continually learning and changing, becoming different people. This chapter covers how learning begins at the level of memory over very short time periods (minutes, usually). We'll also look at how a few of the ways we learn and remember manifest themselves.

Chapter 10, *Other People*

Other people are a fairly special part of our environment, and it's fair to say our brains have special ways of dealing with them. We're great at reading emotions, and we're even better at mimicking emotions and other people in general—so good we often can't help it. We'll cover both of those.

Conventions Used in This Book

The following typographical conventions are used in this book:

Italics

> Used to indicate URLs, filenames, filename extensions, and directory/folder names. For example, a path in the filesystem will appear as */Developer/Applications*.

Color

> The second color is used to indicate a cross-reference within the text.

You should pay special attention to notes set apart from the text with the following icons:

> This is a tip, suggestion, or general note. It contains useful supplementary information about the topic at hand.

> This is a warning or note of caution, often indicating that your money or your privacy might be at risk.

> This is an aside, a tangential or speculative comment. We thought it interesting, although not essential.

Using Material from This Book

We appreciate, but do not require, attribution. An attribution usually includes the title, author, publisher, and ISBN. For example: "*Mind Hacks* by Tom Stafford and Matt Webb. Copyright 2005 O'Reilly Media, Inc., 0-596-00779-5."

If you feel your use of material from this book falls outside fair use or the permission given earlier, feel free to contact us at *permissions@oreilly.com*.

How to Contact Us

We have tested and verified the information in this book to the best of our ability, but you may find that there's new experimental evidence or that the prevailing scientific understanding has changed. As a reader of this book, you can help us to improve future editions by sending us your feedback. Please let us know about any errors, inaccuracies, bugs, misleading or confusing statements, and typos that you find anywhere in this book.

Please also let us know what we can do to make this book more useful to you. We take your comments seriously and will try to incorporate reasonable suggestions into future editions. You can write to us at:

O'Reilly Media, Inc.
1005 Gravenstein Highway North
Sebastopol, CA 95472
(800) 998-9938 (in the U.S. or Canada)
(707) 829-0515 (international/local)
(707) 829-0104 (fax)

To ask technical questions or to comment on the book, send email to:

bookquestions@oreilly.com

Mind Hacks has its own web site with more about and beyond this book, as well as a *Mind Hacks* weblog:

http://www.mindhacks.com

The O'Reilly web page for *Mind Hacks* lists examples, errata, and plans for future editions. You can find this page at:

http://www.oreilly.com/catalog/mindhks

For more information about this book and others, see the O'Reilly web site:

http://www.oreilly.com

Got a Hack?

To explore Hacks books online or to contribute a hack for future titles, visit:

http://hacks.oreilly.com

Inside the Brain
Hacks 1–12

It's never entirely true to say, "This bit of the brain is solely responsible for function X." Take the visual system [Hack #13], for instance; it runs through many varied parts of the brain with no single area solely responsible for all of vision. Vision is made up of lots of different subfunctions, many of which will be compensated for if areas become unavailable. With some types of brain damage, it's possible to still be able to see, but not be able to figure out what's moving or maybe not be able to see what color things are.

What we can do is look at which parts of the brain are active while it is performing a particular task—anything from recognizing a face to playing the piano—and make some assertions. We can provide input and see what output we get—the black box approach to the study of mind. Or we can work from the outside in, figuring out which abilities people with certain types of damaged brains lack.

The latter, part of neuropsychology [Hack #6], is an important tool for psychologists. Small, isolated strokes can deactivate very specific brain regions, and also (though more rarely) accidents can damage small parts of the brain. Seeing what these people can no longer do in these pathological cases, provides good clues into the functions of those regions of the brain. Animal experimentation, purposely removing pieces of the brain to see what happens, is another.

These are, however, pathology-based methods—less invasive techniques are available. Careful experimentation—measuring response types, reaction times, and response changes to certain stimuli over time—is one such alternative. That's cognitive psychology [Hack #1], the science of making deductions about the structure of the brain through reverse engineering from the outside. It has a distinguished history. More recently we've been able to go one step further. Pairing techniques from cognitive psychology with imaging methods and stimulation techniques   [Hacks #2 through #5], we can manipulate and look at the brain from the outside, without having to, say, remove the skull and pull a bit of the cerebrum out. These imaging methods are so important and referred to so much in the rest of this book, we've provided an overview and short explanation for some of the most common techniques in this chapter.

In order that the rest of the book make sense, after looking at the various neuroscience techniques, we take a short tour round the central nervous system [Hack #7], from the spine, to the brain [Hack #8], and then down to the individual neuron [Hack #9] itself. But what we're really interested in is how the biology manifests in everyday life. What does it really mean for our decision-making systems to be assembled from neurons rather than, well, silicon, like a computer? What it means is that we're not software running on hardware. The two are one and the same, the physical properties of our mental substrate continually leaking into everyday life: the telltale sign of our neurons is evident when we respond faster to brighter lights [Hack #11], and our biological roots show through when blood flow has to increase because we're thinking so hard [Hack #10].

And finally take a gander at a picture of the body your brain thinks you have and get in touch with your inner sensory homunculus [Hack #12].

Find Out How the Brain Works Without Looking Inside

How do you tell what's inside a black box without looking in it? This is the challenge the mind presents to cognitive psychology.

Cognitive psychology is the psychology of the basic mental processes—things like perception, attention, memory, language, decision-making. It asks the question, "What are the fundamental operations on which mind is based?"

The problem is, although you can measure what goes into someone's head (the input) and measure roughly what they do (the output), this doesn't tell you anything about what goes on in between. It's a black box, a classic reverse engineering problem.[1] How can we figure out how it works without looking at the code?

These days, of course, we can use neuroimaging (like EEG [Hack #2], PET [Hack #3], and fMRI [Hack #4]) to look inside the head at the brain, or use information on anatomy and information from brain-damaged individuals [Hack #6] to inform how we think the brain runs the algorithms that make up the mind. But this kind of work hasn't always been possible, and it's never been easy or cheap. Experimental psychologists have spent more than a hundred years refining methods for getting insight into how the mind works without messing with the insides, and these days we call this cognitive psychology.

There's an example of a cognitive psychology–style solution in another book from the hacks series, *Google Hacks* (*http://www.oreilly.com/catalog/googlehks*). Google obviously doesn't give access to the algorithms that run its searches, so the authors of *Google Hacks*, Tara Calishain and Rael Dornfest, were forced to do a little experimentation to try and work it out. Obviously, if you put in two words, Google returns pages that feature both words. But does the order matter? Here's an experiment. Search Google for "reverse engineering" and then search for "engineering reverse." The results are different; in fact, they are sometimes different even when searching for words that aren't normally taken together as some form of phrase. So we might conclude that order does make a difference; in some way, the Google search algorithm takes into account the order. If you try to whittle a search down to the right terms, something that returned only a couple of hits, perhaps over time you could figure out more exactly how the order mattered.

This is basically what cognitive psychology tries to do, reverse engineering the basic functions of the mind by manipulating the inputs and looking at the results. The inputs are often highly restricted situations in which people are asked to make judgments or responses in different kinds of situations. *How many words from the list you learned yesterday can you still remember? How many red dots are there? Press a key when you see an X appear on the screen.* That sort of thing. The speed at which they respond, the number of errors, or the patterns of recall or success tell us something about the information our cognitive processes use, and how they use it.

A few things make reverse engineering the brain harder than reverse engineering software, however.

Biological systems are often complex, sometimes even chaotic (in the technical sense). This means that there isn't necessarily a one-to-one correspondence in how a change in input affects output. In a logic-based or linear system, we can clearly see causes and effects. The mind, however, doesn't have this orderly mapping. Small things have big effects and sometimes big changes in circumstance can produce little obvious difference in how we respond. Biological functions—including cognition—are often supported by multiple processes. This means they are robust to changes in just one supporting process, but it also means that they don't always respond how you would have thought when you try and influence them.

People also aren't consistent in the same way software or machines usually are. Two sources of variability are noise and learning. We don't automatically respond in the same way to the same stimulus every time. This sometimes happens for no apparent reason, and we call this randomness *noise*. But sometimes our responses change for a reason, not because of noise, and that's because the very act of responding first time around creates feedback that informs our response pattern for the next time (for example, when you get a new bike, you're cautious with your stopping distance at first, but each time you have to stop suddenly, you're better informed about how to handle the braking next time around). Almost all actions affect future processing, so psychologists make sure that if they are testing someone the test subject has either done the thing in question many times before, and hence stopped changing his response to it, or he has never done it before.

Another problem with trying to guess how the mind works is that you can't trust people when they offer their opinion on *why* they did something or *how* they did it. At the beginning of the twentieth century, psychology relied heavily on introspection and the confusion generated led to the movement that dominated psychology until the '70s: behaviorism. *Behaviorism* insisted that we treat only what we can reliably measure as part of psychology and excluded all reference to internal structures. In effect we were to pretend that psychology was just the study of how stimuli were linked to outputs. This made psychology much more rigorous experimentally (although some would argue less interesting). Psychology today recognizes the need to posit mind as more than simple stimulus-response matching, although cognitive psychologists retain the behaviorists' wariness of introspection. For cognitive psychologists, why you think you did something is just another bit of data, no more privileged than anything else they've measured, and no more likely to be right.2

Cognitive psychology takes us a long way. Many phenomena discovered by cognitive and experimental psychology are covered in this book—things like the attentional blink [Hack #39] and state-dependent recall [Hack #87]. The rigor and precision of the methods developed by cognitive psychology are still vital, but now they can be used in tandem with methods that give insight into the underlying brain structure and processes that are supporting the phenomenon being investigated.

End Notes

1. Daniel Dennett has written a brief essay called "Cognitive Science as Reverse Engineering" (*http://pp.kpnet.fi/seirioa/cdenn/cogscirv.htm*) in which he discusses the philosophy of this approach to mind.

2. A psychologist called Daryl Bem formalized this in "self-perception theory." He said "Individuals come to know their own attitudes, emotions and internal states by inferring them from observations of their own behavior and circumstances in which they occur. When internal cues are weak, ambiguous, or uninterpretable, the individual is in the same position as the outside observer." Bem, D. J., "Self Perception Theory." In L. Berkowitz (ed.), *Advances in Experimental Social Psychology*, volume 6 (1972).

H A C K
#2
Electroencephalogram: Getting the Big Picture with EEGs

EEGs give you an overall picture of the timing of brain activity but without any fine detail.

An *electroencephalogram* (EEG) produces a map of the electrical activity on the surface of the brain. Fortunately, the surface is often what we're interested in, as the cortex—responsible for our complex, high-level functions—is a thin sheet of cells on the brain's outer layer. Broadly, different areas contribute to different abilities, so one particular area might be associated with grammar, another with motion detection. Neurons send signals to one another using electrical impulses, so we can get a good measure of the activity of the neurons (how busy they are doing the work of processing) by measuring the electromagnetic field nearby. Electrodes outside the skull on the surface of the skin are close enough to take readings of these electromagnetic fields.

Small metal disks are evenly placed on the head, held on by a conducting gel. The range can vary from two to a hundred or so electrodes, all taking readings simultaneously. The output can be a simple graph of signals recorded at each electrode or visualised as a map of the brain with activity called out.

Pros

- The EEG technique is well understood and has been in use for many decades. Patterns of electrical activity corresponding to different states are now well-known: sleep, epilepsy, or how the visual cortex responds when the eyes are in use. It is from EEG that we get the concepts of alpha, beta, and gamma waves, related to three kinds of characteristic oscillations in the signal.

- Great time resolution. A reading of electrical activity can be taken every few milliseconds, so the brain's response to stimuli can be precisely plotted.

- Relatively cheap. Home kits are readily available. OpenEEG (*http://openeeg.sourceforge.net*), EEG for the rest of us, is a project to develop low-cost EEG devices, both hardware and software.

Cons

- Poor spatial resolution. You can take only as many readings in space as electrodes you attach (up to 100, although 40 is common). Even if you are recording from many locations, the electrical signals from the scalp don't give precise information on where they originate in the brain. You are getting only information from the surface of the skull and cannot perfectly infer what and where the brain activity was that generated the signals. In effect this means that it's useful for looking at overall activity or activity in regions no more precise than an inch or so across.

—*Myles Jones & Matt Webb*

Positron Emission Tomography: Measuring Activity Indirectly with PET

PET is a radioactivity-based technique to build a detailed 3D model of the brain and its activity.

Positron emission tomography (PET) is more invasive than any of the other imaging techniques. It requires getting a radioactive chemical into the bloodstream (by injection) and watching for where in the brain the radioactivity ends up—the "positron emission" of the name. The level of radioactivity is not dangerous, but this technique should not be used on the same person on a regular basis.

When neurons fire to send a signal to other neurons, they metabolize more energy. A few seconds later, fresh blood carrying more oxygen and glucose is carried to the region. Using a radioactive isotope of water, the amount of blood flow to each brain location can be monitored, and the active areas of the brain that require a lot of energy and therefore blood flow can be deduced.

Pros

- A PET scan will produce a 3D model of brain activity.

Cons

- Scans have to take place in bulky, expensive machinery, which contain the entire body.
- PET requires injecting the subject with a radioactive chemical.
- Although the resolution of images has improved over the last 30 years, PET still doesn't produce as fine detail as other techniques (it can see activity about 1 cm across).
- PET isn't good for looking at how brain activity changes over time. A snapshot can take minutes to be assembled.

—*Myles Jones & Matt Webb*

HACK #4 Functional Magnetic Resonance Imaging: The State of the Art

fMRI produces high-resolution animations of the brain in action.

Functional magnetic resonance imaging (fMRI) is the king of brain imaging. Magnetic resonance imaging is noninvasive and has no known side effects—except, for some, claustrophobia. Having an MRI scan requires you to lie inside a large electromagnet in order to be exposed to the high magnetic field necessary. It's a bit like being slid inside a large white coffin. It gets pretty noisy too.

The magnetic field pushes the hydrogen atoms in your brain into a state in which they all "line up" and spin at the same frequency. A radio frequency pulse is applied at this exact frequency, making the molecules "resonate" and then emit radio waves as they lose energy and return to "normal." The signal emitted depends on what type of tissue the molecule is in. By recording these signals, a 3D map of the anatomy of the brain is built up.

MRI isn't a new technology (it's been possible since the '70s), but it's been applied to psychology with BOLD functional MRI (abbreviated to fMRI) only as recently as 1992. To obtain functional images of the brain, BOLD (blood oxygen level dependent) fMRI utilizes the fact that deoxygenated blood is magnetic (because of the iron in hemoglobin) and therefore makes the MRI image darker. When neurons become active, fresh blood washes away the deoxygenated blood in the precise regions of the brain that have been more active than usual.

While structural MRI can take a long time, fMRI can take a snapshot of activity over the whole brain every couple of seconds, and the resolution is still higher than with PET [Hack #3]. It can view activity in volumes of the brain only 2 mm across and build a whole map of the brain from that. For a particular experiment, a series of fMRI snapshots will be animated over a single high-resolution MRI scan, and experimenters can see in exactly which brain areas activity is taking place.

Much of the cognitive neuroscience research done now uses fMRI. It's a method that is still developing and improving, but already producing great results.

Pros

- High spatial resolution and good enough time resolution to look at changing patterns of activity. While not able to look at the changing brain as easily as EEG [Hack #2], its far greater spatial resolution means fMRI is suitable for looking at which parts of the brain are active in the process of recalling a fact, for example, or seeing a face.

Cons

- Bulky, highly magnetic, and very expensive machinery.

- fMRI is still new. It's a complex technique requiring computing power and a highly skilled team with good knowledge both of physics and of the brain.

—Myles Jones & Matt Webb

HACK #5 Transcranial Magnetic Stimulation: Turn On and Off Bits of the Brain

Stimulate or suppress specific regions of the brain, then sit back and see what happens.

Transcranial magnetic stimulation (TMS) isn't an imaging technique like EEG [Hack #2] or fMRI [Hack #4], but it can be used along with them. TMS uses a magnetic pulse or oscillating magnetic fields to temporarily induce or suppress electrical activity in the brain. It doesn't require large machines, just a small device around the head, and—so far as we know—it's harmless with no aftereffects.

Neurons communicate using electrical pulses, so being able to produce electrical activity artificially has its advantages. Selected regions can be excited or suppressed, causing hallucinations or partial blindness if some part of the visual cortex is being targeted. Both uses help discover what specific parts of the brain are for. If the subject experiences a muscle twitching, the TMS has probably stimulated some motor control neurons, and causing hallucinations at different points in the visual system can be used to discover the order of processing (it has been used to discover where vision is cut out during saccades [Hack #17], for example).

Preventing a region from responding is also useful: if shutting down neurons in a particular area of the cortex stops the subject from recognizing motion, that's a good clue as to the function of that area. This kind of discovery was possible before only by finding people with localized brain damage; now TMS allows more structured experiments to take place.

Coupled with brain imaging techniques, it's possible to see the brain's response to a magnetic pulse ripple through connected areas, revealing its structure.

Pros

- Affects neural activity directly, rather than just measuring it.

Cons

- Apparently harmless, although it's still early days.

See Also

- "Savant For a Day" by Lawrence Osbourne (*http://www.nytimes.com/ 2003/06/22/magazine/22SAVANT.html* or *http://www.cognitiveliberty. org/neuro/TMS_NYT.html*, an alternative URL), an article in the *New York Times*, which describes Lawrence Osborne's experience of TMS, having higher-level functions of his brain suppressed, and a different type of intelligence exposed.

—Myles Jones & Matt Webb

HACK #6 Neuropsychology, the 10% Myth, and Why You Use All of Your Brain

Neuropsychology is the study of what different parts of the brain do by studying people who no longer have those parts. As well as being the oldest technique of cognitive neuroscience, it refutes the oft-repeated myth that we only use 10% of our brains.

Of the many unscientific nuggets of wisdom about the brain that many people believe, the most common may be the "fact" that we use only 10% of our brains.

In a recent survey of people in Rio de Janeiro with at least a college education, approximately half stated that the 10% myth was true.[1] There is no reason to suppose the results of a similar survey conducted anywhere else in the world would be radically different. It's not surprising that a lot of people believe this myth, given how often it is claimed to be true. Its continued popularity has prompted one author to state that the myth has "a shelf life longer than lacquered Spam".[2]

> **Where does this rather popular belief come from?**
>
> It's hard to find out how the myth started. Some people say that something like it was said by Einstein, but there isn't any proof. The idea that we have lots of spare *capacity* is certainly true and fits with our aspirational culture, as well as with the Freudian notion that the mind is mostly unconscious. Indeed, the myth was being used to peddle self-help literature as early as 1929.[3] The neatness and numerological potency of the 10% figure is a further factor in the endurance of the myth.
>
> —A.B.

Neuropsychology is the study of patients who have suffered brain damage and the psychological consequences of that brain damage. As well as being a vital source of information about which bits of the brain are involved in doing which things, neuropsychology also provides a neat refutation of the 10% myth: if we use only 10% of our brains, which bits would you be happy to lose? From neuropsychology, we know that losing *any* bit of the brain causes you to stop being able to do something or being able to do it so well. It's all being used, not just 10% of it.

Admittedly we aren't clear on exactly what each bit of the brain does, but that doesn't mean that you can do without 90% of it.

Neuropsychology has other uses aside from disproving unhelpful but popularly held trivia. By looking at which psychological functions remain after the loss of a certain brain region, we can tell what brain regions are and are not necessary for us to do different things. We can also see how functions group and divide by looking at whether they are always lost together or lost only in dissimilar cases of brain damage. Two of the famous early discoveries of neuropsychology are two distinct language processing regions in the brain. *Broca's area* (named after the neuropsychologist Paul Broca) is in the frontal lobe and supports understanding and producing structure in language. Those with damage to Broca's area speak in stilted, single words. *Wernicke's area* (on the junction between the temporal and parietal lobes and named after Carl Wernicke) supports producing and understanding the semantics of language. People with brain damage to Wernicke's area can produce grammatically correct sentences, but often with little or no meaning, an incomprehensible "word salad."

Another line of evidence against the 10% myth is brain imaging research [Hacks #2 through #4], which has grown exponentially in the last couple of decades. Such techniques allow the increased blood flow to be measured in certain brain regions during the performance of cognitive tasks. While debate continues about the degree to which it is sensible to infer much about functional localization from imaging studies, one thing they make abundantly clear is that there are no areas of the brain that are "black holes"—areas that never "light up" in response to some task or other. Indeed, the neurons that comprise the cortex of the brain are active to some degree all the time, even during sleep.

A third line of argument is that of evolutionary theory. The human brain is a very expensive organ, requiring approximately 20% of blood flow from the heart and a similar amount of available oxygen, despite accounting for only 2% of body weight. The evolutionary argument is straightforward: is it really plausible that such a demanding organ would be so inefficient as to have spare capacity 10 times greater than the areas being usefully employed?

Fourth, developmental studies indicate that neurons that are not employed early in life are likely never to recover and behave normally. For example, if the visual system is not provided with light and stimulation within a fairly narrow developmental window, the neurons atrophy and vision never develops. If the visual system is deprived of a specific kind of stimulation, such as vertical lines, it develops without any sensitivity to that kind of stimulus. Functions in other parts of the brain similarly rely on activation to develop normally. If there really were a large proportion of neurons that were not used but were instead lying in wait, likely they would be useless by puberty.

It can be seen, then, that the 10% myth simply doesn't stand up to critical thinking. Two factors complicate the picture slightly, however; both have been used to muddy the waters around the claim at some stage.

First, people who suffer hydrocephalus in childhood have been seen to have large "holes" in the middle of their brains and yet function normally (the holes are fluid-filled *ventricles* that are present in every brain but are greatly enlarged in hydrocephalus). This condition has been the focus of sensationalist television documentaries, the thrust of which is that we can get on perfectly well without much of our brains. Such claims are willfully misleading—what such examples actually show is the remarkable capacity of the brain to assign functioning to alternative areas if there are problems with the "standard" areas during a specific time-point in development. Such "neuronal plasticity," as it is known, is not seen following brain damage acquired in adulthood. As discussed earlier, development of the brain depends on activity—this same fact explains why hydrocephalitic brains can function normally and makes having an unused 90% extremely unlikely.

Second, there is actually a very disingenuous sense in which we do "use" only 10% of our brains. The glial cells of the brain outnumber the neurons by a factor of roughly 10 to 1. Glial cells play a supporting role to the neurons, which are the cells that carry the electrochemical signals of the brain. It is possible, therefore, to note that only approximately 10% of the cells of the cortex are directly involved in cognition.

This isn't what proponents of the 10% theory are referring to, however. Instead, the myth is almost always a claim about mind, not brain. The claim is analogous to arguing that we operate at only 10% of our potential (although "potential" is so immeasurable a thing, it is misleading from the start to throw precise percentages around).

Uri Geller makes explicit the "untapped potential" interpretation in the introduction to *Uri Geller's Mind-Power Book:*

> Our minds are capable of remarkable, incredible feats, yet we don't use them to their full capacity. In fact, most of us only use about 10 per cent of our brains, if that. The other 90 per cent is full of untapped potential and undiscovered abilities, which means our minds are only operating in a very limited way instead of at full stretch.

The confusion between brain and mind blurs the issue, while lending the claim an air of scientific credibility because it talks about the physical brain rather than the unknowable mind.

But it's just not true that 90% of the brain's capacity is just sitting there unused. It is true that our brains adjust their function according to experience [Hack #12]—good news for the patients studied by neuropsychology. Many of them recover some of the ability they have lost. It is also true that the brain can survive a surprisingly large amount of damage and still sort of work (compare pouring two pints of beer down your throat and two pints of beer into your computer's hard disk drive for an illustration of the brain's superior resistance to insults). But neither of these facts mean that you have exactly 90% of untapped potential—you need all your brain's plasticity and resistance to insult to keep learning and functioning across your life span.

In summary, the 10% myth isn't true, but it does offer an intuitively seductive promise of the possibility of self-improvement. It has been around for at least 80 years, and despite having no basis in current scientific knowledge and being refuted by at least 150 years of neuropsychology, it is likely to exist for as long as people are keen to aspire to be something more than they are.

End Notes

1. Herculano-Houzel, S. (2002). Do you know your brain? A survey on public neuroscience literacy at the closing of the decade of the brain. *The Neuroscientist 8*, 98–110.

2. Radford, B. (1999). The ten-percent myth. *Skeptical Inquirer*. March–April (*http://www.csicop.org/si/9903/ten-percent-myth.html*).

3. You can read all about the 10% myth in Beyerstein, B. L. (1999), Whence cometh the myth that we only use 10% of our brains? In Della Sala (ed.), *Mind Myths—Exploring Popular Assumptions About the Mind and Brain.* New York: John Wiley and Sons, 4–24, at snopes.com (*http://www.snopes. com/science/stats/10percnt.htm*), and in these two online essays by Eric Chudler, "Do We Use Only 10% of Our Brain?" (*http://faculty.washington. edu/chudler/tenper.html*) and "Myths About the Brain: 10 Percent and Counting" (*http://www.brainconnection.com/topics/?main=fa/brain-myth*).

—*Andrew Brown*

Get Acquainted with the Central Nervous System

Take a brief tour around the spinal cord and brain. What's where, and what does what?

Think of the central nervous system like a mushroom with the spinal cord as the stalk and the brain as the cap. Most of the hacks in this book arise from features in the cortex, the highly interconnected cells that make a thin layer over the brain...but not all. So let's start outside the brain itself and work back in.

Senses and muscles all over the body are connected to nerves, bundles of neurons that carry signals back and forth. Neurons come in many types, but they're basically the same wherever they're found in the body; they carry electric current and can act as relays, passing on information from one neuron to the next. That's how information is carried from the sensory surface of the skin, as electric signals, and also how muscles are told to move, by information going the other way.

Nerves at this point run to the spinal cord two by two. One of each pair of nerves is for receptors (a sense of touch for instance) and one for *effectors*—these trigger actions in muscles and glands. At the spinal cord, there's no real intelligence yet but already some decision-making—such as the withdrawal reflex—occurs. Urgent signals, like a strong sense of heat, can trigger an effector response (such as moving a muscle) before that signal even reaches the brain.

The spinal cord acts as a conduit for nerve impulses up and down the body: sensory impulses travel up to the brain, and the motor areas of the brain send signals back down again. Inside the cord, the signals converge into 31 pairs of nerves (sensory and motor again), and eventually, at the top of the neck, these meet the brain.

At about the level of your mouth, right in the center of your head, the bundles of neurons in the spinal cord meet the brain proper. This tip of the spinal cord, called the *brain stem*, continues like a thick carrot up to the direct center of your brain, at about the same height as your eyes.

This, with some other central regions, is known as the *hindbrain*. Working outward from the brain stem, the other large parts of the brain are the *cerebellum*, which runs behind the soft area you can feel at the lower back of your head, and the *forebrain*, which is almost all the rest and includes the cortex.

Hindbrain activities are mostly automatic: breathing, the heartbeat, and the regulation of the blood supply.

The cerebellum is old brain—almost as if it were evolution's first go at performing higher-brain functions, coordinating the senses and movement. It plays an important role in learning and also in motor control: removing the cerebellum produces characteristic jerky movements. The cerebellum takes input from the eyes and ears, as well as the balance system, and sends motor signals to the brain stem.

Sitting atop the hindbrain is the *midbrain*, which is small in humans but much larger in animals like bats. For bats, this corresponds to a relay station for auditory information—bats make extensive use of their ears. For us, the midbrain acts as a connection layer, penetrating deep into the forebrain (where our higher-level functions are) and connecting back to the brain stem. It acts partially to control movement, linking parts of the higher brain to motor neurons and partially as a hub for some of the nerves that don't travel up the spinal cord but instead come directly into the brain: eye movement is one such function.

Now we're almost at the end of our journey. The *forebrain*, also known as the *cerebrum*, is the bulbous mass divided into two great hemispheres—it's the distinctive image of the brain that we all know. Buried in the cerebrum, right in the middle where it surrounds the tip of the brain stem and midbrain, there's the limbic system and other primitive systems. The limbic system is involved in essential and automatic responses like emotions, and includes the very tip of the temporal cortex, the hippocampus and the amygdala, and, by some reckonings, the hypothalamus. In some animals, like reptiles, this is all there is of the forebrain. For them, it's a sophisticated olfactory system: smell is analyzed here, and behavioral responses like feeding and fighting are triggered.

> Neuroscientist joke: the hypothalamus regulates the four essential *F*s of life: fighting, fleeing, feeding, and mating.
>
> —T.S.

For us humans, the limbic system has been repurposed. It still deals with smell, but the *hippocampus*, for example—one part of the system—is now heavily involved in long-term memory and learning. And there are still routing systems that take sensory input (from everywhere but the nose, which is routed directly to the limbic system), and distribute it all over the forebrain. Signals can come in from the rest of the cerebrum and activate or modulate limbic system processing common to all animals—things like emotional arousal. The difference, for us humans, is that the rest of the cerebrum is so large. The cap of the mushroom consists of four large lobes on each hemisphere, visible when you look at the picture of the brain. Taken together, they make up 90% of the weight of the brain. And spread like a folded blanket over the whole of it is the layer of massively interconnected neurons that is the *cerebral cortex*, and if any development can be said to be responsible for the distinctiveness of humanity, this is it. For more on what functions the cerebral cortex performs, read "Tour the Cortex and the Four Lobes" [Hack #8].

As an orienting guide, it's useful to have a little of the jargon as well as the map of the central nervous system. Described earlier are the regions of the brain based mainly on how they grow and what the brain looks like. There are also functional descriptions, like the visual system [Hack #13], that cross all these regions. They're mainly self-explanatory, as long as you remember that functions tend to be both regions in the brain and pathways that connect areas together.

There are also positional descriptions, which describe the brain geographically and seem confusing on first encounter. They're often used, so it's handy to have a crib, as shown in Figure 1-1.

These terms are used to describe direction within the brain and prefix the Latin names of the particular region they're used with (e.g., posterior occipital cortex means the back of the occipital cortex).

Unfortunately, a number of different schemes are used to name the subsections of the brain, and they don't always agree on where the boundaries of the different regions are. Analogous regions in different species may have different names. Different subdisciplines use different schemes and conventions too. A neuropsychologist might say "Broca's areas," while a neuroanatomist might say "Brodman areas 44, 45, and 46"—but they are both referring to the same thing. "Cortex" is also "neocortex" is also "cerebrum." The analogous area in the rat is the forebrain. You get the picture. Add to this the fact that many regions have subdivisions (the somatosensory cortex is in the parietal lobe, which is in the neocortex, for example) and some subdivisions can be put by different people in different supercategories, and it can get very confusing.

See Also

- Three excellent online resources for exploring neuroanatomy are Brain Info (*http://www.med.harvard.edu/AANLIB/home.html*), The Navigable Atlas of the Human Brain (*http://www.msu.edu/~brains/humanatlas*), and The Whole Brain Atlas (*http://braininfo.rprc.washington.edu/mainmenu.html*).

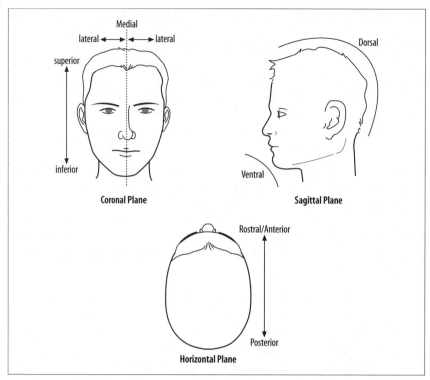

Figure 1-1. Common labels used to specify particular parts of neuroanatomical areas

- The Brain Museum (*http://brainmuseum.org*) houses lots of beautifully taken pictures of the brains from more than 175 different species.

- BrainVoyager (*http://www.brainvoyager.com*), which makes software for processing fMRI data, is kind enough to provide a free program that lets you explore the brain in 3D.

- Nolte, J. (1999). *The Human Brain: An Introduction to Its Functional Anatomy*.

- Crossman, A. R., & Neary, D. (2000). *Neuroanatomy: An Illustrated Colour Text*.

Tour the Cortex and the Four Lobes

The forebrain, the classic image of the brain we know from pictures, is the part of the brain that defines human uniqueness. It consists of four lobes and a thin layer on the surface called the cortex.

When you look at pictures of the human brain, the main thing you see is the rounded, wrinkled bulk of the brain. This is the *cerebrum*, and it caps off the rest of the brain and central nervous system **[Hack #7]**.

To find your way around the cerebrum, you need to know only a few things. It's divided into two hemispheres, left and right. It's also divided into four lobes (large areas demarcated by particularly deep wrinkles). The wrinkles you can see on the outside are actually folds: the cerebrum is a very large folded-up surface, which is why it's so deep. Unfolded, this surface—the *cerebral cortex*—would be about 1.5 m² (a square roughly 50 inches on the side), and between 2 and 4 mm deep. It's not thick, but there's a lot of it and this is where all the work takes place. The outermost part, the top of the surface, is *gray matter*, the actual neurons themselves. Under a few layers of these is the *white matter*, the fibers connecting the neurons together. The cortex is special because it's mainly where our high-level, human functions take place. It's here that information is integrated and combined from the other regions of the brain and used to modulate more basic functions elsewhere in the brain. The folds exist to allow many more neurons and connections than other animals have in a similar size area.

Cerebral Lobes

The four cerebral lobes generally perform certain classes of function.

You can cover the *frontal lobe* if you put your palms on your forehead with your fingers pointing up. It's heavily involved in planning, socializing, language, and general control and supervision of the rest of the brain.

The *parietal lobe* is at the top and back of your head, and if you lock your fingers together and hook your hands over the top back, that's it covered there. It deals a lot with your senses, combining information and representing your body and movements. The object recognition module for visual processing [Hack #13] is located here.

You can put your hands on only the ends of the *temporal lobe*—it's right behind the ears. It sits behind the frontal lobe and underneath the parietal lobe and curls up the underside of the cerebrum. Unsurprisingly, auditory processing occurs here. It deals with language too (like verbal memory), and the left hemisphere is specialized for this (non-linguistic sound is on the right). The curled-up ends of the temporal lobe join into the limbic system at the hippocampus and are involved in long-term memory formation.

Finally, there's the *occipital lobe*, right at the back of the brain, about midway down your head. This is the smallest lobe of the cerebrum and is where the visual cortex is located.

The two hemispheres are joined together by another structure buried underneath the lobes, called the *corpus callosum*. It's the largest bundle of nerve fibers in the whole nervous system. While sensory information, such as vision, is divided across the two hemispheres of the brain, the corpus callosum brings the sides back together. It's heavily coated in a fatty substance called *myelin*, which speeds electrical conduction along nerve cells and is so efficient that the two sides of the visual cortex (for example) operate together almost as if they're adjacent. Not bad considering the corpus callosum is connecting together brain areas a few inches apart when the cells are usually separated by only a millimeter or two.

Cerebral Cortex

The cortex, the surface of these lobes, is divided into areas performing different functions. This isn't exact, of course, and they're highly interconnected and draw information from one another, but more or less there are small areas of the surface that perform edge detection for visual information or detect tools as opposed to animate objects in much higher-level areas of the brain.

> How these areas are identified is covered in the various brain imaging and methods hacks earlier in this chapter.

The sensory areas of the cortex are characterized by maps, representations of the information that comes in from the senses. It's called a map because continous variations in the value of inputs are represented by continuous shifts in distance between where they are processed in the cortical space. In the visual cortex, visual space is preserved on the retina. This spatial map is retained for each stage of early visual processing. This means that if two things are next to each other out there in the world they will, at least initially, be processed by contiguous areas of the visual cortex. This is just like when a visual image is stored on photographic negative but unlike when a visual image is stored in a JPEG image file. You can't automatically point to two adjoining parts of the JPEG file and be certain that they will appear next to each other in the image. With a photographic film and with the visual cortex, you can. Similarly, the auditory cortex creates maps of what you're hearing, but as well as organizing things according to where they appear in space, it also has maps that use frequency of the sound as the coordinate frame (i.e., they are *tonotopic*). And there's an actual map in physical space, on the cortex, of the whole body surface too, called the sensory homunculus [Hack #12]. You can tell how much importance the brain gives to areas of the map, comparatively, by looking at how large they are. The middle of the map of the primary visual cortex corresponds with the fovea in the retina, which is extremely high resolution. It's as large as the rest of the visual map put together.

When the cortex is discussed, that means the function in question is highly integrated with the rest of the brain. When we consider what really makes us human and where consciousness is, it isn't solely the cortex: the rest of the brain has changed function in humans, we have human bodies and nervous systems, and we exist within environments that our brains reflect in their adaptations. But it's definitely mostly the cortex. You are here.

The Neuron

There's a veritable electrical storm going on inside your head: 100 billion brain cells firing electrical signals at one another are responsible for your every thought and action.

A *neuron*, a.k.a. *nerve cell* or *brain cell*, is a specialized cell that sends an electrical impulse out along fibers connecting it, in turn, to other neurons. These guys are the wires of your very own personal circuitry.

What follows is a simplistic description of the general features of nerve cells, whether they are found sending signals from your senses to your brain, from your brain to your muscles, or to and from other nerve cells. It's this last class, the kind that people most likely mean when they say "neurons," that we are most interested in here. (All nerve cells, however, share a common basic design.)

Don't for a second think that the general structure we're describing here is the end of the story. The elegance and complexity of neuron design is staggering, a complex interplay of structure and noise; of electricity, chemistry, and biology; of spatial and dynamic interactions that result in the kind of information processing that cannot be defined using simple rules.[1] For just a glimpse at the complexity of neuron structure, you may want to start with this free chapter on nerve cells from the textbook *Molecular Cell Biology* by Harvey Lodish, Arnold Berk, Lawrence S. Zipursky, Paul Matsudaira, David Baltimore, and James Darnell and published by W. H. Freeman (*http://www.ncbi.nlm.nih.gov/books/bv.fcgi?call=bv.View..ShowSection&rid=mcb.chapter.6074*), but any advanced cell biology or neuroscience textbook will do to give you an idea of what you're missing here.

The neuron is made up of a cell body with long offshoots—these can be very long (the whole length of the neck, for some neurons in the giraffe, for example) or very short (i.e., reaching only to the neighboring cell, scant millimeters away). Signals pass only one way along a neuron. The offshoots receiving incoming transmissions are called *dendrites*. The outgoing end, which is typically longer, is called the *axon*. In most cases there's only one, long, axon, which branches at the tip as it connects to other neurons—up to 10,000 of them. The junction where the axon of one cell meets the dendrites of another is called the *synapse*. Chemicals, called *neurotransmitters*, are used to get the signal across the synaptic gap. Each neuron will release only one kind of neurotransmitter, although it may have receptors for many different kinds. The arrival of the electric signal at the end of the axon triggers the release of stores of the neurotransmitter that move across the gap (it's very small, after all) and bind to receptor sites on the other side, places on the neuron that are tuned to join with this specific type of chemical.

Whereas the signal between neurons uses neurotransmitters, internally it's electrical. The electrical signal is sent along the neuron in the form of an *action potential*.[2] This is what we mean when we say *impulses*, *signals*, *spikes*, or refer, in brain imaging speak, to the *firing* or *lighting up* of brain areas (because this is what activity looks like on the pictures that are made). Action potentials are the fundamental unit of information in the brain, the universal currency of the neural market.

The two most important computational features are as follows:

- They are binary. A neuron either fires or doesn't, and each time it fires, the signal is the same size (there's more on this later). Binary signals stop the message from becoming diluted as neurons communicate with one another over distances that are massive compared to the molecular scale on which they operate.

- Neurons encode information in the rate at which they send signals, not in the size of the signals they send. The signals are always the same size, information encoded in the frequency at which signals are sent. A stronger signal is indicated by a higher frequency of spikes, not larger single spikes. This is called *rate coding*.

Together these two features mean that the real language of the brain is not just a matter of spikes (signals sent by neurons), but spikes in time.

Whether or not a new spike, or impulse, is generated by the postsynaptic neuron (the one on the receiving side of the synapse) is affected by the following interwoven factors:

- The amount of neurotransmitter released
- The interaction with other neurotransmitters released by other neurons
- How near they are and how close together in space and time
- In what order they release their neurotransmitters

All of this short-term information is affected by any previous history of interaction between these two neurons—times one has caused the other to fire and when they have both fired at the same time for independent reasons—and slightly adjusts the probability of interaction happening again.[3]

> Spikes happen pretty often: up to once every 2 milliseconds at the maximum rate of the fastest-firing cells (in the auditory system; see Chapter 4 for more on that). Although the average rate of firing is responsive to the information being represented and transmitted in the brain, the actual timing of individual spikes is unpredictable. The brain seems to have evolved an internal communication system that has noise added to only one aspect of the information it transmits—the timing, but not the size of the signals transmitted. Noise is a property of any biological system, so it's not surprising that it persists even in our most complex organ. It could very well also be the case that the noise [Hack #33] is playing some useful role in the information processing the brain does.

After the neurotransmitter has carried (or not carried, as the case may be) the signal across the synaptic gap, it's then broken down by specialized enzymes and reabsorbed to be released again when the next signal comes along. Many drugs work by affecting the rate and quantity of particular neurotransmitters released and the speed at which they are broken down and reabsorbed.

Hacks such as "Why People Don't Work Like Elevator Buttons" [Hack #11] and "Get Adjusted" [Hack #26] show some of the other consequences for psychology of using neurons to do the work. Two good introductions to how neurons combine on a large scale can be found at *http://www.foresight.gov.uk/cognitive.html*. This is a British government Department of Trade and Industry project that aimed to get neuroscientists and computer scientists to collaborate in producing reviews of recent advances in their fields and summarize the implications for the development of artificial cognitive systems.

End Notes

1. Gurney, K. N. (2001). Information processing in dendrites II. Information theoretic complexity. *Neural Networks, 14,* 1005–1022.

2. You can start finding out details of the delicate electrochemical dance that allows the transmission of these binary electrical signals on the pages about action potentials that are part of a series of lecture notes on human physiology (*http://members.aol.com/Bio50/LecNotes/lecnot11.html*), the Neuroscience for Kids site (*http://faculty.washington.edu/chudler/ap.html*), and The Brain from Top to Bottom project (*http://www.thebrain.mcgill.ca/flash/a/a_01/a_01_m/a_01_m_fon/a_01_m_fon.html*).

3. But this is another story—a story called learning.

See Also

- How neurons are born, develop, and die is another interesting story and one that we're not covering here. These notes from the National Institutes of Health are a good introduction: *http://www.ninds.nih.gov/health_and_medical/pubs/NINDS_Neuron.htm*.

- Neurons actually make up less than a tenth of the cells in the brain. The other 90–98%, by number, are glial cells, which are involved in development and maintenance—the sysadmins of the brain. Recent research also suggests that they play more of a role in information processing than was previously thought. You can read about this in the cover story from the April 2004 edition of *Scientific American* (volume 290 #4), "The Other Half of the Brain."

HACK #10   Detect the Effect of Cognitive Function on Cerebral Blood Flow

When you think really hard, your heart rate noticeably increases.

The brain requires approximately 20% of the oxygen in the body, even during times of rest. Like the other organs in our body, our brain needs more glucose, oxygen, and other essential nutrients as it takes on more work. Many of the scanning technologies that aim to measure aspects of brain function take advantage of this. Functional magnetic resonance imaging (fMRI) [Hack #4] benefits from the fact that oxygenated blood produces slightly different electromagnetic signals when exposed to strong magnetic fields than deoxygenated blood and that oxygenated blood is more concentrated in active brain areas. Positron emission tomography (PET) [Hack #3] involves being injected with weakly radioactive glucose and reading the subsequent signals from the most active, glucose-hungry areas of the brain.

A technology called *transcranial Doppler sonography* takes a different approach and measures blood flow through veins and arteries. It takes advantage of the fact that the pitch of reflected ultrasound will be altered in proportion to the rate of flow and has been used to measure moment-to-moment changes in blood supply to the brain. It has been found to be particularly useful in making comparisons between different mental tasks. However, even without transcranial Doppler sonography, you can measure the effect of increased brain activity on blood flow by measuring the pulse.

In Action

For this exercise you will need to get someone to measure your *carotid pulse*, taken from either side of the front of the neck, just below the angle of the jaw. It is important that only very light pressure be used—a couple of finger-tips pressed lightly to the neck, next to the windpipe, should enable your friend to feel your pulse with little trouble.

First you need to take a measure of a resting pulse. Sit down and relax for a few minutes. When you are calm, ask your friend to count your pulse for 60 seconds. During this time, close your eyes and try to empty your mind.

With a baseline established, ask your friend to measure your pulse for a second time, using exactly the same method. This time, however, try and think of as many species of animals as you can. Keeping still and with your eyes closed, think hard, and if you get stuck, try thinking up a new strategy to give you some more ideas.

During the second session, your pulse rate is likely to increase as your brain requires more glucose and oxygen to complete its task. Just how much increase you'll see varies from person to person.

How It Works

Thinking of as many animals as possible is a type of *verbal fluency* task, testing how easily you can come up with words. To complete the task successfully, you needed to be able to coordinate various cognitive skills, for example, searching your memory for category examples, generating and using strategies to think up more names (perhaps you thought about walking through the jungle or animals from your local area) and checking you were not repeating yourself.

Neuropsychologists often use this task to test the *executive system*, the notional system that allows us to coordinate mental tasks to solve problems and work toward a goal, skills that you were using to think up examples of animals. After brain injury (particularly to the frontal cortex), this system can break down, and the verbal fluency task can be one of the tests used to assess the function of this system.

Research using PET scanning has shown similar verbal fluency tasks use a significant amount of brain resources and large areas of the cortex, particularly the frontal, temporal, and parietal areas.[1]

Interestingly, in this study people who did best used less blood glucose than people who did not perform as well. You can examine this relationship yourself by trying the earlier exercise on a number of people. Do the people who do best show a slightly lower pulse than others? In these cases, high performers seem to be using their brain more efficiently, rather than simply using more brain resources.

Although measuring the carotid pulse is a fairly crude measure of brain activity compared to PET scanning, it is still a good indirect measure of brain activity for this type of high-demand mental task, as the carotid arteries supply both the middle and anterior cerebral arteries. They supply blood to most major parts of the cortex, including the frontal, temporal, parietal, and occipital areas, and so would be important in supplying the needed glucose and oxygen as your brain kicks into gear.

One problem with PET scanning is that, although it can localize activity to certain brain areas, it has poor temporal resolution, meaning it is not very good at detecting quick changes in the rate of blood flow. In contrast, transcranial Doppler sonography can detect differences in blood flow over very short periods of time (milliseconds). Frauenfelder and colleagues used this technique to measure blood flow through the middle and anterior cerebral arteries while participants were completing tasks that are known to need similar cognitive skills as the verbal fluency exercise.[2] They found that the rate of blood flow changed second by second, depending on exactly which part of the task the participant was tackling. While brain scanning can provide important information about which areas of the brain are involved in completing a mental activity, sometimes measuring something as simple as blood flow can fill in the missing pieces.

End Notes

1. Parks, R. W., Loewenstein, D. A., Dodrill, K. L., Barker, W. W., Yoshii, F., Chang, J. Y., Emran, A., Apicella, A., Sheramata, W. A., & Duara, R. (1988). Cerebral metabolic effects of a verbal fluency test: A PET scan study. *Journal of Clinical and Experimental Neuropsychology, 10*(5), 565–575.

2. Schuepbach, D., Merlo, M. C., Goenner, F., Staikov, I., Mattle, H. P., Dierks, T., & Brenner, H. D. (2002). Cerebral hemodynamic response induced by the Tower of Hanoi puzzle and the Wisconsin card sorting test. *Neuropsychologia, 40*(1), 39–53.

—*Vaughan Bell*

HACK #11 Why People Don't Work Like Elevator Buttons

More intense signals cause faster reaction times, but there are diminishing returns: as a stimulus grows in intensity, eventually the reaction speed can't get any better. The formula that relates intensity and reaction speed is Pieron's Law.

It's a common illusion that if you are in a hurry for the elevator you can make it come quicker by pressing the button harder. Or more often. Or all the buttons at once. It somehow feels as if it ought to work, although of course we know it doesn't. Either the elevator has heard you, or it hasn't. How loud you call doesn't make any difference to how long it'll take to arrive.

But then elevators aren't like people. People *do* respond quicker to more stimulation, even on the most fundamental level. We press the brake quicker for brighter stoplights, jump higher at louder bangs. And it's because we all do this that we all fall so easily into thinking that things, including elevators, should behave the same way.

In Action

Give someone this simple task: she must sit in front of a screen and press a button as quickly as she can as soon as she sees a light flash on. If people were like elevators, the time it takes to press the button wouldn't be affected by the brightness of the light or the number of lights.

But people aren't like elevators and we respond quicker to brighter lights; in fact, the relationship between the physical intensity of the light and the average speed of response follows a precise mathematical form. This form is captured by an equation called Pieron's Law. Pieron's Law says that the time to respond to a stimulus is related to the stimulus intensity by the formula:

$$\text{Reaction Time} \approx R_0 + kI^{-\beta}$$

Reaction Time is the time between the stimulus appearing and you responding. I is the physical intensity of the signal. R_0 is the minimum time for any response, the asymptotic value representing all the components of the reaction time that don't vary, such as the time for light to reach your eye. k and β are constants that vary depending on the exact setup and the particular person involved. But whatever the setup and whoever the person, graphically the equation looks like Figure 1-2.

How It Works

In fact, Pieron's Law holds for the brightness of light, the loudness of sound, and even the strength of taste.[1] It says something fundamental about how we process signals and make decisions—the physical nature of a stimulus carries through the whole system to affect the nature of the response. We are not binary systems! The actual number of photons of light or the amplitude of the sound waves that triggers us to respond influences how we respond. In fact, as well as affecting response time, the physical intensity of the stimulus also affects response force as well (e.g., how hard we press the button).

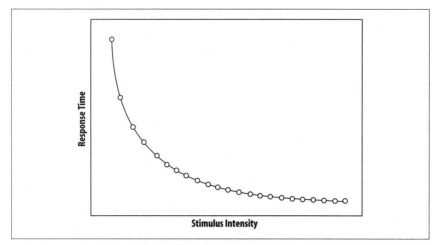

Figure 1-2. How reaction time changes with stimulus intensity

A consequence of the form of Pieron's Law is that increases in speed are easy for low-intensity stimuli and get harder as the stimulus gains more intensity. It follows a log scale, like a lot of things in psychophysics. The converse is also true: for quick reaction times, it's easier to slow people down than to speed them up.

Pieron's Law probably results because of the fundamental way the decisions have to be made with uncertain information. Although it might be clear to you that the light is either there or not, that's only because your brain has done the work of removing the uncertainty for you. And on a neural level, everything is uncertain because neural signals always have noise in them.

So as you wait for light to appear, your neuronal decision-making hardware is inspecting noisy inputs and trying to decide if there is enough evidence to say "Yes, it's there!" Looking at it like this, your response time is the time to collect enough neural evidence that something has really appeared. This is why Pieron's Law applies; more intense stimuli provide more evidence, and the way in which they provide more evidence results in the equation shown earlier.

To see why, think of it like this: Pieron's Law is a way of saying that the response time improves but at a decreasing rate, as the intensity (i.e., the rate at which evidence accumulates) increases. Try this analogy: stimulus intensity is your daily wage and making a response is buying a $900 holiday. If you get paid $10 a day, it'll take 90 days to get the money for the holiday. If you get a raise of $5, you could afford the holiday in 60 days—30 days sooner. If you got two $5 raises, you'd be able to afford the holiday in 45 days—only 15 days sooner than how long it would take with just one $5 raise. The time until you can afford a holiday gets shorter as your wage goes up, but it gets shorter more slowly, and if you do the math it turns out to be an example of Pieron's Law.

End Note

1. Pins, D., & Bonnet, C. (1996). On the relation between stimulus intensity and processing time: Pieron's law and choice reaction time. *Perception & Psychophysics, 58*(3), 390–400.

See Also

- Stafford, T., & Gurney, K. G. (in press). The role of response mechanisms in determining reaction time performance: Pieron's law revisited. *Psychonomic Bulletin & Review* (in press).
- Luce, R. D. (1986). *Response Times: Their Role in Inferring Elementary Mental Organisation*. New York: Clarendon Press. An essential one stop for all you need to know about modeling reaction times.
- Pieron, H. (1952). *The Sensations: Their Functions, Processes and Mechanisms*. London: Frederick Muller Ltd. The book in which Pieron first proposed his law.

Build Your Own Sensory Homunculus

All abilities are skills; practice something and your brain will devote more resources to it.

The sensory homunculus looks like a person, but swollen and out of all proportion. It has hands as big as its head; huge eyes, lips, ears, and nose; and skinny arms and legs. What kind of person is it? It's you, the person in your head. Have a look at the sensory homunculus first, then make your own.

In Action

You can play around with Jaakko Hakulinen's homunculus applet (*http://www.cs.uta.fi/~jh/homunculus.html*; Java) to see where different bits of the body are represented in the sensory and motor cortex. There's a screenshot of it in Figure 1-3.

This is the person inside your head. Each part of the body has been scaled according to how much of your sensory cortex is devoted to it. The area of cortex responsible for processing touch sensations is the *somatosensory cortex*. It lives in the parietal lobe, further toward the back of the head than the motor cortex, running alongside it from the top of the head down each side of the brain. Areas for processing neighboring body parts are generally

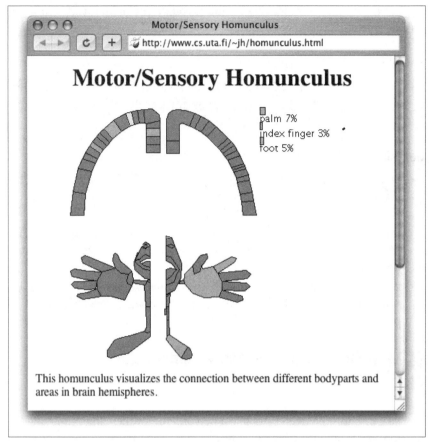

Figure 1-3. The figure shown is scaled according to the relative sizes of the body parts in the motor and sensory cortex areas; motor is shown on the left, sensory on the right

next to each other in the cortex, although this isn't always possible because of the constraints of mapping the 3D surface of your skin to a 2D map. The area representing your feet is next to the area representing your genitals, for example (the genital representation is at the very top of the somatosensory cortex, inside the groove between the two hemispheres).

The applet lets you compare the motor and sensory maps. The motor map is how body parts are represented for movement, rather than sensation. Although there are some differences, they're pretty similar. Using the applet, when you click on a part of the little man, the corresponding part of the brain above lights up. The half of the man on the left is scaled according to the representation of the body in the primary motor cortex, and the half on the right is scaled to represent the somatosensory cortex. If you click on a brain section or body part, you can toggle shading and the display of the percentage of sensory or motor representation commanded by that body part. The picture of the man is scaled, too, according to how much cortex each part corresponds to. That's why the hands are so much larger than the torso.

Having seen this figure, you can see the relative amount of your own somatosensory cortex devoted to each body part by measuring your touch resolution. To do this, you'll need a willing friend to help you perform the two-point discrimination test.

Ask your friend to get two pointy objects—two pencils will do—and touch one of your palms with both of the points, a couple of inches apart. Look away so you can't see him doing it. You'll be able to tell there are two points there. Now get your friend to touch with only one pencil—you'll be able to tell you're being touched with just one. The trick now is for him to continue touching your palm with the pencils, sometimes with both and sometimes with just one, moving the tips ever closer together each time. At a certain point, you won't be able to tell how many pencils he's using. In the center of your palm, you should be able to discriminate between two points a millimeter or so apart. At the base of your thumb, you've a few millimeters of resolution.

Now try the same on your back—your two-point discrimination will be about 4 or 5 centimeters.

To draw a homunculus from these measurements, divide the actual width of your body part by the two-point discrimination to get the size of each part of the figure.

My back's about 35 centimeters across, so my homunculus should have a back that's 9 units wide (35 divided by 4 centimeters, approximately). Then the palms should be 45 units across (my palm is 9 centimeters across; divide that by 2 millimeters to get 45 units). Calculating in units like this will give you the correct scales—the hand in my drawing will be five times as wide as the back.

That's only two parts of your body. To make a homunculus like the one in Hakulinen's applet (or, better, the London Natural History Museum's sensory homunculus model: *http://owen.nhm.ac.uk/piclib/www/image.php?img=87494&cat=6*), you'll also need measurements all over your face, your limbs, your feet, fingers, belly, and the rest. You'll need to find a fairly close friend for this experiment, I'd imagine.

How It Works

The way the brain deals with different tactile sensations is the way it deals with many different kinds of input. Within the region of the brain that deals with that kind of input is a surface over which different values of that input are processed—different values correspond to different actual locations in physical space. In the case of sensations, the body parts are represented in different parts of the somatosensory cortex: the brain has a *somatotopic* (body-oriented) map. In hearing, different tones activate different parts of the auditory cortex: it has a *tonotopic* map. The same thing happens in the visual system, with much of the visual cortex being organized in terms of feature maps comprised of neurons responsible for representing those features, ordered by where the features are in visual space.

Maps mean that qualities of stimuli can be represented continuously. This becomes important when you consider that the evidence for each quality—in other words, the rate at which the neurons in that part of the map are firing—is noisy, and it isn't the absolute value of neural firing that is used to calculate which is the correct value but the relative value. (See "See Movement When All Is Still" [Hack #25] on the motion aftereffect for an example of this in action.)

The more cells the brain dedicates to building the map representing a sense or motor skill, the more sensitive we are in discriminating differences in that type of input or in controlling output. With practice, changes in our representational maps can become permanent.

Brain scanning of musicians has shown that they have larger cortical representations of the body parts they use to play their instruments in their sensory areas—more neurons devoted to finger movements among guitarists, more neurons devoted to lips among trombonists. Musicians' auditory maps of "tone-space" are larger, with neurons more finely tuned to detecting differences in sounds,[1] and orchestra conductors are better at detecting where a sound among a stream of other sounds is coming from.

It's not surprising that musicians are good at these things, but the neuroimaging evidence shows that practice alters the very maps our brains use to understand the world. This explains why small differences are invisible to beginners, but stark to experts. It also offers a hopeful message to the rest of us: all abilities are skills, if you practice them, your brain will get the message and devote more resources to them.

End Note

1. Münte, T. F., Altenmüller, E., & Jäncke, L. (2002). The musician's brain as a model for neuroplasticity. *Nature Neuroscience Reviews, 3,* 473–478. (This is a review paper rather than an original research report.)

See Also

- Pantev, C., Oostenveld, R., Engelien, A., Ross, B., Roberts, L. E., & Hoke, M. (1998). Increased auditory cortical representation in musicians. *Nature, 392,* 811–814.

- Pleger B., Dinse, H. R., Ragert, P., Schwenkreis, P., Malin, J. P., & Tegenthoff, M. (2001). Shifts in cortical representations predict human discrimination improvement. *Proceedings of the National Academy of Sciences of the USA, 98,* 12255–12260.

Seeing
Hacks 13–33

The puzzle that is vision lies in the chasm between the raw sensation gathered by the eye—light landing on our retinas—and our rich perception of color, objects, motion, shape, entire 3D scenes. In this chapter, we'll fiddle about with some of the ways the brain makes this possible.

We'll start with an overview of the visual system [Hack #13], the limits of your vision [Hack #14], and the active nature of visual perception [Hack #15].

There are constraints in vision we usually don't notice, like the blind spot [Hack #16] and the 90 minutes of blindness we experience every day as vision deactivates while our pupils jump around [Hack #17]. We'll have a look at both these and also at some of the shortcuts and tricks visual processing uses to make our lives easier: assuming the sun is overhead [Hacks #20 and #21], jumping out of the way of rapidly expanding dark shapes [Hack #32] (a handy shortcut for faster processing if you need to dodge quickly), and tricks like the use of noisy neurons [Hack #33] to extract signal out of visual noise.

Along the way, we'll take in how we perceive depth [Hacks #22 and #24], and motion [Hacks #25 and #29]. (That's both the correct and false perception of motion, by the way.) We'll finish off with a little optical illusion called the Rotating Snakes Illusion [Hack #30] that has all of us fooled. After all, sometimes it's fun to be duped.

Understand Visual Processing
#13
The visual system is a complex network of modules and pathways, all specializing in different tasks to contribute to our eventual impression of the world.

When we talk about "visual processing," the natural mode of thinking is of a fairly self-contained process. In this model, the eye would be like a video camera, capturing a sequence of photographs of whatever the head happens to be looking at at the time and sending these to the brain to be processed. After "processing" (whatever that might be), the brain would add the photographs to the rest of the intelligence it has gathered about the world around it and decide where to turn the head next. And so the routine would begin again. If the brain were a computer, this neat encapsulation would be how the visual subsystem would probably work.

With that (admittedly, straw man) example in mind, we'll take a tour of vision that shows just how nonsequential it all really is.

And one need go no further than the very idea of the eyes as passive receptors of photograph-like images to find the first fault in the straw man. Vision starts with the entire body: we walk around, and move our eyes and head, to capture depth information [Hack #22] like parallax and more. Some of these decisions about how to move are made early in visual processing, often before any object recognition or conscious understanding has come into play.

This pattern of vision as an interactive process, including many feedback loops before processing has reached conscious perception, is a common one. It's true there's a progression from raw to processed visual signal, but it's a mixed-up, messy kind of progression. Processing takes time, and there's a definite incentive for the brain to make use of information as soon as it's been extracted; there's no time to wait for processing to "complete" before using the extracted information. All it takes is a rapidly growing dark patch in our visual field to make us flinch involuntarily [Hack #32], as if something were looming over us. That's an example of an effect that occurs early in visual processing.

But let's look not at the mechanisms of the early visual system, but how it's used. What are the endpoints of all this processing? By the time perception reaches consciousness, another world has been layered on top of it. Instead of seeing colors, shapes, and changes over time (all that's really available to the eyes), we see whole objects. We see depth, and we have a sense of when things are moving. Some objects seem to stand out as we pay attention to them, and others recede into the background. Consciously, we see both the world and assembled result of the processing the brain has performed, in order to work around constraints (such as the eyes' blind spot [Hack #16]), and to give us a head start in reacting with best-guess assumptions. The hacks in this chapter run the whole production line of visual processing, using visual illusions and anomalies to point out some detail of how vision works.

But before diving straight into all that, it's useful to have an overview of what's actually meant by the *visual system*. We'll start at the eye, see how signals from there go almost directly to the primary visual cortex on the back of the brain, and from there are distributed in two major streams. After that, visual information distributes and merges with the general functions of the cortex itself.

Start at the Retina

In a sense, light landing on the retina—the sensory surface at the back of the eye—is already inside the brain. The whole central nervous system (the brain and spinal column [Hack #7]) is contained within a number of membranes, the outermost of which is called the *dura mater*. The white of your eye, the surface that protects the eye itself, is a continuation of this membrane, meaning the eye is inside the same sac. It's as if two parts of your brain had decided to bulge out of your head and become your eyes, but without becoming separate organs.

The retina is a surface of cells at the back of your eye, containing a layer of *photoreceptors*, cells that detect light and convert it to electrical signals. For most of the eye, signals are aggregated—a hundred photoreceptors will pass their signal onto a single cell further along in the chain. In the center of the eye, a place called the fovea, there is no such signal compression. (The population density of photoreceptors changes considerably across the retina [Hack #14].) The resolution at the fovea is as high as it can be, with cells packed in, and the uncompressed signal dispatched, along with all the other information from other cells, down the *optic nerve*. The optic nerve is a bundle of projections from the neurons that sit behind the photoreceptors in the retina, carrying electrical information toward the brain, the path of information out of the eye. The size of the optic nerve is such that it creates a hole in our field of vision, as photoreceptors can't sit over the spot where it quits the eyeball (that's what's referred to as the blind spot [Hack #16]).

Behind the Eyes

Just behind the eyes, in the middle, the optic nerves from each eye meet, split, and recombine in a new fashion, at the *optic chiasm*. Both the right halves of the two retinas are dispatched to the left of the brain and vice versa (from here on, the two hemispheres of the brain are mirror images of each other). It seems a little odd to divide processing directly down the center of the visual field, rather than by eye, but this allows a single side of the brain to compare the same scene as observed by both eyes, which it needs to get access to depth information.

The route plan now is a dash from the optic chiasm right to the back of the brain, to reach the visual cortex, which is where the real work starts happening. Along the way, there's a single pit stop at a small region buried deep within the brain called the *lateral geniculate nucleus*, or LGN (there's one of these in each hemisphere, of course).

Already, this is where it gets a little messy. Not every signal that passes through the optic chiasm goes to the visual cortex. Some go to the superior colliculus, which is like an emergency visual system. Sitting in the midbrain, it helps with decisions on head and eye orienting. The midbrain is an evolutionary, ancient part of the brain, involved with more basic responses than the cortex and forebrain, which are both better developed in humans. (See "Get Acquainted with the Central Nervous System" **[Hack #7]** for a quick tour.) So it looks as if this region is all low-level functioning. But also, confusingly, the superior colliculus influences high-level functions, as when it suddenly pushes urgent visual signals into conscious awareness **[Hack #37]**.

Actually, the LGN isn't a simple relay station. It deals almost entirely with optical information, all 1.5 million cells of it. But it also takes input from areas of the brain that deal with what you're paying attention to, as well as from the cortex in general, and mixes that in too. Before visual features have been extracted from the raw visual information, sophisticated input from elsewhere is being added—we're not really sure of what's happening here.

There's another division of the visual signal here, too. The LGN has processing pathways for two separate signals: coarse, low-resolution data (lacking in color) goes into the *magnocellular* pathway. High-resolution information goes along the *parvocellular* pathway. Although there are many subsequent crossovers, this division remains throughout the visual system.

Enter the Visual Cortex

From the LGN, the signals are sent directly to the visual cortex. At the lower back of the cerebrum (so about a third of the way up your brain, on the back of your head, and toward the middle) is an area of the cortex called either the striate or primary visual cortex. It's called "striate" simply because it contains a dark stripe when closely examined.

Why the stripes? The primary visual cortex is literally six layers of cells, with a thicker and subdivided layer four where the two different pathways from the LGN land. These projections from LGN create the dark band that gives the striate cortex its name. As visual information moves through this region, cells in all six layers play a role in extracting different features. It's way more complex than the LGN—the striate contains about 200 million cells.

The first batch of processing takes place in a module called V1. *V1* holds a map of the retina as source material, which looks more or less like the area of the eye it's dealing with, only distorted. The part of the map that represents the fovea—the high-resolution center of the eye—is all out of proportion because of the number of cells dedicated to it. It's as large as the rest of the map put together.

Physically standing on top of this map are what are called hypercolumns. A hypercolumn is a stack of cells performing processing that sits on top of an individual location and extracts basic information. So some neurons will become active when they see a particular color, others when they see a line segment at a particular angle, and other more complex ones when they see lines at certain angles moving in particular directions. This first map and its associated hypercolumns constitute the area V1 (*V* for "vision"); it performs really simple feature extraction.

The subsequent visual processing areas named *V2* and *V3* (again, *V* for "vision," the number just denotes order), also in the visual cortex, are similar. Information gets bumped from V1 to V2 by dumping it into V2's own map, which acts as the center for its batch of processing. V3 follows the same pattern: at the end of each stage, the map is recombined and passed on.

"What" and "Where" Processing Streams

So far visual processing has been mostly linear. There are feedback (the LGN gets information from elsewhere on the cortex, for example) and crossovers, but mostly the coarse and fine visual pathways have been processed separately and there's been a reasonably steady progression from the eye to the primary visual cortex.

From V3, visual information is sent to dozens of areas all over the cortex. These modules send information to one another and draw from and feed other areas. It stops being a production line and turns into a big construction site, with many areas extracting and associating different features, all simultaneously.

There's still a broad distinction between the two pathways though. The coarse visual information, the *magnocellular pathway*, flows up to the top of the head. It's called the *dorsal stream*, or, more memorably, the "where" stream. From here on, there are modules to spot motion and to look for broad features.

The fine detail of vision from the *parvocellular pathway* comes out of the primary visual cortex and flows down the *ventral stream*—the "what" stream. The destination for this stream is the inferior temporal lobe, the underside of the cerebrum, above and behind the eyes.

As the name suggests, the "what" stream is all about object recognition. On the way to the temporal lobe, there's a stop-off for a little further processing at a unit called the *lateral occipital complex* (LOC). What happens here is key to what'll happen at the final destination points of the "what" stream. The LOC looks for similarity in color and orientation and groups parts of the visual map together into objects, separating them from the background.

Later on, these objects will be recognized as faces or whatever else. It represents a common method: the visual information is processed to look for features. When found, information about those features is added to the pool of data, and the whole lot is sent on.

Processing with Built-in Assumptions

The wiring diagram for all the subsequent motion detection and object recognition modules is enormously complex. After basic feature extraction, there's still number judgment, following moving objects, and spotting biological motion [Hack #77] to be done. At a certain point, the defining characteristic of the cortex as a whole must come into play, and visual information is processed enough to be associated with memory, language, and reading emotions. This is where it blends in to the higher-order functions of the whole brain.

In the hacks that follow, we'll explore the effects of early and late visual processing. A common thread through these effects will be the assumptions the visual system has made about the visual world to expedite its computation— and by looking at the quirks of vision, we can draw some of these out. Assumptions like the visual world remaining relatively stable from second to second (so we don't notice if it doesn't [Hack #40]) and supposing that dark areas are shadows, which is the quirk that makeup takes advantage of [Hack #20].

In a sense, the fact that we can observe these assumptions suggests that the visual system assumes as much about the external environment as about its own modules. The visual system's expectation that the motion module will report motion correctly (and therefore our confusion when the module doesn't identify motion correctly [Hack #25]) is much the same as the visual system's expectation that a shadow is reporting 3D shape correctly. While we could think of the visual system as entirely in the brain, really we should include the eyes, the head, the body, and the environment as components in this big, messy, densely connected human visual processing system, all of which report their conclusions into the mix.

And somehow, in all of this, the visual perception we know and love somehow springs into existence. There doesn't seem to be a single place where all this visual processing is reassembled, no internal television screen that we watch (and even if there were, who would watch it?). It's distributed over the whole visual system, and over the environment too. Not just a picture at the retina, after all.

See the Limits of Your Vision

The high-resolution portion of your vision is only the size of your thumbnail at arm's length. The rest of your visual input is low res and mostly colorless, although you seldom realize it.

Your vision isn't of uniform resolution. What we generally think of as our visual ability, the sharpness with which we see the world, is really only the very center of vision, where resolution is at its highest. From this high-resolution center, the lower-resolution periphery, and using continual movements of our head and eyes [Hack #15], we construct a seamless—and uniformly sharp—picture of the universe. But how much are we compensating? What is the resolution of vision?

The eye's resolution is determined by the density of light-sensitive cells on the *retina*, which is a layer of these cells on the back of the eye (and also includes several layers of cells to process and aggregate the visual signals to send on to the rest of the brain). If the cells were spread evenly, we would see as well out of the corners of our eyes as directly ahead, but they're not. Instead, the cells are most heavily packed right in the center of the retina, a small region called the *fovea*, so the highest-resolution part of the vision is in the middle of your visual field. The area corresponding to this is small; if you look up at the night sky, out of everything you see, your fovea just about covers the full moon. Away from this, in your peripheral vision, resolution is much coarser.

Color also falls off in peripheral vision. The light-sensitive cells, called *photoreceptors*, come in different types according to what kinds of light they convert into neural signals. Almost all the photoreceptors that can discriminate colors of light are in the fovea. Outside of this central area you can still make out color, but it's harder; the other type of cell, more sensitive but able to recognize only brightness, is more abundant.

In Action

Figure 2-1 is a variant of the usual eye chart you will have encountered at the optometrist, constructed by Stuart Anstis. Hold it in front of you, and rest your gaze on the central dot. The letters in the chart are smallest in the middle and largest at the outer edge; they scale up at a rate to exactly compensate for your eyes' decrease in resolution from the central fovea to the periphery.

That means that, holding your gaze on the center of the chart, it should be as easy for you to read one of the letters near the middle as one of the bigger ones at the edge.

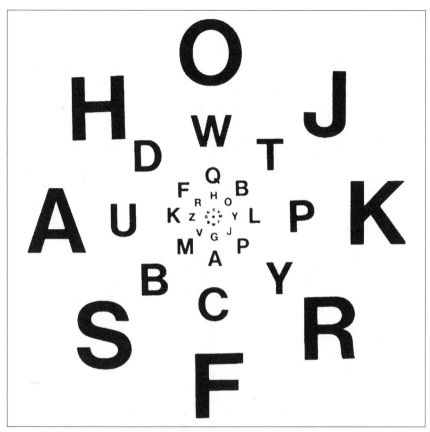

Figure 2-1. When you fixate on the center of this chart, all the letters are scaled to have the same resolution[1]

What this eye chart doesn't show is our relative decrease in color-sensing ability as we edge toward peripheral vision. Have a friend hold pieces of colored card up to the side of your face while you keep your head, and eyes, looking forward. Notice that, while you can see that she's moving the card off in the corner of your eye, you can't tell what color the card is.

Because peripheral vision is still good at brightness, you'll need to use pieces of card that won't give you any clues simply from how bright the card looks. A dull yellow and a bright blue will do. If you'd like to perform a more rigorous experiment, the Exploratorium museum provides instructions on how to make yourself a collar to measure the angles at which your color vision becomes useful (*http://www.exploratorium.edu/snacks/peripheral_vision.html*).

Since trying this experiment, I've been playing a similar game walking along the side of the road. When cars are coming from behind me, and I'm looking strictly ahead, at what point can I see there's something there, and how much later is it that I can tell the color? I know a car's in my peripheral vision for a surprisingly long time before I can make the color out. Even though it would be in the name of science, please do be careful not to get run over.

—M.W.

How It Works

When you're looking at Anstis' eye chart, Figure 2-1, all the letters are equally legible because the light from each is falling on the same number of photoreceptors at the back of the eye. The central letters fall in the center of your retina, where the photoreceptors are densest; the outer letters fall in the periphery where the cells are spread thinner, but the letters are larger so the same number of cells are covered.

The distribution of light-sensitive cells across the retina is shown in Figure 2-2. There are two different curves, one for *rods* and one for *cones*, corresponding to the two types of photoreceptor cells we possess, so named because of their shapes. You can see how they're both densest toward the center of the eye and drop away toward the periphery, although at different rates. Assuming you're reading this book in anything above dim light, you'll have been using your cones to look at the eye chart—they're the ones that drop away fastest, and that rate determines the resolution of vision.

That's why our color vision suffers outside the fovea. Cones work best in normal, daytime light levels, and they also respond to color. But the rods are relatively more numerous outside the fovea, and they don't respond to color. They're also extremely sensitive to light, so during the day they're not too much help at all, but you can still see how they're useful when cones are sparse. They're why you could see your friend moving the colored card in the earlier experiment, but they couldn't help you figure out whether the card was yellow, blue, or whatever.

Rods, because of their sensitivity to light, are also handy when light is very poor. In dim conditions, our cones shut down (over a period of about 5 minutes) and we use our rods to see (the rods reach maximum sensitivity after about half an hour). But notice that rods are actually densest just outside the

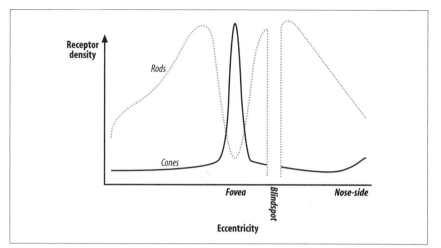

Figure 2-2. The distribution of different photoreceptors on the retina[2]

fovea, which means the best way to spot really faint light is to look at it slightly off-center. You can use this to look for faint stars on a dark night, and you'll see slightly more stars slightly outside the exact center of your vision.

Curiously, aside from experiments like the colored card one, you don't normally notice that not all of your visual world is high resolution. This is because you move your eyes to what you want to look at, and as you move your eyes, the area of high resolution follows. This process of active vision [Hack #15] is much more efficient than having high resolution everywhere.

Of course, before you move your eyes to something, your visual system has to preconsciously spot it using your peripheral vision and move your attention there. The events best noticed by peripheral vision are described in "Grab Attention" [Hack #37] and are mainly sudden changes of movement and light. These are events that signify that something needing an urgent response could be happening—it's not surprising we are designed to notice them even outside the high-resolution center of the eye.

End Notes

1. Reprinted from Vision Research, volume 14, Anstis, S., "A chart demonstrating variations in acuity with retinal position," p. 591, copyright (1974), with permission from Elsevier.

2. For a diagram that shows the detail rather than the general features, see: Østerberg, G. A. (1935). Topography of the layer of rods and cones in the human retina. *Acta Ophthalmologica, 13* (Supplement 6), 1–97.

See Also

- Illustrations of how resolution decreases in the periphery (*http://psy.ucsd.edu/~sanstis/SABlur.html*).

- A brief introduction to the human eye and the implication for page design (*http://www.awpa.asn.au/tipstrix/eyeball1.htm* and *http://www.awpa.asn.au/tipstrix/eyeball2.htm*).

- "The Rods and Cones of the Human Eye" (*http://hyperphysics.phy-astr.gsu.edu/hbase/vision/rodcone.html*), a good introduction and resource, which is part of the innovative and informative HyperPhysics hypertext (*http://hyperphysics.phy-astr.gsu.edu/hbase/hph.html*).

- A list of facts and figures on the eye, its capabilities, and a little about visual processing (*http://white.stanford.edu/~brian/numbers/node1.html*).

- More facts and figures concerning the human retina (*http://webvision.med.utah.edu/facts.html*), with references.

HACK #15 To See, Act

Think of perception as a behavior, as something active, rather than as something passive. Perception exists to guide action, and being able to act is key to the construction of the high-resolution illusion of the world we experience.

The other hacks in this chapter could give the impression that seeing is just a matter of your brain passively processing the information that comes in through the eyes. But perception is far more of an active process. The impression we have of the world is made up by sampling across times, as well as just by sampling across the senses. The sensation we receive at any moment prompts us to change our head position, our attention, maybe to act to affect something out in the world, and this gives us different sensations in the next moment to update our impression of the world.

It's easier for your brain to take multiple readings and then interpolate the answers than it is to spend a long time processing a single scene. Equally important, if you know what you want to do, maybe you don't need to completely interpret a scene; you may need to process it just enough to let you decide what to do next and in acting give yourself a different set of sensations that make the scene more obvious.

This school of thought is an "ecological" approach to perception and is associated with the psychologist J. J. Gibson.[1] He emphasized that perception is a cognitive process and, like other cognitive processes, depends on interacting with the world. The situations used by vision scientists in which people look at things without moving or reaching out to touch them are extremely unnatural, as large as the difference between a movie at the the-ater directed by someone else and the freewill experience of regular real life.

If you want people to see something clearly, give them the chance to move it around and see how it interacts with other objects. Don't be fooled into thinking that perception is passive.

In Action

One example of active vision that always happens, but that we don't nor-mally notice, is moving our eyes. We don't normally notice our blind spots [Hack #16] or our poor peripheral vision [Hack #14], because our gaze constantly flits from place to place. We sample constantly from the visual world using the high-resolution center of the eye—the *fovea*—and our brain constructs a constant, continuous, consistent, high-resolution illusion for us.

Constant sampling means constant eye movement: automatic, rapid shifts of gaze called *saccades*. We saccade up to five times a second, usually without noticing, even though each saccade creates a momentary gap in the flow of visual information into our brains [Hack #17]. Although the target destination of a saccade can be chosen consciously, the movement of the eyes isn't itself consciously controlled. A saccade can also be triggered by an event we're not even consciously aware of—at least not until we shift our gaze, placing it at the center of our attention. In this case, our attention's been captured involuntarily, and we had no choice but to saccade to that point [Hack #37].

Each pause in the chain of saccades is called a *fixation*. Fixations happen so quickly and so automatically that it's hard to believe that we don't actually hold our gaze on anything. Instead, we look at small parts of a scene for just fractions of a second and use the samples to construct an image.

Using eye tracking devices, it is possible to construct images of where peo-ple fixate when looking at different kinds of objects—a news web site, for instance. The Poynter Institute's Eyetrack III project (*http://www.poynterextra.org/eyetrack2004/*) investigates how Internet news readers go about perusing news online (Figure 2-3) and shows the results of their study as a pattern of where eye gaze lingers while looking over a news web site.

Part of developing speed-reading skills is learning to make fewer fixations on each line of text and take in more words at each fixation. If you're good—and the lines are short enough—you can get to the point of one fixation per line, scanning the page from top to bottom rather than side to side. Figure 2-4 shows typical fixation patterns while reading.

Marriott HOTELS & RESORTS
Click for Rates
The Times
Online Edition · Mon Dec 1 11:39:17 PST 2003
Sex Offenders On the Loose
'Bunker Buster' Missiles Aim at Moon
Troops From Iraq War Can't Donate Blood
Amorous Athletes
World's fastest couple: Tim Montgomery & Marion Jones
Get $100 for banking online.
Markets
COLUMBIA
7-day forecast
Features
Today's Highlights
BE THANKFUL FOR SOON THERE WILL BE NOTHING

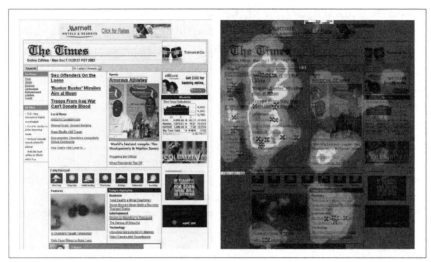

Figure 2-3. The pattern of eye fixations looking over a news web site; the brighter patches show where eyes tend to fixate[2]

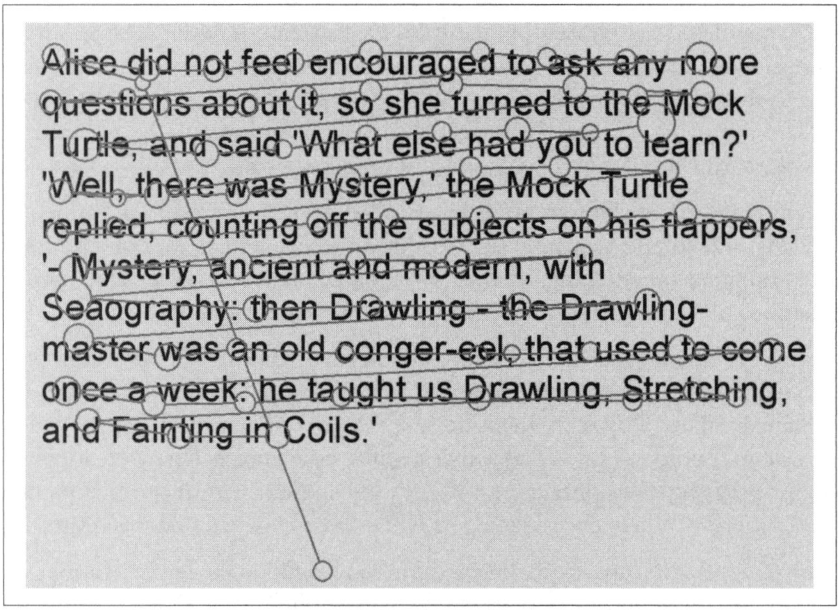

Alice did not feel encouraged to ask any more
questions about it, so she turned to the Mock
Turtle, and said 'What else had you to learn?'
'Well, there was Mystery,' the Mock Turtle
replied, counting off the subjects on his flappers,
'- Mystery, ancient and modern, with
Seaography: then Drawling - the Drawling-
master was an old conger-eel, that used to come
once a week: he taught us Drawling, Stretching,
and Fainting in Coils.'

Figure 2-4. A typical pattern of eye fixations when reading[3]

Figure 2-5 shows a typical pattern of what happens when you look at a face. You fixate enough to get a good idea of the shape of the whole face with your peripheral vision, fixating most on those details that carry the most information: the eyes.

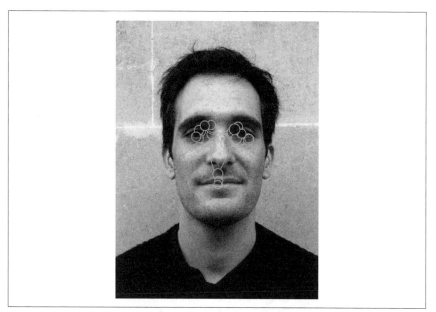

Figure 2-5. A pattern of fixations over 8 seconds when looking at a face (Matt's, in this case)[4]

End Notes

1. Gibson, J. J. (1979). *The Ecological Approach to Visual Perception*. Boston: Houghton Mifflin.

2. Heatmap image produced by Eyetools Inc. as part of the Poynter Institute's Eyetrack III project (*http://www.poynter.com/eyetrack*).

3. Scanpath produced using BeGaze software from eye movements recorded with the iView X Hi-Speed system, courtesy of SensoMotoric Instruments GmBH.

4. Photo of Matt by Dorian Mcfarland. Many thanks to Lizzie Crundall for creating this scanpath image.

See Also

- Eye tracking and visual attention demos and movies from the University of Southern California (*http://ilab.usc.edu/bu*).

- A tutorial on the mechanics of saccades (*http://www.personal.psu.edu/users/e/l/elm173/schlwork/semester3/psych/complete.htm*).

Map Your Blind Spot

#16   Find out how big your visual blind spot is and how your brain fills the hole so
you don't notice it.

Coating the back of each eye are photoreceptors that catch light and convert it to nerve impulses to send to the brain. This surface, the *retina*, isn't evenly spread with receptors—they're densest at the center and sparse in peripheral vision **[Hack #14]**. There's also a patch that is completely devoid of receptors; light that falls here isn't converted into nerve signals at all, leaving a blind spot in your field of view—or actually two blind spots, one for each eye.

In Action

First, here's how to notice your blind spot (later we'll draw a map to see how big it is). Close your left eye and look straight at the cross in Figure 2-6. Now hold the book flat about 10 inches from your face and slowly move it towards you. At about 6 inches, the black circle on the right of the cross will disappear, and where it was will just appear grey, the same color as the page around it.

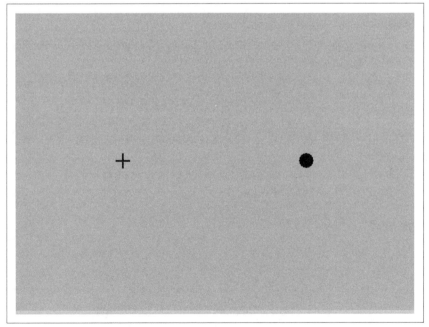

Figure 2-6. A typical blind spot pattern

You may need to move the book back and forth a little. Try to notice when the black circle reappears as you increase the distance, then move the book closer again to hide the circle totally. It's important you keep your right eye fixed on the cross, as the blind spot is at a fixed position from the center of vision and you need to keep it still to find it.

Now that you've found your blind spot, use Jeffrey Oristaglio and Paul Grobstein's Java applet at the web site Serendip (*http://serendip.brynmawr.edu/bb/blindspot*; Java) to plot its size.

The applet shows a cross and circle, so, as before, close your left eye, fix your gaze on the cross, and move your head so that the circle disappears in your blind spot. Then click the Start button (at the bottom of the applet) and move your cursor around within the blind spot. While it's in there, you won't be able to see it, but when you can (only just), click, and a dot will appear. Do this a few times, moving the cursor in different directions starting from the circle each time.

Again, be careful not to move your head, and keep focused on the cross. You'll end up with a pattern like Figure 2-7. The area inside the ring of dots is your blind spot.

> Here's a fun way of playing with your blind spot. In a room of people, close one eye and focus on your index finger. Pick a victim and adjust where your finger is until your blind spot makes his head disappear and the background takes its place. Not very profitable, but fun, and not as obvious as making as if to crush his head between your thumb and index finger.
>
> —T.S.

How It Works

The blind spot for each eye corresponds to a patch on the retina that is empty of photoreceptors. With no photoreceptors, there's nothing to detect light and turn it into information for use by the visual system, hence the blind spot.

Each receptor cell is connected to the brain via a series of cells that aggregate the signal before reporting it to the brain by an information-carrying fiber called an *axon* (see "The Neuron" [Hack #9]). Bizarrely, the part of the photoreceptor responsible for detecting light is *behind* the fibers for carrying the information into the brain. That's right—the light-sensitive part is on the side furthest from the light. Not only does this seem like bad design, but also it means that there has to be a gap in surface of the retina where the

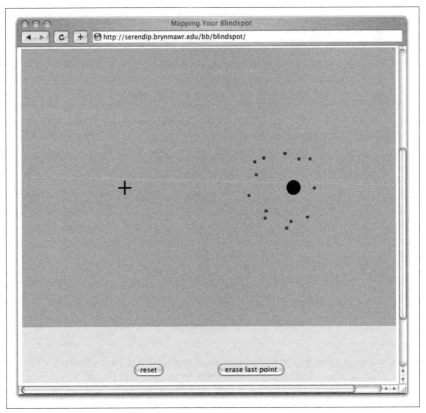

Figure 2-7. Matt's blind spot mapped

fibers gather together to exit the eyeball and run to the brain—and that exit point is the blind spot.

At first sight, there doesn't appear to be any particular reason for this structure other than accident. It doesn't have to be this way. If the light-detecting parts of the cells were toward the light, you wouldn't need a blind spot; the fibers could exit the eye without interrupting a continuous surface of photoreceptors on the retina.

Can we be sure that this is a bug and not a feature? One bit of evidence is that in the octopus eye it was done differently. The eye evolved independently in octopuses, and when it did, the retinal cells have the photoreceptors in front of the nerve fibers, not behind, and hence no blind spot.

Conversely, there are benefits to the arrangement of the human retina: it allows a good blood supply close to the retina to both nourish the photoreceptors and help metabolize debris that accumulates there. Both orientations of the retina have their advantages.

We don't normally notice these two great big holes in our field of vision. Not only do our eyes move around so that there's no one bit of visual space we're ignoring, but the blind spots from the two eyes don't overlap, so we can use information from one eye to fill in the missing information from the other.

However, even in situations in which the other eye isn't providing useful information and when your blind spot is staying in the same place, the brain has evolved mechanisms to fill in the hole.[1] This filling in is why, in the demostration above, you see a continuous grey background rather than a black hole.

Hacking the Hack

The Cheshire Cat experiment (*http://www.exploratorium.edu/snacks/ cheshire_cat.html*; full instructions) shows a really good interaction of the blind spot, the filling-in mechanisms and our innate disposition to notice movement competing against our innate disposition to pay attention to faces. With a blank wall, a mirror, and a friend, you can use your blind spot to give yourself the illusion that you can slowly erase your friend's head until just her smile remains.

End Note

1. "Seeing More Than Your Eye Does" (*http://serendip.brynmawr.edu/bb/ blindspot1.html*) is a fun tour through the capabilities of your blind spot (the link at the bottom of each page's article will lead you to the next page). It demonstrates how your brain uses colors and patterns in the area surrounding the blind spot to make a good guess of what should be in the blind spot itself and will report that to your conscious mind.

See Also

- Ramachandran, V. S. "Blind Spots." *Scientific American*, May 1992, 86–91.
- Ramachandran, V. S., & Gregory, R. L. (1991). Perceptual filling in of artificially induced scotomas in human vision. *Nature, 350,* 699–702.

- There is an interesting discussion of the blind spot, filling in, and what that implies for the nature of experience in Daniel Dennett's *Consciousness Explained*, 344–366. Boston: Little, Brown and Co., 1991.

Glimpse the Gaps in Your Vision

Our eyes constantly dart around in extremely quick movements called saccades. During each movement, vision cuts out.

Despite the fact that the eye has a blind spot, an uneven distribution of color perception, and can make out maximal detail in only a tiny area at the center of vision, we still manage to see the world as an uninterrupted panorama. The eye jumps about from point to point, snapshotting high-resolution views, and the brain assembles them into a stunningly stable and remarkably detailed picture.

These rapid jumps with the eyes are called *saccades*, and we make up to five every second. The problem is that while the eyes move in saccade all visual input is blurred. It's difficult enough for the brain to process stable visual images without having to deal with motion blur from the eye moving too. So, during saccades, it just doesn't bother. Essentially, while your eyes move, you can't see.

In Action

Put your face about 6 inches from a mirror and look from eye to eye. You'll notice that while you're obviously switching your gaze from eye to eye, you can't see your own eyes actually moving—only the end result when they come to rest on the new point of focus. Now get someone else to watch you doing so in the mirror. They can clearly see your eyes shifting, while to you it's quite invisible.

With longer saccades, you can consciously perceive the effect, but only just.

Hold your arms out straight so your two index fingers are at opposite edges of your vision. Flick your eyes between them while keeping your head still. You can just about notice the momentary blackness as all visual input from the eyes is cut off. Saccades of this length take around 200 ms (a fifth of a second), which lies just on the threshold of conscious perception.

What if something happens during a saccade? Well, unless it's really bright, you'll simply not see it. That's what's so odd about saccades. We're doing it constantly, but it doesn't look as if the universe is being blanked out a hundred thousand times a day for around a tenth of a second every time.

> Saccadic suppression may even be one of the ways some magic tricks work. We know that sudden movements grab attention [Hack #37]. The magician's flourish with one hand grabs your attention, and as your eyes are moving, you aren't able to see what he does with the other hand to pull off the trick.
>
> —N.H.

How It Works

Saccadic suppression exists to stop the visual system being confused by blurred images that the eye gets while it is moving rapidly in a saccade. The cutout begins just before the muscles twitch to make the eyes move. Since that's before any blur would be seen on the retina, we know the mechanism isn't just blurred images being edited out at processing time. Instead, whatever bit of the brain prepares the eyes to saccade must also be sending a signal that suppresses vision. Where exactly does that signal come from? That's not certain yet.

One recent experiment proves that suppression definitely occurs before any visual information gets to the cortex. This isn't the kind of experiment that can be done at home, unfortunately, as it requires *transcranial magnetic stimulation* (TMS). TMS [Hack #5] essentially lets you turn on, or turn off, parts of the brain that are close enough to the surface to be affected by a magnet. The device uses rapid electromagnetic pulses to affect the cells carrying signals in the brain. Depending on the frequency of the pulses, you can enhance or suppress neuronal activity.

Kai Thilo and a team from Oxford University[1] used TMS to give volunteers small illusionary spots, called phosphenes, in their vision.

When phosphenes were made at the retina, by applying TMS to the eye, saccadic suppression worked as normal. During a saccade, the phosphenes disappeared, as would be expected. The phosphenes were being treated like normal images on the retina. But when the spots were induced later in visual processing, at the cortex, saccades didn't affect them. They appeared regardless of eye movements.

So, suppression acts between the retina and the cortex, stopping visual information before the point where it would start entering conscious experience. Not being able to see during a saccade isn't the same kind of obstruction as when you don't see because your attention is elsewhere. That is what happens during change blindness [Hack #40]—you don't notice changes because your attention is engaged by other things, but the changes are still potentially visible.

Instead, saccadic suppression is a more serious limitation. What happens during a saccade makes it nowhere near awareness. It's not just that you don't see it, it's that you can't.

End Note

1. Thilo, K. V., Santoro, L., Walsh, V., & Blakemore, C. (2004). The site of saccadic suppression. *Nature Neuroscience, 7*(1), 13–14.

See Also

• Saccadic suppression also lies behind the stopped clock illusion [Hack #18].

When Time Stands Still

Our sense of time lends a seamless coherence to our conscious experience of the world. We are able to effortlessly distinguish between the past, present, and future. Yet, subtle illusions show that our mental clock can make mistakes.

You only have to enjoy the synchrony achieved by your local orchestra to realize that humans must be remarkably skilled at judging short intervals of time. However, our mental clock does make mistakes. These anomalies tend to occur when the brain is attempting to compensate for gaps or ambiguities in available sensory information.

Such gaps can be caused by self-generated movement. For example, our knowledge about how long an object has been in its current position is compromised by the suppression of visual information [Hack #17] that occurs when we move our eyes toward that object—we can have no idea what that object was actually doing for the time our eyes were in motion. This uncertainty of position, and the subsequent guess the brain makes, can be felt in action by saccading the eyes toward a moving object.

In Action

Sometimes you'll glance at a clock and the second hand appears to hang, remaining stationary for longer than it ought to. For what seems like a very long moment, you think the clock may have stopped. Normally you keep looking to check and see that shortly afterward the second hand starts to move again as normal—unless, that is, it truly has stopped.

This phenomenon has been dubbed the *stopped clock illusion*. You can demonstrate it to yourself by getting a silently moving clock and placing it off to one side. It doesn't need to be an analog clock with a traditional second hand; it can be a digital clock or watch, just so long as it shows seconds. Position the clock so that you aren't looking at it at first but can bring the second hand or digits into view just by moving your eyes. Now, flick your eyes over to the clock (i.e., make a saccade [Hack #15]). The movement needs to be as quick as possible, much as might happen if your attention had been grabbed by a sudden sound or thought [Hack #37]; a slow, deliberate movement won't cut it. Try it a few times and you should experience the "stopped clock" effect on some attempts at least.

Whether or not this works depends on exactly when your eyes fall on the clock. If your eyes land on the clock just when the second hand is on the cusp of moving (or second digits are about to change), you're less likely to see the illusion. On the other hand, if your eyes land the instant after the second hand has moved, you're much more likely to experience the effect.

How It Works

When our gaze falls on an object, it seems our brain makes certain assumptions about how long that object has been where it is. It probably does this to compensate for the suppression of our vision that occurs when we move our eyes [Hack #17]. This suppression means vision can avoid the difficult job of deciphering the inevitable and persistent motion blur that accompanies each of the hundred thousand rapid saccadic eye movements that we make daily. So when our gaze falls on an object, the brain assumes that object has been where it is for at least as long as it took us to lay eyes on it. Our brain *antedates* the time the object has been where it is. When we glance at stationary objects like a lamp or table, we don't notice this antedating process. But when we look at a clock's second hand or digits, knowing as we do that they ought *not* be in one place for long, this discord triggers the illusion.

This explanation was supported and quantified in an experiment by Keilan Yarrow and colleagues at University College, London and Oxford University.[1] They asked people to glance at a number counter. The participants' eye movements triggered the counter, which then began counting upward from 1 to 4. Each of the numerals 2, 3, and 4 was displayed for 1 second, but the initial numeral 1 was displayed for a range of different intervals, from 400 ms to 1600 ms, starting the moment subjects moved their eyes toward the counter. The participants were asked to state whether the time they saw the numeral 1 was longer or shorter than the time they saw the subsequent numerals. Consistent with the stopped clock illusion, the participants consistently overestimated how long they thought they had seen the number 1. And crucially, the larger the initial eye movement made to the counter, the more participants tended to overestimate the duration for which the initial number 1 was visible. This supports the saccadic suppression hypothesis, because larger saccades are inevitably associated with a longer period of visual suppression. And if it is true that the brain assumes a newly focused–on target has been where it is for at least as long as it took to make the orienting saccade, then it makes sense that longer saccades led to greater overestimation. Moreover, the stopped clock illusion was found to occur only when people made eye movements to the counter, not when the counter jumped into a position before their eyes—again consistent with the saccadic suppression explanation.

You'll experience an effect similar to the stopped clock illusion when you first pick up a telephone handset and get an intermittent tone (pause, beeeep, pause, beeeep, repeat). You might find that the initial silence appears to hang for longer than it ought to. The phone can appear dead and, consequently, the illusion has been dubbed the *dead phone illusion*.

The clock explanation, however, cannot account for the dead phone illusion since it doesn't depend on saccadic eye movement.[2] And it can't account, either, for another recent observation that people tend to overestimate how long they have been holding a newly grasped object,[3] which seems like a similar effect: the initial encounter appears to last longer.

One suggestion for the dead phone illusion is that shifting our attention to a new auditory focus creates an increase in arousal, or *mental interest*. Because previous research has shown that increased arousal—when we're stressed, for instance—speeds up our sense of time, this could lead us to overestimate the duration of a newly attended–to sound. Of course, this doesn't fit with the observation mentioned before, that the stopped clock illusion fails to occur when the clock or counter moves in front of our eyes—surely that would lead to increased arousal just as much as glancing at a clock or picking up a telephone.

So, a unifying explanation for "when time stands still" remains elusive. What *is* clear is that most of the time our brain is extraordinarily successful at providing us with a coherent sense of what happened when.

End Notes

1. Yarrow, K., Haggard, P., Heal, R., Brown, P., & Rothwell, J. C. (2001). Illusory perceptions of space and time preserve cross-saccadic perceptual continuity. *Nature, 414*(6861), 302–305.

2. Hodinott-Hill, I., Thilo, K. V., Cowey, A., & Walsh, V. (2002). Auditory chronostasis: Hanging on the telephone. *Current Biology, 12,* 1779–1781.

3. Yarrow, K., & Rothwell, J. C. (2003). Manual chronostasis: Tactile perception precedes physical contact. *Current Biology, 12*(13), 1134–1139.

—*Christian Jarrett*

Release Eye Fixations for Faster Reactions

#19 It takes longer to shift your attention to a new object if the old object is still there.

Shifting attention often means shifting your eyes. But we're never fully in control of what our eyes want to look at. If they're latched on to something, they're rather stubborn about moving elsewhere. It's faster for you to look at something new if you don't have to tear your eyes away—if what you were originally looking at disappears and then there's a short gap, it's as if your eyes become unlocked, and your reaction time improves. This is called the *gap effect*.

In Action

The gap effect can be spotted if you're asked to stare at some shape on a screen, then switch your gaze to a new shape that will appear somewhere else on the screen. Usually, switching to the new shape takes about a fifth of a second. But if the old shape vanishes shortly before the new shape flashes up, moving your gaze takes less time, about 20% less.

It has to be said: the effect—on the order of just hundredths of a second—is tiny in the grand scheme of things. You're not going to notice it easily around the home. It's a feature of our low-level cognitive control: voluntarily switching attention takes a little longer under certain circumstances. In other words, voluntary behavior isn't as voluntary as we'd like to think.

How It Works

We take in the world piecemeal, focusing on a tiny part of it with the high-resolution center of our vision for a fraction of a second, then our eyes move on to focus on another part. Each of these mostly automatic moves is called a saccade [Hack #15].

We make saccades continuously—up to about five every second—but that's not to say they're fluid or all the same. While you're taking in a scene, your eyes are locked in. They're resistant to moving away, just for a short time. So what happens when another object comes along and you want to move your eyes toward it? You have to overcome that inhibition, and that takes a short amount of time.

Having to overcome resistance to saccades is one way of looking at why focusing on a new shape takes longer if the old one is still there. Another way to look at it is to consider what happens when the old shape disappears. Then we can see that the eyes are automatically released from their fixation, and no longer so resistant to making a saccade—which is why, when the old shape disappears before the new shape flashes up, it's faster to gaze-shift. In addition, the disappearing shape acts as a warning signal to the early visual system ("There's something going on, get ready!"), which serves to speed up the eyes' subsequent reaction times. It's a combination of both of these factors—the warning and the eyes no longer being held back from moving—that results in the speedup.

In Real Life

Just for completeness, it's worth knowing that the old point of fixation should disappear 200 milliseconds (again, a fifth of a second) before the new object appears, to get maximum speedup. This time is used for the brain to notice the old object has vanished and get the eyes ready to move again. Now, in the real world, objects rarely just vanish like this, but it happens a lot on computer screens. So it's worth knowing that if you want someone to shift his attention from one item to another, you can make it an easier transition by having the first item disappear shortly before the second appears (actually vanish, not just disappear behind something, because we keep paying attention to objects even when they're temporarily invisible [Hack #36]). This will facilitate your user's disengagement from the original item, which might be a dialog box or some other preparatory display and put her into a state ready for whatever's going to need her attention next.

See Also

- Taylor, T. L., Kingstone, A., & Klein, R. M. (1998). The disappearance of foveal and non-foveal stimuli: Decomposing the gap effect. *Canadian Journal of Experimental Psychology, 52*(4), 192–199.

Fool Yourself into Seeing 3D

How do you figure out the three-dimensional shape of objects, just by looking? At first glance, it's using shadows.

Looking at shadows is one of many tricks we use to figure out the shape of objects. As a trick, it's easy to fool—shading alone is enough for the brain to assume what it's seeing is a real shadow. This illusion is so powerful and so deeply ingrained, in fact, that we can actually feel depth in a picture despite knowing it's just a flat image.

In Action

Have a look at the shaded circles in Figure 2-8, following a similar illustration in Kleffner and Ramachandran's "On the Perception of Shape from Shading."[1]

I put together this particular diagram myself, and there's nothing to it: just a collection of circles on a medium gray background. All the circles are gradient-filled black and white, some with white at the top and some with white at the bottom. Despite the simplicity of the image, there's already a sense of depth.

The shading seems to make the circles with white at the top bend out of the page, as though they're bumps. The circles with white at the bottom look more like depressions or even holes.

To see just how strong the sense of depth is, compare the shaded circles to the much simpler diagram in Figure 2-9, also following Kleffner and Ramachandran's paper.

The only difference is that, instead of being shaded, the circles are divided into solid black and white halves. Yet the depth completely disappears.

How It Works

Shadows are identified early in visual processing in order to get a quick first impression of the shape of a scene. We can tell it's early because the mechanism it uses to resolve light source ambiguities is rather hackish.

Ambiguities occur all the time. For instance, take one of the white-at-top circles from Figure 2-8. Looking at it, you could be seeing one of two shapes depending on whether you imagine the shape was lit from the top or the bottom of the page. If light's coming from above, you can deduce it's a bump because it's black underneath where the shadows are. On the other hand, if the light's coming from the bottom of the page, only a dent produces the same shading pattern. Bump or dent: two different shapes can make the same shadow pattern lit from opposite angles.

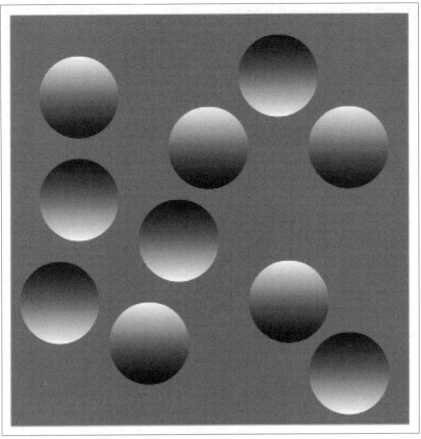

Figure 2-8. Shaded figures give the illusion of three-dimensionality

There's no light source in the diagram, though, and the flat gray background gives no clues as to where the light might be coming from. That white-at-top circle should, by rights, be ambiguous. You should sometimes see a bump and sometimes see a dent.

What's remarkable is that people see the white-at-top circles as bumps, not dents, despite the two possibilities. Instead of leaving us in a state of confusion, the brain has made a choice: light comes from above.[2]

Assuming scenes are lit from above makes a lot of sense: if it's light, it's usually because the sun is overhead. So why describe this as a hackish mechanism?

Although the light source assumption seems like a good one, it's actually not very robust. Try looking at Figure 2-8 again. This time, prop the book against a wall and turn your head upside-down. The bumps turn into dents

Figure 2-9. Binary black-and-white "shading" doesn't provide a sense of depth

and the dents turn into bumps. Instead of assuming the light comes from high up in the sky, your brain assumes it comes from the top of your visual field.

Rather than spend time figuring out which way up your head is and then deducing where the sun is likely to be, your brain has opted for the "good enough" solution. This solution works most, not all, of the time (not if you're upside-down), but it also means the light source can be hardcoded into shape perception routines, allowing rapid processing of the scene.

It's this rapidity that allows the deduction of shape from shadows to occur so early in processing. That's important for building a three-dimensional mental scene rather than a flat image like a photograph. But the shaded circles have been falsely tagged as three-dimensional, which gives them a compelling sense of depth.

What's happened to the shaded circles is called "pop-out." Pop-out means that the circles jump out from the background at you—they're easier to notice or give attention to than similar flat objects. Kleffner and Ramachandran, in the same paper as before, illustrate this special property by timing how long it takes to spot a single bump-like circle in a whole page of dents. It turns out to not matter how many dents are on the page hiding the bump. Due to pop-out, the bump is immediately seen.

If the page of bumps and one dent is turned on its side, however, spotting the dent takes much longer. Look one more time at Figure 2-8, this time holding the book on its side. The sense of depth is much reduced and, because the light-from-above assumption favors neither type of circle, it's pretty much random which type appears indented and which appears bent out of the page. In fact, timings show that spotting the one different circle is no longer immediate. It takes longer, the more circles there are on the page.

The speed advantage for pop-out is so significant that some animals change their coloring to avoid popping out in the eyes of their predators. Standing under a bright sun, an antelope would be just like one of the shaded circles with a lit-up back and shadows underneath. But the antelope is dark on top and has a white belly. Called "countershading," this pattern opposes the shadows and turns the animal an even shade, weakening the pop-out effect and letting it fade into the background.

In Real Life

Given pop-out is so strong, it's not surprising we often use the shading trick to produce it in everyday life.

The 3D beveled button on the computer desktop is one such way. I've not seen any experiments about this specifically, but I'd speculate that Susan Kare's development of the beveled button in Windows 3.0 (*http://www.kare.com/ MakePortfolioPage.cgi?page=6*) is more significant than we'd otherwise assume for making more obvious what to click.

My favorite examples of shade from shading are in Stuart Anstis' lecture on the use of this effect in the world of fashion (*http://psy.ucsd.edu/~sanstis/ SAStocking.htm*). Anstis points out that jeans faded white along the front of the legs are effectively artificially shadowing the sides of the legs, making them look rounder and shapelier (Figure 2-10). The same is true of stockings, which are darker on the sides whichever angle you see them from.

Among many examples, the high point of his presentation is how the apparent shape of the face is changed with makeup—or in his words, "painted-on shadows." The with and without photographs (Figure 2-11) demonstrate

Figure 2-10. Shaded jeans add shape to legs

with well-defined cheekbones and a sculpted face just how compelling shape for shading really is.

End Notes

1. Kleffner, D. A., & Ramachandran, V. S. (1992). On the perception of shape from shading. *Perception and Psychophysics, 52*(1), 18–36.

2. Actually, more detailed experiments show that the brain's default light source isn't exactly at the top of the visual field, but to the top left. These experiments detailed in this paper involve more complex shadowed shapes than circles and testing to see whether they pop out or appear indented when immediately glanced. Over a series of trials, the position of the assumed light source can be deduced by watching where the brain assumes the light source to be. Unfortunately, why that position is top left rather than top anywhere else is still unknown. See Mamassian, P., Jentzsch, I., Bacon, B. A., & Schweinberger, S. R. (2003). Neural correlates of shape from shading. *NeuroReport, 14*(7), 971–975.

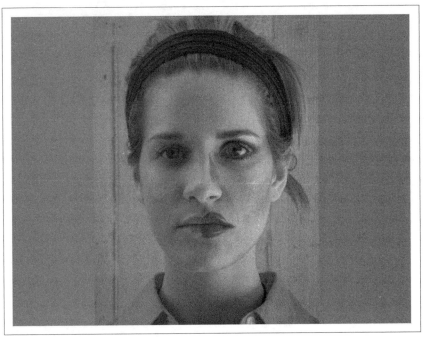

Figure 2-11. With only half the face in makeup, the apparent shape difference is easy to see

Objects Move, Lighting Shouldn't

Moving shadows make us see moving objects rather than assume moving light sources.

Shadows get processed early when trying to make sense of objects, and they're one of the first things our visual system uses when trying to work out shape. "Fool Yourself into Seeing 3D" [Hack #20] further showed that our visual system makes the hardwired assumption that light comes from above. Another way shadows are used is to infer movement, and with this, our visual system makes the further assumption that a moving shadow is the result of a moving object, rather than being due to a moving light source. In theory, of course, the movement of a shadow could be due to either cause, but we've evolved to ignore one of those possibilities—rapidly moving objects are much more likely than rapidly moving lights, not to mention more dangerous.

In Action

Observe how your brain uses shadows to construct the 3D model of a scene. Watch the ball-in-a-box movie at:

- *http://gandalf.psych.umn.edu/~kersten/kersten-lab/images/ball-in-a-box.mov* (small version)

- *http://gandalf.psych.umn.edu/~kersten/kersten-lab/demos/BallInaBox.mov* (large version, 4 MB)

 If you're currently without Internet access, see Figure 2-12 for movie stills.

The movie is a simple piece of animation involving a ball moving back and forth twice across a 3D box. Both times, the ball moves diagonally across the floor plane. The first time, it appears to move along the floor of the box with a drop shadow directly beneath and touching the bottom of the ball. The second time the ball appears to move horizontally and float up off the floor, the shadow following along on the floor. The ball actually takes the same path both times; it's just the path of the shadow that changes (from diagonal along with the ball to horizontal). And it's that change that alters your perception of the ball's movement. (Figure 2-12 shows stills of the first (left) and second (right) times the ball crosses the box.)

Now watch the more complex "zigzagging ball" movie (*http://www.kyb.tue.mpg.de/links/demo.html*; Figure 2-13 shows a still from the movie), again of a ball in motion inside a 3D box.

This time, while the ball is moving in a straight line from one corner of the box to the other (the proof is in the diagonal line it follows), the shadow is darting about all over the place. This time, there is even strong evidence that it's the light source—and thus the shadow—that's moving: the shading and colors on the box change continuously and in a way that is consistent with a moving light source rather than a zigzagging ball (which doesn't produce any shading or color changes!). Yet still you see a zigzagging ball.

How It Works

Your brain constructs an internal 3D model of a scene as soon as you look at one, with the influence of shadows on the construction being incredibly strong. You can see this in action in the first movie: your internal model of

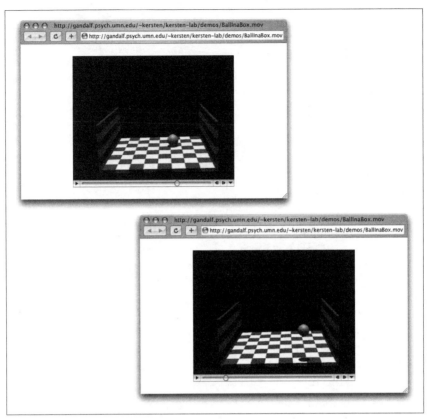

Figure 2-12. Stills from the "ball-in-a-box" movie

the scene changes dramatically based solely on the position and motion of a shadow.

> I feel bad saying "internal model." Given that most of the information about a scene is already in the universe, accessible if you move your head, why bother storing it inside your skull too? We probably store internally only what we need to, when ambiguities have been involved. Visual data inside the head isn't a photograph, but a structured model existing in tandem with extelligence, information that we can treat as intelligence but isn't kept internally.
>
> —T.S.

The second movie shows a couple more of the assumptions (of which there are many) the brain makes in shadow processing. One assumption is that darker coloring means shadow. Another is that light usually comes from

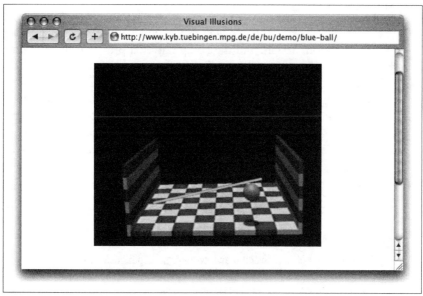

Figure 2-13. A still from the "zigzagging ball" movie[1]

overhead (these assumptions are so natural we don't even notice they've been made). Both of these come into play when two-dimensional shapes—ordinary pictures—appear to take on depth with the addition of judicious shading [Hack #20].

Based on these assumptions, the brain prefers to believe that the light source is keeping still and the moving object is jumping around, rather than that the light source is moving. And this despite all the cues to the contrary: the lighting pattern on the floor and walls, the sides of the box being lit up in tandem with the shifting shadow—these should be more than enough proof. Still, the shadow of the ball is all that the brain takes into account. In its quest to produce a 3D understanding of a scene as fast as possible, the brain doesn't bother to assimilate information from across the whole visual field. It simplifies things markedly by just assuming the light source stays still.

It's the speed of shadow processing you have to thank for this illusion. Conscious knowledge is slower to arise than the hackish-but-speedy early perception and remains influenced by it, despite your best efforts to see it any other way.

End Note

1. Zigzagging ball animation thanks to D. Kersten (University of Minnesota, U.S.) and I. Bülthoff (Max-Planck-Institut für biologische Kybernetik, Germany)

See Also

- The Kersten Lab (*http://gandalf.psych.umn.edu/~kersten/kersten-lab*) researches vision, action, and the computational principles behind how we turn vision into an understanding of the world. As well as publications on the subject, their site houses demos exploring what information we can extract from what we see and the assumptions made. One demo of theirs, Illusory Motion from Shadows (*http://gandalf.psych. umn.edu/~kersten/kersten-lab/images/kersten-shadow-cine.mov*), demonstrates how the assumption that light sources are stationary can be exploited to provide another powerful illusion of motion.

- Kersten, D., Knill, D., Mamassian, P., & Buelthoff, I. (1996). Illusory motion from shadows. *Nature, 379*(6560), 31.

Depth Matters

Our perception of a 3D world draws on multiple depth cues as diverse as atmospheric haze and preconceptions of object size. We use all together in vision and individually in visual design and real life.

Our ability to see depth is an amazing feature of our vision. Not only does depth make what we see more interesting, it also plays a crucial, functional role. We use it to navigate our 3D world and can employ it in the practice of visual communication design to help organize what we see through depth's ability to clarify through separation[1].

Psychologists call a visual trigger that gives us a sense of depth a *depth cue*. Vision science suggests that our sense of depth originates from at least 19 identifiable cues in our environment. We rarely see depth cues individually, since they mostly appear and operate in concert to provide depth information, but we can loosely organize them together into several related groups:

Binocular cues (stereoscopic depth, eye convergence)
    With binocular (two-eye) vision, the brain sees depth by comparing angle differences in the images from each eye. This type of vision is very important to daily life (just try catching a ball with one eye closed), but there are also many monocular (single-eye) depth cues. Monocular cues have the advantage that they are easier to employ for depth in images on flat surfaces (e.g., in print and on computer screens).

Perspective-based cues (size gradient, texture gradient, linear perspective)
    The shape of a visual scene gives cues to the depth of objects within it. Perspective lines converging/diverging or a change in the image size of patterns that we know to be at a constant scale (such as floor tile squares) can be used to inform our sense of depth.

Occlusion-based cues (object overlap, cast shadow, surface shadow)
> The presence of one object partially blocking the form of another and the cast shadows they create are strong cues to depth. See "Fool Yourself into Seeing 3D" [Hack #20] for examples.

Focus-based cues (atmospheric perspective, object intensity, focus)
> Greater distance usually brings with it a number of depth cues associated with conditions of the natural world, such as increased atmospheric haze and physical limits to the eye's focus range. We discuss one of these cues, object intensity, next.

Motion-based cues (kinetic depth, a.k.a. motion parallax)
> As you move your head, objects at different distances move at different relative speeds. This is a very strong cue and is also the reason a spitting cobra sways its head from side to side to work out how far away its prey is from its position.

There isn't room to discuss all of these cues here, so we'll look in detail at just two depth cues: object intensity and known size (a cue that is loosely connected to the prespective-based cue family). More information on depth cues and their use in information design can be found in the references at the end of this hack.

Object Intensity

Why do objects further away from us appear to be faded or faint? Ever notice that bright objects seem to attract our attention? It's all about intensity.

If we peer into the distance, we notice that objects such as buildings or mountains far away appear less distinct and often faded compared to objects close up. Even the colors of these distant objects appear lighter or even washed out. The reason for this is something psychologists call atmospheric perspective or object intensity. It is a visual cue our minds use to sense depth; we employ it automatically as a way to sort and prioritize information about our surroundings (foreground as distinct from background).

Designers take advantage of this phenomenon to direct our attention by using bold colors and contrast in design work. Road safety specialists make traffic safety signs brighter and bolder in contrast than other highway signs so they stand out, as shown in Figure 2-14. You too, in fact, employ the same principle when you use a highlighter to mark passages in a book. You're using a depth cue to literally bring certain text into the foreground, to prioritize information in your environment.

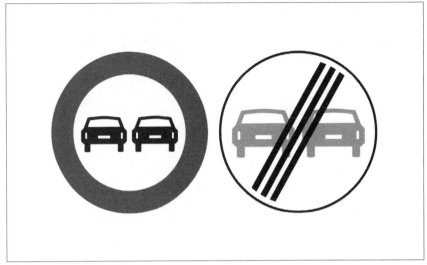

Figure 2-14. Important street signs often use more intense colors and bolder contrast elements so they stand out from other signage[2]

In action. Close one eye and have a look at the two shaded blocks side by side in Figure 2-15. If you had to decide which block appears to be visually closer, which would you choose? The black block seems to separate and appear forward from the gray block. It is as if our mind wants it to be in front.

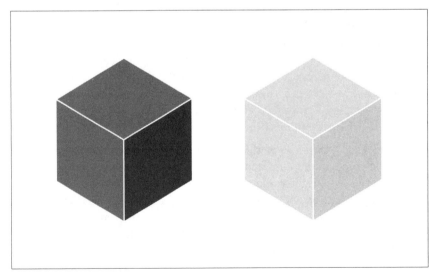

Figure 2-15. Which block appears closer?

How it works. The reason for this experience of depth, based on light-dark value differences, is *atmospheric perspective* and the science is actually quite simple. Everywhere in the air are dust or water particles that partially obscure our view of objects, making them appear dull or less distinct. Up close, you can't see these particles, but as the space between you and an object increases, so do the numbers of particles in the air. Together these particles cause a gradual haze to appear on distant objects. In the daytime, this haze on faraway objects appears to be colored white or blue as the particles scatter the natural light. Darker objects separate and are perceived as foreground and lighter ones as background. At night, the effect is the same, except this time the effect is reversed: objects that are lit appear to be closer, as shown in Figure 2-16. So as a general rule of thumb, an object's intensity compared to its surroundings helps us generate our sense of its position. Even colors have this same depth effect because of comparative differences in their value and chroma. The greater the difference in intensity between two objects, the more pronounced the sense of depth separation between them.

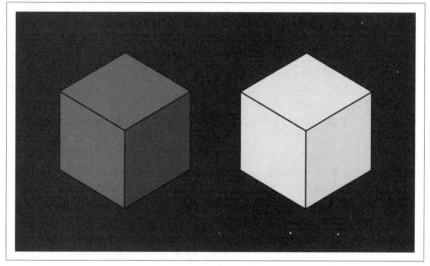

Figure 2-16. At night, lit objects appear closer

So how does intensity relate to attention? One view is that we pay more attention to objects that are closer, since they are of a higher concern to our physical body. We focus on visually intense objects because their association with the foreground naturally causes us to assign greater importance to them. Simply put, they stand out in front.

In real life. Since weather can affect the atmosphere's state, it can influence perceived depth: the more ambient the air particles, the more acute the atmospheric perspective. Hence, a distance judged in a rainstorm, for example, will be perceived as further than that same distance judged on a clear, sunny day.

Known Size

How do we tell the distance in depth between two objects if they aren't the same?

We all know that if you place two same-size objects at different distances and look at them both, the object further away appears smaller. But have you ever been surprised at an object's size when you see it for the first time from afar and discover it is much bigger up close? Psychologists call this phenomenon *size gradient* and *known size*. Size gradient states that as objects are moved further away, they shrink proportionally in our field of view. From these differences in relative size, we generate a sense of depth. This general rule holds true, but our prior knowledge of an object's size can sometime trip us up because we use the known size of an object (or our assumptions of its size) to measure the relative size of objects we see.

Being aware of a user's knowledge of subjects and objects is key if comparative size is an important factor. Many visual communication designers have discovered the peril of forgetting to include scale elements in their work for context reference. A lack of user-recognizable scale can render an important map, diagram, or comparative piece completely useless. An unexpected change in scale can disorientate a user—or, if employed right, can help grab attention.

In action. Have a look at the mouse and elephant in Figure 2-17. We know about their true relative sizes from our memory, even though the mouse appears gigantic in comparison.

But what about Figure 2-18, which shows a mouse and a zerk (a made-up animal). Since we've never seen a zerk before, do we know which is truly bigger or do we assume the scale we see is correct?

How it works. Our knowledge of objects and their actual size plays a hidden role in our perception of depth. Whenever we look at an object, our mind recalls memories of its size, shape, and form. The mind then compares this memory to what we see, using scale to calculate a sense of distance. This quick-and-dirty comparison can sometimes trip us however, especially when we encounter something unfamiliar. One psychologist, Bruce Goldstein, offers a cultural example of an anthropologist who met an African bushman living in dense rain forest. The anthropologist led the bushman out to an

Figure 2-17. An elephant and a mouse—you know from memory that elephants are bigger

Figure 2-18. A zerk and a mouse—since a zerk is made up, you can use only comparison with the mouse to judge size

open plain and showed him some buffalo from afar. The bushman refused to believe that the animals were large and said they must be insects. But when he approached them up close, he was astounded as they appeared to grow in size, and attributed it to magic. The dense rain forest and its limitations on viewing distance, along with the unfamiliar animal, had distorted his ability to sense scale.

In real life. Some designers have captured this magic to their benefit. The movie industry has often taken our assumptions of known size and captivated us by breaking them, making the familiar appear monstrous and novel. For example, through a distortion of scale and juxtaposition, we can be fooled into thinking that 50-foot ants are wreaking havoc on small towns and cities.

End Notes

1. Bardel, W. (2001). "Depth Cues for Information Design." Thesis, Carnegie Mellon University (*http://www.bardel.info/downloads/Depth_cues.pdf*).

2. Street sign symbols courtesy of Ultimate Symbol Inc. (*http://www.ultimatesymbol.com*).

See Also

- Goldstein, E. B. (1989). *Sensation & Perception*. Pacific Grove: Brooks/Cole Publishing.
- Ware, C. (1999). *Information Visualization*. London: Academic Press.
- Tufte, E. (1999). *Envisioning Information*. Cheshire: Graphics Press.
- Braunstein, M. L. (1976). *Depth Perception Through Motion*. London: Academic Press.
- Reagan, D. (2000). *Human Perception of Objects*. Sunderland: Sinauer Assoc.

—*William Bardel*

HACK #23 See How Brightness Differs from Luminance: The Checker Shadow Illusion

A powerful illusion of brightness shows how our brain takes scene structure and implied lighting into account when calculating the shade of things.

A major challenge for our vision is the reconstruction of a three-dimensional visual world from a two-dimensional retinal picture. The projection from three to two dimensions irrevocably loses information, which somehow needs to be reconstructed by the vision centers in our brain. True, we have two eyes, which helps a bit in the horizontal plane, but the vivid self-experience of seeing a 3D world clearly persists after covering one eye [Hack #22].

In the process of reconstructing 3D from 2D, our brain cleverly relies on previous experience and assumptions on the physics of the real world. Since information is thus fabricated, the process is prone to error, especially in appropriately manipulated pictures, which gives rise to various large classes of optical illusions. We will concentrate here on a fairly recent example, Ted Adelson's checker shadow illusion.[1]

In Action

Take a look at Adelson's checker shadow illusion in Figure 2-19.

Figure 2-19. Adelson's checker shadow—which is brighter, A or B?

We would all agree that one sees a checkerboard with a pillar standing in one corner. Illumination obviously comes from the top-right corner, as the shadow on the checkerboard tells us immediately (and we know how important shadows are for informing what we see **[Hack #20]**). All of this is perceived at one rapid glance, much faster than this sentence can be read (lest written!).

Now let's ask the following question: which square is brighter, A or B? The obvious answer is B, and I agree. But now change the context by looking at Figure 2-20. The unmasked grays are from the two squares A and B, and unquestioningly the two shades of gray are identical (in fact, the entire figure was constructed just so).

You can prove it to yourself by cutting out a mask with two checker square–size holes in it, one for A and one for B, and putting it over the original checkerboard (Figure 2-19).

Figure 2-20. This checkerboard is the same as the first, except for the added bars—now does A look brighter than B?

How It Works

If squares A and B in the first case have clearly differing brightness and in the second case they have the same, what gives? Surely the two alternatives exclude each other? The solution in a nutshell: brightness depends on context.

There is a good reason that visual scientists describe their experiments using the term *luminance* rather than brightness. Luminance is a physical measure, effectively counting the number of light quanta coming from a surface, then weighting them by wavelength with regard to their visibility. (The unit of measurement, by the way, is candela per square meter, cd/m^2. A candela was originally defined as the light from a standard candle 1 foot away.)

Brightness, on the other hand, is a subjective measure—something your brain constructs for your conscious experience. It depends on previous history (light adaptation), the immediate surroundings (contrast effects), and context (as here). It has no dimension but can be measured using psychophysical techniques.

Contrast in vision science has two meanings. First, it can refer to the perceptual effect that the brightness of a region in the visual field depends on the luminance of the adjacent regions (mediated by "lateral inhibition," a sort of spatial high-pass filtering of the scene). Second, it is the technical term for how luminance differences are measured. With the term "context" here, we denote the interpretation of figural elements—or scene structure—which here is changed by the gray bars.

What exactly is happening when comparing Figure 2-19 and Figure 2-20? Well, when I initially asked, "Which square is brighter?", I knew you would give the deeper answer, namely the lightness quality of the substance the squares are made of. I knew you—or your smart visual system—would assess the scene, interpret it as a 3D scene, guess the shadowed and lit parts, predict an invisible light source, measure incoming light from the squares, subtract the estimated effect of light versus shadow, and give a good guess at the true lightness—the lightness that we would expect the checker squares to really have given the way they appear in the scene they're in. With the mask applied (Figure 2-20), however, we create a very different context in which a 3D interpretation does not apply. Now the two squares are not assumed to be lit differently, no correction for light and shadow needs to be applied, and the brightness becomes equal. The luminance of squares A and B is always identical, but due to different context, the perceived brightness changes.

By the way: there are more places in that figure where luminances are equal, but brightness differs, and hunting for those is left as an exercise for the gentle reader.

This striking checker shadow illusion by Ted Adelson teaches us quite a number of things: it demonstrates how much unconscious scene computation goes on in our visual brain when it applies inverse perspective and inverse lighting models. It shows us how strongly luminance and brightness can differ, giving rise to perceptual constancies, here light constancy. It also demonstrates the "unfairness" of the term "optical illusion": the first answer you gave was not wrong at all; in fact, it was the answer one would be interested in, most of the time. Imagine the checkerboard were like a puzzle, with missing pieces, and you had to hunt for a matching piece. Material property is what we need then, independent of lighting. In fact, estimating the "true" material properties independent of context is a very hard computational problem and one that hasn't been solved to a satisfying degree by computer vision systems.

In Real Life

Correction of surface perception for light and shadow conditions is such a basic mechanism of our perception—and one that normally operates nearly perfectly—that very artificial situations must be created by the accompanying figures for it to reveal itself. That is why we need technical help taking photographs: since photos are normally viewed under different lighting conditions compared to the original scene, professional photographers need to go a long way arranging lighting conditions so that the impression at viewing is the one that is desired.

End Note

1. The checker shadow illusion, together with Ted Adelson's explanation, is online (*http://web.mit.edu/persci/people/adelson/checkershadow_illusion.html*).

See Also

- You can also use an interactive version of the illusion to verify the colors of the checks do indeed correspond (*http://www.michaelbach.de/ot/lum_adelson_check_shadow*).
- Adelson, E. H. (1993). Perceptual organization and the judgment of brightness. *Science 262*, 2042–2044.
- Adelson, E. H. (2000). Lightness Perception and Lightness Illusions. In *The New Cognitive Neurosciences*, 2nd edition, 339–351. M. Gazzaniga (ed.). Cambridge, MA: MIT Press.
- Todorovic, D. (1997). Lightness and junctions. *Perception 26*, 379–395.
- Blakeslee, B. & McCourt, M. E. (2003). A multiscale spatial filtering account of brightness phenomena. In: L. Harris & M. Jenkin (eds.), *Levels of Perception*. New York: Springer-Verlag.

— *Michael Bach*

Create Illusionary Depth with Sunglasses

#24   We can use a little-known illusion called the Pulfrich Effect to hack the brain's computation of motion, depth, and brightness—all it takes is a pair of shades and a pendulum.

This is a journey into the code the visual system uses to work out how far away things are and how fast they are moving. Both of the variables—depth and velocity—can be calculated by comparing measurements of object position over time. Rather than have separate neural modules to figure out each variable, performing the same fundamental processing, the brain combines the two pieces of work and uses some of the same cells in calculating both measures. Because depth and motion are jointly encoded in these cells, it's possible (under the right circumstances) to convert changes in one into changes in another. An example is the *Pulfrich Effect*, in which a moving pendulum and some sunglasses create an illusion of the pendulum swinging in ellipses rather than in straight lines. It works because the sunglasses create an erroneous velocity perception, which gets converted into a depth change by the time it reaches your perception. It's what we'll be trying out here.

In Action

Make a pendulum out of a piece of string and something heavy to use as a weight, like a bunch of keys. You'll also need a pair of sunglasses or any shaded material.

Ask a friend to swing the pendulum in front of you in a perpendicular plane, and make sure it's going exactly in a straight line, left to right. Now, cover one of your eyes with the shades (this is easiest if you have old shades and can poke one of the lenses out). Keep both eyes open! You'll see that the pendulum now seems to be swinging back and forth as well as side to side, so that it appears to move in an ellipse. The two of you will look something like Figure 2-21.

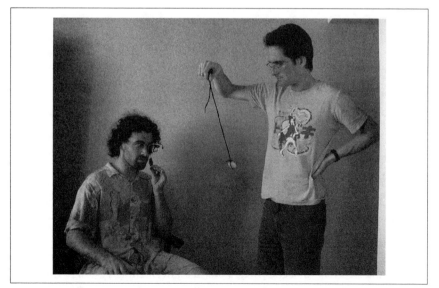

Figure 2-21. Matt and Tom use sunglasses and a pendulum made out of a bootlace to test the Pulfrich Effect

Show your friend swinging the pendulum how you see the ellipse, and ask her to swing the pendulum in the opposite manner to counteract the illusion. Now the pendulum appears to swing in a straight line, and the thing that seems odd is not the distance from you, but the velocity of the pendulum. Because it really is swinging in an elliptical pattern, it covers perceived distance at an inconsistent rate. This makes it seem as if the pendulum is making weird accelerations and decelerations.

How It Works

The classic explanation for the Pulfrich is this: the shading slows down the processing of the image of the object in one eye (lower brightness means the neurons are less stimulated and pass on the signal at a slower rate **[Hack #11]**); in effect, the image reaches one eye at a delay compared to when it reaches the other eye. Because the object is moving, this means the position of the image on the retina is slightly shifted. The difference in image perception between the two retinas is used by the visual system to compute depth **[Hack #22]**. The slight displacement of the image on the retina of the shaded eye is interpreted as an indication of depth, as in Figure 2-22.

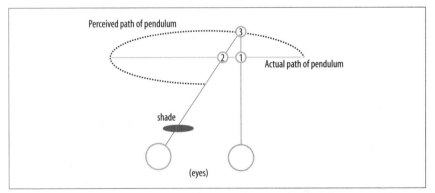

Figure 2-22. The geometry of the Pulfrich Effect: although the pendulum is, in reality, at point 1, the delay in processing makes it appear to be at point 2 to the shaded eye. When the eyes are taken together, the pendulum therefore appears to be at point 3, at a different depth.

This explanation puts the confounding of depth and motion on the geometry of the situation—the point of confusion lies in the world, not in the brain.

Taking recordings of the responses of individual brain cells, Akiyuki Anzai and colleagues have shown that this isn't the whole story. The confounding of motion and depth goes deeper than a mathematical ambiguity that arises from computing real-world interpretations from the visual images on the retinas.

It seems that most of the neurons in the primary visual cortex are sensitive to motion and depth in combination. These neurons are optimally responsive to some combination of motion and depth; what makes up that optimum combination can be varying amounts of motion and depth. This means when you see something and judge its distance your brain always also makes a judgment about its velocity, and vice versa. From the first point in your primary visual cortex where information from the two eyes is combined (i.e., very early in visual processing), motion and depth are coupled. You don't get a sense of one without getting a sense of the other.

This may result from the use of motion parallax to detect depth [Hack #22]. Moving your head is one of the basic ways of telling how far away something is (you can see spitting cobras using motion parallax by shifting their heads from side to side to work out how far to spit). It works even if you have the use only of one eye.

The joint encoding theory explains why you can get Pulfrich-like effects in situations with less obvious geometry. If you watch television snow with one eye shaded, you will see two sheets of dots, one in front of the other and one moving to the left and one moving to the right. The reasons for this are complex but rest on the way our eyes try and match dots in the images for both eyes and use this matching to calculate depth (stereoscopic vision). Adding a shade to the image in one eye creates a bias so that instead of perceiving all the dots at a single average depth we see two sets of skewed averages, and because depth and motion are jointly encoded, these two planes move as well (in opposite directions).

In Real Life

The Pulfrich Effect can be used to create 3D effects for television, as long as people are willing to watch with one eye shaded. It's hard to do since the motion of the image/camera has to be smooth to create a consistent illusion of depth, but it has been done.[1]

End Note

1. Descriptions of some TV shows that have included applications of the Pulfrich Effect (*http://www.combsmusic.com/RosesReview.html*).

See Also

• Anzai, A., Ohzawa, I., & Freeman, R. D. (2001). Joint-encoding of motion and depth by visual cortical neurons: Neural basis of the Pulfrich Effect. *Nature Neuroscience, 4,* 513–518.

- The Psychology Department at Southern Illinois University Carbondale's Pulfrich Effect page (*http://www.siu.edu/~pulfrich*) has many links for further information.

See Movement When All Is Still

Aftereffect illusions are caused by how cells represent motion in the brain.

Why, when the train stops, does the platform you are looking at out the window appear to creep backward? The answer tells us something important about the architecture of the visual system and about how, in general, information is represented in the brain.

The phenomenon is the *motion aftereffect.* Just as when you go from very bright sunlight to the indoors, everything looks dark, or if you are in a very quiet environment, loud noises seem even louder, so continuous motion in a certain direction leaves us with a bias in the other—an aftereffect.

In Action

Watch the video of a waterfall (*http://www.biols.susx.ac.uk/home/George_ Mather/Motion/MAE.HTML*; QuickTime) for a minute or so, staring at the same position, then hit pause. You'll have the illusion of the water flowing upward. It works best with a real waterfall, if you can find one, although pausing at the end is harder, so look at something that isn't moving instead, like the cliff next to the waterfall.

The effect doesn't work for just continuous downward motion. Any continuous motion will create an opposite aftereffect; that includes spiral motion, such as in the Flash demo at *http://www.at-bristol.org.uk/Optical/ AfterEffects_main.htm*.

The effect works only if just part of your visual field is moving (like the world seen through the window of a train). It doesn't occur if everything is moving, which is why, along with the fact that your motion is rarely continuous in a car, you don't suffer an aftereffect after driving.

How It Works

Part of what makes this effect so weird is the experience of motion without any experience of things actually changing location. Not only does this feel pretty funny, but it suggests that motion and location are computed differently within the architecture of the brain.

Brain imaging confirms this. In some areas of the visual cortex, cells respond to movement, with different cells responding to different types of movement. In other areas of the visual cortex, cells respond to the location of objects in different parts of the visual field. Because the modules responsible for the computation of motion and the computation of location are separate, it is possible to experience motion without anything actually moving.

The other way is to be able to perceive static images but be unable to experience motion, and this happens to some stroke victims whose motion module is damaged. Their life is experienced as a series of strobe-like scenes, even though—theoretically—their visual system is receiving all the information it would need to compute motion (that is, location and time).

You don't need brain imaging to confirm that this effect takes place at the cortex, integrating all kinds of data, rather than being localized at each eye. Look at the movie image of the waterfall again but with one eye closed. Swap eyes when you pause the video—you'll still get the effect even with the eye that was never exposed to motion. That shows that the effect is due to some kind of central processing and is not happening at the retina.

To understand why you get aftereffects, you need to know a little about how information is represented in the brain. Different brain cells in the motion-sensitive parts of the visual system respond, or "fire," to different kinds of motion. Some fire most for quick sideways motion, some most to slow motion heading down to the bottom left at an angle of 27 degrees, and so on for different angles and speeds. Each cell is set to respond most to a different type of motion, with similar motions provoking almost as much response, and they won't respond at all to motions with completely different angles and speeds.

The kind of motion we perceive depends on the pattern of activation across the whole range of motion-sensitive cells. Relative activation of the cells compared to one another matters, not just how much each one individually is activated. But if some cells fire continuously, their level of response drops (a process called adaptation). So as you watch the waterfall, the cells coding for that particular motion adapt and stop firing so much.

Pausing the waterfall means normal service is resumed but not for the adapted cells. Relatively, they're responding much less than the cells looking for motion in the opposite sense, which haven't been firing. Usually these two groups of cells should balance each other out, but now the cells for the opposite direction are firing more. Despite a stationary input, overall your brain interprets the response pattern as movement occurring in the opposite direction.

Hacking the Hack

Originally some people thought that adaptation in the motion aftereffect may have been caused by simple fatigue of the motion-sensitive cells. We

know now that this isn't the case. Instead, the mechanism is far more interesting and far cleverer. To demonstrate, simply try the original waterfall
effect, but before watching the static pattern, close your eyes for 20 seconds. Now if the effect were due to fatigue and the effect itself lasted for 10
seconds, a wait of 20 seconds should remove the effect completely. But
instead, you get an aftereffect nearly as long as you would have if you hadn't
waited for 20 seconds with your eyes closed. The motion-sensitive neurons
should have had time to recover—why are they still adapted?

They are still adapted because your baseline for motion perception hasn't
been reset (because you've had your eyes closed). Adaptation worked as a
kind of gain control, adjusting the sensitivity of your motion perception to the
new expected level of input provided by the constant motion of the waterfall.

Aftereffects are common illusions; they don't occur just for motion. The relative activation and habituation of neurons are general features of the brain.
The reason aftereffects are built into neural processing is to adjust our sensations to cancel out continuous—and therefore uninformative—information. It operates to make us sensitive to changes around the adapted-to
baseline, rather than being overwhelmed by one dominant level of input.
Think about how your eyes adjust to the dark for a good example of useful
adaptation that can result in an unpleasant aftereffect. Adaptation is discussed further in "Get Adjusted" [Hack #26].

See Also

- A motion aftereffect with scrolling text (*http://www.naturalhighs.net/
  waterfalls/illusion.htm*).
- A good demo and good explanation of the effect (*http://psylux.psych.tu-
  dresden.de/i1/kaw/diverses%20Material/www.illusionworks.com/html/
  motion_aftereffect.html*).
- Mather, G., Verstraten, F., & Anstis, S. (1998). *The Motion Aftereffect: a
  Modern Perspective*. Cambridge, MA: MIT Press.
- Grunewald, A., & Mingolla, E. (1998). Motion after-effect due to binocular sum of adaptation to linear motion. *Vision Research*. 38(19), 2963–
  2971.
- Rees, G., Frith, C. D., & Lavie, N. (1997). Modulating irrelevant motion
  perception by varying attentional load in an unrelated task. *Science*,
  278(5343), 1616–1619.

Get Adjusted

#26 We get used to things because our brain finds consistency boring and adjusts to filter it out.

My limbs feel weightless. I can't feel my clothes on my body. The humming of my laptop has disappeared. The flicker of the overhead light has faded out of my consciousness. I know it all must still be happening—I just don't notice it anymore.

In other words, it's just another normal day in the world with my brain.

Our brains let us ignore any constant input. A good thing too; otherwise, we'd spend all our time thinking about how heavy our hands are, how exactly our T-shirts feel on our backs, or at precisely what pitch our computers are humming, instead of concentrating on the task at hand.

The general term for this process of adjusting for constant input is called *adaptation*. Combined with relative representation of input, adaptation gives us aftereffects. The motion aftereffect is a good example of a complex adaptation process, so we'll walk through a detailed story about that here in a moment.

 Both relative representation and the motion aftereffect are described in "See Movement When All Is Still" **[Hack #25]**. Simply put, how much "movement up" we perceive depends on the activation of up-sensitive neurons compared against the activation of down-sensitive neurons, not just the absolute level of activity.

Adaptation is a feature of all the sensory systems. You'll notice it (or, on the contrary, most likely not notice it) for sound, touch, and smells particularly. It affects vision **[Hack #25]**, too. If you stop to consider it for a moment, you'll appreciate just how little of the world you actually notice most of the time.

Adaptation is a general term for a number of processes. Some of these processes are very basic, are of short term, and occur at the level of the individual sense receptor cells. An example is neuronal fatigue, which means just what it sounds as if it means. Without a break, individual neurons stop responding as vigorously to the same input. They get tired. Strictly speaking, ion channels in the membrane that regulate electrical changes in the cell become inactivated, but "tired" is a close enough approximation.

The most basic form of memory is a kind of adaptation, called habituation. This is just the diminishing of a response as the stimulus that provokes it happens again. The shock of a cold shower might make you gasp at first, but with practice you can get in without flinching. It was neuroscientists using a similar kind of situation—poking sea slugs until they got used to it—that first demonstrated that learning happens due to changes in the strength and structure of connections between individual neurons.

In Action

Aftereffects are the easiest way to see adaptation occurring. You can have aftereffects with most things—sounds, touch pressure, brightness, tilt, and motion are just some. Some, like the motion aftereffect [Hack #25], are due to adaptation processes that happen in the cortex. But others happen at the point of sensation. The adaptation of our visual system to different light levels happens directly in the eyes, not in the cortex.

To see this, try adapting to a darkened room with both eyes and then walking into a bright room with only one eye open. If you then return to the darkened room, you will be able to see nothing with one eye (it has quickly adapted to a high level of light), yet plenty with the eye you kept closed in the light room (this eye is still operating at the dark-adapted baseline). The effect is very strong as you switch between having alternate eyes open and the whole lighting and tone of the room you're looking at changes instantly.

Why It Works

Adaptation operates for a perceptual purpose, rather than being a reflection of neural fatigue or being a side effect of some kind of long-term memory phenomenon. It seems to be that sensory systems contain an intrinsic and ongoing mechanism for correcting drift in the performance of components of the system. Constant levels of input are an indication that either some part of the neural machinery has gone wrong and is over-responding, or at the least the input isn't as relevant as other stuff and should be canceled out of your sensory processing to allow you to perceive variations around the new baseline.

This relates to the idea of *channel decorrelation*[1]—that sensory channels, as far as possible, should be providing independent evidence, not correlated evidence about the world. If the input is correlated, then it isn't adding any extra information, and large, constant, moving stimuli create a load of correlation, across visual space and across time, among the neurons responsible for responding to motion.

Not all cells adapt to all stimuli. Most subcortical sensory neurons don't adapt.[2] Some kinds of stimuli aren't worth learning to ignore—such as potentially dangerous looming stimuli [Hack #32]—and so aren't adapted to.

Adaptation lets us ignore the stuff that's constant, so we can concentrate on things that are either new or changing. This isn't just useful, it is essential for the constant ongoing calibration we do of our senses. Adaptation isn't so much a reduction in response as a recalibration of our responses to account for the recent history of our sensory neurons. Neurons can vary the size of their response over only a limited range. Momentarily changing the level that the baseline of this range represents allows the neurons to better represent the current inputs.

In Real Life

You can see the changing baseline easily in the adaptation of our eyes to different levels of brightness. Perhaps more surprising is the adaptation to constant motion, such as you get on a boat. Continuous rocking from side to side might cause seasickness on the first day aboard, but soon adaptation removes it. Upon returning to land, many suffer a syndrome called "mal de debarquement" in which everything seems to be rocking (no doubt in the opposite direction, not that you could tell!).

The "deafening silence" which results from the disappearance of a constant sound is due to auditory adaptation. Our hearing has adapted to a loud baseline so that when the sound disappears we hear a silence more profound (neurally) than we can normally hear in continuously quiet conditions.

Adaptation allows us to ignore things that are constant or predictable. I'm guessing that this is why mobile phone conversations in public places are so distracting. Normal conversations have a near-constant volume and a timing and rhythm that allow us to not be surprised when the conversation switches between the two speakers. With a mobile phone conversation, we don't hear any of the clues that would allow our brains to subconsciously predict when the other person is going to speak. Consequence: large and unpredictable variations in volume. Just the sort of stimuli that it's hard to adapt to and hence hard to filter out.

End Notes

1. Barlow, H. B. (1990). A theory about the functional role and synaptic mechanism of visual after-effects. In C. Blakemore (ed.), *Vision: Coding and Efficiency*, 363–375. Cambridge, U.K.: Cambridge University Press.

2. There is a good introduction to adaptation in this paper (which is interesting in its own right too). Kohn, A., & Movshon, J. A. (2003). Neuronal adaptation to visual motion in area MT of the macaque. *Neuron, 39*, 681–691.

See Also

- There's a discussion of olfactory (smell) adaptation at the Neuroscience for Kids web site (*http://faculty.washington.edu/chudler/chems.html*).

 ## Show Motion Without Anything Moving

#27 Find out why static pictures can make up a moving image on your TV screen.

The motion aftereffect [Hack #25] shows that motion is computed in your brain separately from location. For instance, becoming accustomed to the moving surface of a waterfall causes you to see stationary surfaces as moving the other way, although they're quite still. In theory, motion can be calculated from position and time information, but that's not how your brain does it—there's a specialized brain region for detecting motion directly. Since location and motion are perceived separately, this can lead to some odd illusions, the motion aftereffect chief among them: you get the illusion of motion *without anything actually changing position*.

The motion aftereffect relies on an initial moving scene to set it up, but we can go one better and get an impression of movement when there's been no actual thing present, moving or otherwise. The effect is *apparent motion*, and even if you haven't heard of it, you'll have experienced it.

Look at two pictures one after the other, very rapidly, showing objects in slightly different positions. Get the timing right, and your brain fills in the gap: You get an illusion of the objects in the first picture moving smoothly to their position in the second. There's no single, moving object out there in the world, but your brain's filling in of the assumed path of movement gives you that impression.

Sound familiar? It should; it's the effect that all television and cinema is based on, of course.

In Action

The easiest way to experience this effect is, of course, to turn on your television or go to the cinema. Movie projectors show 24 frames (pictures) a second, and that's good enough for everyone to perceive continuous motion in the change from one frame to the next.

In the old days of cinema, the film had 16 frames a second, which were projected using a three-bladed shutter to increase the flicker frequency above the rate necessary for flicker fusion. Despite seeing the same frame three times, your brain would fill in the gaps between the images, whether they were the same or different, so that you'd get the impression of continuous motion.

Television and computer screens are more complex cases, because the refresh doesn't happen for the whole image at once as it does with cinema but the principle is the same.

To demonstrate the effect to yourself in a more low-tech way, try this old child's game. Take a notebook and in the page corners draw the successive frames of a moving scene. I'm not very good at drawing stickmen, so when I did it I just tried drawing small, filled circles moving up from the bottom corner to the top of the page. Alternately, you may find a flip book in your local bookshop.

Flip through the pages of the book using your thumb and—at a particular speed—you'll see the scene come to life. They're not just single pictures any more; together they form an animation. In my case, I see the little dot shoot up the side of the page. If I flip through the pages more slowly, the dot moves more slowly—but still continuously, as if it moves through every position on its path. Then, as I slow down even more, there comes a certain point at which the feeling of watching a single moving circle disappears and I'm just looking at a bunch of pages populated with slightly different shapes in slightly different positions.

How It Works

This apparent motion effect is also sometimes called the phi phenomenon. The simplest form in which you've probably encountered it before is two lights flashing at such an interval that you see one light moving from the first position to the second, as on an LED ticker display. Imagine only two lights from such a display. If the delay between the lights flashing is too short, the lights seem to flash on simultaneously. If it is too long, you just see two lights flashing on, one after the other. But if just right, you'll be treated to some apparent motion.

Although the optimum time varies with circumstance, 50 milliseconds is approximately the delay you need between the first light blinking out and the second light flashing on, in order to get a strong illusion of a single light moving between the two locations. Note that that's 20 flashes a second, close to the rate of image change in cinema. (Just so you know, as the physical distance between the two light flashes increases, so does the optimum time delay.[1])

The effect is most powerful when you see the light appearing at several locations, making a consistent movement—exactly like LED tickers, on which a message appears to scroll smoothly across despite really being made out of sequentially flashing lights. In fact, it isn't just that we feel there's an illusion of movement: the apparent motion effect activates a region called MT (standing for *middle temporal gyrus*, a folded region on the temporal lobe) in the visual cortex, one primarily responsible for motion processing. Apparent motion is just as valid as real motion, according to the brain.

And this makes sense. The only difference with apparent motion, as far as visual perception is concerned, is that some of the information is missing (i.e., everything that happens in the locations between the flashing lights). Since there's no way to detect motion directly—we can't *see* momentum, for example—and visual information is all we have to go on, apparent motion is just a legacy of our tolerance for missing data and our ability to adjust.

A visual system that wasn't susceptible to the effect would be overdesigned. The capacity to perceive apparent motion lets us see consistency in images that are moving too rapidly for us to comprehend individually.

In Real Life

The obvious benefit of the phenomenon is that we can sit back and watch television and movies.

It also explains why wheels can look as if they are going backward slowly when they are actually going forward extremely quickly. Remember that apparent motion is strongest when adjacent lights, or images, flash up approximately 50 milliseconds apart. Caught on film, a wheel rotating forward may be turning at such a speed that, after 50 milliseconds (or a frame), it's made almost a full turn, but not quite. The apparent motion effect is stronger for the wheel moving the short distance backward in that short time rather than all the way round forward, and so it dominates: We see the wheel moving slowly backward, rather than fast and forward.

Hacking The Hack

The phi phenomenon also seems to say something important about the relationship of real time to perceived time. If you show two flashing lights of different colors so as to induce the phi phenomenon, you still get an effect of apparent motion.[2] For some people, the light appears to change from the first color to the second as it moves from the first spot (where the first light was shown) to the second spot (where the second light was shown).

Now the thing about this is—*how did your brain know what color the light was going to change to?* It seems as if what you "saw" (the light changing color) was influenced by something you were about to see. Various theories had been put forward to explain this, either about the revision of our perceptions by what comes after or about the revision of our memories. Philosopher Daniel Dennett[3] says that both of these types of theory are misleading because they both imply that conscious experience travels forward in time along a single, one-step-forward-at-a-time-and-no-steps-back track.

Instead, he suggests, there are multiple drafts of what is going on being continuously updated and revised. Within an editorial window (of, some have suggested, about 200 milliseconds of real time), any of these drafts can outcompete the others to become what we experience .[4]

End Notes

1. You can measure how the optimum timing of the flashes is affected by distance with the Apparent Motion Experiment maintained by Purdue University's Visual Perception Online Laboratory (*http://www.psych. purdue.edu/~coglab/VisLab/ApparentMotion/AM.html*; Java).

2. You can see a demo of the changing color phi phenomenon here at Ken Kreisman's Phi Phenomenon Demo page (*http://www.cs.tufts.edu/ ~kreisman/phi/index.html*; requires Java).

3. Dennett, D. C. (1991). *Consciousness Explained.* Boston: Little, Brown.

4. Obviously there's a lot more to both Dennett's theory and to the philosophy of consciousness in general. "Multiple Drafts: an Eternal Golden Braid?" (*http://ase.tufts.edu/cogstud/papers/multdrft.htm*) by Daniel Dennett and Marcel Kinsbourn, and this summary of Chapter 5 of Dennett's book *Consciousness Explained*, "Multiple Drafts Versus the Cartesian Theater" (*http://epmalab.uoregon.edu/writings/Chapter%205%20summary.pdf*; PDF), both discuss the mental world as a parallel process that is edited down into a single experience for conscious consumption.

See Also

- Greg Egan's science fiction short story "Mister Volition" (part of the excellent collection *Luminous*) is inspired by the multiple drafts theory of consciousness and, to understand the theory, a good a place as any to start. See Egan's bibliography for availability (*http://gregegan.customer. netspace.net.au/BIBLIOGRAPHY/Online.html*).

Motion Extrapolation: The "Flash-Lag Effect"

#28   If there's a flash of light on a moving object, the flash appears to hang a little behind.

How quickly we can act is slow compared to how quickly things can happen to us—especially when you figure that by the time you've decided to respond to something that is moving it will already be in a new position. How do you coordinate your slow reactions to deal with moving objects? One way is to calibrate your muscles to deal with the way you expect things to be, so your legs are prepared for a moving escalator [Hack #62], for example, before you step on it, to avoid the round-trip time of noticing the ground is moving, deciding what to do, adjusting your movements, and so on. Expectations are built into your perceptual system as well as your motor system, and they deal with the time delay from sense data coming in to the actual perception being formed. You can see this coping strategy with an illusion called the flash-lag effect.[1]

In Action

Watch Michael Bach's Flash Lag demo at *http://www.michaelbach.de/ot/ mot_flashlag1* (Flash). A still from it is shown in Figure 2-23. In it, a blue-filled circle orbits a cross—hold your eyes on the cross so you're not looking directly at the moving circle. This is to make sure the circle is moving across your field of view.

Occasionally the inside of the ring flashes yellow, but it looks as if the yellow flash happens slightly behind the circle and occupies only part of the ring. This is the flash-lag illusion. You can confirm what's happening by clicking the Slow button (top right). The circle moves slower and the flash lasts longer, and it's now clear that the entire center of the circle turns yellow and the lag is indeed only an illusion.

How It Works

The basic difficulty here is that visual perception takes time; almost a tenth of a second passes between light hitting your retina to the signal being processed and reaching your cortex (most of this is due to how long it takes the receptors in the eye to respond). The circle in Bach's demo moves a quarter of an inch in that time, and it's not even going that fast. Imagine perpetually interacting with a world that had already moved on by the time you'd seen it.

So we continuously extrapolate the motion of anything we see, and our brain presents us with a picture of where the world most likely is now, rather than where it was a fraction of a second ago. This applies only to moving objects, not to stationary ones, and that's why the disparity opens

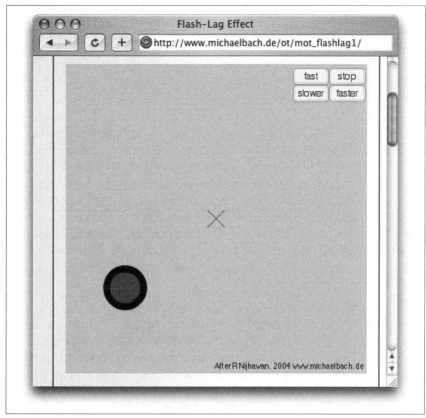

Figure 2-23. In the movie, the circle orbits the cross and flashes from time to time

up between the moving blue circle and the static yellow flash—one is being extrapolated; the other isn't.

Straightforward extrapolation of the path of moving objects is one way in which this effect can take place, and this happens as early as the retina itself during visual processing. The cells in the eye compensate for its slow response by being most active at the front edge of a moving object. (Without this, the most active cells would be the ones that had been exposed to the object the longest, that is, the ones at the back.[2])

That's one way in which the flash-lag effect could come about, because the delay for visual processing is compensated for with moving objects, but flashes still pay the penalty and are seen later. But that doesn't explain the demonstration movies constructed by David Eagleman and Terrence Sejnowski (*http://nba.uth.tmc.edu/homepage/eagleman/flashlag*; QuickTime). Essentially the same as Bach's demo, these movies have an erratically moving ring that should confuse the brain's motion prediction.

In Experiment 1 (*http://nba.uth.tmc.edu/homepage/eagleman/flashlag/r1.html*; QuickTime), the ring abruptly changes direction at the same time as the flash. Still we see the flash lag behind the moving ring, even though prediction of the future motion of the ring could not have occurred.

Eagleman and Sejnowski's explanation is that vision is *postdictive*. They argue that the brain takes into account changes in the scene that occur after the flash, for a very short time (less than a tenth of a second), and the motion preceding the flash isn't relevant at all. This is similar to the way two flashing dots can appear to be a single dot apparently moving [Hack #27] smoothly from one position to another, if the timing is right. Your brain must have filled in the interim motion retrospectively, because you can't know what in-between would be before the second dot appears. Similarly, the circle in this flash-lag experiment and the following fraction of a second comprise a period to be assembled retrospectively. The ring is moving smoothly after the flash, so you have to see it moving smoothly, and the flash appears slightly behind, because by the time you've mentally assembled the scene, the ring has moved on.

The situation is muddied because flash lag isn't unique to motion. One experiment[3] found the same effect with color. Imagine a green dot slowly becoming red by passing through all intermediate shades. At a certain point, another dot flashes up next to it, with the same color for that time. Looking at it, you'd see the flash-lag effect as if the changing dot were moving along the color dimension: the flashed dot would appear lagged. That is, the flashed dot would appear greener than the changing dot.

That flash lag appears for phenomena other than motion supports that postdiction position. It could be the case that we don't see the world at an instant, but actually as an average over a short period of time. The moving ring appears to be ahead of the flash because, over a very short period, on average it *is* ahead of the flash. The colored dot appears to be redder than the flashed dot because it *is* redder, over the averaged period.

In Real Life

The effect was first noticed with the taillights of a car in the dark (the car being invisible except for the rear lights). A flash of lightning lets you see the car, and the lights appear to be halfway along it: the car—which is flashed—lags behind the taillights—which are extrapolated.

It should also be evident in reverse. If you're photographed from a moving car, the flash of the camera should appear a little behind the car itself.

End Notes

1. Nijhawan, R. (1994). Motion extrapolation in catching. *Nature, 370,* 256–257.

2. Berry, M. J. 2nd, Brivanlou, I. H., Jordan, T. A., & Meister M. (1999). Anticipation of moving stimuli by the retina. *Nature, 398* (6725), 334–338.

3. Krekelberg, B., & Lappe, M. (2001). Neuronal latencies delay the registration of the visual signal. *Trends in Neurosciences, 24*(6), 335–339.

See Also

- Flash lag may also contribute to controversial offside decisions in soccer. The offside rule is notorious for its opaqueness, so it's best, if you're a follower of the game, to read the paper yourself. It's about how a linesman observes both a moving player and the ball being played forward (which acts as the flash). The percept of the flash can lag behind the moving player, leading to an incorrect call of offside. Baldo, M. V. C., Ranvaud, R. D., & Morya, E. (2002). Flag errors in soccer games: The flash-lag effect brought to real life. *Perception, 31,* 1205–1210. (*http://fisio.icb.usp.br/~vinicius/Public_pdf/Baldo_Ranvaud_Morya.pdf*)

Turn Gliding Blocks into Stepping Feet

Motion detection uses contrast information first, not color.

The moral of this story is that if you want people to see moving objects, make them brighter or darker than the background, not just a different color.

Motion is important stuff for the brain. Information about movement gets routed from the eye to the visual cortex—the final destination for all visual information—along its own pathway (you can take a tour round the visual system [Hack #13]), the *magnocellular pathway.* (Like a lot of things in neuroscience, this sounds more technical than it is; *magnocellular* means "with large cells.")

Color and form information travels along the *parvocellular pathway* (yup, "small cells") to the visual cortex, which means any motion has to be processed without access to that information. This functional division makes sense for a brain that wants to know immediately if there's a movement, and only secondly what exactly that moving something looks like. Problems arise only when movement processing is trying to figure out what sort of motion is occurring but the clues it needs are encoded in color and so not available.

In Action

Stuart Anstis has constructed just such a problematic situation, and it leads to the nifty stepping feet illusion[1] (*http://psy.ucsd.edu/~sanstis/Foot.html*; Shockwave). Blue and yellow blocks move smoothly in tandem from side to side. Click the Background button to bring up the striped background, and look again. It should look like Figure 2-24.

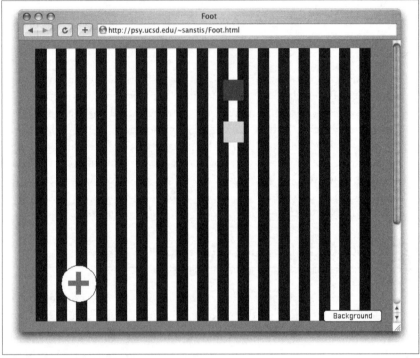

Figure 2-24. The stepping feet illusion, with the striped background

Even though they're still moving in the same direction, the blocks now appear to be alternately jerking forward, like little stepping feet. Like a lot of illusions, the effect is stronger in your peripheral vision; fix the center of your gaze at the cross off to the side and the stepping feet will be even clearer.

How It Works

The easiest way to see why the stepping feet occur is to look at the same pattern, but without any color—the yellow becomes white and the blue becomes black. Michael Bach's animation of stepping feet (*http://www.michaelbach.de/ot/mot_feet_lin*; Flash) allows you to remove the color with a click of the Color Off button.

With no color, there's no illusion: the moving blocks appear like stepping feet even when you look straight at them. When the black (previously blue) block overlaps a black stripe, you can't see its leading edge so it isn't apparent that it's moving. Given no cues, your motion processing centers assume no movement. Then as the black block begins to move over a white stripe, you can suddenly see the leading edge again, and it's moved from where your brain had thought it was. That's when you see the block apparently jump forward and then move normally—at least until it overlaps the black stripe again. The same is true for the white (previously yellow) block over white stripes, only it moves when the black block looks still and vice versa.

So that's what the blocks look like in black and white. Losing the movement information of the leading edge over one stripe in two makes the blocks look like stepping feet. And that's what the motion-sensitive and color-insensitive magnocellular pathway sees. The color information is added back in only later, reattached in the visual cortex after the motion has been computed. In the end, you're able to simultaneously see the stepping feet motion via one pathway and the colors via the other.

Low-contrast patterns in general produce a less vigorous response from the motion-sensitive parts of the brain,[2] which may explain why objects seen in fog appear to drift serenely, even though they may actually be moving quite fast.

End Notes

1. Anstis, S. M. (2003). Moving objects appear to slow down at low contrasts. *Neural Networks, 16,* 933–938.

2. Thiele A., Dobkins, K. R., & Albright, T. D. (2000). Neural correlates of contrast detection at threshold. *Neuron, 26,* 715–724.

See Also

- Stuart Anstis's publications online (*http://psy.ucsd.edu/~sanstis/SAPub.html*).

- Anstis discusses the effect of contrast on motion perception (*http://psy.ucsd.edu~sanstis/PDFs/YorkChapter.pdf*).

Understand the Rotating Snakes Illusion

HACK #30

Shading in pictures combined with the continuous random jiggling our eyes make can generate compelling movement illusions.

We've all seen optical illusions in which parts of a completely static picture appear to drift and swirl. One of the most famous examples is Professor

Akiyoshi Kitaoka's rotating snake illusion (Figure 2-25), commonly passed around via email, but, sadly, rarely with explanation.

Figure 2-25. The rotating snake illusion, Akiyoshi Kitaoka © 2003, is available in color at http://www.ritsumei.ac.jp/~akitaoka/index-e.html

This is really a story about why you don't see everything moving all the time rather than about why you see movement sometimes when it isn't there. Your eyes constantly move in your head [Hack #15], your head moves on your body, and your body moves about space. Your brain has to work hard to disentangle those movements in incoming visual information that are due to your movement and those due to real movement in the world.

Another source of confusion for our visual system is a constant random drift in the exact focus of our eyes.[1] This happens between saccades (see Figure 2-5, for example, in "To See, Act" [Hack #15]). Our muscles are constantly sending little corrective signals to keep our eyes in the same place. These signals never keep the eyes exactly still, producing so-called *fixational movements*. This is a good thing. If visual input is completely constant (i.e., if your eyes become paralyzed), the neurons in the eye stop responding to the constant input (because that is what they do [Hack #26]) and everything fades out.

The Vestibular-Ocular Reflex

One way your brain cuts down on confusion is shutting down visual input during rapid eye movements [Hack #17].

Another mechanism is used to cancel out visual blur that results from head movements. Signals from how your head is moving are fed to the eyes to produce opposite eye movements that keep the visual image still.

Try this experiment. Hold the book in one hand and shake your head from side to side. You can still read the book. Now shake the book from side to side at the same speed at which you shook your head. You can't read a word, even though the words are moving past your head in the same way, and at the same speed, as when you were shaking your head. The *vestibular-ocular reflex* feeds a signal from your inner ear [Hack #47] to your eyes in such a way that they move in the opposite direction and at the correct rate to correct the visual displacement produced by the movement of your head.

You can readily demonstrate that this is a reflex hardwired to your inner ear, rather than a clever compensatory mechanism that depends on the motor signals you are sending to shake your head. If you get a friend to move your head from side to side while you relax completely (be sure your friend is careful and gentle!), you'll see that you can still read. This compensation doesn't depend on your knowing to where your head is going to move.

Normally your brain uses the structure of the current scene combined with the assumption that small random movements are due to eye movement so as not to get distracted by these slight constant drifts. To actually see these fixational movements, you have to look at something without any structure and without any surrounding frame of reference.

In Action

We need to get a handle on various principles of vision and motion computation before we can understand the rotating snakes illusion. Fortunately, each step comes with a practical demonstration of the principle.

The autokinetic effect. You will need a small point of light. A lit cigarette in an ashtray is ideal—slow-burning, small, and dim enough not to illuminate anything else near it. Place it at the other end of a completely darkened room so that all you can see is the light, not the table it is sitting on or the wall it is in front of. Stand back at the other end of the room from the light and watch it. You'll see it start to move of its own accord. This movement is due to the random drift of your eyes, which can't be compensated for by your brain because it has no frame of reference.

You can get the same effect by looking at a single star through a tube. Without the other stars visible as a reference, it can look as if the single star is dancing slightly in the night sky.

This *autokinetic* effect is famous for being influenced by suggestion. If you're introducing this effect to someone else, see if you can make him see the kind of motion you want by saying something like, "Look, it's going round in circles" or "Hey, it's swinging back and forth."

Ouchi illusion. So while we normally have these jiggly eye movements going on all the time, we use the structure of what we're seeing to discount them. But certain visual structures can co-opt these small random movements to create illusions of movement in static pictures. The rotating snakes illusion is one, but to understand the principle, it's easier to start with an older visual illusion called the Ouchi illusion, shown in Figure 2-26.[2]

Figure 2-26. The Ouchi illusion—the central circle appears to float above the other part of the design

Here the central disk of vertical bars appears to move separately from the rest of the pattern, floating above the background of horizontal bars. You can increase the effect by jiggling the book.

Your fixational eye movements affect the two parts of the pattern in different ways. The dominant direction of the bars, either horizontal or vertical, means that only one component of the random movements stands out. For the "background" of horizontal bars, this means that the horizontal component of the movements is eliminated, while for the "foreground" disk the vertical component of the movements is eliminated. Because the fixational movements are random, the horizontal and vertical movements are independent. This means that the two parts of the pattern appear to move independently, and your visual system interprets this as meaning that there are two different objects, one in front of the other.

Peripheral drift. The rotating snakes illusion (Figure 2-25) uses a different kind of structure to co-opt these small random eye movements, one that relies on differential brightness in parts of the pattern (color isn't essential to the effect[3]). To understand how changes in the brightness of the pattern create an illusion of motion in the periphery, see Figure 2-27.

In this simple pattern, the difference in the shading of the figure creates the impression of illusory movement. It makes use of the same principles as the rotating snakes, but it's easier to work out what's happening. Brighter things are processed faster in the visual system (due to the stronger response they provoke in neurons [Hack #11]), so where the spokes meet, as one fades out into white and meets the black edge of another, the white side of the edge is processed faster that the black edge. The difference in arrival times is interpreted as a movement but only in the peripheral vision where your resolution is low enough to be fooled. The illusion of motion occurs only when the information first hits the eye, so you need to "reset" by blinking or quickly shifting your eyes. It works really well with two patterns next to each other, because your eye flicks between the two as the illusory motion in the periphery grabs your attention. Try viewing two copies of this illusion at the same time; open *http://viperlib.york.ac.uk/Pimages/Lightness-Brightness/Shading/8cycles.DtoL. CW.jpg* in two browser windows on opposite sides of your desktop.

How It Works

You are now equipped to understand why Professor Kitaoka's rotating snakes illusion (Figure 2-25) works. Because the shape has lots of repeating parts, it is hard for your visual system to lock on to any part of the pattern to get a frame of reference. The shading of the different parts of the squares creates illusory motion that combines with motion from small eye movements

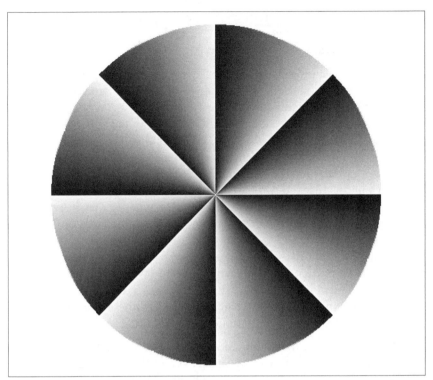

Figure 2-27. The peripheral drift illusion, in which the spokes appear to rotate in the corner of your eye[4]

that are happening constantly. The effect is greatest in your peripheral vision, where your visual resolution is most susceptible to the illusionary motion cue in the shading of the patterns. Your eyes are attracted by the illusory motion, so they flit around the picture and the movement appears everywhere apart from where you are directly looking. The constant moving of your eyes results in a kind of reset, which triggers a new interpretation of the pattern and new illusory motions and prevents you from using consistency of position across time to figure out that the motion is illusory.

In Real Life

Professor Kitaoka's web page (*http://www.ritsumei.ac.jp/~akitaoka/index-e. html*) contains many more examples of this kind of anomalous motion and his scientific papers in which he explores the mechanisms behind them.

We are constantly using the complex structure of the world to work out what is really moving and to discount movements of our eyes, heads, and bodies. These effects show just how artificial patterns have to be to fool our visual system. Patterns like this are extremely unlikely without human intervention.

Professor Kitaoka has spotted one example of anomalous motion similar to his rotating snakes illusion that may not have been intentional. The logo of the Society For Neuroscience, used online (*http://web.sfn.org*), appears to drift left and right in the corner of their web site! Now you know what to look for, maybe you will see others yourself.

End Notes

1. Martinez-Conde, S., Macknik, S. L., & Hubel, D. H. (2004). The role of fixational eye movements in visual perception. *Nature Reviews Neuroscience, 5*, 229–240.

2. Figure reprinted from: Ouchi, H. (1977). *Japanese Optical and Geometrical Art: 746 Copyright-Free Designs.* New York: Dover. See also *http://mathworld.wolfram.com/OuchiIllusion.html.*

3. Olveczky, B., Baccus, S., & Meister, M. (2003). Segregation of object and background motion in the retina. *Nature, 423*, 401–408.

4. Faubert, J., & Herbert, A. (1999). The peripheral drift illusion: A motion illusion in the visual periphery. *Perception, 28*, 617–622. Figure reprinted with permission from Pion Limited, London.

Minimize Imaginary Distances

#31 If you imagine an inner space, the movements you make in it take up time according to how large they are. Reducing the imaginary distances involved makes manipulating mental objects easier and quicker.

Mental imagery requires the same brain regions that are used to represent real sensations. If you ask someone to imagine hearing the first lines to the song "Purple Haze" by Jimi Hendrix, the activity in her auditory cortex increases. If you ask someone to imagine what the inside of a teapot looks like, his visual cortex works harder. If you put a schizophrenic who is hearing voices into a brain scanner, when she hears voices, the parts of the brain that represent language sounds really are active—she's not lying; she really is hearing voices.

Any of us can hear voices or see imaginary objects at will; it's only when we lose the ability to suppress the imaginings that we think of it as a problem.

When we imagine objects and places, this imagining creates mental space that is constrained in many of the ways real space is constrained. Although you can imagine impossible movements like your feet lifting up and your body rotating until your head floats inches above the floor, these movements take time to imagine and the amount of time is affected by how large they are.

In Action

Is the left shape in Figure 2-28 the same as the right shape?

Figure 2-28. Is the left shape the same as the right shape?

How about the left shape in Figure 2-29—is it the same as the right shape?

Figure 2-29. Is the left shape the same as the right shape?

And is the left shape in Figure 2-30 the same as the one on the right?

Figure 2-30. Is the left shape the same as the right shape?

To answer these questions, you've had to mentally rotate one of each pair of the shapes. The first one isn't too hard—the right shape is the same as the left but rotated 50°. The second pair is not the same; the right shape is the mirror inverse of the left and again rotated by 50°. The third pair is identical, but this time the right shape has been rotated by 150°. To match the right shape in the third example to the left shape, you have to mentally rotate 100° further than to match the first two examples. It should have taken you extra seconds to do this. If you'd like to try an online version, see the demonstration at *http://www.uwm.edu/People/johnchay/mrp.htm* (requires Shockwave). When we tried it, the long version didn't save our data (although it claimed it did) so don't get excited about being able to analyze your results; at the moment, you can use it only to get a feel for how the experiment works.

How It Works

These shapes are similar to the ones used by Robert Shepard and Jacqueline Metzler[1] in their seminal experiments on mental rotation. They found that the time to make a decision about the shapes was linearly related to the angle of rotation. Other studies have shown the mental actions almost always take up an amount of time that is linearly related to the amount of imaginary movement required.

This shows that mental images are analog representations of the real thing—we don't just store them in our head in some kind of abstract code. Also interesting is the fact that mental motions take up a linearly increasing amount of time as mental distance increases; in the original experiments by Shepard and Metzler, it was one extra second for every extra 50°. This relationship implies that the mental velocity of our movements is constant (unlike our actual movements, which tend to accelerate sharply at the beginning and decelerate sharply at the end, meaning that longer movements have higher velocities).

Further studies of mental rotation[2] showed that the mental image does indeed move through all the transitional points as it is rotated in and that at least in some experiments, rotating complex shapes didn't take any longer than rotating simple shapes.

Other experiments[3] have also shown that moving your mind's eye over a mental space (such as an imagined map) takes time that is linearly related to the imagined distance. If you "zoom in" on a mental image, that takes time as well. So if you ask people to imagine an elephant next to a rabbit, they will take longer to answer a question about the color of the rabbit's eyes than about the color of the elephant's eyes. You can partially avoid this zooming-in time by getting people to imagine the thing really large to start with—asking them to start, say, by imagining a fly and then the rabbit next to it.

Recent neuroimaging research[4] has shown that mentally rotating objects may involve different brain regions from mentally rotating your own body through space. Studies that compare the difficulty of the two have found that it is easier and faster to imagine yourself mentally rotating around a display of objects than it is to imagine the objects rotating around their own centers.[5] So if you are looking at a pair of scissors that have the handle pointing away from you, it will be easier to imagine yourself rotating around the scissors in order to figure out if they are lefthanded or righthanded scissors, rather than imaging the scissors rotating around so that the handle faces you. And easiest of all is probably to imagine just your own hand rotating to match the way the handle is facing.

All this evidence suggests that mental space exists in analog form in our minds. It's not just statements about the thing, but a map of the thing in your mind's eye. There is some evidence, however, that the copy in your mind's eye isn't an exact copy of the visual input—or at least that it can't be used in exactly the same way as visual input can be. Look at Figure 2-31, which shows an ambiguous figure that could be a duck or could be a rabbit. You'll see one of them immediately, and if you wait a few seconds, you'll spot the other one as well. You can't see both at once; you have to flip between them and there will always be one you saw first (and which one you see first is the sort of thing you can affect by priming [Hack #81], exposing people to concepts that influence their later behavior).

If you flash a figure up to people for just long enough for them to see it and make one interpretation—to see a duck or a rabbit, but not both—then they can't flip their mental image in their mind's eye to see the other interpretation. If they say they saw a duck, then if you ask them if the duck could be a rabbit, they just think you're mad.[6]

Perceiving the ambiguity seems to require real visual input to operate on. Although you have the details of the image in your mind's eye it seems you need to experience them anew, to refresh the visual information, to be able to make a reinterpretation of the ambiguous figure.

In Real Life

We use mental imagery to reason about objects before we move them or before we move around them. Map reading involves a whole load of mental rotation, as does fitting together things like models or flat-pack furniture. Assembly instructions that involve rotating the object will be harder to compute, all other things being equal. But if you can imagine the object staying

Figure 2-31. You can see this picture as a duck or a rabbit, but if you'd seen only one interpretation at the time, could you see the other interpretation in your mind's eye?[7]

in the same place with you rotating around it, you can partially compensate for this. The easier it is to use mental rotation, the less physical work we actually have to do and the more likely we are to get things right the first time.

End Notes

1. Shepard, R. N., & Metzler, J. (1971). Mental rotation of three dimensional objects. *Science, 171*, 701–703.

2. Cooper, L. A., & Shepard, R. N. (1973). Chronometric studies of the rotation of mental images. In W. G. Chase (ed.), *Visual Information Processing*, 75–176. New York: Academic Press.

3. Kosslyn, S., Ball, T., & Reiser, B. (1978). Visual images preserve metric spatial information: Evidence from studies of image scanning. *Journal of Experimental Psychology: Human Perception and Performance, 4*, 47–60.

4. Parsons, L. M. (2003). Superior parietal cortices and varieties of mental rotation. *Trends in Cognitive Sciences, 7*(12), 515–517.

5. Wraga, M., Creem, S. H., & Proffitt, D. R. (2000). Updating displays after imagined object and viewer rotations. *Journal of Experimental Psychology: Learning, Memory, and Cognition, 26*, 151–168.

6. Chambers, D., & Reisberg, D. (1985). Can mental images be ambiguous? *Journal of Experimental Psychology: Human Perception and Performance, 11*(3), 317–328.

7. *Fliegende Blätter* (1892, No. 2465, p. 17). Munich: Braun & Schneider. Reprinted in: Jastrow, J. (1901). *Fact & Fable in Psychology*. London: Macmillan.

See Also

- Great short notes on mental imagery from Barnes & Noble (*http://www. sparknotes.com/psychology/cognitive/perception/section1.html*).

 Explore Your Defense Hardware

#32   We have special routines that detect things that loom and make us flinch in response.

Typically, the more important something is, the deeper in the brain you find it, the earlier in evolution it arose, and the quicker it can happen.

Avoiding collisions is pretty important, as is closing your eyes or tensing if you can't avoid the collision. What's more, you need to do these things to a deadline. It's no use dodging after you've been hit.

Given this, it's not surprising that we have some specialized neural mechanisms for detecting collisions and that they are plugged directly into motor systems for dodging and defensive behavior.

In Action

The startle reaction is pretty familiar to all of us—you blink, you flinch, maybe your arms or legs twitch as if beginning a motion to protect your vulnerable areas. We've all jumped at a loud noise or thrown up our arms as something expands toward us. It's automatic. I'm not going to suggest any try-it-at-home demonstrations for this hack. Everyone knows the effect, and I don't want y'all firing things at each other to see whether your defense reactions work.

How It Works

Humans can show response to a collision-course stimulus within 80 ms.[1] This is far too quick for any sophisticated processing. In fact, it's even too quick for any processing that combines information across both eyes.

It's done, instead, using a classic hack—a way of getting good-enough 3D direction and speed information from crude 2D input. It works like this: symmetrical expansion of darker-than-background areas triggers the startle response.

"Darker-than-background" because this is a rough-and-ready way of deciding what to count as an object rather than just part of the background. "Symmetrical expansion" because this kind of change in visual input is characteristic of objects that are coming right at you. If it's not expanding, it's probably just moving, and if it's not expanding symmetrically, it's either changing shape or not moving on a collision course.

These kind of stimuli capture attention [Hack #37] and cause a startle response. Everything from reptiles to pigeons to human infants will blink and/or flinch their heads when they see this kind of input. You don't get the same effects with contracting patches, rather than expanding patches, or with light patches, rather than dark patches .[2]

Looming objects always provoke a reaction, even if they are predictable; we don't learn to ignore them as we learn to ignore other kinds of event.[3] This is another sign that they fall in a class for which there is dedicated neural machinery—and the reason why is pretty obvious as well. A looming object is always potentially dangerous. Some things you just shouldn't get used to.

In pigeons, the cells that detect looming exist in the midbrain. They are very tightly tuned so that they respond only to objects that look as if they are going to collide—they don't respond to objects that are heading for a near miss, even if they are still within 5° of collision.[4] These neurons fire at a consistent time before collision, regardless of the size and velocity of the object.

This, and the fact that near misses don't trigger a response, shows that path and velocity information is extracted from the rate and shape of expansion. Now this kind of calculation can be done cortically, using the comparison of information from both eyes, but for high-speed, non-tiny objects at anything more than 2 m away, it isn't.[5] You don't need to compare information from both eyes; the looming hack is quick and works well enough.

End Notes

1. Busettini, C., Masson, G. S., Miles, F. A. (1997). Radial optic flow induces vergence eye movements with ultra-short latencies. *Nature, 390*(6659), 512–515.

2. Nanez, J. E. (1988). Perception of impending collision in 3- to 6-week-old human infants. *Infant Behaviour and Development, 11,* 447–463.

3. Caviness, J. A., Schiff, W., & Gibson, J. J. (1962). Persistent fear responses in rhesus monkeys to the optical stimulus of "looming." *Science, 136,* 982–983.

4. Wang, Y., & Frost, B. J. (1992). Time to collision is signalled by neurons in the nucleus rotundus of pigeons. *Nature, 356,* 236–238.

5. Rind, F. C., & Simmons, P. J. (1999). Seeing what is coming: Building collision-sensitive neurones. *Trends in Neurosciences, 22,* 215–220. (This reference contains some calculations showing exactly what size of approaching objects, at what distances, are suitable for processing using the looming system and what are suitable for processing by the stereo-vision system.)

 ## Neural Noise Isn't a Bug; It's a Feature

Neural signals are innately noisy, which might just be a good thing.

Neural signals are always noisy: the timings of when they fire, or even whether they fire at all, is subject to random variation. We make generalizations at the psychological level, such as saying that the speed of response is related to intensity by a certain formula—Pieron's Law [Hack #11]. And we also say that cells in the visual cortex respond to different specific motions [Hack #25]. But both of these are true only *on average*. For any single cell, or any single test of reaction time, there is variation each time it is measured. Not all the cells in the motion-sensitive parts of the visual cortex will respond to motion, and those that do won't do it exactly the same each time we experience a particular movement.

In the real world, we take averages to make sense of noisy data, and somehow the brain must be doing this too. We know that the brain is pretty accurate, despite the noisiness of our neural signals. A prime mechanism for compensating for neural noise is the use of lots of neurons so that the average response can be taken, canceling out the noise.

But it may also be the case that noise has some useful functions in the nervous system. Noise could be a feature, rather than just an inconvenient bug.

In Action

To see how noise can be useful, visit Visual Perception of Stochastic Resonance (*http://neurodyn.umsl.edu/sr/*; Java) designed by Enrico Simonotto,[1] which includes a Java applet.

A grayscale picture has noise added and the result filtered through a threshold. The process is repeated and results played like a video. Compare the picture with various levels of noise included. With a small amount of noise, you see some of the gross features of the picture—these are the parts with high light values so they always cross the threshold, whatever the noise, and produce white pixels—but the details don't show up often enough for you to make them out. With lots of noise, most of the pixels of the picture are frequently active and it's hard to make out any distinction between true parts of the picture and pixels randomly activated by noise.

But with the right amount of noise, you can clearly see what the picture is and all the details. The gross features are always there (white pixels), the fine features are there consistently enough (with time smoothing they look gray), and the pixels that are supposed to be black aren't activated enough to distract you.

How It Works

Having evolved to cope with noisy internal signals gives you a more robust system. The brain has developed to handle the odd anomalous data point, to account for random inputs thrown its way by the environment. We can make sense of the whole even if one of the parts doesn't entirely fit (you can see this in our ability to simultaneously process information [Hack #52], as well). "Happy Birthday" sung down a crackly phone line is still "Happy Birthday." Compare this with your precision-designed PC; the wrong instruction at the wrong time and the whole thing crashes. The ubiquity of noise in neural processing means your brain is more of a statistical machine than a mechanistic one.

That's just a view of noise as something to be worked around, however. There's another function that noise in neural systems might be performing—it's a phenomenon from control theory called *stochastic resonance*. This says that adding noise to a signal raises the maximum possible combined signal level. Counterintuitively, this means that adding the right amount of noise to a weak signal can raise it above the threshold for detection and make it easier to detect and not less so. Figure 2-32 shows this in a graphical form. The smooth curve is the varying signal, but it never quite reaches the activation threshold. Adding noise to the signal produces the jagged line that, although it's messy, still has the same average values *and* raises it over the threshold for detection at certain points.

Just adding noise doesn't always improve things of course: you might now have a problem with your detection threshold being crossed even though there is no signal. A situation in which stochastic resonance works best is one in which you have another dimension, such as time, across which you can compare signals. Since noise changes with time, you can make use of the frequency at which the detection threshold is crossed too.

In Simonotto's applet, white pixels correspond to where the detection threshold has been crossed, and a flickering white pixel averages to gray over time. In this example, you are using time and space to constrain your judgment of whether you think a pixel has been correctly activated, and

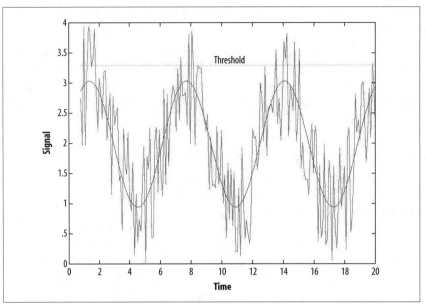

Figure 2-32. Adding noise to a signal brings it above threshold, without changing the mean value of the signal

you're working in cooperation with the noise being added inside the applet, but this is exactly what your brain can do too.

End Note

1. Simonotto, E., Riani, M., Seife, C., Roberts, M., Twitty, J., & Moss, F. (1997). Visual perception of stochastic resonance. *Physical Review Letters, 78*(6), 1186–1189.

See Also

- An example of a practical application of stochastic resonance theory, in the form of a hearing aid: Morse, R. P., & Evans, E. F. (1996). Enhancement of vowel coding for cochlear implants by addition of noise. *Nature Medicine, 2*(8), 928–932.

CHAPTER THREE

Attention
Hacks 34–43

It's a busy world out there, and we take in a lot of input, continuously. Raw sense data floods in through our eyes, ears, skin, and more, supplemented by memories and associations both simple and complex. This makes for quite a barrage of information; we simply haven't the ability to consider all of it at once.

How, then, do we decide what to attend to and what else to ignore (at least for now)?

Attention is what it feels like to give more resources over to some perception or set of perceptions than to others. When we talk about attention here, we don't mean the kind of concentration you give to a difficult book or at school. It's the momentary extra importance you give to whatever's just caught your eye, so to speak. Look around the room briefly. What did you see? Whatever you recall seeing—a picture, a friend, the radio, a bird landing on the windowsill—you just allocated attention to it, however briefly.

Or perhaps attention isn't a way of allocating the brain's scarce processing resources. Perhaps the limiting factor isn't our computational capacity at all, but, instead, a physical limit on action. As much as we can perceive simultaneously, we're able to act in only any one way at any one time. Attention may be a way of throwing away information, of narrowing down all the possibilities, to leave us with a single conscious experience to respond to, instead of millions.

It's hard to come up with a precise definition of attention. Psychologist William James,[1] in his 1890 *The Principles of Psychology*, wrote: "Everyone knows what attention is." Some would say that a more accurate and useful definition has yet to be found.

That said, we can throw a little light on attention to see how it operates and feels. The hacks in this chapter look at how you can voluntarily focus your visual attention [Hack #34], what it feels like when you do (and when you remove it again) [Hack #36], and what is capable of overriding your voluntary behavior and grabbing attention [Hack #37] automatically. We'll do a little counting [Hack #35] too. We'll also test the limits of shifting attention [Hacks #38 and #39] and run across some situations in which attention lets you down [Hacks #40 and #41]. Finally, we'll look at a way your visual attention capacity can be improved [Hack #43].

End Note

1. The Stanford Encyclopedia of Philosophy has a good biography of William James (*http://plato.stanford.edu/entries/james*).

Detail and the Limits of Attention
Focusing on detail is limited by both the construction of the eye and the attention systems of the brain.

What's the finest detail you can see? If you're looking at a computer screen from about 3 meters away, 2 pixels have to be separated by about a millimeter or more for them not to blur into one. That's the highest your eye's resolution goes.

But making out detail in real life isn't just a matter of discerning the difference between 1 and 2 pixels. It's a matter of being able to focus on fine-grain detail among enormously crowded patterns, and that's more to do with the limits of the brain's visual processing than what the eye can do. What you're able to see and what you're able to look at aren't the same.

In Action

Figure 3-1 shows two sets of bars. One set of bars is within the resolution of attention, allowing you to make out details. The other obscures your ability to differentiate particularly well by crowding .[1]

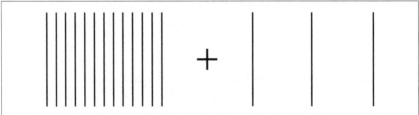

Figure 3-1. One set of bars is within the resolution of attention (right), the other is too detailed (left)[1]

Hold this book up and fix your gaze on the cross in the middle of Figure 3-1. To notice the difference, you have to be able to move your focus around without moving your eyes—it does come naturally, but it can feel odd doing it deliberately for the first time. Be sure not to shift your eyes at all, and notice that you can count how many bars are on the righthand side easily. Practice moving your attention from bar to bar while keeping your eyes fixed on the cross in the center. It's easy to focus your attention on, for example, the middle bar in that set.

Now, again without removing your gaze from the cross, shift your attention to the bars on the lefthand side. You can easily tell that there are a number of bars there—the basic resolution of your eyes is more than good enough to tell them apart. But can you count them or selectively move your attention from the third to the fourth bar from the left? Most likely not; they're just too crowded.

How It Works

The difference between the two sets of bars is that the one on the right is within the resolution of *visual selective attention* because it's spread out, while the one on the left is too crowded with detail.

"Attention" in this context doesn't mean the sustained concentration you give (or don't give) the speaker at a lecture. Rather, it's the prioritization of some objects at the expense of others. Capacity for processing is limited in the brain, and attention is the mechanism to allocate it. Or putting it another way, you make out more detail in objects that you're paying attention to than to those you aren't. Selective attention is being able to apply that processing to a particular individual object voluntarily. While it feels as if we should be able to select anything we can see for closer inspection, the diagram with the bars shows that there's a limit on what can be picked out, and the limit is based on how fine the detail is.

We can draw a parallel with the resolution of the eye. In the same way the resolution of the eye is highest in the center [Hack #14] and decreases toward the periphery, it's easier for attention to select and focus on detail in the center of vision than it is further out. Figure 3-2 illustrates this limit.

On the left, all the dots are within the resolution required to select any one for individual attention. Fix your gaze on the central cross, and you can move your attention to any dot in the pattern. Notice how the dots have to be larger the further out from the center they are in order to still be made out. Away from the center of your gaze, your ability to select a dot deteriorates, and so the pattern has to be much coarser.

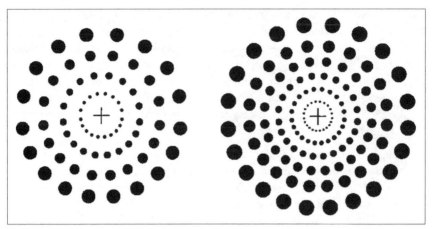

Figure 3-2. Comparing a pattern within the resolution of attention (left) with one that is too fine (right)

The pattern on the right shows what happens if the pattern isn't that much coarser. The dots are crowded together just a little too much for attention to cope, and if you keep your eyes on the central cross, you can't voluntarily focus your attention on any particular dot any more. (This is similar to the lefthand side set of bars in the first diagram, as shown in Figure 3-1.)

Also notice, in Figure 3-2, left, that the dots are closer together at the bottom of the patterns than at the top. They're able to sit tighter because we're better at making out detail in the lower half of vision—the resolution of attention is higher there. Given eye level and below is where all the action takes place, compared to the boring sky in the upper vision field, it makes sense to be optimized that way round. But precisely where this optimization arises in the structure of the brain, and how the limit on attentional resolution in general arises, isn't yet known.

Why is selective attention important, anyway? Attention is used to figure out what to look at next. In the dot pattern on the left, you can select a given dot before you move your eyes, so it's a fast process. But in the other diagram, on the right, moving your eyes to look directly at a dot involves more hunting. It's a hard pattern to examine, and that makes examination a slow process.

In Real Life

Consider attentional resolution when presenting someone with a screen full of information, like a spreadsheet. Does he have to examine each cell laboriously to find his way around it, like the crowded Figure 3-2, right? Or, like the one on the left, is it broken up into large areas, perhaps using color and contrast to make it comprehensible away from the exact center of the gaze and to help the eyes move around?

End Note

1. Figures reprinted from *Trends in Cognitive Sciences*, 1(3), He, S., Cavanagh, P., & Intriligator, J., Attentional Resolution, 115–21, Copyright (1997), with permission from Elsevier.

Count Faster with Subitizing

#35 You don't need counting if a group is small enough; subitizing will do the job, and it's almost instant.

The brain has two methods for counting, and only one is officially called counting. That's the regular way—when you look at a set of items and check them off, one by one. You have some system of remembering which have already been counted—you count from the top, perhaps—and then increment: 7, 8, 9...

The other way is faster, up to five times faster per item. It's called *subitizing*. The catch: subitizing works for only really small numbers, up to about 4. But it's fast! So fast that until recently it was believed to be instantaneous.

In Action

See how many stars there are in the two sets in Figure 3-3. You can tell how many are in set A just by looking (there are three), whereas it takes a little longer to see there are six in set B.

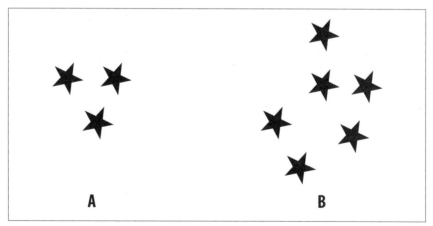

Figure 3-3. The set of stars on the left can be subitized; the one on the right cannot

I know this feels obvious, that it takes longer to see how many stars there are in the larger set. After it, there are more of them. But that's exactly the point. If you can tell, and it feels like immediately, how many stars there are when there are three of them, why not when there are six? Why not when there are 100?

How It Works

Subitizing and counting do seem like different processes. If you look at studies of how long it takes for a person to look at some shapes on the screen and report how many there are, the time grows at 40–80 ms per item up to four, then increases at 250–350 milliseconds beyond that.[1] Or to put it another way, assessing the first four items takes only a quarter of a second. It takes another second for every four items after that. That's a big jump.

The difference between the two is borne out by the subjective experience. Counting feels to be a very deliberate act. You must direct your attention to each item. Your eyes move from star to star. Subitizing, on the other hand, feels preattentive. Your eyes don't need to move from star to star at all. There's no deliberate act required; you just know that there are four coffee mugs on the table or three people in the lobby, without having to check. You just look. It's this that leads some researchers to believe that subitizing isn't an act in itself, but rather a side effect of visual processing.

We know that we are able to keep track of a limited number of objects automatically and follow them as they move around and otherwise change. Like looking at shadows to figure out the shape of the environment [Hack #20], object tracking seems to be a built-in feature of visual processing—an almost involuntary ability to keep persistent files open for objects in vision [Hack #36]. The limit on how many objects can be tracked and how many items can be subitized is curiously similar. Perhaps, say some, the reason subitizing is so quick is that the items to be "counted" have already been tagged by the visual processing system, and so there's no further work required to figure out how many there are .[2]

In this view, counting is an entirely separate process that occurs only when the object tracking capacity is reached. Counting then has to remember which items have been enumerated and proceed in a serial way from item to item to see how many there are. Unfortunately, there's no confirmation of this view when looking at which parts of the brain are active while each of the two mechanisms is in use.[1] Subitizing doesn't appear to use any separate part of the brain that isn't also used when counting is employed. That's not to say the viewpoint of fast subitizing as a side effect is incorrect, only that it's still a conjecture.

Regardless of the neural mechanism, this does give us a hint as to why it's quicker to count in small clusters rather than one by one. Say you have 30 items on the table. It's faster to mentally group them into clusters of 3 each (using the speedy subitizing method to cluster) and slowly count the 10 clusters, than it is to use no subitizing and count every one of the 30 individually. And indeed, counting in clusters is what adults do.

In Real Life

You don't have to look far to see the real-life impact of the speed difference between sensing the quantity of items and having to count them.

Some abaci have 10 beads on a row. These would be hard—and slow—to use if it weren't for the Russian design of coloring the two central beads.[3] This visual differentiation divides a row into three groups with a top size of four beads—perfect for instantly subitizing with no need for actual counting. It's a little design assistance to work around a numerical limitation of the brain.

We also subitize crowds of opponents in fast-moving, first-person shooter video games to rapidly assess what we're up against (and back off if necessary). The importance of sizing up the opposition as fast as possible in these types of games has the nice side effect of training our subitizing routines [Hack #43].

End Notes

1. Piazza, M., Mechelli, A., Butterworth, B., & Price, C. J. (2002). Are subitizing and counting implemented as separate or functionally overlapping processes? *NeuroImage, 15*, 435–446.

2. Trick, L. M., & Pylyshyn, Z. W. (1994). Why are small and large numbers enumerated differently? A limited-capacity preattentive stage in vision. *Psychological Review, 101*(1), 80–102.

3. "The Material Culture of Mathematics in a Historical Perspective." University of Cambridge, Department of History and Philosophy of Science (*http://www.hps.cam.ac.uk/readinglists/p5mcm-2.html*; includes illustrations).

HACK #36 Feel the Presence and Loss of Attention

Following seemingly identical objects around with your eyes isn't an easy job. Concentrating, it's possible, and the brain can even track objects when they momentarily pass behind things and disappear, but only in certain circumstances.

The problem with attention as a mechanism is that we use it continuously—it's an intrinsic part of perception—and consequently it's very hard to spot what it actually does or what giving attention to something actually feels like.

This hack has a go at showing you what allocating attention actually feels like, by getting you to voluntarily give attention to some fairly generic objects—in this case, you'll be tracking small, colored shapes as they move around. And you'll be able to feel what happens to these shapes when you take attention away. These are humble beginnings—attention allocation to moving shapes—but we use these mechanisms for following any *thing* as it moves around: tennis balls, dogs, ants, and cursors.

In Action

Watch the sequence of *multiple object tracking* (MOT) demonstrations at Dr. Zenon Pylyshyn's Visual Attention Lab (*http://ruccs.rutgers.edu/finstlab/ demos.htm*).[1] Multiple object tracking is a class of experiment based around trying to keep track of many objects (small circles in the first demonstration) simultaneously, as they jiggle about. It tests the limits of your attention and specialized tracking skills.

> Just in case you're not online at the moment, Figures 3-4 through 3-6 provide screenshots of the experiments for your convenience.

Start with the General MOT experiment (*http://ruccs.rutgers.edu/finstlab/ mot.mov*; QuickTime; Figure 3-4). In this demo, you're required to track four of the eight circles as they move around; you're told which four as they flash briefly at the beginning of the movie.

The point of this demonstration is simply to point out that you can indeed attend to more than one object at a time. It's not a trivial matter to follow all four circles around simultaneously, but you'll find that you can gaze at the center of the screen and track your four chosen circles fairly easily, without even having to stare directly at each in turn.

In the Occluder task (*http://ruccs.rutgers.edu/finstlab/mot-occ-occlusion.mov*; QuickTime; Figure 3-5), the circles have been replaced by identical white squares, and now they disappear occasionally behind bars placed over the field of movement.

Aside from the newly introduced bars, the experiment is the same as the General MOT experiment; four of the eight squares flash at the beginning, your task being to track those four for the duration of the movie. This certainly isn't as easy as the general MOT experiment and may take a couple of attempts, but you should be able to complete the task.

The Virtual Occluder MOT movie (*http://ruccs.rutgers.edu/finstlab/mot-occ- virtocc.mov*; QuickTime; Figure 3-6), on the other hand, requires serious concentration. Now instead of sliding behind visible bars, the white squares

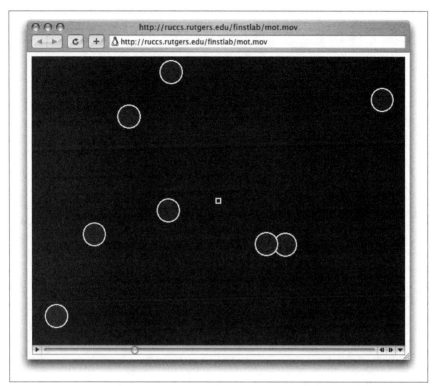

Figure 3-4. You have to track four of these circles as they move around the screen

momentarily vanish. The occluders—the bars that occlude, or hide, the squares behind them—are now the same color as the background and have become invisible. Tracking the four white squares that flash at the beginning for the duration of the whole experiment is now a real challenge. You have to give the task your full concentration, and any distraction will cause you to confuse one of your chosen white squares with one of the other, apparently identical, distracter objects. It doesn't help that they all keep disappearing and reappearing—the two smaller white rectangles in Figure 3-6 are just reappearing from behind one of the invisible virtual occluders.

While it is still possible to do a reasonable job of tracking the four targets, we've now reached the limits of your attention. But there's one more movie to go: the Implode/Explode task (*http://ruccs.rutgers.edu/finstlab/mot-occ-implosion.mov*; QuickTime). The single difference between this experiment and the previous (Virtual Occluder) is that here the squares shrink down to a dot when they encounter one of the invisible black bars instead of slipping behind it. On the other side of the bar, they grow back from a dot into a square instead of appearing from underneath the bar's edge.

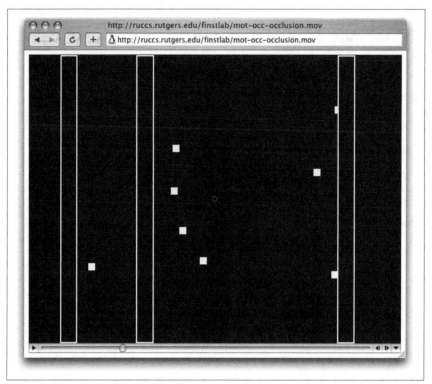

Figure 3-5. Tracking the moving shapes becomes harder when they periodically move behind the black bars (outlined in white)

Give it a whirl. It's not just difficult this time, it's more or less impossible. You can't complete this multiple object tracking task at all.

How It Works

The ability to perform multiple object tracking (MOT) is the skill we get by giving attention to objects: without attention, you can't keep track of which object is which (let alone more than one at a time). Attention is both a mechanism the brain uses for giving some objects more processing time and what you feel is an extra layer on your visual perception. Despite all eight circles in the General MOT experiment having the same visual appearance, you perceive four of them as somehow different, just because they flashed at the beginning. That's the feeling of attention feeding into your visual perception.

If you had followed around only a single circle in that first movie, you would have very easily been able to distinguish it from all of the others. But you wouldn't have been able to distinguish the other seven from one another. That's what attention does.

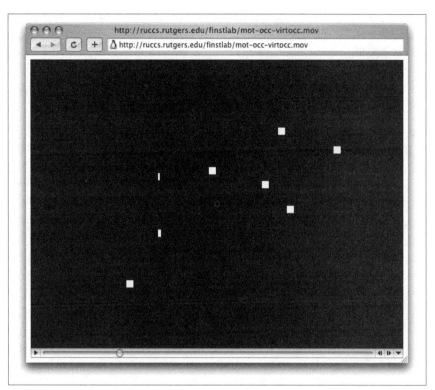

Figure 3-6. Tracking gets harder still: the slimmer white shapes are squares half-hidden behind invisible obstructing bars

Although in this case you've applied attention voluntarily to certain objects, it's actually a semiautomatic process. Attention can be captured [Hack #37] by sudden movements, for example. And it doesn't always feel as obvious as "I am now able to distinguish these objects"—you momentarily give your attention to every single car that passes you when you're waiting to cross the road, but not in the same way as you give attention to these multiple object tracking demonstrations—it's not a concentrated kind of attention, just an awareness that you've seen it.

Attention is something that can be allocated piecemeal. You can choose to notice certain colors, for example, or look out for particular movements. Conversely, you can choose to suppress attention for those features (that's what negative priming [Hack #42] is all about). In this case, you're choosing to allocate attention to collections of features that appear to move round together: blue-ness, circle-ness, move-at-a-certain-speed-ness. We tend to refer to bundles of features as *objects*. (It's possible that attention has a role to play in bundling the features together.)

We deal with objects in our attention in a special way, setting up *object files* that can persist through time. The brain automatically says, "This is an object I need to remember" and sets up a *file* (a kind of invisible sticky tag on the object) to do it. Imagine if you used your finger to point at something as it moved about, like running your finger along a row in a table of figures. It helps you remember which row, out of all the similar-looking rows, was the one you were following. Object files are like finger pointing, but using attention instead. That's how you know that the circle at the end of the task is the same as the one you identified at the beginning: your brain set up a file about it—an index to the bundle of features that are appearing in your visual perception—and kept that for as long as your attention was on that object.

Given this, the brain must have some automatic processes to reclaim attention as soon as it's no longer needed. One way of doing this would be to close the object file as soon as the object disappears. That would often be a hindrance however—imagine if you, as an early human living on the African savannah, lost track of a predator every time it went behind a bush.

That's what the Occluder demonstration shows. Object files are kept open when it looks as if the object being tracked is slipping behind some other object in the visual field, in this case black bars. The Virtual Occluder demo is hard because you're maxing out your attentional resources tracking four objects (four or five objects is about the maximum we have room for) and relying entirely on your automatic processes to imagine where the objects are even when they're hidden and reattach the object file when the squares reappear from behind the invisible bars. But it's still possible because this is the kind of situation visual perception needs to deal with: an animal darting around in a forest will keep disappearing behind branches or greenery, and the dense foliage in the foreground has the same pattern as everything else and is basically invisible against the background.

Here's the trick your object files system is using to know not to shut down the file: As the squares disappear behind the bars—that is, as they are occluded—they disappear line by line. They vanish from one edge. That's the cue your brain uses to know occlusion is occurring.

The final demo, the Imploder/Exploder, is a bit of a cheat. It's supposed to be impossible. Tracking that many objects is deliberately hard so it fills your voluntary attentional capacity and forces you to rely on your automatic brain functions. That's a way of getting the automatic functions to reveal themselves.

In this case, the demonstration disrupts the occlusion cue. Shrinking down to a dot, the squares instead present the cue that they're moving away into the distance. Thinking the object has disappeared from the vicinity and is no longer important, your brain immediately swings in and closes the object file, reclaiming the attention for use elsewhere. When the square reappears from a dot a moment later, it's as if it's coming back from a long way away. But the object file has already been closed, it's as if it's a different white square entirely.

It's cues as small as how objects disappear behind other objects that your brain uses, even in cartoons such as these movies (which don't have shadows, or perspective, or even 3D depth—anything that we'd usually say makes a scene feel real or physical), to figure out what to track and what to give attention to.

End Note

1. Scholl, B. J., & Pylyshyn, Z. W. (1999). Tracking multiple items through occlusion: clues to visual objecthood. *Cognitive Psychology, 38,* 259–290. Reprint available on the Visual Attention Lab's publications page (*http://ruccs.rutgers.edu/finstlab/ZPPublications.htm*).

Grab Attention

Sudden movement or light can grab your attention, thanks to a second region for visual processing.

What are you paying attention to? These words? In a minute it could switch to a friend or to making coffee or to the person on the bus who just stood up and you noticed out of the corner of your eye. We don't pay attention to everything we see or experience. Following two conversations at the same time is hard, even though we hear both perfectly well, and, likewise, it's simply not possible to read every word on the page of a book simultaneously, although they're all in plain view.

While your senses work overtime to provide as much input as possible, there's a bottleneck in the brain's limited capacity for attention. So we consciously decide which line of text to focus on and read across and down the page, line by line. And this happens at the expense of all the other stimuli we could have attended to, such as the color of the walls or the traffic noise from the road outside.

Choosing what to give attention to is voluntary...mostly. But attention can also be captured.

In Action

Stand so that you're facing a crowded scene. Watching a crowded theater settle down is ideal. A busy street corner is a good choice, too. A TV screen or video game will do as well, as long as there's a lot going on in the frame.

Don't try to direct your attention; just let it wander and feast your eyes on the full field of view.

Notice that when a person waves, or stands up, your attention is grabbed and snaps to focus on the person's position. It's not so much that you notice the waving or standing up itself; the event simply captures your attention and you properly focus on that place a fraction of a second afterward.

Since you're relaxed, your attention soon drifts away, until someone else moves and captures it again. Your attention scintillates across your whole field of view, darting from point to point.

How It Works

After visual information leaves the eye, it doesn't just go to one place for processing; the signal divides. Our conscious appreciation of visual information is provided by processing done in the visual cortex. It sits at the back of the brain in the area called the *occipital lobe* and performs what we typically associate with the job of vision: figuring out exactly what shape the thing you're looking at is, what color, if it's moving, then in what direction and how fast, what it means, and so on—providing the raw information needed to put names to faces and avoid stepping in front of a car while crossing a road.

Attention capture, on the other hand, relies on processing done by a region of the brain called the *superior colliculus*. It gets a copy of the same visual information the visual cortex does from the retina, but processes it in a different way. This region is evolutionarily ancient, which means the basic structure was established and refined in brains far simpler than our own, through many species of animals. (Rather than relegating it to second place, fish and amphibians do most of their visual processing with their equivalent of the superior colliculus, called the *optic lobe*.) So as one might expect, it's not particularly sophisticated, compared to the visual cortex. And it doesn't use much of the information it receives; the superior colliculus looks at a black-and-white world through frosted glass. Then again, it doesn't need much. This processing is for rapid response, when it appears something potentially dangerous is happening and urgent action is needed quicker than the complex visual cortex can respond. It's just useful enough to guide reflex movements, tell the head and body to orient in a particular direction, and force attention to snap to important-seeming events.

The visual cortex and superior colliculus aren't the only regions of the brain that process signals from the eye; there are about 10 in total. Basic visual information also informs pupil size for different light levels, influences our day-night cycle, and influences head and eye movement.

That's what's going on when attention is captured. There's a sudden movement and the rapid response bit of your brain says, "Hey, I don't know what that was, but pay it some attention and figure out what to do in case it attacks us." Looking at the crowd, your attention darts around automatically because this bit of your brain feels startled enough to interrupt consciousness every time somebody waves suddenly.

When you're sitting in a darkened theater, absorbed in the dialog on stage, think about what happens when a door opens at the side of the room. The sudden appearance of light grabs your attention. If it happens again, despite the fact that you know you're not interested, it still grabs your attention and demands a response. It's distracting. That's the automatic nature of attention capture coming into play.

On the upside, that bright light flashing in the corner of your eye could well be a ray of sunlight being revealed as a large dangerous *something* lumbering out of the shadows toward you. The automatic capture of attention serves to orient conscious perception in important directions.

 Automatic responses can go further than just grabbing your attention. This part of the brain is also responsible for the looming instinct [Hack #32], which, given a growing dark shadow anywhere in the field of vision, can trigger not just attention but a physical flinch.

Events that capture attention include the two already mentioned: sudden light (actually, a sudden change in contrast) and sudden movement. In keeping with the purpose of facilitating rapid response, it's only new movement that captures attention. Ongoing motion, like a moving car or a walking person, doesn't trigger the automatic shift in attention.

Two other triggers provide hints as to what else our brains regard as so critical to survival that they deserve a rapid response. One is an object appearing abruptly. In general, our brains give special treatment to objects—as opposed to backgrounds and shadows, which are given less attention. This makes sense, as objects such as other people, animals or food usually require a response of some kind. There are even dedicated routines to object tracking [Hack #36]. An extra person, rock, or car in the scene—especially if it appears suddenly—is likely to be a big deal, so attentional capture is triggered.[1]

John Eastwood and his colleagues also suggest another trigger that is worth mentioning as it shows just how deep our social nature goes. The trigger here is facial expression.2 Eastwood's team made simple line-drawing faces, happy and sad ones, and asked people to count certain of the lines that made up the drawings. When the drawings were upside-down, so they were unrecognizable as faces, people did the counting exercise easily. But when the drawings were the right way up, counting took longer for drawings of faces that displayed negative emotions rather than for drawings of positive expressions. Why? The team's conclusion is that negative expressions—sad or angry faces—distract you, in just the same way as light through a theater door grabs your attention away from the main action.

End Notes

1. Enns, J. T., Austen, E. L., Di Lollo, V., Rauschenberger, R., & Yantis, S. (2001). New objects dominate luminance transients in setting attentional priority. *Journal of Experimental Psychology—Human Perception and Performance, 27*(6), 1287–1302.

2. Eastwood, J. D., Smilek, D., & Merikle, P. M. (2003). Negative facial expression captures attention and disrupts performance. *Perception & Psychophysics, 65*(3), 353–358.

See Also

- A curious side effect of having two regions devoted to visual processing is when the conscious region, the visual cortex, is damaged but the other, automatic one remains intact. *Blindsight* emerges, in which a person believes herself to be blind but is somehow able to reach directly for a flashing light accurately every time. Visual information has reached the person subconsciously, and she puts it down to guesswork. Professor Ramachandran covers blindsight, and more, in the second of his series of BBC Reith Lectures from 2003, "The Emerging Mind" (*http://www.bbc.co.uk/radio4/reith2003/lecture2.shtml*).

HACK #38 Don't Look Back!

Your visual attention contains a basic function that puts the dampers on second glances.

There are layers and layers of functions and processing in the brain. One—attention—is a collaborative exercise between voluntary application of attention and automatic mechanisms to snap attention to where it's needed [Hack #37]. Even the voluntary application of attention is a negotiation with what evolution has taught the brain is most sensible. In particular, the brain doesn't like to return attention to a place or object it has just left. This phenomenon is called *inhibition of return*.

In Action

Like negative priming **[Hack #42]**, which is how contextual features are suppressed from attention, inhibition of return is such a low-level effect that it's hard to show without precision timing equipment. Again, just like those other effects, it turns up in all kinds of cases because attention is so widely employed.

Imagine you're taking part in an experiment in which an icon flashes up on a screen and you have to touch that position. It'll take you longer to move and touch the icon if some other icon had previously, and recently, been in that position.

Inhibition doesn't kick in immediately. Let's say you're playing Whack-A-Mole,[1] in which moles emerge from holes and you have to hit them with a hammer. A hole could light up momentarily before the mole appears. This would be a prime candidate for the inhibition-of-return effect. If the brightening occurs very shortly before the mole appears, only a fifth of a second or so, it serves to draw your attention to that place and you'll actually respond to the mole faster.

If, on the other hand, the brightening occurs and then there's a longer pause—more than a fifth of a second and up to 3 or 4 seconds—that's enough time for your attention to be dragged to the brightness change then shift away again. Inhibition of return kicks in, and when the mole appears in that same spot, you have to overcome the inhibition. It'll take longer for you to react to the mole (although it's not likely you'll miss it. Reaction time increases only on the order of a twentieth of a second or so—enough to make a difference in some circumstances, but hard to spot.) One caveat: if the brightening happens before the mole pops up every single time, you're going to learn that pattern and end up being better at whacking the mole every time instead.

How It Works

The big question is why this happens. One possibility is that it's because we prefer novelty and want to suppress distracting stimuli. An attention-grabbing event is good if it's useful, but if it's not the event we're looking for, then we're better off focusing our attention elsewhere in the future and ignoring that distracting location.

Raymond Klein, in his review paper "Inhibition of Return,"[2] gives the example of efficient foraging for food. He suggests that potential locations that have been found bare should be remembered as places to be avoided, and this acts as a mechanism to orient toward novel locations. This could be used just standing in one place and looking ahead to find edible plants on the ground. For a task like visually searching straight ahead, it would be extremely useful to have a mechanism that allows you to briefly look harder (for a fifth of a second) and helps you to look for novel locations (for a few seconds after).

Current research indicates there may be two ways in which inhibition of return is produced. One is at a very low level, subcortically in the *superior colliculus*, which does rapid visual processing (but isn't responsible for our conscious visual processing [Hack #13], which takes longer) and helps orient the pupils and body. Indeed, damage to this part of the brain stops inhibition of return from taking place[3], at least for stopping the eyes moving back to locations they've previously been.

Inhibition of return could also be triggered by higher-level operations in the allocation of attention. The fact that the inhibition remains in place even when the objects are moving around supports this—it can no longer rely on just eye position. Think of counting a crowd of people when they're all moving around: you're able to do this because you can *deselect* people who have already been counted. This is the inhibition of return in play.

In Real Life

In fact, that this mechanism crops up in more than one place in the brain points to it being a good, generic solution to tricky search problems, rather than a workaround for some problem specific to a particular function like feature processing. I can see the same strategy coming into play when I'm looking for something I've lost in my house. I'll search one location pretty thoroughly, then move on to the next, and the next, and the next. If someone suggests I return to my first location and look there again, I'm pretty reluctant. After all, I would have found it first time around, right?

If this is a common strategy in search, there are some pointers for interface design. Don't attract people's attention to a place briefly if you really want to grab their attention there shortly after. So if a news ticker on a web site, for example, appears with a flash but then has a 2-second pause before the news appears on it, people aren't going to notice the news coming up. The initial flash will have inhibited their attention returning there for the subsequent few seconds. If something is going to happen, make it happen immediately, not after a brief pause. When people are skimming over stuff, they don't want to have their attention squandered—inhibition of return makes second glances less likely.

End Notes

1. Spy Whack-A-Mole, using Flash (*http://www.spymuseum.org/games/mole.html*), lets you play the game and simultaneously learn about the past 100 years of spying.

2. Klein, R. M. (2000). Inhibition of return. *Trends in Cognitive Science,* 4(4), 138–147.

3. Sapir, A., Soroker, N, Berger, A., & Henik, A. (1999). Inhibition of return in spatial attention: Direct evidence for collicular generation. *Nature Neuroscience,* 2(12), 1053–1054.

Avoid Holes in Attention

HACK #39

Our ability to notice things suffers in the half-second after we've just spotted something else.

A good way to think about *attention* is as the brain's way of paring down the sheer volume of sensory input into something more manageable. You can then concentrate your resources on what's important (or at least perceived to be so on first blush) and ignore the rest. If processing capacity weren't limited, perhaps we wouldn't need attention at all–we'd be able to give the same amount of concentration to everything in our immediate environment, simultaneously.

> Another reason we continually pare down perception, using attention as a final limiting stage before reaching conscious awareness, could be that perception causes action. Maybe processing capacity doesn't intrinsically need to be limited, but our ability to act definitely is: we can do only one major task at a time. Attention might just be a natural part of conflict resolution over what to do next.
>
> —M.W.

Attention isn't the end of the chain, however. There's conscious awareness too. The difference between the two is subtle but important. Think of walking down a street and idly looking at the faces going by. Each face as it passes has a moment of your attention, but if you were asked how many brown-haired people you'd seen, you wouldn't have the slightest idea.

Say somebody you recognize passes. Suddenly this semiautomatic, mostly backgrounded looking-at-faces routine jumps to the foreground and pushes the face into conscious awareness. This is the act of *noticing*.

It turns out the act of noticing takes up resources in the brain too, just as paying attention does. Once you've noticed a face in the crowd, there's a gap where your ability to consciously notice another face is severely reduced. It's a big gap too—about half a second. This phenomenon has been dubbed the *attentional blink*, drawing a parallel with the physical eye blink associated with visual surprise.

Attention—just like vision, which cuts out during eye movements [Hack #17]—is full of holes that, as a part of everyday life, we're built to ignore.

In Action

There's a standard experiment used to induce the attentional blink, using a technique called rapid serial visual presentation (RSVP). RSVP consists of projecting black letters onto a gray screen, one at a time, at about 10 letters a second.

You're instructed to watch the stream of letters and be on the lookout for two particular targets: a white letter and the letter X. Spotting either on its own is easy enough. One-tenth of a second (the length of time a letter is on-screen) is enough time for recognition and awareness. Spotting the targets when they're close together in time, however, is much harder.

If the letter X follows the white letter by five places or fewer, you'll probably miss it. Spotting the white letter, the first target, stops the second target, the X, from reaching conscious awareness. That's the attentional blink.

Obviously this isn't an easy test to do at home, but we can approximate it using speed-reading software. Speed-reading software often has a function to run through a text file, flashing the words up sequentially—and that's what we'll use here.

You can use whichever software you like. I used AceReader Pro (*http://www. stepware.com/acereader.html*; $49.95; trial version available).

> Although the AceReader Pro trial version is suitable for this small test, it is available only on Mac and Windows. Flash-Ware (*http://www.flashreader.com*) is a simple, freeware Java applet that takes a file as input for rapid serial visual presentation. GnomeRSVP (*http://www.icebreaker.net/gnomersvp*) and kRSVP (*http://krsvp.sourceforge.net*) are speed-reading applications for the Gnome and KDE Linux desktops, respectively.

Whichever piece of software you choose, you'll need it to have a mode that lets you load an arbitrary file and step through it at about 300–400 words a minute. For AceReader Pro, that means choosing the Online Reader & Expert Mode option.

You'll need a text file, preferably one you haven't read. Ask a friend to choose two relatively unusual words for you from a random place in the text, making sure they're only two or three words apart. These are the words you have to look out for—your targets.

Now load the text into the speed-reader software (in AceReader Pro, choose File → Load File), set the words per minute (WPM) to 400, and click the Play button (the green triangle) to begin. What you're expecting to experience is that you'll spot the first word easily and miss the next one completely. Figure 3-7 shows AceReader Pro in action; you'd notice the first (left), but the second (right) would go utterly without notice.

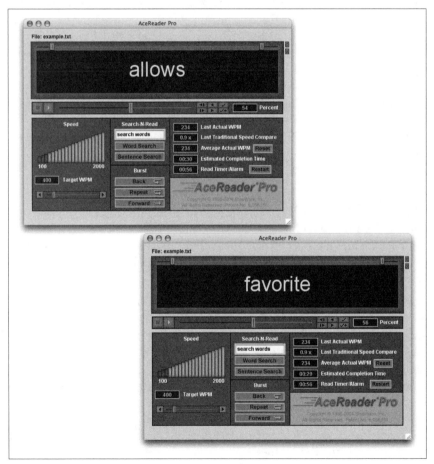

Figure 3-7. AceReader Pro presenting target words

With this particular experiment, nobody experiences the attentional blink every time. For instance, if you're already good at speed-reading or it's easy to guess the sentences in the text document as they come up, it probably won't work. We're using this software to simulate the controlled RSVP experiment, which uses random letters. Doing it this way isn't as reliable.

That said, it worked for me about half the time, and I can only describe the attentional blink itself as a peculiar experience. At about five words a second (300 words a minute), I wasn't overwhelmed by having to read every word and decide whether it was one of my targets—but I was certainly on the cusp of being overwhelmed. I had to sustain a high level of concentration on the screen.

The first word jumped out at me, as I expected it would. OK, I'd recognized that one; now I could look out for the next. But the next word I remember reading properly was four places after. I'd somehow missed my second target. What had occurred in between was my attentional blink. Thinking back, I could remember the sensation of having seen my second word on the screen, but somehow, although I'd seen it, I hadn't twigged that it was actually my target. My memory was distinctly less visual and sure than for the first word, and all I could really remember, for the duration of the blink, was the feeling of doing two things at once: processing the first target and trying to keep up with the fresh words on-screen. If I hadn't been able to stop and figure out why I hadn't noticed my second target, knowing it had to have flashed up, I would've missed it completely.

How It Works

Clearly the attentional blink does exist. The half-second recovery time after noticing a target has been shown many times in experiments. Like attention in general, however, precisely how it arises in the brain is still subject to research.

One strong theory assumes there's a limited amount of attention to go round, which is rapidly transferred from one letter to the next in the rapid serial visual presentation task. Due to the amount of processing each letter needs—to see if it's white or if it's the X—and the speed of change of letters, attention is forced to operate at maximum capacity. When the white letter, the first target, is spotted, additional attentional resources are suddenly needed to lift it to a level of conscious awareness. These extra resources have to come from somewhere, and the process of raising one's awareness takes time; for that period of time, new incoming letters aren't given as much attention as they really need.

That's not to say new letters aren't given any attention at all, and that's where the analogy with eye blinking breaks down. Eye blinks shut off vision almost completely, but attentional blinks just reduce the *probability* of spotting a target during the blink. The success rate for spotting the second target, the X, dips to its minimum of 50% if the second target occurs a quarter of a second (250 ms) after the first target and then gradually recovers as the half-second plays out.

In this view, it's not so much that the second target doesn't get seen at all, it's that it gets processed but there just isn't enough attentional resource to go around and so it isn't brought up to conscious awareness. Additional, random letters keep coming in and claim the processing resource for themselves, and so you never notice that second target.

Two pieces of evidence back this up. First, the processing demand contributed by the random letters is essential for the attentional blink to show up. If the letters aren't there, or instead something that is easily ignored is used (like blocks of random colors, perhaps), they don't act as a processing drain. The second target is seen as easily as the first target in that case.

Second, although the second target may never reach conscious awareness, it can still influence the subconscious mind. There's an effect called *priming*, in which seeing a word once will make it, or a related word, easier to notice the second time **[Hack #81]**. So, for example, in the RSVP task, if shown the word "doctor," the subsequent word is faster and easier to spot if it's the word "doctor" or "nurse."[1] It turns out that the second target, even if it isn't consciously noticed, can prime the next item. This means that the items shown during the attentional blink reach the level of processing required for meaning, at least, and aren't just discarded. The limited-resources-for-attention theory appears to be a good one: there's just not enough attention to lift two items to awareness in quick succession.

> There's one exception to the attentional blink, and that's when the second target, the X, immediately follows the first one, the white letter, with no random letters in between. Curiously, this enables both to be lifted to awareness together.

Think of the attentional blink next time you're looking along a bookshelf for particular titles or down a list of names for people you know. I've had experiences looking down lists when I miss one of the names I'm after time after time, only to look again—slower the second time—and see it was shortly after another name that had jumped out at me each time for some other reason.

End Note

1. An excellent review paper on the subject, especially the priming effect, is: Shapiro, K. L., Arnell, K. M., & Raymond, J. E. (1997). The attentional blink. *Trends in Cognitive Science, 1*(8), 291–296.

See Also

- Two good introductions to the general topic of attention are: Styles, E. A. (1997). *The Psychology of Attention*. Hove: U.K.: Psychology Press. And: Pashler, H. (1998). *The Psychology of Attention*. Cambridge, MA: MIT Press.

Blind to Change

We don't memorize every detail of a visual scene. Instead, we use the world as its own best representation—continually revisiting any bits we want to think about. This saves the brain time and resources, but can make us blind to changes.

Both our vision [Hack #14] and attention [Hack #34] have far coarser resolutions than we'd have thought. What's more, there are gaps in our vision across time [Hack #17] and in space [Hack #16], but our brains compensate for these gaps and knit together a rather seamless impression of the world.

And this gapless impression is utterly convincing. Most of the time we don't even realize that there are holes in the information we're getting. And so we believe we experience more of the world than we actually do. There are two possibilities as to what's going on here. The first is that we build a model inside our heads of the world we can see. You can test to see whether this is the case.

Imagine you are looking at a picture. There's a flicker as the picture disappears and appears again. What's different? If we made and kept a full internal representation of the visual world inside our heads, it would be easy to spot the difference. In theory—before memory decay set in—it should be as easy as comparing two pictures (before and after) side by side on a page. But it isn't.

So that puts paid to the first possibility. The other is that you don't build a full internal model of what you're seeing at all—you just think you do. The illusion is maintained by constant sampling as you move your eyes around, a part of what is called active vision [Hack #15]. After all, why bother to store information about the world in your head when the information is freely available right in front of your very eyes?

The proof of the pudding for *active vision* is testing the consequence that, if true, you should find it very difficult to spot changes between two scenes, even with just a short flicker in between. Since most of the two separated images aren't stored in memory, there's no way to compare them. And, true enough, spotting any difference is very difficult—so hard, in fact, that the phenomenon's been labeled *change blindness*.

In Action

You can try an animated GIF demo, which we made, at *http://www. mindhacks.com/book/40/changeblindness.gif*, both frames of which are shown in Figure 3-8. Shown side by side, the difference between the two versions of this picture is obvious.

Figure 3-8. The difference is easy to spot when you're allowed to look at both versions of the "same" picture at once[1]

But if you don't know what you're looking for, it can be impossible to spot. Load the images in the following URLs and have a look. If you're finding the first one hard, have a look at the man's nose—you can be looking right at the change in the image and still not spot it for a frustratingly long time.

- *http://nivea.psycho.univ-paris5.fr/ASSChtml/couple.gif* (an animated GIF)
- *http://www.usd.edu/psyc301/Rensink.htm* (a Java applet)

How It Works

You need the momentary blink between the pictures so you are actually forced to compare the two pictures in memory rather than noticing the change as it happens. Interestingly enough, the blink doesn't actually even need to cover the feature that's changing, as another demonstration at *http:// nivea.psycho.univ-paris5.fr/ASSChtml/dottedline.gif* shows. Rather than blanking out the entire image, distracting patterns momentarily appear overlaid on it to divert your attention from the change.

You're just as blind to the altering feature when patterns flash up, even though the picture as a whole remains present the entire time. It's enough that your attention is momentarily distracted from picking up on the change, forcing you to rely on your memory for what the scene looked like half a second ago—we're not talking long-term memory here.

In Real Life

This isn't just lab theory. Change blindness can help you pull some great tricks outside of the lab and without the aid of a computer. A classic experiment by Daniel Simons and Daniel Levin[2] is a perfect example. One of the pair would stop a passerby to ask for directions. In the midst of the kindly passerby's attempt at giving directions, two men would carry a door between the experimenter and passerby. During this distraction, the experimenter switched places with his colleague, who was a different height and build, sounded different, and was wearing different clothes. Despite these blatant differences, a full half of the people they tried this on didn't notice any difference between the man who started asking for directions and the man who finished listening to them.

End Notes

1. The road markings on the right of the picture change location.
2. Simons, D. J., & Levin, D. T. (1998). Failure to detect changes to people during a real-world interaction. *Psychonomic Bulletin and Review, 5,* 644–649.

See Also

- Daniel Simons' lab provides a nice collection of movies they've used to demonstrate change blindness (*http://viscog.beckman.uiuc.edu/djs_lab/demos.html*).
- J. Kevin O'Regan has a great talk entitled "Experience Is Not Something We Feel but Something We Do: a Principled Way of Explaining Sensory Phenomenology, with Change Blindness and Other Empirical Consequences" (*http://nivea.psycho.univ-paris5.fr/ASSChtml/ASSC.html*).

HACK #41 Make Things Invisible by Concentrating (on Something Else)

What you pay attention to determines what you see, so much so that you can miss things that are immensely obvious to others—like dancing gorillas, for instance.

Attention acts as a kind of filter, directing all resources to certain tasks and away from others. Nowhere is the impact of attention on what you actually see more evident than in the various experiments on *inattention blindness*.

Inattention blindness comes up when you're focusing as much attention as you can on a particular task and trying really hard to ignore distractions. It's the name given to the phenomenon of not noticing those distractions, however blatant and bizarre they become. In the most famous experiment on this subject, subjects had to watch a video of a crowd playing basketball. Concentrating on a spurious task, a good number of them were completely blind to the gorilla that walked into view halfway through the game.

In Action

You can watch the basketball video used in the gorilla experiment by Daniel Simons and Christopher Chabris.[1] Find it from the University of Illinois Visual Cognition Lab's page at *http://viscog.beckman.uiuc.edu/media/mindhacks.html*.[2]

OK, because you know what's going to happen, this isn't going to work for you, but here's the procedure anyway. Watch the basketball game, and count the number of passes made by the team in white shirts only. Find a friend and set her on the task.

If you were a subject in this experiment for real, counting those passes, what happens next would be completely unexpected: a woman in a gorilla suit walks through the group playing the game and stands in the middle of the screen before walking off again. About half the observers tested in Simons and Chabris's experiment missed the gorilla.

How It Works

Following the passes in the game and counting only some of them is a difficult task. There are two balls and six players, everyone's moving around, and the balls are often obscured. It's all your brain can do to keep up.

Actually, there's a little too much to keep up with. The bottleneck is in visual short-term memory, where the results of visual processing have to be stashed while the actual analysis—looking for passes by players in white shirts—happens.

Visual short-term memory, or VSTM, can hold only a small amount of information. Its capacity is limited to the equivalent of about four objects. Now, there are tricks we can use to temporarily increase the size of short-term memory. Repeating a word over and over can lengthen the time it's remembered, for example. When two researchers at Vanderbilt University, J. Jay Todd and René Marois, performed experiments to measure the size of short-term memory,[3] they devised their task in such a way that tricks weren't possible. Not only did subjects taking part have to do the memory experiment—looking at a pattern of colored dots and answering a question on it a second later—they also had to speak numbers out loud for the duration, preventing the word repeating trick from being used. While the full load of the experiment was on VSTM, Todd and Marois looked at their subjects' brain activity using functional magnetic resonance imaging [Hack #4], a technique that produces images in which busy parts of the brain show up brighter.

What they found was a small area on the back surface, in a region called the *posterior parietal cortex* where the activity increased as the pattern presented in the experiment became more complex. They could see that, as the pattern contained more colored dots, the brain activity grew proportionately—but only up to four dots. At that point, not only did activity reach its peak, but performance in the short-term memory task did too. This points to a real capacity limit in VSTM.

The capacity is a major factor in counting passes in the basketball game too. There's simply too much going on. That's where attention comes in. Attention is our everyday word for the mechanisms that prioritize processing of some objects, making sure they get into VSTM, and suppress irrelevant information. In this case, when you're watching the gorilla video you have no choice but to pay attention only to fast-moving people dressed in white and concentrate on the ball and whatever it goes behind. That automatically means you're discarding information about slow-moving objects, especially those colored black—like the gorilla.

So when the dark gorilla suit slowly walks into the game, not only is your attention elsewhere, but also your visual processing system actively throws away information about it, to ensure the short-term memory doesn't get swamped. You don't even perceive the gorilla, despite the ball going behind it so that you're looking through it at some points.

To add a little proof to the pudding: when Simons and Chabris asked viewers to count the passes of the team dressed in black, they became significantly more likely to notice the gorilla, as this time the observation of it wasn't being actively discarded by the brain.

This example shows in a fun way just how powerfully attention affects our perception. It's also an example of the moment-by-moment way we allocate attention, picking some things to focus on and some to ignore, and how this is determined within an overall scheme of the priorities we've set ourselves. Psychologists call this the *attentional set*, which is the keyword phrase to use if you'd like to find out more.

End Notes

1. Simons, D. J., & Chabris, C. F. (1999). Gorillas in our midst: Sustained inattentional blindness for dynamic events. *Perception, 28,* 1059–1074. You can get a copy at *http://viscog.beckman.uiuc.edu/reprints/index.php.*

2. The Visual Cognition Lab (*http://viscog.beckman.uiuc.edu/djs_lab*) has additional research and demonstrations on inattentional blindness and on related topics.

3. Todd, J. J., & Marois, R. (2004). Capacity limit of visual short-term memory in human posterior parietal cortex. *Nature, 428,* 751–754.

The Brain Punishes Features that Cry Wolf

#42 The act of focusing on just one object goes hand in hand with actively suppressing everything you have to ignore. This suppression persists across time, in a phenomenon called negative priming.

In the story "The Boy Who Cried Wolf," the young shepherd repeatedly claims a wolf has come to attack his flock. There's no wolf there. The boy just enjoys seeing all the villagers run up the hill, coming to save him and the sheep. The villagers, naturally, get a bit annoyed at getting panicked and trying to scare off the nonexistent wolf, so when they hear the boy cry, "Wolf!" again in the middle of the night, they don't bother getting up. But this time there is a wolf. Oh dear. I could say the boy learns his lesson, but he doesn't: he gets eaten. Morality tale, very sad, etc.

Negative priming is the tiniest psychological root of "The Boy Who Cried Wolf." A stimulus, such as a color, a word, a picture, or a sound acts like the cry of "Wolf!" The brain acts as the villagers did, and it has an inhibition to responding to meaningless cries, and this kicks in after only one cry. But nobody gets eaten.

In Action

Negative priming can be picked up only in experiments with careful timing and many trials—it's a small-scale effect, but it's been demonstrated in many situations.

Look at the flash card in Figure 3-9, and say what the gray picture is as fast as you can. Speak it out loud.

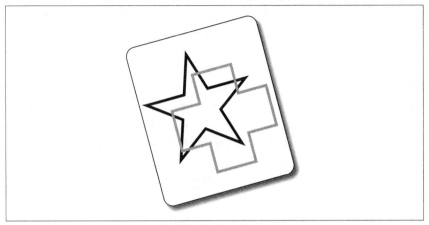

Figure 3-9. An example negative priming flash card

Now look at Figure 3-10, and do the same: name the gray picture, out loud, as quickly as possible.

Figure 3-10. The next flash card in the sequence

You may find the picture in the second flash card slightly harder to make out, although really you need a controlled situation to pick up the reaction time difference. Both cards have a gray drawing to pick out and a black drawing to ignore, and you suppress both the black ink and the black image in order to ignore it. If, as is the case here, the image you have to identify in the second flash card is the same as the one you had to ignore in the first, you'll take a little longer about it. Your brain is acting like the second time the villagers hear the boy shouting "Wolf!"—they still get out of bed, but it takes slightly longer to pull their clothes on.

How It Works

Negative priming has been found in situations much wider than when two colored pictures overlap. In that case, it's one of the pictures that has been negatively primed. But if you set up the experiment so one feature is selected at the expense of another, you can get negative priming for color, location, or shape. All it requires is for a feature to have been in your visual field but actively ignored, then subsequently that feature will take slightly longer to attend to.

What's curious is, in the flash cards used earlier, you're concentrating on the ink color (gray or black), thus ignoring the black ink...but the negative priming occurs for the picture itself too. You've not even had to consciously ignore the distracter picture, because you can just look past the black ink, but it gets suppressed anyway.

In a more extreme way, this is what is happening in inattention blindness [Hack #40]. You're concentrating on a certain set of features (white T-shirts, fast-moving), so you implicitly ignore anything that's colored black and is slow-moving—and that's why an ape walking across the basketball game gets blanked. You're ignoring the features, not the objects themselves.

Looking at the ape in the basketball game [Hack #41] is a good way to figure out what negative priming is happening for. Attention's resources are scarce, and we simply don't have enough to allow them to be consumed by every event that comes along. We need to be able to avoid being distracted by the ape if we're concentrating on basketball. It's the ability to suppress perceptions that makes actions truly voluntary.[1]

What's happening is that attention is being allocated to one set of features, then selectively disabled for potential disrupters. This inhibition function is pretty indiscriminate too, so any feature that's being discarded gets added to the ignore pile, whether it's relevant to the task at hand or not. It looks like a piano? Ignore. It's in black ink? Ignore. Contextual information, whether you focus on it or not, is inhibited, and you'll take longer to notice it when you next have to. Features stay on the ignore pile for much longer than they have to. Traces can be found not just seconds, but days and even weeks later.[2]

(Incidentally, this also provides evidence that we—at least initially—perceive objects as bundles of features that can be separately perceived and inhibited.)

In a sense, negative priming is performing a similar selection function to focusing attention. It narrows down the quantity of perceptions that reach conscious awareness and can be responded to. In everyday life, you can see echoes of information filtering in action: you soon learn what noises foreshadow your car breaking down and which aren't relevant. And then, of course, there's the boy and the villagers. But these are long timescale, large effects. What's surprising is negative priming uses the same strategy, acting very quickly and almost entirely automatically. The narrowing down of information starts here, at the moment-to-moment and completely preconscious level.

End Notes

1. Pipper, S. P., Howard, L. A., & Houghton, G. (1999). Action-based mechanisms of attention. In G. W. Humphreys, J. Duncan, & A. Treisman (eds.), *Attention, Space and Action*, 232–247. Oxford University Press.

2. Treisman, A. (1999). Feature binding, attention and object perception. In G. W. Humphreys, J. Duncan, & A. Treisman (eds.), *Attention, Space and Action*, 91–111. Oxford: Oxford University Press.

See Also

- Damian, M. F. (2000). Semantic negative priming in picture categorization and naming. *Cognition, 76*, B45–B55. This typical, and interesting, negative priming experiment is also available online (*http://eis.bris.ac.uk/~psmfed/papers/np.html*).

- May, C. P., Kane, M. J., & Hasher, L. (1995). Determinants of negative priming. *Psychological Bulletin, 118*, 35–54. This paper explores the mechanisms behind negative priming in depth (*http://www.psych.utoronto.ca/~hasher/abstracts/may_95.htm*).

- Unfortunately, I can't understand Japanese so can't comment on the content of the negative priming intro I found online (*http://www.l.u-tokyo.ac.jp/AandC/HLV/DataBase/NP/intro.html*), but the sample flash cards overlapping green and red line drawings are perfect examples of how to negatively prime certain objects.

**Improve Visual Attention
Through Video Games**

Some of the constraints on how fast we can task-switch or observe
simultaneously aren't fixed. They can be trained by playing first-person
action video games.

Our visual processing abilities are by no means hardwired and fixed from
birth. There are limits, but the brain's nothing if not plastic. With practice,
the attentional mechanisms that sort and edit visual information can be
improved. One activity that requires you to practice lots of the skills
involved in visual attention is playing video games.

So, what effect does playing lots of video games have? Shawn Green and
Daphne Bavelier from the University of Rochester, New York, have
researched precisely this question; their results were published in the paper
"Action Video Game Modifies Visual Attention,"[1] available online at *http://
www.bcs.rochester.edu/people/daphne/visual.html#video*.

Two of the effects they looked at we've talked about elsewhere in this book.
The attentional blink [Hack #39] is that half-second recovery time required to
spot a second target in a rapid-fire sequence. And *subitizing* is that alternative to counting for very low numbers (4 and below), the almost instantaneous mechanism we have for telling how many items we can see [Hack #35].
Training can both increase the subitization limit and shorten the attentional
blink, meaning we're able to simultaneously spot more of what we want to
spot, and do it faster too.

Shortening the Attentional Blink

Comparing the attentional blink of people who have played video games for
4 days a week over 6 months against people who have barely played games
at all finds that the games players have a shorter attentional blink.

The attentional blink comes about in trying to spot important items in a
fast-changing sequence of random items. Essentially, it's a recovery time.
Let's pretend there's a video game in which, when someone pops up, you
have to figure out whether it's a good guy or a bad guy and respond appropriately. Most of the characters that pop up are good guys, it's happening as
fast as you can manage, and you're responding almost automatically—then
suddenly a bad one comes up. From working automatically, suddenly the
bad guy has to be lifted to conscious awareness so you can dispatch him.
What the attentional blink says is that the action of raising to awareness creates a half-second gap during which you're less likely to notice another bad
guy coming along.

Now obviously the attentional blink—this recovery time—is going to have an impact on your score if the second of two bad guys in quick succession is able to slip through your defenses and get a shot in. That's a great incentive to somehow shorten your recovery time and return from "shoot bad guy" mode to "monitor for bad guys" mode as soon as possible.

Raising the Cap on Subitizing

Subitizing—the measure of how many objects you can quantify without having to count them—is a good way of gauging the capacity of visual attention. Whereas counting requires looking at each item individually and checking it off, subitizing takes in all items simultaneously. It requires being able to give a number of objects attention at the same time, and it's not easy; that's why the maximum is usually about four, although the exact cap measured in any particular experiment varies slightly depending on the setup and experimenter.

Green and Bavelier found the average maximum number of items their non-game-playing subjects could subitize before they had to start counting was 3. 3. The number was significantly higher for games players: an average of 4.9—nearly 50% more.

Again, you can see the benefits of having a greater capacity for visual attention if you're playing fast-moving video games. You need to be able to keep on top of whatever's happening on the screen, even when (especially when) it's getting stretching.

How It Works

Given these differences in certain mental abilities between gamers and non-gamers, we might suspect the involvement of other factors. Perhaps gamers are just people who have naturally higher attention capacities (not attention as in concentration, remember, but the ability to keep track of a larger number of objects on the screen) and have gravitated toward video games.

No, this isn't the case. Green and Bavelier's final experiment was to take two groups of people and have them play video games for an hour each day for 10 days.

The group that played the classic puzzle game Tetris had no improvement on subitizing and no shortened attentional blink. Despite the rapid motor control required and the spatial awareness implicit in Tetris, playing the game didn't result in any improvement.

On the other hand, the group that played Medal of Honor: Allied Assault (Electronic Arts, 2002), an intense first-person shooter, could subitize to a higher number and recovered from the attentional blink faster. They had trained and improved both their visual attention capacity and processing time in only 10 days.

In Real Life

Green and Bavelier's results are significant because processes like subitizing [Hack #35] are used continuously in the way we perceive the world. Even before perception reaches conscious attention, our attention is flickering about the world around us, assimilating information. It's mundane, but when you look to see how many potatoes are in the cupboard, you'll "just know" if the quantity fits under your subitization limit and have to count them—using conscious awareness—if not.

Consider the attentional blink, which is usually half a second (for the elderly, this can double). A lot can happen in that time, especially in this information-dense world: are we missing a friend walking by on the street or cars on the road? These are the continuous perceptions we have of the world, perceptions that guide our actions. And the limits on these widely used abilities aren't locked but are trainable by doing tasks that stretch those abilities: fast-paced computer games.

I'm reminded of Douglas Engelbart's classic paper "Augmenting Human Intellect"[2] on his belief in the power of computers. He wrote this in 1962, way before the PC, and argued that it's better to improve and facilitate the tiny things we do every day rather than attempt to replace entire human jobs with monolithic machines. A novel-writing machine, if one were invented, just automates the process of writing novels, and it's limited to novels. But making a small improvement to a pencil, for example, has a broad impact: any task that involves pencils is improved, whether it's writing novels, newspapers, or sticky notes. The broad improvement brought about by this hypothetical better pencil is in our basic capabilities, not just in writing novels. Engelbart's efforts were true to this: the computer mouse (his invention) heightened our capability to work with computers in a small, but pervasive, fashion.

Subitizing is a like a pencil of conscious experience. Subitizing isn't just responsible for our ability at a single task (like novel writing), it's involved in our capabilities across the board, whenever we have to apply visual attention to more than a single item simultaneously. That we can improve such a fundamental capability, even just a little, is significant, especially since the way we make that improvement is by playing first-person shooter video games. Building a better pencil is a big deal.

End Notes

1. Green, C. S., & Bavelier, D. (2003). Action video game modifies visual attention. *Nature, 423,* 534–537.

2. Engelbart, D. (1962). Augmenting human intellect: a conceptual framework located at *http://www.bootstrap.org/augdocs/friedewald030402/augmentinghumanintellect/ahi62index.html.*

CHAPTER FOUR

Hearing and Language
Hacks 44–52

Your ears are not simply "eyes for sound." Sound contains quite different information about the world than does light. Light tends to be ongoing, whereas sound occurs when things change: when they vibrate, collide, move, break, explode! Audition is the sense of events rather than scenes. The auditory system thus processes auditory information quite differently from how the visual system processes visual information: whereas the dominant role of sight is telling where things are, the dominant role of hearing is telling when things happen [Hack #44].

Hearing is the first sense we develop in the womb. The regions of the brain that deal with hearing are the first to finish the developmental process called *myelination*, in which the connecting "wires" of neurons are finished off with fatty sheaths that insulate the neurons, speeding up their electrical signals. In contrast, the visual system doesn't complete this last step of myelination until a few months after birth.

Hearing is the last sense to go as we lose consciousness (when you're dropping off to sleep, your other senses drop away and sounds seem to swell up) and the first to return when we make it back to consciousness.

We're visual creatures, but we constantly use sound to keep a 360° check on the world around us. It's a sense that supplements our visual experience—a movie without a music score is strangely dull, but we hardly notice the sound track normally. We'll look at how we hear some features of that sound track, stereo sound [Hack #45], and pitch [Hack #46].

And of course, audition is the sense of language. Hacks in this chapter show how we don't just hear a physical sound but can hear the meanings they convey [Hack #49], even on the threshold of perception [Hack #48]. Just as with vision, what we experience isn't quite what is physically there. Instead, we experience a useful aural construction put together by our brains.

We'll finish up by investigating three aspects of understanding language: of the hidden sound symbolism in words **[Hack #50]**, of how we break sentences into phrases, **[Hack #51]**, and of how you know excalty waht tehse wrdos maen **[Hack #52]**.

Detect Timing with Your Ears

#44   Audition is a specialized sense for gathering information from the fourth dimension.

If vision lets you see where something is, hearing tells you when it is. The time resolution of audition is way above that of vision. A cinema screen of 24 images a second looks like a constant display, rather than 24 brief images. A selection of 24 clicks a second sounds like a bunch of clicks—they don't blur into a constant tone.

In Action

Listen to these three sound files:

- 24 clicks per second, for 3 seconds (*http://www.mindhacks.com/book/44/24Hz.mp3*; MP3)
- 48 clicks per second, for 3 seconds (*http://www.mindhacks.com/book/44/48Hz.mp3*; MP3)
- 96 clicks per second, for 3 seconds (*http://www.mindhacks.com//book/44/96Hz.mp3*; MP3)

At a frequency of 24 frames per second, film blurs into a continuous image. At 24 clicks per second, you perceive the sound as separate clicks. At four times that rate, you still hear the sound as discontinuous. You may not be able to count the clicks, but you know that the sound is made up of lots of little clicks, not one continuous hum. Auditory "flicker" persists up to higher frequencies than visual flicker before it is integrated to a continuous percept.

How It Works

Specialization for timing is evident in many parts of the auditory system. However, it is the design of the sound receptor device (the ears) that is most crucial. In the eye, light is converted to neural impulses by a slow chemical process in the receptor cells. However, in the ear, sound is converted to neural impulses by a fast mechanical system.

Sound vibrations travel down the ear canal and are transmitted by the tiny ear bones (*ossicles*) to the snail-shaped *cochlea*, a piece of precision engineering in the inner ear. The cochlea performs a frequency analysis of incoming sound, not with neural circuitry, but mechanically. It contains a curled wedge, called the basilar membrane, which, due to its tapering thickness, vibrates to different frequencies at different points along its length. It is here, at the basilar membrane, that sound information is converted into neural signals, and even that is done mechanistically rather than chemically. Along the basilar membrane are receptors, called hair cells. These are covered in tiny hairs, which are in turn linked by tiny filaments. When the hairs are pushed by a motion of the basilar membrane, the tiny filaments are stretched, and like ropes pulling open doors, the filaments open many minute channels on the hairs. Charged atoms in the surrounding fluid rush into the hair cells, and thus sound becomes electricity, the native language of the brain. Even movements as small as those on the atomic scale are enough to trigger a response. And for low frequency sounds (up to 1500 cycles per second), each cycle of the sound can trigger a separate group of electrical pulses. For higher frequencies, individual cycles are not coded, just the average intensity of the cycles. The cells that receive auditory timing input in the brain can fire at a faster rate than any other neurons, up to 500 times a second.

This arrangement means that the auditory system is finely attuned to frequency and timing information in sound waves. Sounds as low as 20 Hz (1 Hz is one beat per second), and as high as 20,000 Hz can be represented. The timing sensitivity is exquisite; we can detect periods of silence in sounds of as little as 1 millisecond (thousandths of a second). Compare this with your visual system, which requires exposure to an image for around 30 milliseconds to report an input to consciousness. Furthermore, thanks to the specialized systems in the ear and in the brain, timing between the ears is even more exquisite. If sound arrives at one ear as little as 20 *microseconds* (millionths of a second) before arriving at the other, this tiny difference can be detected [Hack #45]. For perspective, an eye blink is in the order of 100,000 microseconds, 5000 times slower.

Although vision dominates many other senses in situations of conflicting information [Hack #53], given the sensitivity of our ears, it is not surprising that audition dominates over vision for determing the timing of events

We use this sensitivity to timing in many ways—notably in enjoying music and using the onset of new sounds to warn us that something has changed somewhere.

Detect Sound Direction

#45   Our ears let us know approximately which direction sounds are coming from. Some sounds, like echoes, are not always informative, and there is a mechanism for filtering them out.

A major purpose of audition is telling where things are. There's an analogy used by auditory neuroscientists that gives a good impression of just how hard a job this is. The information bottleneck for the visual system is the ganglion cells that connect the eyes to the brain [Hack #13]. There are about a million in each eye, so, in your vision, there are about two million channels of information available to determine where something is. In contrast, the bottleneck in hearing involves just two channels: one eardrum in each ear. Trying to locate sounds using the vibrations reaching the ears is like trying to say how many boats are out on a lake and where they are, just by looking at the ripples in two channels cut out from the edge of the lake. It's pretty difficult stuff.

Your brain uses a number of cues to solve this problem. A sound will reach the near ear before the far ear, the time difference depending on the position of the sound's source. This cue is known as the *interaural* (between the ears) *time* difference. A sound will also be more intense at the near ear than the far ear. This cue is known as the *interaural level* difference. Both these cues are used to locate sounds on the horizontal plane: the time difference (delay) for low-frequency sounds and the level difference (intensity) for high-frequency sounds (this is known as the Duplex Theory of sound localization). To locate sounds on the vertical plane, other cues in the spectrum of the sound (spectral cues) are used. The direction a sound comes from affects the way it is reflected by the outer ear (the ears we all see and think of as ears, but which auditory neuroscientists call pinnae). Depending on the sound's direction, different frequencies in the sound are amplified or attenuated. Spectral cues are further enhanced by the fact that our ears are slightly different shapes, thus differently distort the sound vibrations.

The main cue is the interaural time difference. This cue dominates the others if they conflict. The spectral cues, providing elevation (up-down) information, aren't as accurate and are often misleading.

In Action

Echoes are a further misleading factor, and seeing how we cope with them is a good way to really feel the complexity of the job of sound localization. Most environments—not just cavernous halls but the rooms in your house too—produce echoes. It's hard enough to work out where a single sound is coming from, let alone having to distinguish between original sounds and their reverberations, all of which come at you from different directions. The distraction of these anomalous locations is mitigated by a special mechanism in the auditory system.

Those echoes that arrive at your ears within a very short interval are grouped together with the original sound, which arrives earliest. The brain takes only the first part of the sound to place the whole group. This is noticeable in a phenomenon known as the Haas Effect, also called *the principle of first arrival* or *precedence effect*.

The Haas Effect operates below a threshold of about 30–50 milliseconds between one sound and the next. Now, if the sounds are far enough apart, above the threshold, then you'll hear them as two sounds from two locations, just as you should. That's what we traditionally call echoes. By making echoes yourself and moving from an above-threshold delay to beneath it, you can hear the mechanism that deals with echoes come into play.

You can demonstrate the Haas Effect by clapping at a large wall.[1] Stand about 10 meters from the wall and clap your hands. At this distance, the echo of your hand clap will reach your ears more than 50 milliseconds after the original sound of your clap. You hear two sounds.

Now try walking toward the wall, while still clapping every pace. At about 5 meters—where the echo reaches your ears less than 50 ms after the original sound of the clap—you stop hearing sound coming from two locations. The location of the echo has merged with that of the original sound; both now appear to come as one sound from the direction of your original clap. This is the precedence effect in action, just one of many mechanisms that exist to help you make sense of the location of sounds.

How It Works

The initial computations used in locating sounds occur in the brainstem, in a peculiarly named region called the superior olive. Because the business of localization begins in the brainstem, surprising sounds are able to quickly produce a turn of the head or body to allow us to bring our highest resolution sense, vision, to bear in figuring out what is going on. The rapidity of this response wouldn't be possible if the information from the two ears were integrated only later in processing.

The classic model for how interaural time differences are processed is called the Jeffress Model, and it works as shown in Figure 4-1. Cells in the midbrain indicate a sound's position by increasing their firing in response to sound, and each cell takes sound input from both ears. The cell that fires most is the one that receives a signal from both ears simultaneously. Because these cells are most active when the inputs from both sides are synchronized, they're known as *coincidence-detector* neurons.

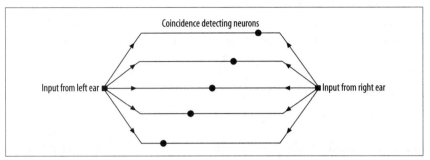

Figure 4-1. *Neurons used in computing sound position fire when inputs from the left and right ear arrive simultaneously. Differences in time delays along the connecting lines mean that different arrival times between signals at the left and right ear trigger different neurons.*

Now imagine if a sound comes from your left, reaching your right ear only after a tiny delay. If a cell is going to receive both signals simultaneously, it must be because the left-ear signal has been slowed down, somewhere in the brain, to exactly compensate for the delay. The Jeffress Model posits that the brain contains an array of coincidence-detector cells, each with particular delays for the signals from either side. By this means, each possible location can be represented with the activity of neurons with the appropriate delays built in.

 The Jeffress Model may not be entirely correct. Most of the neurobiological evidence for it comes from work with barn owls, which can strike prey in complete darkness. Evidence from small mammals suggests other mechanisms also operate.[2]

An ambiguity of localization comes with using interaural time difference, because sounds need not be on the horizontal plane—they could be in front, behind, above, or below. A sound that comes in from your front right, on the same level as you, at an angle of 33° will sound, in terms of the interaural differences in timing and intensity, just like the same sound coming from your back right at an angle of 33° or from above right at an angle of 33°. Thus, there is a "cone of confusion" as to where you place a sound, and that is what is shown in Figure 4-2. Normally you can use the other cues, such as the distortion introduced by your ears (spectral cues) to reduce the ambiguity.

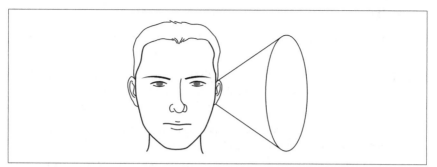

Figure 4-2. Sounds from the surface of the "cone of confusion" produce the same interaural time difference and are therefore ambiguously localized

In Real Life

The more information in a sound, the easier it is to localize. Noise containing different frequencies is easier to localize. This is why they now add white noise, which contains all frequencies in equal proportions, to the siren sounds of emergency vehicles,[3] unlike the pure tones that have historically been used.

If you are wearing headphones, you don't get spectral cues from the pinnae, so you can't localize sounds on the up-down dimension. You also don't have the information to decide if a sound is coming from in front or from behind.

Even without headphones, our localization in the up-down dimension is pretty poor. This is why a sound from down and behind you (if you are on a balcony, for example) can sound right behind you. By default, we localize sounds to either the center left or center right of our ears—this broad conclusion is enough to tell us which way to turn our heads, despite the ambiguity that prevents more precise localization.

This ambiguity in hearing is the reason we cock our heads when listening. By taking multiple readings of a sound source, we overlap the ambiguities and build up a composite, interpolated set of evidence on where a sound might be coming from. (And if you watch a bird cocking its head, looking at the ground, it's listening to a worm and doing the same.[4])

Still, hearing provides a rough, quick idea of where a sound is coming from. It's enough to allow us to turn toward the sound or to process sounds differently depending on where they come from [Hack #54].

End Notes

1. Wall and clapping idea thanks to Geoff Martin and from his web site at *http://www.tonmeister.ca/main/textbook/psychoacoustics/06.html*.

2. McAlpine, D., & Grothe, B. (2003). Sound localization and delay lines—Do mammals fit the model? *Trends in Neurosciences, 26*(7), 347–350.

3. "Siren Sounds: Do They Actually Contribute to Traffic Accidents?" (*http://www.soundalert.com/pdfs/impact.pdf*).

4. Montgomerie, R., & Weatherhead, P. J. (1997). How robins find worms. *Animal Behaviour, 54*, 137–143.

See Also

- Moore, B. C. J. (1997). *An Introduction to the Psychology of Hearing.* New York: Academic Press.

HACK #46 Discover Pitch

Why we perceive pitch at all is a story in itself. Pitch exists for sounds because our brains calculate it, and to do that, they must have a reason.

All sounds are vibrations in air. Different amplitudes create different sound intensities; different frequencies of vibration create different pitches. Natural sounds are usually made up of overlaid vibrations that are occurring at a number of different frequencies. Our experience of pitch is based on the overall pattern of the vibrations. The pitch isn't, however, always a quality that is directly available in the sound information. It has to be calculated. Our brains have to go to some effort to let us perceive pitch, but it isn't entirely obvious why we do this at all. One theory for why we hear pitch at all is because it relates to object size: big things generally have a lower basic frequency than small things.

The pitch we perceive a sound having is based on what is called the *fundamental* of the sound wave. This is the basic rate at which the vibration repeats. Normally you make a sound by making something vibrate (say, by hitting it). Depending on how and what you hit (this includes hitting your vocal cords with air), you will establish a main vibration—this is the fundamental—which will be accompanied by secondary vibrations at higher frequencies, called harmonics. These harmonics vibrate at frequencies that are integer multiples of the fundamental frequency (so for a fundamental at 4 Hz, a harmonic might be at 8 Hz or 12 Hz, but not 10 Hz). The pitch of the sound we hear is based on the frequency of the fundamental alone; it doesn't matter how many harmonics there are, the pitch stays the same.

Amazingly, even if the fundamental frequency isn't actually part of the sound we hear; we still hear pitch based on what it *should be*. So for a sound that repeats four times a second but that is made up of component frequencies at 8 Hz, 12 Hz, and 16 Hz, the fundamental is 4 Hz, and it is based upon this that we experience pitch.

It's not definite how we do this, but one theory runs like this[1]: the physical construction of the basilar membrane in the inner ear means that it vibrates at the frequency of the fundamental as it responds to higher component frequencies. Just the physical design of the cochlea as an object means that it can be used by the brain to reproduce—physically—the calculation needed to figure out the fundamentals of a sound wave. That discovered fundamental is then available to be fed into the auditory processing system as information of equal status to any other sound wave.[2]

So it looks as if a little bit of neural processing has leaked out into the physical design of the ear—a great example of what some people have called extelligence, using the world outside the brain itself to do cognitive work.

In Action

An illusion called the missing fundamental demonstrates the construction of sounds in the ear. The fundamental and then harmonics of a tone are successively removed, but the pitch of the tone sounds the same. Play the sound file at *http://physics.mtsu.edu/~wmr/julianna.html*, and you'll hear a series of bleeps. Even though the lower harmonics are vanishing, you don't hear the sound get higher. It remains at the same pitch.[3]

How It Works

The way pitch is computed from tones with multiple harmonics can be used to construct an illusion in which the pitch of a tone appears to rise continuously, getting higher and higher without ever dropping. You can listen to the continuously rising tone illusion and see a graphical illustration of how the sound is constructed at *http://www.kyushu-id.ac.jp/~ynhome/ENG/Demo/2nd/05.html#20*.

Each tone is made up of multiple tones at different harmonics. The harmonics shift up in frequency with each successive tone. Because there are multiple harmonics, evenly spaced, they can keep shifting up, with the very highest disappearing as they reach the top of the frequency range covered by the tones and with new harmonics appearing at the lowest frequencies. Because each shift seems like a step up on a normal scale, your brain gives you an experience of a continuously rising tone. This is reinforced because the highest and lowest components of each tone are quieter, blurring the exact frequency boundaries of the whole sound.[4]

End Notes

1. There are other mechanisms, using neural processing, involved too, in reconstructing the fundamental from a harmonic. There are two main theories of what these are. One involves recognizing patterns in the activity level of the receptor cells over the length of the cochlea, and the other involves using the timing of the responses of the cells.

2. McAlpine, D. (2004) Neural sensitivity in the inferior colliculus: Evidence for the role of cochlear distortions. *Journal of Neurophysiology, 92*(3), 1295–1311.

3. The missing fundamental illusion is also found in motion perception at *http://www.umaine.edu/visualperception/summer*.

4. Yoshitaka Nakajima's "Demonstrations of Auditory Illusions and Tricks" (*http://www.kyushu-id.ac.jp/~ynhome/ENG/Demo/illusions2nd.html*) is a fantastic collection of auditory illusions, including examples and graphical explanations. A particular favorite is the "Melody of Silences" (*http://133.5.113.80/~ynhome/ENG/Demo/2nd/03.html*).

HACK #47 Keep Your Balance

The ear isn't just for hearing; it helps you keep your balance.

Audition isn't the only function of the inner ear. We have semicircular channels of fluid, two in the horizontal plane, two in the vertical plane, that measure acceleration of the head. This, our vestibular system, is used to maintain our balance.

Note that this system can detect only acceleration and deceleration, not motion. This explains why we can be fooled into thinking we're moving if a large part of our visual field moves in the same direction—for example, when we're sitting on a train and the train next to ours moves off, we get the impression that we've started moving. For slow-starting movement, the acceleration information is too weak to convince us we've moved.

> It's a good thing the system detects only acceleration, not absolute motion, otherwise we might be able to tell that we are moving at 70,000 mph through space round the sun. Or, worse, have direct experience of relativity—then things would get really confusing.
>
> —T.S.

In Action

You can try and use this blind spot for motion next time you're on a train. Close your eyes and focus on the rocking of the train side to side. Although you can feel the change in motion side to side, without visual information— and if your train isn't slowing down or speeding up—you don't have any information except memory to tell you in which direction you are traveling. Imagine the world outside moving in a different way. See if you can hallucinate for a second that you are traveling very rapidly in the opposite direction. Obviously this works best with a smooth train, so readers in Japan will have more luck.

How It Works

Any change in our velocity causes the fluid in the channels of the vestibular system to move, bending hair cells that line the surface of the channels (these hair cells work the same as the hair cells that detect sound waves in the cochlea, except they detect distortion in fluid, not air). Signals are then sent along the vestibular nerve into the brain where they are used to adjust our balance and warn of changes in motion.

Dizziness can result from dysfunction of the vestibular system or from a disparity between visual information and the information from the vestibular system. So in motion sickness, you feel motion but see a constant visual world (the inside of the car or of the ship). In vertigo, you don't feel motion but you see the visual world move a lot more than it should—because of parallax, a small movement of your head creates a large shift in the difference between your feet and what you see next to them. (Vertigo is more complex than just a mismatch between vestibular and visual detection of motion, but this is part of the story.)

This is why, if you think you might get dizzy, it helps to fix on a moving point if you are moving but your visual world is not (such as the horizon if you are on a ship). But if you are staying still and your visual world is moving, the best thing to do is not to look (such as during vertigo or during a motion sickness–inducing film).

I guess this means I'd have felt less nauseated after seeing the *Blair Witch Project* if I'd watched it from a vibrating seat.

—T.S.

Detect Sounds on the Margins of Certainty

Can you sort the signal from the noise? Patterns and regularity are often deeply hidden, but we're surprisingly adept at finding them.

Our perceptual abilities and sensory acumen differ from one individual to another, making our threshold for detecting faint or ambiguous stimuli vary considerably. The brain is particularly good at making sense of messy data and can often pick out meaning in the noisiest of environments, filtering out the chaotic background information to pick out the faintest signals.

In Action

A sample of Bing Crosby's "White Christmas" has been hidden in the sound file on our book web site (*http://www.mindhacks.com/book/48/whitechristmas.mp3; MP3*). The sound file is 30 seconds long and is mostly noise, so you will have to listen carefully to detect when the song starts. The song will start either in the first, second, or third 10 seconds and will be very faint, so pay close attention.

> You'll get more out of this hack if you listen to the sound file before knowing how the music has been hidden, so you're strongly recommended not to read ahead to the next section until you've done so.

How It Works

If you managed to hear the strains of Bing Crosby in the noisy background of the sound file, you may be in for a surprise. The sound file is pure noise, and despite what we promised earlier, "White Christmas" is not hidden in there at all (if you read ahead without trying it out for yourself, try it out on someone else). Not everyone is likely to detect meaningful sounds in the background noise, but it's been shown to work on a certain subset of the population. An experiment conducted by Merckelbach and van de Ven[1] reported that almost a third of students reported hearing "White Christmas" when played a similar noisy sound track.

There's been a lot of debate about why this might happen and what sort of attributes might be associated with the tendency to detect meaning in random patterns. In the study mentioned earlier, the authors found that this ability was particularly linked to measures of fantasy proneness—a measure of richness and frequency of imagination and fantasy—and hallucination proneness—a measure of vividness of imagery and unusual perceptual experiences. If you, or someone you tested, heard "White Christmas" amid the noise and are now worried, there's no need to be. The tendencies measured by Merckelbach and van de Ven's study were very mild and certainly not a marker of anything abnormal (after all, it worked in a third of people!), and we all hallucinate to some degree (not seeing the eye's blind spot [Hack #16] is a kind of hallucination).

However, there is evidence that people who believe in certain paranormal phenomena may be more likely to find patterns in unstructured information. Brugger and colleagues[2] found that people who believe in ESP are more likely to detect meaningful information in random dot patterns than people who do not. Skeptics are often tempted to argue that this sort of experiment *disproves* ESP and the like, but the other finding reported in the same study was that meaningful patterns were more likely to be detected if the random dot pattern was presented to the left visual field, regardless of the participant's belief in ESP. The left visual field crosses over to connect to the right side of the brain, meaning that random patterns presented to be preferentially processed by the right hemisphere, seem to be more "meaningful" than those presented either to both or to the left hemisphere alone. This demonstrates another aspect of hemispheric asymmetry [Hack #69] but also hints that people who have high levels of paranormal beliefs may be more likely to show greater activation in their right hemisphere than their left, an effect that has been backed up by many further studies.

This pattern of hemispheric activation is linked to more than paranormal beliefs. Researchers have argued that it may be linked to a cognitive style that promotes "loose" associations between concepts and semantic information, a style people have if they often see connections between ideas that others do not. This is not necessarily a bad thing, as this tendency has been linked to creativity and lateral thinking. Detecting patterns where other people do not may be a very useful skill at times. Although it may result in the occasional false positive, it almost certainly allows genuine patterns to be perceived when other people would be confused by background perceptual noise.

End Notes

1. Merckelbach, H., & van de Ven, V. (2001). Another White Christmas: fantasy proneness and reports of "hallucinatory experiences" in undergraduate students. *Journal of Behavior Therapy and Experimental Psychiatry, 32*(3), 137–144.

2. Brugger, P., Regard, M., Landis, T., Cook, N., Krebs, D., & Niederberger, J. (1993). "Meaningful" patterns in visual noise: Effects of lateral stimulation and the observer's belief in ESP. *Psychopathology, 26*(5–6), 261–265.

—*Vaughan Bell*

Speech Is Broadband Input to Your Head

#49   Once your brain has decided to classify a sound as speech, it brings online a
raft of tricks to extract from it the maximum amount of information.

Speech isn't just another set of noises. The brain treats it very differently
from ordinary sounds. Speech is predominantly processed on the left side of
the brain, while normal sounds are mostly processed on the right.

> This division is less pronounced in women, which is why
> they tend to recover better from strokes affecting their left-
> sided language areas.

Knowing you're about to hear language prepares your brain to make lots of
assumptions specially tailored to extract useful information from the sound.
It's this special way of processing language-classified sounds that allows our
brains to make sense of speech that is coming at us at a rate of up to 50 phonemes a second—a rate that can actually be produced only using an artificially sped-up recording.

In Action

To hear just how much the expectation of speech influences the sounds you
hear, listen to the degraded sound demos created by Bob Shannon et al. at the
House Ear Institute (*http://www.hei.org/research/depts/aip/audiodemos.htm*).

In particular, listen to the MP3 demo that starts with a voice that has been
degraded beyond recognition and then repeated six times, each time increasing the quality (*http://www.hei.org/research/depts/aip/increase_channels.mp3*).

You won't be able to tell what the voice is saying until the third or fourth
repetition. Listen to the MP3 again. This time your brain knows what to
hear, so the words are clearer much earlier. However hard you try, you can't
go back to hearing static.

How It Works

Sentences are broken into words having meaning and organized by grammar, the system by which we can build up an infinite number of complex
sentences and subtle meanings from only a finite pool of words.

Words can be broken down too, into *morphemes*, the smallest units of
meaning. "-ing" is a morpheme and makes the word "run" become "running." It imparts meaning. There are further rules at this level, about how to
combine words into large words.

Morphemes, too, can be broken down, into *phonemes*. Phonemes are the basic sounds a language uses, so the word "run" has three: /r u n/. They don't map cleanly onto the letters of the alphabet; think of the phoneme at the beginning of "shine." Phonemes are different from syllables. So the word "running" is made up of two morphemes and has five phonemes, but just two syllables (and seven letters of course).

Languages have different sets of phonemes; English has about 40–45. There are more than 100 phonemes that the human mouth is capable of making, but as babies, when we start learning language, we tune into the ones that we encounter and learn to ignore the rest.

People speak at about 10–15 phonemes per second, 20–30 if they're speaking fast, and that rate is easily understood by native speakers of the same language (if you fast-forward recorded speech, we can understand up to 50 phonemes per second). Speech this fast can't contain each sound sequentially and independently. Instead, the sounds end up on top of one another. As you're speaking one phoneme, your tongue and lips are halfway to the position required to speak the next one, anticipating it, so words sound different depending on what words are before and after. That's one of the reasons making good speech recognition software is so hard.

The other reason software to turn sounds into words is so hard is that the layers of phonemes, morphemes, and words are messy and influence one another. Listeners know to expect certain sounds, certain sound patterns (morphemes), and even to expect what word is coming next. The stream of auditory input is matched against all of that, and we're able to understand speech, even when phonemes (such as /ba/ and /pa/, which can also be identified by looking at lip movements **[Hack #59]**) are very similar and easily confused. The lack of abstraction layers—and the need to understand the meaning of the sentence and grammar just to figure out what the phonemes are—is what makes this procedure so hard for software.

It's yet another example of how expectations influence perception, in a very fundamental way. In the case of auditory information, knowing that the sound is actually speech causes the brain to route the information to a completely separate region than the one in which general sound processing takes place. When sound is taken to the speech processing region, you're able to hear words you literally couldn't possibly have heard when you thought you were just hearing noise, even for the same sound.

To try this, play for a friend synthesized voices made out of overlapping sine-wave sounds (*http://www.biols.susx.ac.uk/home/Chris_Darwin/SWS*). This site has a number of recorded sentences and, for each one, a generated, artificial version of that sound pattern. It's recognizable as a voice if you know what it is, but not otherwise.

When you play the sine-wave speech MP3 (called SWS on the site) to your friend, don't tell her it's a voice. She'll just hear a beeping sound. Then let her hear the original voice of the same sentence, and play the SWS again. With her new knowledge, the sound is routed to speech recognition and will sound quite different. Knowing that the sound is actually made out of words and is English (so it's made out of guessable phonemes and morphemes), allows the whole recognition process to take place, which couldn't have happened before.

See Also

- Mondegreens occur when our phoneme recognition gets it oh-so-wrong, which happens a lot with song lyrics—so called from mishearing "and laid him on the green" as "and Lady Mondegreen" (*http://www.sfgate. com/cgi-bin/article.cgi?file=/chronicle/archive/1995/02/16/DD31497. DTL*). SF Gate keeps an archive of misheard lyrics (*http://www.sfgate. com/columnists/carroll/mondegreens.shtml*).

Give Big-Sounding Words to Big Concepts

The sounds of words carry meaning too, as big words for big movements demonstrate.

Steven Pinker, in his popular book on the nature of language, *The Language Instinct*[1], encounters the frob-twiddle-tweak continuum as a way of talking about adjusting settings on computers or stereo equipment. The Jargon File, longtime glossary for hacker language, has the following under *frobnicate* (*http://www.catb.org/~esr/jargon/html/F/frobnicate.html*):

> Usage: frob, twiddle, and tweak sometimes connote points along a continuum. 'Frob' connotes aimless manipulation; twiddle connotes gross manipulation, often a coarse search for a proper setting; tweak connotes fine-tuning. If someone is turning a knob on an oscilloscope, then if he's carefully adjusting it, he is probably tweaking it; if he is just turning it but looking at the screen, he is probably twiddling it; but if he's just doing it because turning a knob is fun, he's frobbing it.[2]

Why frob first? Frobbing is a coarse action, so it has to go with a big lump of a word. Twiddle is smaller, more delicate. And tweak, the finest adjustment of all, feels like a tiny word. It's as if the actual sound of the word, as it's spoken, carries meaning too.

In Action

The two shapes in Figure 4-3 are a *maluma* and a *takete*. Take a look. Which is which?

 Don't spoil the experiment for yourself by reading the next paragraph! When you try this out on others, you may want to cover up all but the figure itself.

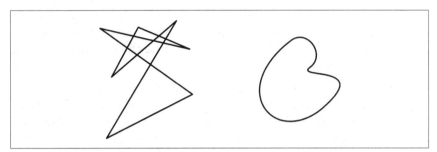

Figure 4-3. One of these is a "maluma," the other a "takete"—which is which?

If you're like most people who have looked at shapes like these since the late 1920s, when Wolfgang Köhler devised the experiment, you said that the shape on the left is a "takete," and the one on the right is a "maluma." Just like "frob" and "tweak," in which the words relate to the movements, "takete" has a spiky character and "maluma" feels round.

How It Works

Words are multilayered in meaning, not just indices to some kind of meaning dictionary in our brains. Given the speed of speech, we need as many clues to meaning as we can get, to make understanding faster. Words that are just arbitrary noises would be wasteful. Clues to the meaning of speech can be packed into the intonation of a word, what other words are nearby, and the sound itself.

Brains are association machines, and communication makes full use of that fact to impart meaning.

In Figure 4-3, the more rounded shape is associated with big, full objects, objects that tend to have big resonant cavities, like drums, that make booming sounds if you hit them. Your mouth is big and hollow, resonant to say the word "maluma." It rolls around your mouth.

On the other hand, a spiky shape is more like a snare drum or a crystal. It clatters and clicks. The corresponding sound is full of what are called *plosives*, sounds like *t-* and *k-* that involve popping air out.

That's the association engine of the brain in action. The same goes for "frob" and "tweak." The movement your mouth and tongue go through to say "frob" is broad and coarse like the frobbing action it communicates. You put your tongue along the base of your mouth and make a large cavity to make a big sound. To say "tweak" doesn't just remind you of finely controlled movement, it really entails more finely controlled movement of the tongue and lips. Making the higher-pitched noise means making a smaller cavity in your mouth by pushing your tongue up, and the sound at the end is a delicate movement.

Test this by saying "frob," "twiddle," and "tweak" first thing in the morning, when you're barely awake. Your muscle control isn't as good as it usually is when you're still half-asleep, so while you can say "frob" easily, saying "tweak" is pretty hard. It comes out more like "twur." If you're too impatient to wait until the morning, just imagine it is first thing in the morning—as you stretch say the words to yourself with a yawn in your voice. The difference is clear; frobbing works while you're yawning, tweaking doesn't.

Aside from denser meaning, these correlations between motor control (either moving your hands to control the stereo or saying the word) and the word itself may give some clues to what language was like before it was really language. Protolanguage, the system of communication before any kind of syntax or grammar, may have relied on these metaphors to impart meaning.[3] For humans now, language includes a sophisticated learning system in which, as children, we figure out what words mean what, but there are still throwbacks to the earlier time: *onomatopoeic* words are ones that sound like what they mean, like "boom" or "moo." "Frob" and "tweak" may be similar to that, only drawing in bigness or roundness from the visual (for shapes) or motor (for mucking around with the stereo) parts of the brain.

In Real Life

Given the relationship between the sound of a word, due to its component phonemes and its feel (some kind of shared subjective experience), sound symbolism is one of the techniques used in branding. Naming consultants take into account the maluma and takete aspect of word meaning, not just dictionary meaning, and come up with names for products and companies on demand—for a price, of course. One of the factors that influenced the naming of the BlackBerry wireless email device was the *b-* sound at the beginning. According to the namers, it connotes reliability.[4]

End Notes

1. Pinker, S. (1994). *The Language Instinct: The New Science of Language and Mind*. London: Penguin Books Ltd.

2. The online hacker Jargon File, Version 4.1.0, July 2004 (*http://www.catb.org/~esr/jargon/index.html*).

3. This phenomenon is called phonetic symbolism, or phonesthesia. Some people have the perception of color when reading words or numbers, experiencing a phenomenon called synaesthesia. Ramachandran and Hubbard suggest that synaesthesia is how language started in the first place. See: Ramachandran, V. S., & Hubbard, E. M. (2001). Synaesthesia—a window into perception, thought and language. *Journal of Consciousness Studies, 8*(12), 3–34. This can also be found online at *http://psy.ucsd.edu/chip/pdf/Synaesth_JCS.pdf*.

4. Begley, Sharon. "Blackberry and Sound Symbolism" (*http://www.stanford.edu/class/linguist34/Unit_08/blackberry.htm*), reprinted from the *Wall Street Journal*, August 26, 2002.

See Also

- Naming consultancies were especially popular during the 1990s dot-com boom. Alex Frenkel took a look for *Wired* magazine in June 1997 in "Name-o-rama" (*http://www.wired.com/wired/archive/5.06/es_namemachine.html*).

HACK #51 Stop Memory-Buffer Overrun While Reading

The length of a sentence isn't what makes it hard to understand— it's how long you have to wait for a phrase to be completed.

When you're reading a sentence, you don't understand it word by word, but rather phrase by phrase. Phrases are groups of words that can be bundled together, and they're related by the rules of grammar. A noun phrase will include nouns and adjectives, and a verb phrase will include a verb and a noun, for example. These phrases are the building blocks of language, and we naturally chunk sentences into phrase blocks just as we chunk visual images into objects.

What this means is that we don't treat every word individually as we hear it; we treat words as parts of phrases and have a buffer (a very short-term memory) that stores the words as they come in, until they can be allocated to a phrase. Sentences become cumbersome not if they're long, but if they overrun the buffer required to parse them, and that depends on how long the individual phrases are.

In Action

Read the following sentence to yourself:

- While Bob ate an apple was in the basket.

Did you have to read it a couple of times to get the meaning? It's grammatically correct, but the commas have been left out to emphasize the problem with the sentence.

As you read about Bob, you add the words to an internal buffer to make up a phrase. On first reading, it looks as if the whole first half of the sentence is going to be your first self-contained phrase (in the case of the first, that's "While Bob ate an apple")—but you're being led down the garden path. The sentence is constructed to dupe you. After the first phrase, you mentally add a comma and read the rest of the sentence...only to find out it makes no sense. Then you have to think about where the phrase boundary falls (aha, the comma is after "ate," not "apple"!) and read the sentence again to reparse it. Note that you have to read again to break it into different phrases; you can't just juggle the words around in your head.

Now try reading these sentences, which all have the same meaning and increase in complexity:

- The cat caught the spider that caught the fly the old lady swallowed.
- The fly swallowed by the old lady was caught by the spider caught by the cat.
- The fly the spider the cat caught caught was swallowed by the old lady.

The first two sentences are hard to understand, but make some kind of sense. The last sentence is merely rearranged but makes no natural sense at all. (This is all assuming it makes some sort of sense for an old lady to be swallowing cats in the first place, which is patently absurd, but it turns out she swallowed a goat too, not to mention a horse, so we'll let the cat pass without additional comment.)

How It Works

Human languages have the special property of being recombinant. This means a sentence isn't woven like a scarf, where if you want to add more detail you have to add it at the end. Sentences are more like Lego. The phrases can be broken up and combined with other sentences or popped open in the middle and more bricks added.

Have a look at these rather unimaginative examples:

- This sentence is an example.

- This boring sentence is a simple example.
- This long, boring sentence is a simple example of sentence structure.

The way sentences are understood is that they're parsed into phrases. One type of phrase is a noun phrase, the object of the sentence. In "This sentence is an example," the noun phrase is "this sentence." For the second, it's "this boring sentence."

Once a noun phrase is fully assembled, it can be packaged up and properly understood by the rest of the brain. During the time you're reading the sentence, however, the words sit in your verbal working memory—a kind of short-term buffer—until the phrase is finished.

> There's an analogy here with visual processing. It's easier to understand the world in chunks—hence the Gestalt Grouping Principles [Hack #75]. With language, which arrives serially, rather than in parallel like vision, you can't be sure what the chunks are until the end of the phrase, so you have to hold it unchunked in working memory until you know where the phrase ends.
>
> —M.W.

Verb phrases work the same way. When your brain sees "is," it knows there's a verb phrase starting and holds the subsequent words in memory until that phrase has been closed off (with the word "example," in the first sentence in the previous list). Similarly, the last part of the final sentence, "of sentence structure," is a prepositional phrase, so it's also self-contained. Phrase boundaries make sentences much easier to understand. Rather than the object of the third example sentence being three times more complex than the first (it's three words: "long, boring sentence" versus one, "sentence"), it can be understood as the same object, but with modifiers.

It's easier to see this if you look at the tree diagrams shown in Figure 4-4. A sentence takes on a treelike structure, for these simple examples, in which phrases are smaller trees within that. To understand a whole phrase, its individual tree has to join up. These sentences are all easy to understand because they're composed of very small trees that are completed quickly.

We don't use just grammatical rules to break sentences in chunks. One of the reasons the sentence about Bob was hard to understand was you expect, after seeing "Bob ate" to learn about *what* Bob ate. When you read "the apple," it's exactly what you expect to see, so you're happy to assume it's part of the same phrase. To find phrase boundaries, we check individual word meaning and likelihood of word order, continually revise the meaning

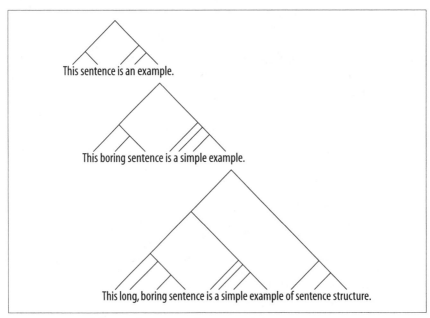

Figure 4-4. How the example sentences form trees of phrases

of the sentence, and so on, all while the buffer is growing. But holding words in memory until phrases complete has its own problems, even apart from sentences that deliberately confuse you, which is where the old lady comes in.

Both of the first remarks on the old lady's culinary habits require only one phrase to be held in buffer at a time. Think about what phrases are left incomplete at any given word. There's no uncertainty over what any given "caught" or "by" words refer to: it's always the next word. For instance, your brain read "The cat" (in the first sentence) and immediately said, "did what?" Fortunately the answer is the very next phrase: "caught the spider." "OK," says your brain, and pops that phrase out of working memory and gets on with figuring out the rest of the sentence.

The last example about the old lady is completely different. By the time your brain gets to the words "the cat," three questions are left hanging. What about the cat? What about the spider? What about the fly? Those questions are answered in quick succession: the fly the old lady swallowed; the spider that caught the fly, and so on.

But because all of these questions are of the same type, the same kind of phrase, they clash in verbal working memory, and that's the limit on sentence comprehension.

In Real Life

A characteristic of good speeches (or anything passed down in an oral tradition) is that they minimize the amount of working memory, or buffer, required to understand them. This doesn't matter so much for written text, in which you can skip back and read the sentence again to figure it out; you have only one chance to hear and comprehend the spoken word, so you'd better get it right the first time around. That's why speeches written down always look so simple.

That doesn't mean you can ignore the buffer size for written language. If you want to make what you say, and what you write, easier to understand, consider the order in which you are giving information in a sentence. See if you can group together the elements that go together so as to reduce demand on the reader's concentration. More people will get to the end of your prose with the energy to think about what you've said or do what you ask.

See Also

- Caplan, D., & Waters, G. (1998). "Verbal Working Memory and Sentence Comprehension" (*http://cogprints.ecs.soton.ac.uk/archive/00000623*).
- Steven Pinker discusses parse trees and working memory extensively in *The Language Instinct*. Pinker, S. (2000). *The Language Instinct: The New Science of Language and Mind*. London: Penguin Books Ltd.

Robust Processing Using Parallelism

#52

Neural networks process in parallel rather than serially. This means that as processing of different aspects proceeds, previously processed aspects can be used quickly to disambiguate the processing of others.

Neural networks are massively parallel computers. Compare this to your PC, which is a serial computer. Yeah, sure, it can emulate a parallel processor, but only because it is really quick. However quick it does things, though, it does them only one at a time.

Neural processing is glacial by comparison. A neuron in the visual cortex is unlikely to fire more than every 5 milliseconds even at its maximum activation. Auditory cells have higher firing rates, but even they have an absolute minimum gap of 2 ms between sending signals. This means that for actions that take 0.5 to 1 second—such as noticing a ball coming toward you and catching it (and many of the things cognitive psychologists test)—there are a maximum of 100 consecutive computations the brain can do in this time. This is the so-called *100 step rule*.[1]

The reason your brain doesn't run like a PC with a 0.0001 MHz processor is because the average neuron connects onto between 1000 and 10,000 other neurons. Information is routed, and routed back, between multiple interconnected neural modules, all in parallel. This allows the slow speed of each neuron to be overcome, and also makes it natural, and necessary, that all aspects of a computational job be processed simultaneously, rather than in stages.

Any decision you make or perception you have (because what your brain decides to provide you with as a coherent experience is a kind of decision too) is made up of the contributions of many processing modules, all running simultaneously. There's no time for them to run sequentially, so they all have to be able to run with raw data and whatever else they can get hold of at the time, rather than waiting for the output of other modules.

In Action

A good example of simultaneous processing is in understanding language. As you hear or read, you use the context of what is being said, the possible meaning of the individual words, the syntax of the sentences, and how the sounds of each word—or the letters of each word—look to figure out what is being said.

Consider the next sentence: "For breakfast I had bacon and ****." You don't need to know the last word to understand it, and you can make a good guess at the last word.

Can you tell the meaning of "Buy v!agra" if I email it to you? Of course you can; you don't need to have the correct letter in the second word to know what it is (if it doesn't get stopped by your spam filters first, that is).

How It Works

The different contributions—the different clues you use in reading—inform one another, to fill in missing information and correct mismatched information. This is one of the reasons typos can be hard to spot in text (particularly your own, in which the contribution of your understanding of the text autocorrects, in your mind, the typos before you notice them), but it's also why you're able to have conversations in loud bars. The parallel processing of different aspects of the input provides robustness to errors and incompleteness and allows information from different processes to interactively disambiguate each other.

Do you remember the email circular that went around (*http://www.mrc-cbu. cam.ac.uk/personal/matt.davis/Cmabrigde*) saying that you can write your sentences with the internal letters rearranged and still be understood just as well? Apparently, it deosn't mttaer in waht oredr the ltteers in a wrod are, the olny iprmoetnt tihng is taht the frist and lsat ltteer be at the rghit pclae. The rset can be a toatl mses and you can sitll raed it wouthit a porbelm.

It's not true, of course. You understand such scrambled sentences only *nearly as well* as unscrambled ones. We can figure out what the sentence is in this context because of the high redundancy of the information we're given. We know the sentence makes sense, so that constrains the range of possible words that can be in it, just as the syntax does: the rules of grammar mean only some words are allowed in some positions. The word-length information is also there, as are the letters in the word. The only missing thing is the position information for the internal letters. And compensating for that is an easy bit of processing for your massively parallel, multiple constraint–satisfying, language faculty.

Perhaps the reason it seems surprising that we can read scrambled sentences is because a computer faced with the same problem would be utterly confused. Computers have to have each word fit exactly to their template for that word. No exact match, no understanding. OK, so Google can suggest correct spellings for you, but type in **i am cufosned** and it's stuck, whereas a human could take a guess (they face off in Figure 4-5).

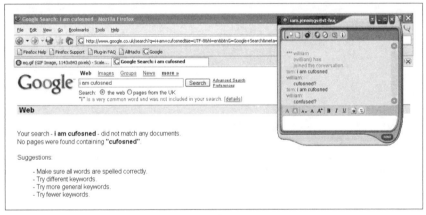

Figure 4-5. Google and my friend William go head to head

This same kind of process works in vision. You have areas of visual cortex responsible for processing different elements. Some provide color information, some information on motion or depth or orientation. The interconnections between them mean that when you look at a scene they all start working and cooperatively figure out what the best fit to the incoming data is. When a fit is found, your perception snaps to it and you realize what you're looking at. This massive parallelism and interactivity mean that it can be misleading to label individual regions as "the bit that does X"; truly, no bit of the brain ever operates without every other bit of the brain operating simultaneously, and outside of that environment single brain regions wouldn't work at all.

End Note

1. Feldman, J. A., & Ballard, D. H. (1982). Connectionist models and their properties. *Cognitive Science, 6,* 205–254 (*http://cognitrn.psych. indiana.edu/rgoldsto/cogsci/Feldman.pdf*).

CHAPTER FIVE

Integrating
Hacks 53–61

This chapter looks at how we integrate our perceptions—images (Chapter 2), sounds (Chapter 4), our own mechanisms of attention (Chapter 3), and our other senses [Hack #12]—into a unified perceptual experience.

For instance, how do we use our eyes and ears together? (We prefer to use our ears for timing and eyes for determining location [Hack #53].) And what are the benefits of doing so? (We feel experiences that happen in two senses simultaneously as more intense [Hacks #57 and #58].)

Sometimes, we overintegrate. The Stroop Effect [Hack #55], a classic experiment, shows that if we try to respond linguistically, irrelevant linguistic input interferes. In its eagerness to assimilate as much associated information, as much context, as possible, the brain makes it very hard to ignore even what we consciously know is unimportant.

We'll also look at one side effect and one curious limitation of the way we integrate sense information. The first goes to show that even the brain's errors can be useful and that we can actually use a mistaken conclusion about a sound's origin to better listen to it [Hack #60]. The second answers the question: do we really need language to perform what should be a basic task, of making a simple deduction from color and geometry? In some cases, it would appear so [Hack #61].

Put Timing Information into Sound and Location Information into Light

#53

The timing of an event will be dominated by the sound it makes, the location by where it looks as if it is happening—this is precisely why ventriloquism works.

Hearing is good for timing [Hack #44] but not so good for locating things in space. On the flip side, vision has two million channels for detecting location in space but isn't as fast as hearing.

What happens when you combine the two? What you'd expect from a well-designed bit of kit: vision dominates for determining location, audition dominates for determining timing. The senses have specialized for detecting different kinds of information, and when they merge, that is taken into account.

In Action

You can see each of the two senses take control in the location and timing domains. In the first part, what you see overrules the conflicting location information in what you hear; in the second part, it's the other way around.

Vision dominates for localization. Go to the theater, watch a film, or play a movie on your PC, listening to it on headphones. You see people talking and the sound matches their lip movement [Hack #59]. It feels as if the sound is coming from the same direction as the images you are watching. It's not, of course; instead, it's coming at you from the sides, from the cinema speakers, or through your headphones.

The effect is strongest at public lectures. You watch the lecturer on stage talking and don't notice that the sound is coming at you from a completely different direction, through speakers at the sides or even back of the hall. Only if you close your eyes can you hear that the sounds aren't coming from the stage. The visual correspondence with the sounds you are hearing causes your brain to absorb the sound information into the same event as the image, taking on the location of the image. This is yet another example (for another, see "Watch Yourself to Feel More" [Hack #58]) of how our most important sense, vision, dominates the other senses.

> Incidentally, this is how ventriloquism works. The ventriloquist knows that if the timings of the dummy's lip movements are close enough to the sounds you hear you will preconsciously locate the sounds as coming from the dummy. Every time we go to the cinema we are experiencing a ventriloquism effect, but it is so finessed that we don't even notice that it is part of the show.
>
> —T.S.

Audition dominates for timing. Vision doesn't always dominate. Watch Ladan Shams's "Sound-induced Illusory Flashing" movies at Caltec (*http://neuro.caltech.edu/~lshams/demo.html*; QuickTime).[1] They show a black dot flashing very briefly on a white background. The only difference between the movie on the left and the movie on the right is the sound played along with the flash of the dot. With one set you hear a beep as the dot appears; with another set you hear two beeps.

 On Ladan Shams's page, you have the option of watching a number of different pairs of movies. These correspond to different computer speeds. Start with the ones at the top and run them all until you find the one with the strongest effect.

Notice how the sound affects what you see. Two beeps cause the dot not to flash but to appear to flicker. Our visual system isn't so sure it is seeing just one event, and the evidence from hearing is allowed to distort the visual impression that our brain delivers for conscious experience.

When the experiment was originally run, people were played up to four beeps with a single flash. For anything more than one beep, people consistently experienced more than one flash.

Aschersleben and Bertelson[2] demonstrated that the same principle applied when people produced timed movements by tapping. People tapping in time with visual signals were distracted by mistimed sound signals, whereas people tapping in time with sound signals weren't as distracted by mistimed visual signals.

How It Works

This kind of dominance is really a bias. When the visual information about timing is ambiguous enough, it can be distorted in our experience by the auditory information. And vice versa—when auditory information about location is ambiguous enough, it is biased in the direction of the information provided by visual information. Sometimes that distortion is enough to make it seem as if one sense completely dominates the other.

Information from the nondominant sense (vision for timing, audition for location) does influence what result the other sense delivers up to consciousness but not nearly so much. The exact circumstances of the visual-auditory event can affect the size of the bias too. For example, when judging location, the weighting you give to visual information is proportional to the brightness of the light and inversely proportional to the loudness of the sound.[3] Nevertheless, the bias is always weighted toward using vision for location and toward audition for timing.

The weighting our brain gives to information from these two senses is a result of the design of our senses, so you can't change around the order of dominance by making sounds easier to localize or by making lights harder to locate. Even if you make the sound location-perfect, people watching are still going to prefer to experience what they see as where they see it, and they'll disregard your carefully localized sounds.

End Notes

1. Shams, L., Kamitani, Y., & Shimojo, S. (2000). What you see is what you hear. *Nature, 408*, 788.

2. Aschersleben, G., & Bertelson, P. (2003). Temporal ventriloquism: crossmodal interaction on the time dimension: 2. Evidence from synchronization. *International Journal of Psychophysiology, 50(1–2)*, 157–63.

3. Radeau, M. (1985). Signal intensity, task context, and auditory-visual interactions. *Perception, 14*, 571–577.

See Also

- Recanzone, G. H. (2003). Auditory influences on visual temporal rate perception. *Journal of Neurophysiology, 89*, 1078–1093.

- The advice in this hack, and other good tips for design can be found in Reeves et al. (2004). Guidelines for multimodal user interface design. *Communications of the ACM—Special Issue on Multimodal Interfaces, 47(1)*, 57–59. It is online at *http://www.niceproject.com/publications/CACM04.pdf*.

Don't Divide Attention Across Locations

Attention isn't separate for different senses. Where you place your attention in visual space affects what you hear in auditory space. Attention exists as a central, spatially allocated resource.

Where you direct attention is not independent across the senses. Where you pay attention to in space with one sense affects the other senses.[1] If you want people to pay attention to information across two modalities (a *modality* is a sense mode, like vision or audition), they will find this easiest if the information comes from the same place in space. Alternatively, if you want people to ignore something, don't make it come from the same place as something they are attending to. These are lessons drawn from work by Dr. Charles Spence of the Oxford University crossmodal research group (*http://www.psych.ox.ac.uk/xmodal/default.htm*). One experiment that everyone will be able to empathize with involves listening to speech while driving a car.[2]

In Action

Listening to a radio or mobile phone on a speaker from the back of a car makes it harder to spot things happening in front of you.

Obviously showing this in real life is difficult. It's a complex situation with lots of variables, and one of these is whether you crash your car—not the sort of data psychologists want to be responsible for creating. So Dr. Spence created the next best thing in his lab—an advanced driving simulator, which he sat people in and gave them the job of simultaneously negotiating the traffic and bends while repeating sets of words played over a speaker (a task called *shadowing*). The speakers were placed either on the dashboard in front or to the side.

Drivers who listened to sounds coming from the sides made more errors in the shadowing task, drove slower, and took longer to decide what to do at junctions.

You can see coping strategy in action if you sit with a driver. Notice how he's happy to talk while driving on easy and known roads, but falls quiet and pops the radio off when having to make difficult navigation decisions.

How It Works

This experiment—and any experience you may have had with trying to drive with screaming kids in the backseat of a car—shows that attention is allocated in physical space, not just to particular things arbitrarily and not independently across modalities. This is unsurprising, given that we know how interconnected cortical processing is [Hack #81] and that it is often organized in maps that use spatial coordinate frames [Hack #12]. The spatial constraints on attention may reflect the physical limits of modulating the activity in cortical processing structures that are themselves organized to mirror physical space.

In Real Life

Other studies of this kind of task, which involve complex real-world tasks, have shown that people are actually very good at coordinating their mental resources. The experiments that motivated this experiment proved that attention is allocated in space and that dividing it in space, even across modalities, causes difficulties. But these experiments tested subjects who weren't given any choice about what they did—the experimental setup took them to the limits of their attentional capacities to test where they broke down.

Whether these same factors had an effect in a real-world task like driving was another question. When people aren't at the limit of their abilities, they can switch between tasks, rather than doing both at once—allocating attention dynamically, shifting it between tasks as the demands of the task change. People momentarily *stop* talking when driving at sections of the road that are nonroutine, like junctions, in order to free up attention, avoiding getting trapped in the equivalent of Spence's shadowing task.

The driving experiment shows that despite our multitasking abilities the spatial demands of crossmodal attention do influence driving ability. The effect might be small, but when you're travelling at 80 mph toward something else that is travelling at 80 mph toward you, a small effect could mean a big difference.

Hacking the Hack

One of the early conclusions drawn from research into crossmodal attention[3] was that it was possible to divide attention between modalities without clashing, so if you wanted users to simultaneously pay attention to two different streams of information, they should appear in two different modalities. That is, if a person needs to keep on top of two rapidly updating streams, you're better off making one operate in vision and one in sound rather than having both appear on a screen, for example. The results discussed in this hack suggest two important amendments to this rule of thumb:[4]

- Dividing attention across modalities—attending to both vision and sound, for example—is more efficient if the streams have a common spatial location.
- If one stream needs to be ignored, don't let it share spatial location with an attended stream.

End Notes

1. Spence, C., & Driver, J. (eds.). (2004) *Crossmodal Space and Crossmodal Attention*. Oxford: Oxford University Press.

2. Spence, C., & Read, L. (2003). Speech shadowing while driving: On the difficulty of splitting attentions between eye and ear. *Psychological Science, 14*(3), 251–256.

3. Wickens, C. D. (1980). The structure of attentional resources. In R. S. Nickerson (ed.), *Attention and Performance*, 8, 239–257. Hillsdale, NJ: Erlbaum.

4. More details about the best way to present two steams of important information to a person, one in vision and one in sound, are discussed by Spence & Driver. *Crossmodal Space and Crossmodal Attention*, 187–188.

HACK #55
Confuse Color Identification with Mixed Signals

When you're speaking, written words can distract you. If you're thinking nonlinguistically, they can't.

The Stroop Effect is a classic of experimental psychology. In fact, it's more than a classic, it's an *industry*. J. Ridley Stroop first did his famous experiment in 1935, and it's been replicated thousands of times since then. The task is this: you are shown some words and asked to name the ink color the words appear in. Unfortunately, the words themselves can be the names of colors. You are slower, and make more errors, when trying to name the ink color of a word that spells the name of a different color. This, in a nutshell, is the Stroop Effect. You can read the original paper online at *http://psychclassics.yorku.ca/Stroop*.

In Action

To try out the Stroop Effect yourself, use the interactive experiment available at *http://faculty.washington.edu/chudler/java/ready.html*[1] (you don't need Java in your web browser to give this a go).

Start the experiment by clicking the "Go to the first test" link; the first page will look like Figure 5-1, only (obviously) in color.

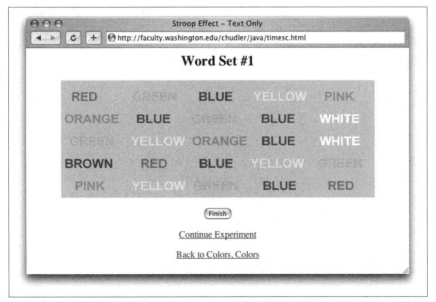

Figure 5-1. In the Stroop experiment, the color of the ink isn't necessarily the same as the color the word declares

As fast as you're able, read out loud the color of each word—not what it spells, but the actual color in which it appears. Then click the Finish button and note the time it tells you. Continue the experiment and do the same on the next screen. Compare the times.

The difference between the two tests is that whereas the ink colors and the words correspond on the first screen, on the second they conflict for each word. It takes you longer to name the colors on the second screen.

How It Works

Although you attempt to ignore the word itself, you are unable to do so and it still breaks through, affecting your performance. It slows your response to the actual ink color and can even make you give an incorrect answer. You can get this effect with most people nearly all of the time, which is one reason why psychologists love it.

The other reason it's a psychologist's favorite is that, although the task is simple, it involves many aspects of how we think, and the experiment has variations to explore these. At first glance, the explanation of the task seems simple—we process words automatically, and this process overrides the processing of color information. But this isn't entirely true, although that's the reason still taught in many classes.

Reading the word interferes only if two conditions are fulfilled. First, the level and focus of your attention has to be broad enough that the word can be unintentionally read. Second, the response you are trying to give must be a linguistic one. In this case, the required response is spoken, so it is indeed linguistic.

Avoiding reading is easier when the color to report is disentangled from the word. If you have to respond to only the color of the first letter of each word and the rest are black, the confusion is reduced. Ditto if the word and block of color are printed separately. In these cases, we're able to configure ourselves to respond to certain stimuli (the color of the ink) and ignore certain others (the word). It's only when we're not able to divide the two types of information that the Stroop Effect emerges.

 It's probably this kind of selective concentration that renders otherwise bizarre events invisible, as with inattention blindness [Hack #41] when attention on a basketball game results in a gorilla walking unseen across the court.

The second condition, that the response is linguistic, is really a statement about the compatibility between the stimulus and response required to it.

Converting a written word into its spoken form is easier than converting a visual color into its spoken form. Because of immense practice, word shapes are already linguistic items, whereas color has to be translated from the purely visual into a linguistic symbol (the sensation of red on the eye, to the word "red").

So the kind of response normally required in the Stroop Effect uses the same code—language—as the word part of the stimulus, not the color part. When we're asked to give a linguistic label to the color information, it's not too surprising that the response-compatible information from the word part of the stimulus distracts us.

But by changing the kind of response required, you can remove the distracting effect. You can demonstrate this by doing the Stroop Effect task from earlier, but instead of saying the color out loud, respond by pointing to a square of matching color on a printout. The interference effect disappears—you've stopped using a linguistic response code, and reading the words no longer acts as a disruption.

Taking this one step further, you can reintroduce the effect by changing the task to its opposite—try responding to what the written word says and attempting to ignore the ink color (still pointing to colors on the chart rather than reading out loud). Suddenly pointing is hard again when the written word and ink color don't match.[2]

You're now getting the reverse effect because your response is in a code that is different from the stimulus information you're trying to use (the word) and the same as the stimulus information you're trying to ignore (the color).

Take-home message: more or less mental effort can be required to respond to the same information, depending on how compatible the response is with the stimulus. If you don't want people to be distracted, don't make them translate from visual and spatial information into auditory and verbal information (or vice versa).

End Notes

1. This experiment is part of the much larger Neuroscience for Kids web site: *http://faculty.washington.edu/chudler/neurok.html*.

2. Durgin, F. H. (2002). The reverse Stroop Effect. *Psychonomic Bulletin & Review,* 7(1), 121–125.

See Also

- Two further papers may be of interest if you'd like to explore the Stroop Effect and the underlying brain regions responsible: Besner, D. (2001).

The myth of ballistic processing: Evidence from Stroop's paradigm. *Psychonomic Bulletin & Review, 8*(2), 324–330. And: MacLeod, C. M., & MacDonald, P. A. (2000). Interdimensional interference in the Stroop Effect: Uncovering the cognitive and neural anatomy of attention. *Trends in Cognitive Sciences, 4*(10), 383–391.

Don't Go There

You're drawn to reach in the same direction as something you're reacting to, even if the direction is completely unimportant.

So much of what we do in everyday life is responding to something that we've seen or heard—choosing and clicking a button on a dialog box on a computer or leaping to turn the heat off when a pan boils over. Unfortunately, we're not very good at reacting *only* to the relevant information. The form in which we receive it leaks over into our response.

For instance, if you're reacting to something that appears on your left, it's faster to respond with your left hand, and it takes a little longer to respond with your right. And this is true even when location isn't important at all. In general, the distracting effect of location responses is called the Simon Effect,[1] named after J. Richard Simon, who first published on it in 1968 and is now Professor Emeritus at the University of Iowa.[2]

The Simon Effect isn't the only example of the notionally irrelevant elements of a stimulus leaking into our response. Similar is the Stroop Effect [Hack #55], in which naming an ink color nets a slower response if the ink spells out the name of a different color. And, although it's brought about by a different mechanism, brighter lights triggering better reaction times [Hack #11] is similar in that irrelevant stimulus information modifies your response (this one is because a stronger signal evokes a faster neural response).

In Action

A typical Simon task goes something like this: you fix your gaze at the center of a computer screen and at intervals a light flashes up, randomly on the left or the right—which side is unimportant. If it is a red light, your task is to hit a button on your left. If it is a green light, you are to hit a button on your right. How long it takes you is affected by which side the light appears on, even though you are supposed to be basing which button you press entirely on the color of the light. The light on the left causes quicker reactions to the red button and slower reactions to the green button (good if the light is red, bad if the light is green). Lights appearing on the right naturally have the opposite effect. Even though you're supposed to disregard the location entirely, it still interferes with your response. The reaction times being measured are usually a half-second or less for this sort of experiment, and the location confusion results in an extension of roughly 5%.

It's difficult to tell what these reaction times mean without trying the experiment, but it is possible to feel, subjectively, the Simon Effect without equipment to measure reaction time.

You need stimuli that can appear on the left or the right with equal measure. I popped outside for 10 minutes and sat at the edge of the road, looking across it, so traffic could come from either my left or my right. (Figure 5-2 shows the view from where I was sitting.) My task was to identify red and blue cars, attempting to ignore their direction of approach.

Figure 5-2. The view from where I sat watching for red and blue cars

In choosing this task, I made use of the fact that color discrimination is poor in peripheral vision [Hack #14]. By fixing my gaze at a position directly opposite me, over the road, and refusing to move my eyes or my head, I would be able to tell the color of each car only as it passed directly in front of me. (If I had chosen to discriminate black cars and white cars, there's no color information required, so I would have been able to tell using my peripheral vision.) I wanted to do this so I wouldn't have much time to do my color task, but would be able to filter out moving objects that weren't cars (like people with strollers).

As a response, I tapped my right knee every time a red car passed and my left for blue ones, trying to respond as quickly as possible.

After 10 minutes of slow but steady traffic, I could discern a slight bias in my responses. My right hand would sometimes twitch a little if cars approached from that direction, and vice versa.

Now, I wouldn't be happy claiming a feeling of a twitchy hand as any kind of confirmation of the Simon Effect. The concept of location in my experiment is a little blurred: cars that appear from the *right* are also in motion to the *left*—which stimulus location should be interfering with my knee-tapping response?

But even though I can't fully claim the entire effect, that a car on the right causes a twitching right hand, I can still claim the basic interference effect: although I'd been doing the experiment for 10 minutes, my responses were still getting mucked up somehow.

To test whether my lack of agility at responding was caused by the location of the cars conflicting with the location of my knees, I changed my output, speaking "red" or "blue" as a response instead. In theory, this should remove the impact of the Simon Effect (because I was taking away the left-or-right location component of my response), and I might feel a difference. If I felt a difference, that would be the Simon Effect, and then its lack, in action.

And indeed, I did feel a difference. Using a spoken output, responding to the color of the cars was absolutely trivial, a very different experience from the knee tapping and instantly more fluid.

How It Works

For my traffic watching exercise, the unimportant factor of the location of the colored cars was interfering with my tapping my left or right knee. Factoring out the location variable by speaking instead of knee tapping—effectively routing around the Simon Effect—made the whole task much easier.

Much like the Stroop Effect [Hack #55] (in which you involuntarily read a word rather than sticking to the task of identifying the color of the ink in which it is printed), the Simon Effect is a collision of different pieces of information. The difference between the two is that the conflict in the Stroop Effect is between two component parts of a stimulus (the color of the word and the word itself), while, in the Simon Effect, the conflict is between the compatibility of stimulus and response. You're told to ignore the location of the stimulus, but just can't help knowing location is important because you're using it in making your response.

The key point here is that location information is almost always important, and so we're hardwired to use it when available. In real life, and especially before the advent of automation, you generally reach to the location of something you perceive in order to interact with it. If you perceive a light switch on your left, you reach to the left to switch off the lights, not to the right—that's the way the world works. Think of the Simon Effect not as location information leaking into our responses, but the *lack* of a mechanism to specifically *ignore* location information. Such a mechanism has never really been needed.

In Real Life

Knowing that location information is carried along between stimulus and response is handy for any kind of interface design. My range has four burners, arranged in a square. But the controls for those burners are in a line. It's because of the Simon Effect that I have to consult the diagram next to the controls each and every time I use them, not yet having managed to memorize the pattern (which, after all, never changes, so it should be easy). When I have to respond to the pot boiling over at the top right, I have the top-right location coded in my brain. If the controls took advantage of that instead of conflicting, they'd be easier to use.

Dialog boxes on my computer (I run Mac OS X) are better aligned with keyboard shortcuts than my stove's controls with the burners. There are usually two controls: OK and Cancel. I can press Return as a shortcut for OK and Escape as a shortcut for Cancel. Fortunately, the right-left arrangement of the keys on my keyboard matches the right-left arrangement of the buttons in the dialog (Escape and Cancel on the left, Right and OK on the right). If they didn't match, there would be a small time cost every time I attempted to use the keyboard, and it'd be no quicker at all.

And a corollary: my response to the color of the cars in the traffic experiment was considerably easier when it was verbal rather than directional (tapping left or right). To make an interface more fluid, avoid situations in which the directions of stimulus and response clash. For technologies that are supposed to be transparent and intuitive—like my Mac (and my stove, come to that)—small touches like this make all the difference.

End Notes

1. Simon, J. R. (1969). Reactions toward the source of stimulation. *Journal of Experimental Psychology, 81,* 174–176.

2. In fairness, we should mention that the Simon Effect was actually noted a hundred years before Simon published, by the pioneering Dutch experimental psychologist Franciscus Donders. Donders, Franciscus C.

(1868). Over de snelheid van psychische processen. Onderzoekingen gedaan in het Physiologisch Laboratorium der Utrechtsche Hooge-school, 1868–1869, Tweede reeks II: 92–120. Reprinted as Donders, Franciscus C. (1969). On the speed of mental processes. *Acta Psychologica, 30*, 412–431.

See Also

- You can read about the early history of measuring reaction times at "Mental Chronometry and Verbal Action—Some Historical Threads" (*http://www.mpi.nl/world/persons/private/ardi/Rts.htm*).

Combine Modalities to Increase Intensity

Events that affect more than one sense feel more intense in both of them.

The vision and audition chapters (Chapters 2 and 4, respectively) of this book look at the senses individually, just as a lot of psychologists have over the years. But interesting things begin to happen when you look at the senses as they interact with one another.[1]

Multisensory information is the norm in the real world, after all. Tigers smell strong and rustle as they creep through the undergrowth toward you. Fire shines and crackles as it burns. Your child says your name as she shakes your shoulder to wake you up.

These examples all suggest that the most basic kind of interaction between two senses should be the enhanced response to an event that generates two kinds of stimulation rather than just one. Information from one sense is more likely to be coincidence; simultaneous information on two senses is a good clue that you have detected a real event.

In Action

We can see the interaction of information hitting two senses at once in all sorts of situations. People sound clearer when we can see their lips [Hack #59]. Movies feel more impressive when they have a sound track. If someone gets a tap on one hand as they simultaneously see two flashes of light, one on each side, the light on the same side as the hand tap will appear brighter.

Helge Gillmeister and Martin Eimer of Birkbeck College, University of London, have found that people experience sounds as louder if a small vibration is applied to their index finger at the same time.[2] Although the vibration didn't convey any extra information, subjects rated sounds as up to twice as loud when they occurred at the same time as a finger vibration. The effect was biggest for quieter sounds.

How It Works

Recent research on such situations shows that the combination of information is wired into the early stages of sensory processing in the cortex. Areas of the cortex traditionally thought to respond to only a single sense (e.g., parts of the visual cortex) do actually respond to stimulation of the other senses too. This makes sense of the fact that many of these effects occur preconsciously, without any sense of effort or decision-making. They are preconscious because they are occurring in the parts of the brain responsible for initial representation and processing of sensation—another example (as in "To See, Act" [Hack #15]) of our perception not being passive but being actively constructed by our brains in ways we aren't always aware of.

Macaluso et al.[3] showed that the effect can work the other way round from the one discussed here: touch can enhance visual discrimination. They don't suggest that integration is happening in the visual cortex initially, but instead that parietal cortex areas responsible for multisensory integration send feedback signals down to visual areas, and it is this that allows enhanced visual sensitivity.

For enhancement to happen, it has to be labeled as belonging to the same event, and this is primarily done by the information arriving simultaneously. Individual neurons [Hack #9] are already set up to respond to timing information and frequently respond strongest to inputs from different sources arriving simultaneously. If information arrives at different times, it can suppress the activity of cells responsible for responding to inputs across senses (senses are called *modalities*, in the jargon).

So, what makes information from two modalities appear simultaneous? Obviously arriving at the *exact* same time is not possible; there must be a resolution of the senses in time below which two events appear to be simultaneous.

Although light moves a million times faster than sound, sound is processed faster once it gets to the ear [Hack #44] than light is processed once it gets to the eye. The relative speed of processing of each sense, coupled with the speed at which light and sound travel, leads to a "horizon of simultaneity"[4] at about 10 meters—where visual and auditory signals from the same source reach the cortex at the same time.

Most events don't occur just on this 10-meter line, of course, so there must be some extra mechanisms at work in the brain to allow sound and light events to appear simultaneous. Previously, researchers had assumed that the calculation of simultaneity was approximate enough that time difference due to arrival time could be ignored (until you get to events very far away—like lightning that arrives before thunder, for example). But now it appears that our brains make a preconscious adjustment for how far away some-thing is when calculating whether the sound and the light are arriving at the same time.[5] Another mechanism that operates is simply to override the tim-ing information that comes from vision with the timing information from auditory information [Hack #53].

End Notes

1. To start following up the research on crossmodal interactions, you could start by reading *Crossmodal Space and Crossmodal Attention* by Charles Spence and Jon Driver. This is an edited book with contribu-tions from many of the people at the forefront of the field. You can read more about the Oxford University crossmodal research group on its home page: *http://www.psych.ox.ac.uk/xmodal/default.htm*.

2. Gillmeister, H., & Eimer, M. (submitted). Multisensory integration in perception: tactile enhancement of perceived loudness.

3. Macaluso, E., Frith, C. D., & Driver, J. (2000). Modulation of human visual cortex by crossmodal spatial attention. *Science, 289*, 1206–1208.

4. Pöppel, E. (1988). *Mindworks: Time and Conscious Experience.* New York: Harcourt Brace Jovanovich.

5. Sugita, Y., and Suzuki, Y. (2003). Audiovisual perception: Implicit esti-mation of sound-arrival time. *Nature, 421*, 911.

Watch Yourself to Feel More

Looking at your skin makes it more sensitive, even if you can't see what it is you're feeling. Look through a magnifying glass and it becomes even more sensitive.

The skin is the shortest-range interface we have with the world. It is the only sense that doesn't provide any information about distant objects. If you can feel something on your skin, it is next to you right now.

Body parts exist as inward-facing objects—they provide touch informa-tion—but they also exist as external objects—we can feel them with other body parts, see them, and (if you're lucky) feel and see those of other peo-ple. "Mold Your Body Schema" [Hack #64] and "Understand What Makes Faces Special" [Hack #93] explore how we use vision to update our internal model of our body parts. But the integration of the two senses goes deeper, so much so that looking at a body part enhances the sensitivity of that body part, even if you aren't getting any useful visual information to illuminate what's happening on your skin.

In Action

Kennett et al.[1] tested how sensitive people were to touch on their forearms. In controlled conditions, people were asked to judge if they were feeling two tiny rods pressed against their skin or just one. The subjects made these judgments in three conditions. The first two are the most important, providing the basic comparison. Subjects were either in the dark or in the light and looking at their arm—but with a brief moment of darkness so they couldn't actually see their arm as the pins touched it. Subjects allowed to look at their arms were significantly more accurate, indicating that looking at the arm, even though it didn't provide any useful information, improved tactile sensitivity.

The third condition is the most interesting and shows exactly how pervasive the effect can be. Subjects were shown their forearm through a magnifying glass (still with darkness at the actual instant of the pinprick). In this condition, their sensitivity was nearly twice as precise as their sensitivity in the dark!

This is astounding for at least two reasons. First, it shows that visual attention can improve our sensitivity in another domain, in this case touch. There is no necessity for touch to interact like this with vision. The senses could be independent until far later in processing. Imagine if the double-click rate setting on your mouse changed depending on what was coming down your Internet connection? You'd think it was pretty odd. But for the brain this kind of interaction makes sense because we control where we look and events often spark input to more than one of our senses at a time.

The second reason this is astounding is because it shows how a piece of technology (the magnifying glass) can be used to adjust our neural processing at a very fundamental level.

How It Works

Touch information is gathered together in the parietal cortex (consult the crib notes in "Get Acquainted with the Central Nervous System" [Hack #7] if you want to know where that is), in an area called the *primary somatosensory cortex*. You'll find neurons here arranged into a map representing the surface of your body [Hack #12], and you'll find *polysensory neurons*. These respond in particular when visual and tactile input synchronize and suppress when the two inputs are discordant; it seems there's a network here that integrates information from both senses, either within the somatosensory map of the body or in a similar map nearby.

This theory explains why brain damage to the parietal cortex can result in distortions of body image. Some patients with damaged parietal lobes will point to the doctor's elbow when asked to point to their own elbow for example.

This hack and "Mold Your Body Schema" [Hack #64] show that short-term changes in our representation of our body are possible. Individual neurons in the cortex that respond to stimulation of the skin can be shown to change what area of skin they are responsible for very rapidly. If, for example, you anesthetize one finger so that it is no longer providing touch sensation to the cortical cells previously responsible for responding to sensation there, these cells will begin to respond to sensations on the other fingers.[2] In the magnifying glass condition, the expanded resolution of vision appears to cause the resources devoted to tactile sensitivity of the skin to adjust, adding resolution to match the expanded resolution the magnifying glass has artificially given vision.

In Real Life

This experiment explains why in general we like to look at things as we do them with our hands or listen to them with our ears—like watching the band at a gig. We don't just want to see what's going on—it actually enhances the other senses as well.

Perhaps this is also why first-person shooter games have hit upon showing an image of the player's hands on the display. Having hands where you can see them may actually remap your bodily representation to make the screen part of your personal—or near-personal—space, and hence give all the benefits of attention [Hack #54] and multimodal integration (such as the better sense discrimination shown in this hack) that you get there.

End Notes

1. Kennett, S., Taylor-Clarke, M., & Haggard, P. (2001). Noninformative vision improves the spatial resolution of touch in humans. *Current Biology, 11*, 1188–1191.

2. Calford, M. B., & Tweedale, R. (1991). Acute changes in cutaneous receptive fields in primary somatosensory cortex after digit denervation in adult flying fox. *Journal of Neurophysiology, 65*, 178–187.

 ## Hear with Your Eyes: The McGurk Effect

#59   Listen with your eyes closed and you'll hear one sound; listen and watch the speaker at the same time and you'll hear another.

If there were ever a way of showing that your senses combine to completely change your ultimate experience, it's the McGurk Effect. This classic illusion, invented by Harry McGurk (and originally published in 1976[1]), makes you hear different sounds being spoken depending on whether or not you can see the speaker's lips. Knowing what's going to happen doesn't help: the effect just isn't as strong.

In Action

Watch Arnt Maasø's McGurk Effect video (*http://www.media.uio.no/ personer/arntm/McGurk_english.html*; QuickTime with sound). You can see a freeze frame of the video in Figure 5-3.

Figure 5-3. Arnt Maasø's McGurk Effect video

When you play it with your eyes closed, the voice says "ba ba." Play the video again, and watch the mouth: the voice says "da da." Try to hear "ba ba" while you watch the lips move. It can't be done.

How It Works

The illusion itself can't happen in real life. McGurk made it by splicing the sound of someone saying "ba ba" over a video of him making a different sound, "ga ga." When you're not watching the video, you hear what's actually being spoken. But when you see the speaker too, the two bits of information clash. The position of the lips is key in telling what sound someone's making, especially for distinguishing between speech sounds (called phonemes) like "ba," "ga," "pa," and "da" (those which you make by popping air out).

> Visual information is really important for listening to people speak. It's a cliché, but I know I can't understand people as well when I don't have my glasses on.
>
> —M.W.

We use both visual and auditory information when figuring out what sound a person is making and they usually reinforce each other, but when the two conflict, the brain has to find a resolution. In the world the brain's used to, objects don't usually look as if they're doing one thing but sound as if they're doing another.

Since visually you're seeing "ga ga" and audition is hearing "ba ba," these are averaged out and you perceive "da da" instead, a sound that sits equally well with both information cues. In other situations, visual information will dominate completely and change a heard syllable to the one seen in the lip movements.[2]

Remarkably, you don't notice the confusion. Sensory information is combined before language processing is reached, and language processing tunes into only certain phonemes [Hack #49]. The decision as to what you hear is outside your voluntary control. The McGurk Effect shows integration of information across the senses at a completely preconscious level. You don't get to make any decisions about this; what you hear is affected by what goes in through your eyes. It's a good thing that in most circumstances the visual information you get matches what you need to hear.

End Notes

1. McGurk, H., & MacDonald, J. (1976). Hearing lips and seeing voices. *Nature, 264*, 746–747.

2. Fusion of the sound and sight information is possible only when you have experience with a suitable compromise phoneme. One of the interesting things about phonemes is that they are perceived as either one thing or the other, but not as in-between values. So although there exists a continuum of physical sounds in between "ba" and "da," all positions along this spectrum will be perceived as either "ba" or "da," not as in-between sounds (unlike, say, colors, which have continuous physical values that you can also perceive). This is called categorical perception.

See Also

- Hearing with Your Eyes (*http://ccms.ntu.edu.tw/~karchung/ Phonetics%20II%20page%20seventeen.htm*; QuickTime) has a collection of McGurk Effect movies.

Pay Attention to Thrown Voices

#60 Sounds from the same spatial location are harder to separate, but not if you use vision to fool your brain into "placing" one of the sounds somewhere else.

Sense information is mixed together in the brain and sorted by location [Hack #54], and we use this organization in choosing what to pay attention to (and therefore tune into). If you're listening to two different conversations simultaneously, it's pretty easy if they're taking place on either side of your head—you can voluntarily tune in to whichever one you want. But let's say those conversations were occurring in the same place, on the radio: it's suddenly much harder to make out just one.

> Which is why we can talk over each other in a bar and still understand what's being said, but not on the radio. On the radio, we don't have any other information to disambiguate who says what and the sounds get confused with each other.
>
> —T.S.

Hang on...how do we decide on the spatial location of a sense like hearing? For sound alone, we use clues implicit in what we hear, but if we can *see* where the sound originates, this visual information dominates [Hack #53].

Even if it's incorrect.

In Action

Jon Driver from University College London[1] took advantage of our experience with syncing language sounds with lip movements to do a little hacking. He showed people a television screen showing a person talking, but instead of the speech coming from the television, it was played through a separate amplifier and combined with a distracting, and completely separate, voice speaking. The television screen was alternately right next to the amplifier or some distance away. The subject was asked to repeat the words corresponding to the talking head on the television.

If they watched the talking head on screen nearby the amplifier, they made more errors than if they watched the talking head on the screen kept distant from the sound. Even though both audio streams were heard from the single amplifier in the two cases, moving the video image considerably changed the listener's ability to tune into one voice.

This experiment is a prime candidate for trying at home. An easy way would be with a laptop hooked up to portable speakers and a radio. Have the laptop playing a video with lots of speech where you can see lip movements. A news broadcast, full of talking heads, is ideal. Now put the radio, tuned into a talk station, and the laptop speaker, in the same location. That's the single amplifier in Driver's experiment. The two different cases in the experiment correspond to your laptop being right next to the speakers or some feet away. You should find that you understand what the talking heads on the video are saying more easily when the laptop is further away. Give it a go.

How It Works

It's easier to understand what's going on here if we think about it as two separate setups. Let's call them "hard," for the case in which you're looking at the television right by the amplifier and "easy," when you're looking at the screen put a little further away.

In the hard case, there's a video of a talking head on the television screen and two different voices, all coming from the same location. The reason it's hard is because it's easier to tune out of one information stream and into another if they're in different locations (which is what "Don't Divide Attention Across Locations" [Hack #54] is all about). The fact there's a video of a talking head showing in this case isn't really important.

The easy setup has one audio stream tucked off to the side somewhere, while a talking head and its corresponding audio play on the television. It's plain to see that tuning into the audio on the television is a fairly simple task—I do it whenever I watch TV while ignoring the noise of people talking in the other room.

But hang on, you say. In Driver's experiment, the easy condition *didn't* correspond to having one audio stream neatly out of the way and the one you're listening to aligned with the television screen. Both audio streams were coming from the same place, from the amplifier, right?

Yes, right, but also no. Strictly speaking, both audio streams do still come from the same place, but remember that we're not very good at telling where sounds come from. We're so poor at it, we prefer to use what we see to figure out the origin of sounds instead [Hack #53]. When you look at the screen, the lip movements of the talking head are so synchronized with one of the audio streams that your brain convinces itself that the audio stream must be coming from the position of the screen too.

It's whether the video is in the same place as the amplifier that counts in this experiment. When the screen is in a different place from the amplifier, your brain makes a mistake and mislocates one of the audio streams, so the audio streams are divided and you can tune in one and out the other.

Never mind that the reason the conversations can be tuned into separately is because of a localization mistake; it still works. It doesn't matter that this localization was an illusion—the illusion could still be used by the brain to separate the information before processing it. All our impressions are a construction, so an objectively wrong construction can have as much validity in the brain as an objectively correct construction.

End Note

1. Driver, J. (1996). Enhancement of selective listening by illusory mislocation of speech sounds due to lip-reading. *Nature, 381*, 66–68.

Talk to Yourself

Language isn't just for talking to other people; it may play a vital role in helping your brain combine information from different modules.

Language might be an astoundingly efficient way of getting information into your head from the outside [Hack #49], but that's not its only job. It also helps you think. Far from being a sign of madness, talking to yourself is something at the essence of being human.

Rather than dwell on the evolution of language and its role in rewiring the brain into its modern form,[1] let's look at one way language may be used by our brains to do cognitive work. Specifically we're talking about the ability of language to combine information in ordered structures—in a word: syntax.

Peter Carruthers, at the University of Maryland,[2] has proposed that language syntax is used to combine, simultaneously, information from different cognitive modules. By "modules," he means specialized processes into which we have no insight,[3] such as color perception or instant number judgments [Hack #35]. You don't know *how* you know that something is red or that there are two coffee cups, you just *know*. Without language syntax, the claim is, we can't combine this information.

The theory seems pretty bold—or maybe even wrong—but we'll go through the evidence Carruthers uses and the details of what exactly he means and you can make up your own mind. If he's right, the implications are profound, and it clarifies exactly how deeply language is entwined with thought. At the very least, we hope to convince you that *something* interesting is going on in these experiments.

In Action

The experiment described here was done in the lab of Elizabeth Spelke.[4] You could potentially do it in your own home, but be prepared to build some large props and to get dizzy.

Imagine a room like the one in Figure 5-4. The room is made up of four curtains, used to create four walls in a rectangle, defined by two types of information: geometric (two short walls and two long walls) and color information (one red wall).

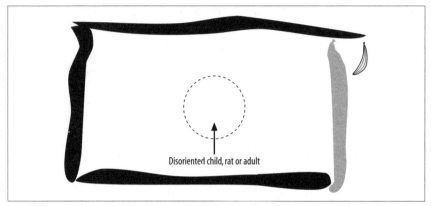

Figure 5-4. Setup for Spelke's experiments—a rectangular room with one colored wall

Now, think about the corners. If you are using only geometric information, pairs of corners are identical. There are two corners with a short wall on the left and a long wall on the right and two corners the other way around. If you are using only color information, there are also two pairs of identical corners: corners next to a red wall and corners *not* next to a red wall.

Using just one kind of information, geometry or color, lets you identify corners with only 50% accuracy. But using both kinds of information in combination lets you identify any of the four corners with 100% accuracy, because although both kinds of information are ambiguous, they are not ambiguous in the same way.

So, here's a test to see if people can use both kinds of information in combination.[5] Show a person something he'd like, like some food, and let him see you hide it behind the curtains in one corner of the room. Now disorient him by spinning him around and ask him to find the food. If he can combine the geometric and the color information, he'll have no problem finding the food—he'll be able to tell unambiguously which corner it was hidden in. If he doesn't combine information across modules, he will get it right 50% of the time and 50% of the time wrong on his first guess and need a second guess to find the food.

Where does language come into it? Well, language seems to define the kinds of subjects who can do this task at better than 50% accuracy. Rats can't do it. Children who don't have language yet can't do it. Postlinguistic children and adults can do it.

Convinced? Here's the rub: if you tie up an adult's language ability, her performance drops to close to 50%. This is what Linda Hermer-Vazquez, Elizabeth Spelke, and Alla Katsnelson did.[6] They got subjects to do the experiment, but all the time they were doing it, they were asked to repeat the text of newspaper articles that were played to them over loudspeakers. This "verbal shadowing task" completely engaged their language ability, removing their inner monologue.

The same subjects could orient themselves and find the correct corner fine when they weren't doing the task. They could do it when they were doing an equivalently difficult task that didn't tie up their language ability (copying a sequence of rhythms by clapping). But they couldn't do it with their language resources engaged in something else. There's something special about language that is essential for reorienting yourself using both kinds of information available in the room.

How It Works

Peter Carruthers thinks that you get this effect because language is essential for conjoining information from different modules. Specifically he thinks that it is needed at the interface between beliefs, desires, and planning. Combining across modalities is possible without language for simple actions (see the other crossmodal hacks [Hacks #57 through #59] in this book for examples), but there's something about planning, and that includes reorientation, that requires language.

This would explain why people sometimes begin to talk to themselves—to instruct themselves out loud—during especially difficult tasks. Children use self-instruction as a normal part of their development to help them carry out things they find difficult.[7] Telling them to keep quiet is unfair and probably makes it harder for them to finish what they are doing.

If Carruthers is right, it means two things. First, if you are asking people to engage in goal-oriented reasoning, particularly if it uses information of different sorts, you shouldn't ask them to do something else that is verbal, either listening or speaking.

> I've just realized that this could be another [Hack #54] part of the reason people can drive with the radio on but need to turn it off as soon as they don't know where they are going and need to think about which direction to take. It also explains why you should keep quiet when the driver is trying to figure out where to go next.
>
> —T.S.

Second, if you do want to get people to do complex multisequence tasks, they might find it easier if the tasks can be done using only one kind of information, so that language isn't required to combine across modules.

End Notes

1. Although if you do want to dwell on the role of language in brain evolution (and vice versa), you should start by reading Terrence Deacon's fantastic *The Symbolic Species: The Co-Evolution of Language and the Brain*. New York: W. W. Norton & Company (1998).

2. The article that contains this theory was published by Peter Carruthers in *Behavioural and Brain Sciences*. It, and the response to comments on it, are at *http://www.philosophy.umd.edu/people/faculty/pcarruthers/ Cognitive-language.htm* and *http://www.philosophy.umd.edu/people/ faculty/pcarruthers/BBS-reply.htm*.

3. OK, by "modules," he means a lot more than that, but that's the basic idea. Read Jerry Fodor's *Modularity of Mind* (Cambridge, MA: MIT Press, 1983) for the original articulation of this concept. The importance of modularity is also emphasized by evolutionary psychologists, such as Steven Pinker.

4. Much of the work Peter Carruthers bases his theory on was done at the lab of Elizabeth Spelke (*http://www.wjh.harvard.edu/~lds*).

5. Strictly, you don't have to use both kinds of information in combination at the same time to pass this test; you could use the geometric information and then use the color information, but there is other good evidence that the subjects of the experiments described here—rats, children, and adults—don't do this.

6. Hermer-Vazquez, L., Spelke, E. S., & Katsnelson, A. S. (1999). Sources of flexibility in human cognition: Dual-task studies of space and language. *Cognitive Psychology, 39*(1), 3–36.

7. Berk, L. E. (November 1994). Why children talk to themselves. *Scientific American*, 78–83 (*http://www.abacon.com/berk/ica/research.html*).

CHAPTER SIX

Moving

Hacks 62–69

The story of the brain is a story of embodiment, of how much the brain takes for granted the world we're in and the body that carries it about.

For instance, we assume a certain level of stability in the world. We make assumptions about how our body is able to move within the environment, and if the environment has changed [Hack #62], we get confused.

As we assume stability in the world, so too do we assume stability from our body. Why should the brain bother remembering the shape of our own body when it's simply there to consult? But when our body's shape doesn't remain stable, the brain can get confused. You start by getting your fingers mixed up when you cross your hands [Hack #63]; you end up convincing your brain that you're receiving touch sensations from the nearby table [Hack #64].

This is also a story of how we interact with the world. Our brains continually assess and anticipate the movements we need to grasp objects, judging correctly even when our eyes are fooled [Hack #66]. We're built for activity, our brains perceiving the uses of an object, its affordances [Hack #67], as soon as we look at it—as soon as we see something, we ready ourselves to use it.

We'll finish on what we use for manipulation: our hands. What makes us right- or left-handed [Hack #68]? And, while we're on the topic, what does all that left-brain, right-brain stuff really mean [Hack #69]?

 ## The Broken Escalator Phenomenon: #62 When Autopilot Takes Over

Your conscious experience of the world and control over your body both feel instantaneous—but they're not.

Lengthy delays in sensory feedback and in the commands that are sent to your muscles mean that what you see now happened a few moments ago and what you're doing now you planned back then. To get around the problem caused by these delays in neural transmission, your brain is active and constructive in its interactions with the outside world, endlessly anticipating what's going to happen next and planning movements to respond appropriately.

Most of the time this works well, but sometimes your brain can anticipate inappropriately, and the mismatch between what your brain thought was going to happen and what it actually encounters can lead to some strange sensations.

In Action

One such sensation can be felt when you walk onto a broken escalator. You know it's broken but your brain's autopilot takes over regardless, inappropriately adjusting your posture and gait as if the escalator were moving. This has been dubbed the *broken escalator phenomenon*.[1] Normally, the sensory consequences of these postural adjustments are canceled out by the escalator's motion, but when it's broken, they lead to some self-induced sensations that your brain simply wasn't expecting. Your brain normally cancels out the sensory consequences of its own actions [Hack #65], so it feels really weird when that doesn't happen.

To try it out yourself, the best place to look is somewhere like the London Underground (where you're sure to find plenty of broken escalators) or your favorite run-down mall. You need an escalator that is broken and not moving but that you're still allowed to walk up. You could also use the moving walkways they have at airports; again, you need one that's stationary but that you're still permitted to walk onto. Now, try not to think about it too much and just go ahead and walk on up the escalator. You should find that you experience an odd sensation as you take your first step or two onto the escalator. People often report feeling as though they've been "sucked" onto the escalator. You might even lose your balance for a moment. If you keep trying it, the effect usually diminishes quite quickly.

How It Works

Unless we've lived our lives out in the wilderness, most of us will have encountered moving escalators or walkways at least a few times. And when we've done so, our brain has learned to adapt to the loss of balance caused by the escalator's motion. It's done this with little conscious effort on our part, automatically saving us from falling over. So when we step onto an escalator or moving walkway now, we barely notice the transition, and continue fluidly on our way. The thing is, when the escalator is broken, our brain adjusts our balance and posture anyway, and it seems we can't stop it from doing so.

Until recently, evidence for this phenomenon was based only on urban anecdotes. But now the phenomenon has actually been investigated in the laboratory using a computer-controlled moving walkway.[1,2] Special devices attached to the bodies and legs of 14 volunteers recorded their posture and muscle activity. Each volunteer then walked 20 times from a fixed platform onto the moving walkway. After that, the walkway was switched off, the volunteers were told it would no longer move, and they then walked from the platform onto the stationary walkway 10 times.

The first time the subjects stepped onto the moving walkway, they lost their balance and grasped the handrail. But over the next few attempts, they learned to anticipate the unbalancing effect of the walkway by speeding up their stride and leaning their body forward.

Then crucially, when the volunteers first walked onto the walkway when it was switched off, they continued to walk at the increased speed and also continued to sway the trunk of their body forward. They performed these inappropriate adjustments even though they could see the walkway was no longer moving and even though they had been told it would no longer move. However, this happened only once. Their brain had apparently realized the mistake and the next time they walked onto the stationary walkway they didn't perform these inappropriate adjustments. Consistent with anecdotal evidence for the broken escalator phenomenon, most of the volunteers expressed spontaneous surprise at the sensations they experienced when they first stepped onto the stationary walkway.

In Real Life

There are obviously differences between the lab experiment and the real-life phenomenon. Our brains have learned to cope with escalators over years of experience, whereas the experimental volunteers adapted to the lab walkway in just a few minutes. But what the real-life phenomenon and lab experiment both represent is an example of dissociation between our conscious knowledge and our brain's control of our actions. The volunteers knew the walkway was motionless, but because it had been moving previously, the brain put anticipatory adjustments in place anyway to prevent loss of balance. Usually these kinds of dissociations work the other way around. Often our conscious perception can be tricked by sensory illusions, but the action systems of our brain are not fooled and act appropriately. For example, visual illusions of size can lead us to perceptually misjudge the size of an object, yet our fingertip grasp will be appropriate to the object's true size.

The motor system gets it right when our conscious perception is fooled by the illusion size (see "Trick Half Your Mind" [Hack #66] to see this in action).

These observations undermine our sense of a unified self: it seems our consciousness and the movement control parts of our brain can have two different takes on the world at the same time. This happens because, in our fast-paced world of infinite information and possibility, our brain must prioritize both what sensory information reaches consciousness and what aspects of movement our consciousness controls. Imagine how sluggish you would be if you had to think in detail about every movement you made. Indeed, most of the time autopilot improves performance—think of how fluent you've become at the boring drive home from work or the benefits of touch-typing. It's just that, in the case of the broken escalator, your brain should really have handed the reins back to "you."

End Notes

1. Reynolds, R. F., & Bronstein, A. M. (2003). The broken escalator phenomenon. aftereffect of walking onto a moving platform. *Experimental Brain Research, 151,* 301–308.

2. Reynolds, R. F., & Bronstein, A. M. (2004). The moving platform aftereffect: Limited generalization of a locomotor adaptation. *Journal of Neurophysiology, 91,* 92–100.

—*Christian Jarrett*

HACK #63 Keep Hold of Yourself

How do we keep the sensations on our skin up to date as we move our bodies around in space?

When an insect lands on your skin, receptors in that area of skin fire and a signal travels up to your brain. The identity of the receptor indicates which part of your skin has been touched. But how do you know exactly where that bit of your body is so you can swat the fly? As we move our bodies around in space we have to remap and take account of our changes in posture to understand the sensations arriving at our skin; very different movements are required to scratch your knee depending on whether you're sitting down or standing up. This might seem like a trivial problem, but it is more complex than it seems at first. We have to integrate information from our joints and muscles about the current position of our body—*proprioceptive information*—as well as touch and vision, for example, to gauge that the sight of a fly landing and the sensation of it contacting your finger are coming from the same place.

In Action

Try closing your eyes and feeling an object on a table in front of you with the fingers of both hands. Now, cross your hands and return your fingers to the object. Despite swapping the point of contact between your two hands, you do not feel that the object has flipped around. The next two illusions attempt to make this remapping fail.

First, try crossing your index finger and middle finger and run the gap between them along the ridge and around the tip of your nose (make sure you do this quite slowly). You will probably feel as if you have two noses. This is because your brain has failed to take account of the fact that you have crossed your fingers. Notice that you are unable to overcome this illusion even if you consciously try to do so. This is sometimes called Aristotle's Illusion, as he was apparently the first person to record it.

Now, try out the *crossed hands illusion*. You'll need a friend to help. Cross your hands over in front of your chest, at arm's length. Then turn your palms inward, so your thumbs point downward and clasp your hands together, so your fingers are interleaved. Next, rotate your hands up toward your chest, until your thumbs are pointing away from you, as shown in Figure 6-1. Now, if a friend points to one of your fingers and asks you to move it, you will probably fail to move the correct finger and instead move the same finger but on the opposite hand. Again, you have failed to take account of your unusual posture; you assume that the finger you see corresponds to the finger that would be in that position if you had simply clasped your hands, without crossing them over. You may find that you are able to overcome the illusion if your friend indicates which finger he wants you to move by touching it. This can help you to remap and take your posture into account.

How It Works

Charles Spence and colleagues[1] have shown that we can update how we bind together vision and touch when we cross our hands over. They asked people to attend to and make judgments about vibrations that they felt on their hands, while ignoring lights presented at the same time. When feeling a vibration on their right hand, the lights on the right side—closest to their right hand—interfered much more (made people slower to carry out the task), than lights on their left side. That is, we tend to bind together vision and touch when they come from the same part of the outside world. So what happened when they crossed their hands over? The interaction between vision and touch changed over: lights over on the left side of their body were now closest to their right hand and interfered more with the right hand than

Figure 6-1. Tom tries out the crossed hands illusion

the lights over on the right side. So, when we change where our hands are in space, we integrate different sets of visual and tactile signals.

But remapping can sometimes fail, even without intertwining our fingers. Two recent experiments[2,3] have shown that we are particularly bad at dealing with information in quick succession. If your hands are in their usual uncrossed position and you are asked to judge which hand is touched first, it is relatively easy. On the other hand, if your hands are crossed, the same task becomes much more difficult. This difficulty in coping with stimuli presented in quick succession, suggests that remapping can be a time-consuming process. Shigeru Kitazawa[4] has suggested we do not become conscious of a sensation on a particular part of our skin and then attribute it to a particular location in space. Rather, our conscious sensation of touch seems to be delayed until we can identify where it's coming from.

So where in the brain do we remap and update our connections? Some clues have come from investigating the monkey brain. Cells that respond to both vision and touch have been found in the parietal and premotor cortex—higher areas, upstream of the somatosensory **[Hack #12]** and visual areas, which deal mainly with touch and vision alone.

The parietal cortex [Hack #8] contains areas that are concerned with visual and spatial representation. The premotor cortex is involved in representing and selecting movements.

These cells usually respond to stimuli coming from the same region of space: a cell might respond to a finger being touched and to a light close to that finger. The most fascinating thing about some of these cells is that when the monkey moves its arm around, the region of visual space to which the cell responds also moves. Such cells are thought to represent the space that is close to our bodies. It is particularly important for us to merge together information from our different senses about this, our peripersonal space, which is within our immediate reach.

Spence and colleagues[5] gave a patient with a split brain (whose left and right hemispheres were disconnected [Hack #69]) the same touch and vision distraction task as described earlier. The patient behaved as normal with his right hand in the right side of space. That is, the lights on the right side produced the greatest interference. In this case, both touch and vision arrived first at the left hemisphere of his brain. When he moved his right hand over to the left side of space, we would now expect his right hand to be disrupted most by the nearby lights on the left side. However, the lights on the right side still interfered most with touches to the right hand (despite being on the opposite side of space to his hand). In this case, the lights on the left arrived first at the right hemisphere and touches to the right hand at the left hemisphere, and without connections between the two halves of his brain, he was unable to update. This shows how important the long-range connections between distant cortical areas of the brain are for remapping.

The fact that the updating of our posture and remapping of our visual-tactile links appears to occur before conscious awareness could explain why we take them for granted in our everyday lives. Some people seem to find such processing easier than others. Could experience affect these abilities? Might drummers who spend many hours playing with their arms crossed find remapping easier?

End Notes

1. Maravita, A., Spence, C., & Driver, J. (2003). Multisensory integration and the body schema: Close to hand and within reach. *Current Biology, 13*, R531–R539.

2. Yamamoto, S., & Kitazawa, S. (2001). Reversal of subjective temporal order due to arm crossing. *Nature Neuroscience 4*, 759–765.

3. Shore, D. I., Spry, E., & Spence, C. (2002). Confusing the mind by crossing the hands. *Cognitive Brain Research, 14*, 153–163.

4. Kitazawa, S. (2002). Where conscious sensation takes place. *Consciousness and Cognition, 11*, 475–477.

5. Spence, C. J., Kingstone, A., Shore, D. I., & Gazzaniga, M. S. (2001). Representation of visuotactile space in the split brain. *Psychological Science, 12*, 90–93.

—Ellen Poliakoff

HACK #64 Mold Your Body Schema

Your body image is mutable within only a few minutes of judicious—and misleading—visual feedback.

Our brains are constantly updated with information about the position of our bodies. Rather than relying entirely on one form of sensory feedback, our bodies use both visual and tactile feedback in concert to allow us to work out where our limbs are likely to be at any one moment. *Proprioception*—generated by sensory receptors located in our joints and muscles that feed back information on muscle stretch and joint position—is another sense that is specifically concerned with body position.

The brain combines all this information to provide a unified impression of body position and shape known as the *body schema*. Nevertheless, by supplying conflicting sensory feedback during movement, we can confuse our body schema and break apart the unified impression.

In Action

Find a mirror big enough so you can stand it on its edge, perpendicular to your body, with the mirrored side facing left. Put your arms at your sides (you'll probably need a friend to hold the mirror). This whole setup is shown in Figure 6-2. Look sideways into the mirror so you can see both your left hand and its reflection in the mirror, so that it appears at first blush to be your hidden right hand. While keeping your wrists still and looking into the mirror, waggle your fingers and move both your hands in synchrony for about 30 seconds. After 30 seconds, keep your left hand moving but stop your right. You should sense a momentary feeling of "strangeness," as if disconnected from your right hand. It looks as if it is moving yet feels as if it has stopped.

Figure 6-2. Matt confuses his body schema using a mirror and curtain rail (being in dire need of a haircut isn't essential for the experiment)

One easy way of moving your hands together is to run a curtain rail under the mirror, if you have one handy, and place each hand on a curtain ring (this is what I'm doing in Figure 6-2). Move your hands toward and away from the mirror for 30 seconds, until your brain has confused your right hand and your reflected left hand in the mirror—then release the curtain ring from your right hand. You can feel the ring has gone, but in the mirror it looks as though you're still holding it. To me, the disconnect felt like pins and needles, all through my right hand.

Alternatively, you can manipulate your body schema into incorporating a table as part of yourself.[1] Sit at a table with a friend at your side. Put one hand on your knee, out of sight under the table. Your friend's job is to tap, touch, and stroke your hidden hand and—with identical movements using her other hand—to tap the top of the table directly above. Do this for a couple of minutes. It helps if you concentrate on the table where your friend is touching, and it's important you don't get hints of how your friend is touching your hidden hand. The more irregular the pattern and the better synchronized the movements on your hand and on the table, the greater the chance this will work for you. About 50% of people begin to feel as if the tapping sensation is arising from the table, where they can see the tapping happening before their very eyes. If you're lucky, the simultaneous touching and visual input have led the table to be incorporated into your body image.

How It Works

These techniques provide conflicting touch and visual feedback, making it difficult to maintain a consistent impression of exactly where body parts are located in space. They're similar to the crossed hands illusion [Hack #63], in which twisting your hands generates visual feedback contradictory to your body schema. In the crossed hands illusion, this leads to movement errors, and in the preceding techniques leads to the sense of being momentarily disconnected from our own movements.

Some of our best information on the body schema has been from patients who have had limbs amputated. More than 90% of amputees with reporting an experience of a "phantom limb": they still experience sensations (sometimes pain) from an amputated body part. This suggests that the brain represents some aspects of body position and sensation as an internal model that does not entirely depend on sensory feedback. Further evidence is provided by a rare disorder called *autotopagnosia:* despite the patients having intact limbs, brain injury (particularly to the left parietal lobe [Hack #8]) causes a loss of spatial knowledge about the body so severe that they are unable to even point to a body part when asked.

These disorders suggest that the brain's system for representing body schema can operate (and be damaged) independently from the sensory feedback provided by the body itself. Sensory feedback must play a role of course, and it seems that it is used to update and correct the model to keep it in check with reality. In some situations, like the ones in the previous exercises, one type of sensory feedback can become out of sync with the others, leading to the experience of mild confusion of the body schema.

Ramachandran and Rogers-Ramachandran applied an understanding of the relationship between sensory feedback and the body schema to create a novel method to help people with phantom-limb pain.[2] They used a mirror to allow people who were experiencing a phantom limb to simulate visual experience of their amputated hand. In the same way as the earlier exercise, the image of their amputated hand was simply a reflection of their remaining hand, but this simulated feedback provided enough information to the brain so they felt as if they could control and move their phantom limb. In some cases, they were able to "move" their limb out of positions that had been causing them real pain.

An fMRI [Hack #4] study by Donna Lloyd and colleagues[3] might explain why visual feedback of body position might have such a dramatic effect. They scanned people while they were receiving tactile stimulation to the right hand, either while they had their eyes closed or while they were looking directly at their hand. When participants had the opportunity to view where they were being stimulated, activation shifted dramatically, not only to the parietal area, known to be involved in representing the body schema, but also to the premotor area, a part of the brain involved in planning and executing movements. This may also explain why the earlier exercises confuse our body schema enough to make accurate movement seem difficult or feel unusual. Visual information from viewing our body seems to activate brain areas involved in planning our next move.

End Notes

1. Ramachandran, V. S., & Blakeslee, S. (1998). Phantoms in the Brain: Human Nature and the Architecture of the Mind. London: Fourth Estate.

2. Ramachandran, V. S., & Rogers-Ramachandran, D. (1996). Synaesthesia in phantom limbs induced with mirrors. *Proceedings of the Royal Society of London. Series B. Biological sciences, 263*(1369), 377–386.

3. Lloyd, D. M., Shore, D. I., Spence, C., & Calvert, G. A. (2002). Multisensory representation of limb position in human premotor cortex. *Nature Neuroscience, 6*(1), 17–18.

See Also

- Tool use extends the body schema with its reach, altering the map the brain keeps of our own body: Maravita, A., & Iriki, A. (2004). Tools for the body (schema). *Trends in Cognitive Sciences, 8*(2), 79–86.

—Vaughan Bell

Why Can't You Tickle Yourself?

#65   Experiments with tickling provide hints as to how the brain registers self-generated and externally generated sensations.

Most of us can identify a ticklish area on our body that, when touched by someone else, makes us laugh. Even chimpanzees, when tickled under their arms, respond with a sound equivalent to laughter; rats, too, squeal with pleasure when tickled. Tickling is a curious phenomenon, a sensation we surrender to almost like a reflex. Francis Bacon in 1677 commented that "[when tickled] men even in a grieved state of mind…cannot sometimes forebear laughing." It can generate both pleasure and pain: a person being tickled might simultaneously laugh hysterically and writhe in agony. Indeed, in Roman times, continuous tickling of the feet was used as a method of torture. Charles Darwin, however, theorized that tickling is an important part of social and sexual bonding. He also noted that for tickling to be effective in making us laugh, the person doing the tickling should be someone we are familiar with, but that there should also be an element of unpredictability.

As psychoanalyst Adam Phillips commented, tickling "cannot be reproduced in the absence of another." So, for tickling to induce its effect, there needs to be both a tickler and a ticklee. Here are a couple of experiments to try in the privacy of your own home—you'll need a friend, however, to play along.

Tickle Predicting

First, you can look at why there's a difference between being tickled by yourself and by someone else.

In action. Try tickling yourself on the palm of your hand and notice how it feels. It might feel a little ticklish. Now, ask a friend to tickle you in the same place and note the difference. This time, it tickles much more.

How it works. When you experience a sensation or generate an action, how do you know whether it was you or someone else who caused it? After all, there is no special signal from the skin receptors to tell you that it was generated by you or by something in the environment. The sensors in your arm cannot tell who's stimulating them. The brain solves this problem using a prediction system called a *forward model*. The brain's motor system makes predictions about the consequences of a movement and uses the predictions to label sensations as self-produced or externally produced.

Every time an action is made, the brain generates an *efference copy* of the actual motor command in parallel. The efference copy is just like a carbon copy, or duplicate, of the real motor command and is used to make a prediction about the effect of the action, for example, the tickling effect of a finger stroke. The predicted sensory effect of the efference copy and the actual sensory effect of the motor command are compared (Figure 6-3). If there is a mismatch, the sensation is labeled as externally generated.

Your accurate prediction of the consequences of the self-tickle reduces the sensory effects (the tickliness) of the action, but this does not happen when someone else tickles you. This explains why the sensation is usually more

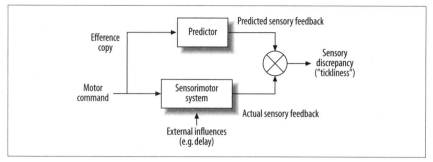

Figure 6-3. Forward model: an internal predictor uses information about movements to distinguish between self-produced and externally produced sensations

intense when another person touches your arm compared with when you touch your own arm.

Neuroimaging studies using a tickling machine (Figure 6-4) at University College London[1] suggest that the distinction between self and other is hardwired in the brain. This device was used to apply a soft piece of foam to the participant's left palm. In one condition, the participant self-produced the touch stimulus with his right hand, and in the other condition, the experimenter produced the stimulus. The participant's brain was scanned during the experiment to investigate the brain basis of self-produced versus externally produced touch. Results show stronger activation of the *somatosensory cortex* and *anterior cingulate*, parts of the brain involved in processing touch and pleasure, respectively, when a person is tickled by someone else, compared with when they tickle themselves. The *cerebellum*, a part of the brain that is generally associated with movement, also responds differently to self-produced and externally produced touch, and it may have a role in predicting the sensory consequences of self-touch but not external touch. (See "Get Acquainted with the Central Nervous System" **[Hack #7]** for more about these parts of the brain.)

One study used two robots to trick the brain into reacting to a self-tickle as if it were an external tickle.[2] In the right hand, participants held an object attached to the first robot. This was connected to a second robot, attached to which was a piece of foam that delivered a touch stimulus to the palm of the left hand. Movement of the participant's right hand therefore caused movement of the foam, as if by remote control. The robotic interface was used to introduce time delays between the movement of the participant's right hand and the touch sensation on the left palm, and participants were asked to rate the "tickliness" (Figure 6-5).

When there was no time delay, the condition was equivalent to a self-produced tickle because the participant determined the instant delivery of the

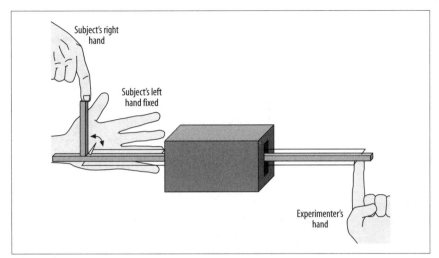

Figure 6-4. Tickling machine: this device was used to apply a soft piece of foam to the participant's left palm

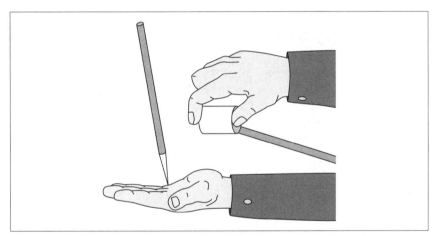

Figure 6-5. Tickling robots: participants found the stimulus more tickly as the time delay increased

touch stimulus by movements of the right hand. Greater delay between the causal action and the sensory effect (up to 300 ms) meant participants experienced the touch as more tickly.This suggests that, when there is no time delay, the brain can accurately predict the touch stimulus so that the sensory effect is attenuated. Introducing a time delay increases the likelihood of a discrepancy between the predicted and actual sensory effect. As a result, there is less attenuation of the tickly sensation, which tricks the brain into labeling the stimulus as external. By making the consequences of our own action unpredictable, therefore, the brain treats the self as another.

Force Prediction

You can see how we anticipate a stimulus and compensate for it, by attempting to estimate a force and seeing whether you can get that right.

In action. Use your right index finger to press down gently on the back of a friend's hand. Your friend should then use her right index finger to press down on the same spot on your hand with the same force that she felt from your finger press. Continue taking turns at this—reproducing the same force each time—and you may notice that after about 10 turns, the forces of your finger presses are getting stronger.

How it works. This predictive process may also be at the root of why physical fights tend to escalate. Notice how tit-for-tat tussles between children (or indeed brawls between adults) intensify, with each person claiming that the other hit him harder. In a recent study,[3] a motor was used to apply a brief force to the tip of each participant's left index finger. Participants were then asked to match the force they felt using their right index finger to push down on their left index finger through a force transducer.

Results showed that participants consistently applied a stronger force than that which was applied to them. The authors suggest that, just as when we try to tickle ourselves, the brain predicts the sensory consequences of the self-generated force and then reduces the sensation. We can only predict the outcome of our own actions and not of someone else's, so an externally generated force feels more intense. As a result, if you were to deliver a vengeful punch to match the force of your opponent's blow, it is likely that you would overestimate the strength of the opponent's punch and strike back harder.

Why have we evolved the inability to tickle ourselves? The force generation experiment shows that sensations that are externally caused are enhanced. Similarly, our reactions to tickling may have evolved to heighten our sensitivity to external stimuli that pose a threat. Our sensory systems are constantly bombarded with sensory stimulation from the environment. It is therefore important to filter out sensory stimulation that is uninteresting—such as the results of our own movements—in order to pick out, and attend to, sensory information that carries more evolutionary importance, such as someone touching us. When a bee lands on your shoulder or a spider climbs up your leg, the brain ensures that you attend to these potentially dangerous external stimuli by ignoring feelings from your own movements. The predictive system therefore protects us and tickling may just be an accidental consequence.

End Notes

1. Blakemore, S-J, Wolpert, D. M., & Frith, C. D. (1998). Central cancellation of self-produced tickle sensation. *Nature Neuroscience, 1*(7), 635–640.

2. Blakemore, S-J, Frith, C. D., & Wolpert, D. W. (1999). Spatiotemporal prediction modulates the perception of self-produced stimuli. *Journal of Cognitive Neuroscience, 11*(5), 551–559.

3. Shergill, S., Bays, P. M., Frith, C. D., & Wolpert, D. M. (2003). Two eyes for an eye: The neuroscience of force escalation. *Science, 301*(5630), 187.

See Also

- Weiskrantz, L., Elliot, J., & Darlington, C. (1971). Preliminary observations of tickling oneself. *Nature, 230*(5296), 598–599.

- Wolpert, D. M., Miall, C. M., & Kawato, M. (1998). Internal models in the cerebellum. *Trends in Cognitive Sciences, 2*(9), 338–347.

—Suparna Choudhury and Sarah-Jayne Blakemore

HACK #66 Trick Half Your Mind

When it comes to visual processing in the brain, it's all about job delegation. We've got one pathway for consciously perceiving the world—recognizing what's what—and another for getting involved—using our bodies to interact with the world out there.

The most basic aspects of the visual world are processed altogether at the back of your brain. After that, however, the same visual information is used for different purposes by two separate pathways. One pathway flows forward from the back of your brain to the *inferior temporal cortex* near your ears, where memories are stored about what things are. The other pathway flows forward and upward toward the crown of your head, to the *posterior parietal cortex*, where your mental models of the outside world reside. Crudely speaking, the first pathway (the "ventral" pathway) is for recognizing things and consciously perceiving them, whereas the second (the "dorsal" pathway) is for interacting with them. (Well, that's according to the dual-stream theory of visual processing [Hack #13].)

The idea was developed by David Milner and Melvyn Goodale in the 1990s, inspired in part by observation of neurological patients with damage to one pathway but not the other. Patients with damage to the temporal lobe often have difficulty recognizing things—a toothbrush, say—but when asked to interact with the brush they have no problems. In contrast, patients with damage to the parietal lobe show the opposite pattern; they often have no trouble recognizing an object but are unable to reach out and grasp it appropriately.

Since then, psychologists have found behavioral evidence for this separation of function in people without neurological problems, using visual illusions.

In Action

In the mid-'90s, Salvatore Aglioti[1] and colleagues showed that when people are presented with the Ebbinghaus illusion (see Figure 6-6) they find the disk surrounded by smaller circles seems larger than an identically sized disk surrounded by larger circles, and yet, when they reach for the central disks, they use the same, appropriate, finger-thumb grip shape for both disks. The brain's conscious perceptual system (the ventral pathway) appears to have been tricked by the visual illusion, whereas the brain's visuomotor (hand-eye) system (the dorsal pathway) appears immune.

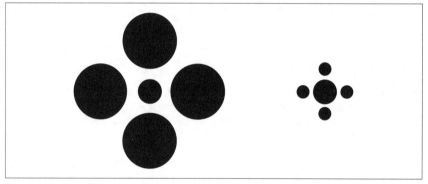

Figure 6-6. The Ebbinghaus Illusion. Both central circles are the same size; although they don't look it to your perceptual system, your visuomotor system isn't fooled

There are many examples of situations in which our perception seems to be tricked while our brain's visuomotor system remains immune. Here's one you can try. You'll need a friend and a tape measure. Find a sandy beach so you can draw in the sand or a tarmac area where you can draw on the ground with chalk. Tell your friend to look away while you prepare things.

Part 1. Draw a line in the sand, between 2 and 3 meters long. Now draw a disk at the end, about 70 cm in diameter, as in Figure 6-7A. Ask your friend to stand so her toes are at the start of the line, with the disk at far end, and get her to estimate how long the line is, using whichever units she's happy with. Then blindfold her, turn her 90°, and get her to pace out how long she thinks the line is. Measure her "walked" estimate with your tape measure.

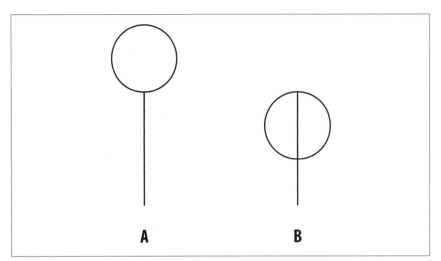

Figure 6-7. A draw-it-yourself visual illusion

Part 2. Tell your friend to look away again, get rid of the first line, and draw another one of identical length. (You could use another length if you think your friend might suspect what's going on—it just makes comparing estimates easier if you use the same length twice.) This time, draw the disk at the end so that it overlays the line, as in Figure 6-7B. Now do exactly as before: get your friend to stand with her toes at the line start and guess the length verbally from where she is, blindfold her, and ask her to walk the same length as she thinks the line is.

Part 3. You should find that your friend's spoken estimate of the second line is less than her estimate of the first, even though both lines were the same length. That's the visual illusion. (If you used different length lines, this difference will be in relative terms.) And yet her walked-out estimates should be pretty much the same (i.e., not tricked by the illusion), or at least you should find she underestimates the second line's length far less when walking. That is, her conscious judgment should be tricked more by this illusion (a version of a famous illusion called the Muller-Lyer illusion), than her walked-out estimate, controlled by her dorsal stream.

How It Works

How it works depends upon whom you ask. Advocates of the dual-stream theory of visual processing argue that these demonstrations, of the immunity of our actions to visual illusions, are evidence for the separateness of the dorsal (action) and ventral (perception) streams. The ventral stream is susceptible, they argue, because it processes objects relative to their surroundings, assessing the current context in order that we might recognize things.

The dorsal stream, by contrast, is invulnerable to such illusions because it processes objects of interest in egocentric coordinates, relative to the observer, so that we might accurately interact with them.

Doubters of the dual-stream theory take a different view. One reason we are sometimes duped by illusions, and sometimes not, they argue, is all to do with the type of task, far less to do with there being separate processing pathways in our brain. For instance, when we view the Ebbinghaus illusion (Figure 6-6), we are typically asked to compare the two central disks. Yet, when we reach for one of the disks, we are focused on only one disk at a time. Perceptual tasks tend to involve taking context and nearby objects into account, whereas motor tasks tend to involve focusing on one object at a time and, by necessity, using egocentric coordinates to interact accurately. When changing the task conditions reverses these tendencies, the visuomotor system can be found to be susceptible to illusion or the perceptual system invulnerable.

Which argument is right? Well, there's evidence both ways and the debate will probably roll on for some time yet.[2,3] What is clear, is that this phenomenon provides yet another example [Hack #62] of how our illusory sense of a unified self keeps all these conflicting processes conveniently out of mind.

Does the world really appear as you're seeing it? Who cares? Just sit back and enjoy the view, accurate or not, while your neurons fight things out.

End Notes

1. Aglioti, S. et al. (1995). Size contrast illusions deceive the eye but not the hand. *Current Biology, 5*, 679–685.

2. Franz, V. H. (2001). Action does not resist visual illusions. *Trends in Cognitive Sciences, 5*, 457–459.

3. Milner, D., & Dyde, R. (2003). Why do some perceptual illusions affect visually guided action, when others don't? *Trends in Cognitive Sciences, 7*, 10–11.

—Christian Jarrett

Objects Ask to Be Used
HACK #67

When we see objects, they automatically trigger the movements we'd make to use them.

How do we understand and act upon objects around us? We might perceive the shape and colors of a cup of coffee, recognize what it is, and then decide that the most appropriate movement would be to lift it by the handle toward our mouth. However, there seems to be something rather more direct and automatic going on. In the 1960s, James Gibson developed the idea of object *affordances*. Objects appear to be associated with (or *afford*) a particular action or actions, and the mere sight of such an object is sufficient to trigger that movement in our mind. There are obvious advantages to such a system: it could allow us to respond quickly and appropriately to objects around us, without having to go to the bother of consciously recognizing (or thinking about) them. In other words, there is a direct link between perceiving an object and acting upon it. I don't just see my cup of coffee; it also demands to be picked up and drunk.

In Action

You may not believe me yet, but I'm sure you can think of a time when your movements appeared to be automatically captured by something in your environment. Have you ever seen a door handle with a "Push" sign clearly displayed above it, yet found yourself automatically pulling the door toward you? The shape of the pullable handle suggests that you should pull it, despite the contradictory instruction to push it. I go through such a door several times a week and still find myself making that same mistake!

Try finding such a door near where you live or work. Sit down and watch how people interact with it. What happens if you cover up the "Push" sign with a blank piece of paper? Or cover it with a piece of paper labeled "Pull"; does this appear to affect how often people pull rather than push, or is the shape of the handle all they're really paying attention to?

Perhaps you've found yourself picking up a cup or glass from the table in front of you, even though you didn't mean to (or even knowing that it belonged to someone else)?

Effects of object affordances have been found in experiments: Tucker and Ellis[1] asked subjects to press a button with their left or right hand, to indicate whether a picture of an object was the right way up or inverted. Even though subjects were not thinking about the action they would use for that object, it had an effect. If they saw a cup with a handle pointing toward the right—evoking a right-hand grasp—they were faster to react if their response also happened to require a right-hand response. That is, the reaction time improved if the hand used for the button press coincided with the hand that *would* be used for interacting with the object. This is called a *compatibility effect*. (The Simon Effect [Hack #56] shows that reaction times improve when stimuli and response match in the more general case. What's happening here is that the stimulus includes not just what you perceive directly, but what affordances you can perceive too.)

The graspability of objects can affect judgments, even when people are not making any kind of movement. de'Sperati and Stucchi[2] asked people to judge which way a moving screwdriver was rotating on a computer screen. People were slower to make a judgment if the handle were in a position that would involve an awkward grasping movement with their dominant hand. That is, although they had no intention to move, their own movement system was affecting their perceptual judgment.

How It Works

Brain imaging has helped us to understand what is happening when we see action-relevant objects. Grèzes and Decety[3] looked at which brain areas are active when people do the Tucker and Ellis judgment task. Bits of their brain become active, like the supplementary motor area and the cerebellum, which are also involved in making real movements. In related research in monkeys, cells have also been discovered that respond both when the monkey sees a particular object and also when it observes the type of action that object would require.

People with damage to their frontal lobes sometimes have problems suppressing the tendency to act upon objects. They might automatically pick up a cup or a pair of glasses, without actually wishing to do so (or even when they're told not to). It is thought that we all share these same tendencies, but with our intact frontal lobes, we are better at stopping ourselves from acting them out. (Frontal patients can also have trouble suppressing other impulses; for instance, some become compulsive gamblers.)

So, objects can produce movements within our mind, but just how do they do so? We don't know the answer to this yet. One possibility is that these effects happen automatically, as Gibson suggested. Our system for visual perception has two routes [Hack #66]: the ventral (or "what?") route, concerned with the identity of the object and the dorsal ("where?" or "how?") route, concerned with location and action. Affordances may act directly on the dorsal stream, without relying on any higher processing; information about the type of movement might be extracted directly from the shape or location of the object.

However, our knowledge about objects must play a role. We certainly couldn't have evolved to respond to everyday objects of today—prehistoric man didn't live in a world filled with door handles and coffee mugs! These automatic responses must be learned through experience. Recently, Tucker and Ellis[4] found that merely seeing an object's name was enough to speed reaction times to produce the relevant size of grasp. Thus, our previous experience and knowledge about acting upon objects become bound up with the way that we represent each object in our brains. So, whenever you see (or simply consider) an object, the possibility of what you might do with it is automatically triggered in your mind.

> One point to remember from this research is that objects will exert a constant "pull" on people to be used in the ways that they afford. Don't be surprised if people who are tired, in a hurry, or simply not paying attention (or who just have a lack of respect for how you wanted the object to be used) end up automatically responding to the actions the object offers. One practical example: if you don't want something to be used by accident (e.g., an ejector seat), don't have it triggered by the same action as something else that is used constantly without much thought (e.g., have it triggered by a twist switch, rather than by a button like the ignition).
>
> —T. S.

End Notes

1. Tucker, M., & Ellis, R. (1998). On the relationship between seen objects and components of potential actions. *Journal of Experimental Psychology: Human Perception and Performance, 24,* 830–846.

2. de'Sperati, C., & Stucchi, N. (1997). Recognizing the motion of a graspable object is guided by handedness. *NeuroReport, 8,* 2761–2765.

3. Grezes, J., & Decety, J. (2002). Does visual perception of object afford action? Evidence from a neuroimaging study. *Neuropsychologia, 40,* 212–222.

4. Tucker, M., & Ellis, R. (2004). Action priming by briefly presented objects. *Acta Psychologica, 116,* 185–203.

—*Ellen Poliakoff*

Test Your Handedness

HACK #68

We all have a hand preference when undertaking manual tasks. But why is this so? And do you always prefer the same hand, or does it vary with what you are doing? Does the way people vary their hand preference differ between right- and left-handers?

The world is a right-handed one, as will be obvious to left-handers. Most tools are made for right-handed people. Implements such as scissors, knives, coffee pots, and so on are all constructed for the right-handed majority. In consequence, the accident rate for left-handers is higher than for right—and not just in tool use; the rate of traffic fatalities among left-handers is also greater than for right.[1]

> The word "sinister," which now means "ill-omened," originally meant "left-handed." The corresponding word for "right-handed" is "dexter," from which we get the word "dexterous."
>
> —T.S.

Nine out of 10 people are right-handed.[2] The proportion appears to have been stable over thousands of years and across all cultures in which handedness has been examined. Anthropologists have been able to determine the incidence of handedness in ancient cultures by examining artifacts, such as the shape of flint axes. Based on evidence like this and other evidence such as writing about handedness in antiquity, our species appears always to have been a predominantly right-handed one.

But even right-handers vary in just how right-handed they are, and this variation may have a link to how you use the different sides of your brain [Hack #69].

In Action

Have a go at the following tests to determine which is your dominant hand and just how dominant it is. Do each test twice—once with each hand—and record your score, in seconds, both times. You don't have to do all of them; just see which you can do given the equipment you have on hand.

Darts
> Throw three darts at a dartboard. (Be very careful when doing this with your off-hand!) Add up the distances from the bull's-eye.

Handwriting
> Measure the time that it takes to write the alphabet as one word, six times. Start with the hand you normally write with and rest for 1 minute before starting with the other hand.

Drawing
> Measure the time that it takes to draw a line between two of the lines of some lined paper. Add a penalty of 2 seconds for each time your line touches one of the ruled lines.

Picking up objects with tweezers
> Using tweezers, measure the time that it takes to pick up and transfer 12 pieces of wire from one container to another.

Stoppering bottles

Measure the time, in seconds, it takes to put the lids on five jars, the corks back in five wine bottles, or the cap back on five beer bottles.

Here's how to calculate your handedness quotient:

```
(Left-hand score - Right-hand score) / (Right-hand score + Left-hand score)
x 100
```

You can now see how the score differs for the different tasks and take an average to see your average dominance. Positive numbers mean right-handedness, negative numbers mean left-handedness. Bigger numbers mean greater dominance by one hand.

How It Works

By doing the previous tests, you can see that you can still use your off-hand for some things and that it is easier to use your off-hand for some things than for other things. Most people have some things for which they use their dominant hand, some things they may use both for, and some for which they use their off-hand.

So, in a sense, describing people as left-handed or right-handed is limiting because it puts them into only one category and ignores the extent to which they may be in that category—or in between the two. This is why, of course, we used behavioral measures to work out the handedness quotient, rather than just asking people.[3]

Handedness is only weakly genetic. The child of two left-handers has a 45–50% chance of being left-handed, and thus handedness must partly be to do with how the child is brought up as well, so we know that there is a large nongenetic influence on whether you turn out to be a left-hander. Evidence also suggests that left-handedness may be associated with neurological insult in the womb or during delivery.[4]

If you try the test out on a few people, you will see that left-handed people more easily use their right hand than right-handed people use their left hand. In part, this is probably because our right-handed world forces left-handers to learn to use their right more, and it could also be for deeper reasons to do with brain lateralization as well.

Nine out of 10 people use their right hand predominantly, and at least 9 out of 10 people have their major functions on their left side.[5] This includes around two-thirds of left-handers. Everyone else, a significant minority, either uses the right hemisphere for speech or uses both hemispheres.[6]

One test of which half of the brain is dominant for language is the Wada test. This involves a short-acting anesthetic (e.g., sodium amytal) being injected into the carotid artery. This transiently anesthetizes the left hemisphere, thus testing the functional capabilities of the affected half of the brain. People for whom the left hemisphere is indeed dominant for language (i.e., most of us) will temporarily become aphasic, losing the ability to comprehend or produce language. If counting at the time, you'll stop being able to do so for a few beats when injected with the anesthetic.

The reason most people are still left-brainers for language may be due to how our brain functions became lateralized [Hack #69] before the evolution of language, the brain lateralizing separately from the use of our hands.

It has been suggested that the speech areas of the brain developed near the motor cortex because hand gestures were the principal form of communication before speech.[7] Studies show that, when a participant observes hand and mouth gestures, parts of the motor cortex (F5) and Broca's area (found in the left frontal lobe, specifically involved in the production of language) are stimulated. It is argued that before speech our ancestors used gestures to communicate, much as monkeys and apes do now (i.e., lip smacks). And so the human speech circuit is a consequence of the precursor of Broca's area, which was endowed (before speech) with mechanisms to recognize action made by others, from which speech developed.

It is plausible that only the one hand (the right) was used for a more efficient and simple way of communicating. This would explain why language and hand dominance are on the same side (remember, the left side of the brain controls the right side of the body, so left-language dominance and right-hand dominance are both due to the left side of the brain).

If this were the norm during evolution, it may help to explain why most left-handers still have speech areas in the left hemisphere. However, this still doesn't answer the question of why the right hand was dominant in the beginning. At present, this can be only speculation; the important point is that right- and left-handedness are distributed differently—they are not mirror images of each other, which has implications for the genetics of handedness and the laterality of other functions.

It has been argued that the original hand preferences evolved from a postural position preference of the right hand and consequently a left preference for reaching in *arboreal* (tree-living) species.[8] So, with postural demands becoming less pronounced in ground-dwelling species, the left hand remained the dominant one for highly stereotyped tasks like simple reaching, whereas the right became the preferred one for more manipulative tasks or tasks requiring some skill. In other words, we would hang on with the left hand and pick fruit with the right.

Although this is an interesting theory for why the majority of the population is right-handed, it does not give any indication as to why some people are left-handed. Are left-handed people highly skilled in reaching? Are left-handed people as skilled in manipulative tasks as their right-handed counterparts? Regretfully, these questions have to wait for further research.

End Notes

1. Salive, M. E., Guralink, J. M., & Glynn, R. J. (1993). Left-handedness and mortality. *American Journal of Public Health, 83*, 265–267.

2. Annet, M. (1972). The distribution of manual asymmetry. *The British Journal of Psychology, 63*, 343–358.

3. Hartlage, L. C., & Gage, R. (1997). Unimanual performance as a measure of laterality. *Neuropsyhological Review, 7*(3), 143–156.

4. Bakan, P. (1971). Handedness and birth order. *Nature, 229*, 195.

5. Davidson, R. J., & Hugdahl, K (eds.) (1995). *Brain Asymmetry*. Cambridge, MA: MIT Press.

6. Rasmussen, T., & Milner, B. (1977). The role of early left-brain injury in determining lateralization of cerebral speech functions. *Annals of the New York Academy of Sciences*, 299, 355–369.

7. Rizzolatti, G., & Arbib, A. (1998). Language within our grasp. *Trends in Neurosciences, 21*, 188–194.

8. MacNeilage, P. E. (1990). The "Postural Origins" theory of primate neurobiological asymmetries. In N. A. Krasneger et al. (eds.), *Biological and Behavioural Determinants of Language Development*, 165–168, Hillsdale, NJ: Erlbaum.

See Also

- Laska, M. (1996). Manual laterality in spider monkeys (Ateles geoffroyi) solving visually and tactually guided food-reaching tasks. *Cortex, 32*(4), 717–726.

—*Karen Bunday*

Use Your Right Brain—and Your Left, Too

HACK #69

The logical left brain and intuitive right brain metaphor is popular, but the real story of the difference between the two halves of your brain is more complex and more interesting.

There's a grain of truth in all the best myths, and this is true for the left-brain/right-brain myth. Our cortex is divided into left and right hemispheres, and they do seem to process information differently, but exactly how they do this isn't like the story normally told by management gurus and the self-help literature. As with many scientific myths, the real story is less intuitive but more interesting.

Our brains follow the general pattern of the rest of our bodies: two of everything down the sides and one of everything down the middle. With the brain, the two halves are joined directly in the *subcortex*, but in the cortex the two halves, called *hemispheres*, have a gap between them. They are connected by a tight bunch of some 250 million nerve fibers, called the *corpus callosum*, which runs between the two hemispheres (it's not the only way for information to cross the hemispheres, but it's the most important).

Each hemisphere is wired up to sense and act on the opposite side of the body. So information from your right goes to the left side of the visual cortex, and signals from your left motor cortex control your right hand. For higher functions, in which information from both senses is combined, the two hemispheres seem to have different strengths and weaknesses, so that for certain tasks one hemisphere or the other will be dominant.

The origins of the popular myth were studies of patients who had their corpus callosum severed as part of a radical surgical intervention for epilepsy. These "split-brain" patients could function seemingly normally on many tasks, but displayed some quirks when asked to respond to the same material with different hands or when speaking (left brain) rather than pointing with their left hand (right brain).[1]

A simple distinction between a left brain specialized for language and cold logic and an oppressed right brain that specializes in intuition grew into the myth we know today. Similar to the 10% myth [Hack #6], this led to the further conclusion that most of us use only half of our brains. Although this distinction may or may not be a useful metaphor in talking about styles of thinking, it is certainly not a useful metaphor for conducting research nor for giving insight into the true differences between the hemispheres.

Any real difference between the hemispheres may be the opposite of what people raised on the left brain bad, right brain good myth would expect. Michael Gazzaniga, who was part of the team that did the original split-brain experiments and is now a very senior cognitive neuroscientist, recently wrote in *Scientific American* of an "inventive and interpreting" left brain, a hemisphere for structure and meaning, and a "truthful, literal" right brain, limited by a preoccupation with general surface features.[2] In his research, he found that the right hemisphere contained modules specializing for computationally analyzing perceptions, in a very straightforward way, not looking for any deeper meaning. It's not good at smart search strategies, for example. The left hemisphere is better at high-level associations and problem solving, including language, looking for meaning, and patterns.

In Action

Many of the original demonstrations of hemispheric specialization involve showing an image to just one *hemifield* of the eyes. Information from both eyes is processed by both hemispheres of the brain, but in both eyes, the information to the left of the focal point is processed by the right hemisphere and vice versa. By making sure someone is looking straight ahead, you can control which hemisphere processes an image by presenting it to the left or the right of his focal point—one hemifield. You have to do it very quickly; as soon as an image appears before them, people will move their eyes to look at it and thus feed the information to both hemispheres. Since this is difficult to do with vision, here's a nonvisual demo you can try at home.[3]

The left hemisphere is better at processing rapidly occurring sounds and seems better at keeping rhythm; it can hold fancier rhythms and keep them synchronized with a beat better than the right hemisphere.

To show this in action, start tapping a regular beat with your left hand (1-2-3-4- etc.) and then start tapping a fancy beat at the same time with the right hand (jazzy, syncopated, like a melody line to accompany the regular beat). Now, try starting with the regular beat on the right hand (1-2-3-4- etc.), and after a measure or two, start the fancy beat on the left. See what happens. You should find it easier the first way round, with your left hemisphere controlling the more difficult rhythm (your right hand).

Many left-handers actually get the same result as right-handers on this test, so it is not just to do with mere handedness. It probably isn't a coincidence that a piano keyboard is organized with the lower notes, which are used for simpler rhythms, on the left side where they can be delegated to the right hemisphere.

How It Works

By comparing the performance of normal people on tasks that give information to different hemispheres and by comparing responses controlled by different hemispheres, cognitive neuroscientists have uncovered a number of
functions that are done differently by the different hemispheres, and some
patterns are beginning to appear in the data.

The most obvious specialized function is language. Speech is controlled by
the left brain, and understanding the literal meaning of words and sentence
grammar is supported by the left brain in most people (but not all). But that
doesn't mean that the right brain has no role in language processing. Studies of people with right-brain damage, along with other evidence, have suggested that the right brain may support analyzing global features of language
such as mood and implication. If I say, "Can you close the window?" I'm
not asking if you are able, I'm asking if you will. A step more complex is to
say, "It's cold in here," which is the same request, but more oblique (but
maybe not as oblique as "Why are you so selfish?"). It is this kind of pragmatic reasoning in language that some researchers think is supported by the
right brain.

The left-brain specialization for language carries over to an advantage in
sequential ordering and symbolic, logical reasoning.

The right brain seems specialized for visual and spatial processing, such as
mental rotation or remembering maps and faces, dealing with the appearance of things, and with understanding the overall pattern. We have a bias
whereby we judge faces by their left side.[4] You can see a demonstration of
this at *http://perception.st-and.ac.uk/hemispheric/explanation.html*. The web
site shows two faces, one looking more female than the other (see
Figure 6-8). In fact, the faces are both equally male and female, but the one
that looks female has the more female half on the left side (right-hemisphere
processing) and the male half on the right side, where it doesn't affect your
judgment of gender. Test this now by covering the left sides of the faces in
Figure 6-8 and looking again; you can now see that the face you first judged
as female is half-male and the face you judged as male is half-female.

Like perceiving gender and moods, musical appreciation also appears to
mostly involve right-brain-dominant processes (although, as we've seen, for
keeping complex rhythms, the left brain is dominant).

Brain imaging studies have suggested that these kind of results can be understood by thinking of the hemispheres as specialized for different kinds of processing, not as specialized for processing different kinds of things. One study[6]
involved showing subjects letters made up of lots of little letters (e.g., the letter *A* made up of lots of little *S*s). The left brain responded to the detail (the

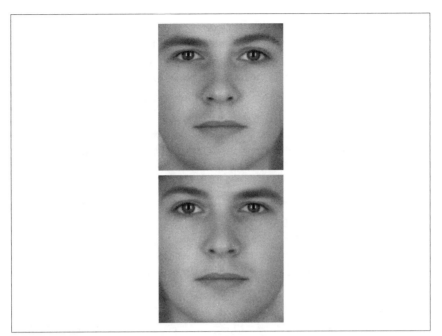

Figure 6-8. Both faces are equally male and female, but on different sides; your right brain dominates the perception of gender in faces, so you see one as more male and the other as more female[5]

small letters) and the right brain to the global picture (the large letter constructed out of small letters). Subsequent work has shown that the story isn't as clear as this study suggests. It seems you can get the left-detail/right-global pattern to reverse with the correct kinds of stimulus-task combination—but it has confirmed that the hemispheric dominance is due to the demands of the task, not due to the nature of the information being processed.[7] This gives some tentative legitimacy to the idea that there are left-brain and right-brain styles of processing.

But the important thing is how the two hemispheres combine, not how they perform in artificial situations like those of the split-brain patients. Brain imaging studies of normal people are based on the average results across many brains, and this tends to play down the large variation between different individuals in how the functions are distributed across the brain. Ultimately, however people's brains are wired, they will be using both sides to deal with situations they encounter—so it isn't too helpful to become preoccupied with which half does what and whether they are processing with their left or their right.

End Notes

1. It was even claimed the two hemispheres of a patient's split brain were conscious in different ways (*http://www.macalester.edu/~psych/whathap/UBNRP/Split_Brain/Split_Brain_Consciousness.html*).

2. Gazzaniga, M. S. (1998). The split brain revisited. *Scientific American, 279*(1), 50–55. (reprinted and updated 2002).

3. This demo is from the book *The Lopsided Ape* by Michael C. Corballis (Oxford University Press, paperback, 1991), p.267. Many thanks to Michael Parker (*http://www.michaelparker.com*) for bringing it to our attention.

4. At least we judge *holistic* features of faces (like gender or mood) by their left side, using our right hemisphere. Neuroimaging research shows left hemisphere involvement in analyzing the *parts* of faces. Rossion, B. et al. (2000). Hemispheric asymmetries for whole-based and part-based face processing in the human fusiform gyrus. *Journal of Cognitive Neuroscience, 12*, 793–802.

5. © Michael Burt, Perception Lab, *http://perception.st-and.ac.uk*.

6. Fink, G. R., Halligan, P. W., Marshall, J. C., et al. (1996). Where in the brain does visual attention select the forest and the trees? *Nature 382* (6592), 626–628. There is a great discussion of this article by John McCrone in *New Scientist* (13 July 1999), reprinted online (*http://web.archive.org/web/*/http://www.btinternet.com/~neuronaut/webtwo_features_leftbrain.html*).

7. Stephan, K. E., Marshall, J. C., Friston, K. J., Rowe, J. B., Ritzl, A., Zilles, K., et al. (2003). Lateralized cognitive processes and lateralized task control in the human brain. *Science, 301*(5631), 384–386.

See Also

- Other good starting points for reading about the neuroscience between the right and left brain story are ABC's "All in the Mind" (*http://www.abc.net.au/rn/science/mind/stories/s1137394.htm*), "Hemispheres" at Neuroscience for Kids (*http://faculty.washington.edu/chudler/split.html*), and "New Theories of Expression Focus on Brain's Two Sides," article by Sandra Blakeslee (*http://members.aol.com/sakrug/dualbrain.html*; reprinted from the *New York Times*).

Reasoning
Hacks 70–74

We consider ourselves pretty rational animals, and we can indeed be pretty logical when we put our minds to it. But you only have to scratch the surface to find out how easily we're misled by numbers [Hack #70], and it's well-known that statistics are really hard to understand [Hack #71]. So how good are we at being rational? It depends: our logic skills aren't too hot, for instance, until we need to catch people who might be cheating on us [Hack #72] instead of just logically solving sums. And that's the point. We have a very pragmatic kind of rationality, solving complex problems as long as they're real-life situations.

Pure rationality is overrated anyway. Figuring out logic is slow going when we can have gut feelings instead, and that's a strategy that works. Well, the placebo effect [Hack #73] works at least—belief is indeed a powerful thing. And we have a strong bias toward keeping the status quo [Hack #74] too. It's not rational, that's for sure, but don't worry; the "If it ain't broke, don't fix it" policy is a pragmatic one, at least.

Use Numbers Carefully

Our brains haven't evolved to think about numbers. Funny things happen to them as they go into our heads.

Although we can instantly appreciate how many items comprise small groups (small meaning four or fewer [Hack #35]), reasoning about bigger numbers requires counting, and counting requires training. Some cultures get by with no specific numbers higher than 3, and even numerate cultures took a while to invent something as fundamental as zero.[1]

So we don't have a natural faculty to deal with numbers explicitly; that's a cultural invention that's hitched onto natural faculties we do have. The difficulty we have when thinking about numbers is most apparent when you ask people to deal with very large numbers, with very small numbers, or with probabilities [Hack #71].

This hack shows where some specific difficulties with numbers come from and gives you some tests you can try on yourself or your friends to demonstrate them.

The biases discussed here and, in some of the other hacks in this chapter, don't affect everyone all the time. Think of them as forces, like gravity or tides. All things being equal, they will tend to push and pull your judgments, especially if you aren't giving your full attention to what you are thinking about.

In Action

How big is:

    9 x 8 x 7 x 6 x 5 x 4 x 3 x 2 x 1

How about:

    1 x 2 x 3 x 4 x 5 x 6 x 7 x 8 x 9

Since you've got both in front of you, you can easily see that they are equivalent and so must therefore equal the same number. But try this: ask someone the first version. Tell her to estimate, not to calculate—have her give her answer within 5 seconds. Now find another person and ask him to estimate the answer for the second version. Even if he sees the pattern and thinks to himself "ah, 9 factorial," unless he has the answer stored in his head, he will be influenced by the way the sum is presented.

Probably the second person you asked gave a smaller answer, and both people gave figures well below the real answer (which is a surprisingly large 362,880).

How It Works

When estimating numbers, most people start with a number that comes easily to mind—an "anchor"—and adjust up or down from that initial base. The initial number that comes to mind is really just your first guess, and there are two problems. First, people often fail to adjust sufficiently away from the first guess. Second, the guess can be easily influenced by circumstances. And the initial circumstance, in this case, is the number at the beginning of the sum.

In the previous calculations, anchors people tend to use are higher or lower depending on the first digit of the multiplication (which we read left to right). The anchors then unduly influence the estimate people make of the answer to the calculation. We start with a higher anchor for the first series than for the second. When psychologists carried out an experimental test of these two questions, the average estimate for the first series was 4200, compared to only 500 for the second.

Both estimates are well below the correct answer. Because the series as a whole is made up of small numbers, the anchor in both cases is relatively low, which biases the estimate most people make to far below the true answer.

In fact, you can give people an anchor that has nothing to do with the task you've set for them, and it still biases their reasoning. Try this experiment, which is discussed in Edward Russo and Paul Schoemaker's book *Decision Traps*.[2]

Find someone—preferably not a history major—and ask her for the last three digits of her phone number. Add 400 to this number then ask "Do you think Attila the Hun was defeated in Europe before or after X," where X is the year you got by the addition of 400 to the telephone number. Don't say whether she got it right (the correct answer is A.D. 451) and then ask "In what year would you guess Attila the Hun was defeated?" The answers you get will vary depending on the initial figure you gave, even though it is based on something completely irrelevant to the question—her own phone number!

When Russo and Schoemaker performed this experiment on a group of 500 Cornell University MBA students, they found that the number derived from the phone digits acted as a strong anchor, biasing the placing of the year of Attila the Hun's defeat. The difference between the highest and lowest anchors corresponded to a difference in the average estimate of more than 300 years.

In Real Life

You can see charities using this anchoring and adjustment hack when they send you their literature. Take a look at the "make a donation" section on the back of a typical leaflet. Usually this will ask you for something like "$50, $20, $10, $5, or an amount of your choice." The reason they suggest $50, $20, $10, then $5 rather than $5, $10, $20, then $50 is to create a higher anchor in your mind. Maybe there isn't ever much chance you'll give $50, but the "amount of your choice" will be higher because $50 is the first number they suggest.

Maybe anchoring explains why it is common to price things at a cent below a round number, such as at $9.99. Although it is only 1 cent different from $10, it feels (if you don't think about it much) closer to $9 because that's the anchor first established in your mind by the price tag.

Irrelevant anchoring and insufficient adjustment are just two examples of difficulties we have when thinking about numbers. ("Think About Frequencies Rather than Probabilities" [Hack #71] discusses extra difficulties we have when thinking about a particularly common kind of number: probabilities.)

The difficulty we have with numbers is one of the reasons people so often try to con you with them. I'm pretty sure in many debates many of us just listen to the numbers without thinking about them. Because numbers are hard, they lend an air of authority to an argument and can often be completely misleading or contradictory. For instance, "83% of statistics are completely fictitious" is a sentence that could sound convincing if you weren't paying attention—so watch out! It shows just how unintuitive this kind of reasoning is, that we still experience such biases despite most of us having done a decade or so of math classes, which have, as a major goal, to teach us to think carefully about numbers.

The lesson for communicating is that you shouldn't use numbers unless you have to. If you have to, then provide good illustrations, but beware that people's first response will be to judge by appearance rather than by the numbers. Most people won't have an automatic response to really think about the figures you give unless they are motivated, either by themselves or by you and the discussion you give of the figures.

End Notes

1. The MacTutor History of Mathematics Archive: a History of Zero (*http://www-gap.dcs.st-and.ac.uk/~history/HistTopics/Zero.html*).

2. Russo, J. E., and Schoemaker, P. J. H. (1989). *Decision Traps*. New York: Doubleday.

HACK #71 Think About Frequencies Rather than Probabilities

Probability statistics are particularly hard to think about correctly. Fortunately you can make it easier by presenting the same information in a way that meshes with our evolved capacity to reason about how often things happen.

Mark Twain once said, "People commonly use statistics like a drunk uses a lamppost: for support rather than for illumination."[1] Things haven't changed. It's strange, really, given how little people trust them, that statistics get used so much.

Our ability to think about probabilities evolved to keep us safe from rare events that would be pretty serious if they did happen (like getting eaten) and to help us learn to make near-correct estimates about things that aren't quite so dire and at which we get multiple attempts (like estimating the chances of finding food in a particular part of the valley for example). So it's not surprising that, when it comes to formal reasoning about single-case probabilities, our evolved ability to estimate likelihood tends to fail us.

One example is that we overestimate low-frequency events that are easily noticed. Just ask someone if he gets more scared traveling in a car or by airplane. Flying is about the safest form of transport there is, whether you calculate it by miles flown or trips made. Driving is pretty risky in comparison, but most people would say that flying feels like the more dangerous of the two.

Another thing we have a hard time doing is accounting for the basic frequency at which an event occurs, quite aside from the specific circumstances of its occurrence on the current occasion. Let me give an example of this in action…

In Action

This is a famous demonstration of how hard we find it to work out probabilities. When it was published in *Parade* magazine in 1990, the magazine got around 10,000 letters in response—92% of which said that their columnist, Marilyn vos Savant, had reached the wrong conclusion.[2] Despite the weight of correspondence, vos Savant *had* reached the correct conclusion, and here's the confusing problem she put forward, based roughly on the workings of the old quiz show *Let's Make a Deal* presented by Monty Hall.

Imagine you're a participant on a game show, hoping to win the big prize. The final hoop to jump through is to select the right door from a choice of three. Behind each door is either a prize (one of the three doors) or a booby prize (two of the doors). In this case, the booby prizes are goats.

You choose a door.

To raise the tension, the game-show host, Monty, looks behind the other doors and throws one open (not yours) to reveal a goat. He then gives you the choice of sticking with your choice or switching to the remaining unopened door.

Two doors are left. One *must* have a goat behind it, one *must* have a prize. Should you stick, or should you switch? Or doesn't it matter?

 This is not a trick question, like some lateral thinking puzzles. It's the statistics that are tricky, not the wording.

Most people get this wrong—even those with formal mathematics training. Many of the thousands who wrote to Marilyn vos Savant at *Parade* were university professors who were convinced that she had got it wrong and insisted she was misleading the nation. Even the famous Paul Erdos, years before the *Parade* magazine incident, had got the answer wrong and he was one of the most talented mathematicians of the century (and inspiration for Erdos numbers, which you may have heard of[3]).

The answer is that you should switch—you are twice as likely to win the prize if you switch doors than if you stick with your original door. Don't worry if you can't see why this is the right answer; the problem is famous precisely because it is so hard to get your head around. If you did get this right, try telling it to someone else and then explaining *why* switching is the right answer. You'll soon see just how difficult the concepts are to get across.

How It Works

The chance you got it right on the first guess is 1 in 3. Since by the time it comes to sticking or switching, the big prize (often a car) must be behind one of the two remaining doors, there must be a 2 in 3 chance that the car is behind the other door (i.e., a 2 in 3 chance your first guess was wrong).

Our intuition seems compelled to ignore the prior probabilities and the effect that the game show host's actions have. Instead, we look at the situation as it is when we come to make the choice. Two doors, one prize. 50-50 chance, right? Wrong. The host's actions make switching a better bet. By throwing away one dud door from the two you didn't choose initially, he's essentially making it so that switching is like choosing between *two* doors and you win if the prize is behind either of them.

Another way to make the switching answer seem intuitive is to imagine the situation with 1000 doors, 999 goats, and still just one prize. You choose a door (1 in 1000 chance it's the right door) and your host opens all the doors you didn't choose, which have goats behind them (998 goats). Stick or switch? Obviously you have a 999 in 1000 chance of winning if you switch, even though as you make the choice there are two doors, one prize, and one goat like before. This variant highlights one of the key distractions in the original problem—the host knows where the prize is and acts accordingly to eliminate dud doors. You choose without knowing where the prize is, but given that the host acts *knowing* where the prize is, your decision to stick or switch should take that into account.

Part of the problem is that we are used to thinking about probabilities as things attached to objects or events in simple one-to-one correspondence.

But probabilities are simply statements about what can be known about uncertain situations. The probabilities themselves can be affected by factors that don't actually affect the objects or events they label (like base rates and, in this case, the game show host's actions).

Evolutionary psychologists Leda Cosmides and John Tooby[4] argue that we have evolved to deal with frequency information when making probability judgments, not to do abstract probability calculations. Probabilities are not available directly to perception, whereas how often something happens is. The availability of frequencies made it easier for our brains to make use of them as they evolved. Our evolved faculties handle probabilities better as frequencies because this is the format of the information as it is naturally present in the environment. Whether something occurs or not can be easily seen (is it raining or is it not raining, to take an example), and figuring out a frequency of this event is a simple matter of addition and comparison: comparing the number of rainy days against the number of days in spring would automatically give you a good idea whether this current day in spring is likely to be rainy or not. One-off probabilities aren't like this; they are a cultural invention—and like a lot of cultural inventions, we still have difficulty dealing with them.

The idea that we are evolved to make frequency judgments, not probability calculations, is supported by evidence that we use frequencies as inputs and outputs for our likelihood estimates. We automatically notice and remember the frequency of events (input) and have subjective feelings of confidence that an event will or will not occur (output).

If you rephrase the Monty Hall problem in terms of frequencies, rather than in terms of a one-off decision, people are more likely to get it right.[5] Here's a short version of the same problem, but focusing explicitly on frequencies rather than one-off probabilities. Is it easier to grasp intuitively?

Take the same routine as before—three doors, one prize, and two duds. But this time consider two different ways of playing the game, represented here by two players, Tom and Helen. Tom always chooses one door and sticks with it. Helen is assigned the other two doors. Monty always lets out a goat from behind one of these two doors, and Helen gets the prize if it is behind the remaining door. They play the game, say, 30 times. How often is it likely Tom will win the prize? How often is it likely Helen will win the prize? Given this, which is the better strategy, Tom's (stick) or Helen's (switch)?

In Real Life

An example of an everyday choice that is affected by our problems with probabilities is thinking about weather forecasts. It can be simultaneously true that the weather forecasts are highly accurate and that you shouldn't believe them. The following quote is from a great article by Neville Nicholls about errors and biases in our commonsense reasoning and how they affect the way we think about weather prediction:[6]

> The accuracy of the United Kingdom 24-hour rain forecast is 83%. The climatological probability of rain on the hourly timescale appropriate for walks is 0.08 (this is the base rate). Given these values, the probability of rain, given a forecast of rain, is 0.30. The probability of no rain, given a forecast of rain, is 0.70. So, it is more likely that you would enjoy your walk without getting wet, even if the forecast was for rain tomorrow.

It's a true statement but not easy to understand, because we don't find probability calculations intuitive. The trick is to avoid them. Often probability statistics can be equally well-expressed using frequencies, and they will be better understood this way. We know the probabilities concerning base rates will be neglected, so you need to be extra careful if the message you are trying to convey relies on this information. It also helps to avoid conditional probabilities—things like "the probability of X given Y"—and relative risks—"your risk of X goes down by Y% if you do Z." People just don't find it easy to think about information given in this way.[7]

End Notes

1. Or at least it's commonly attributed to Mark Twain. It's one of those free-floating quotations.

2. vos Savant, M. (1997). *The Power of Logical Thinking*. New York: St Martin's Press.

3. Paul Erdos published a colossal number of papers in his lifetime by collaborating with mathematicians around the world. If you published a paper with Erdos, your Erdos number is 1; if you published with someone who published with Erdos, it is 2. The mathematics of these indices of relationship can be quite interesting. See "The Erdos Number Project," *http://www.oakland.edu/enp*.

4. Cosmides, L., & Tooby, J. (1996). Are humans good intuitive statisticians after all? Rethinking some conclusions from the literature on judgment under uncertainty. *Cognition, 58*(1), 1–73.

5. Krauss, S., & Wang, X. T. (2003). The psychology of the Monty Hall problem: Discovering psychological mechanisms for solving a tenacious brain teaser. *Journal of Experimental Psychology: General, 132*(1), 3–22.

6. Nicholls, N. (1999). Cognitive illusions, heuristics, and climate prediction. *Bulletin of the American Meteorological Society, 80*(7), 1385–1397 (*http://ams.allenpress.com/pdfserv/i1520-0477-080-07-1385.pdf*).

7. Gigerenzer, G., & Edwards, A. (2003). Simple tools for understanding risks: From innumeracy to insight. *British Medical Journal, 327*, 741–744 (*http://bmj.bmjjournals.com/cgi/reprint/327/7417/741*). This article is great on ways you can use frequency information as an alternative to help people understand probabilities.

See Also

- A detailed discussion of the psychology of the Monty Hall dilemma, but one that doesn't focus on the base-rate interpretation highlighted here is given by Burns, B. D., & Wieth, M. (in press). The collider principle in causal reasoning: Why the Monty Hall dilemma is so hard. *Journal of Experimental Psychology: General.* More discussion of the Monty Hall dilemma and a simulation that lets you compare the success of the stick and switch strategies is at *http://www.cut-the-knot.org/hall.shtml.*

Detect Cheaters
#72

Our sense of logic is much better when applied to social situations than used in abstract scenarios.

Despite the old saying that we're ruled by our emotions, it's tempting to believe that we have at least *some* intuitive sense of logic. The various forms of logic such as syllogisms and deductive and inductive reasoning[1] seem so simple and fundamental that you might expect that the rules are hardwired into our brains. After all, since we're constantly told that our neurons are the equivalent of computer processors, shouldn't our brains be able to handle a little bit of logic?

See how you do on these logical puzzles.

In Action

Each of the cards in Figure 7-1 has a letter on one side and a number on the reverse. If I told you there was a rule stating that a card with a vowel on one side must have an even number on the reverse, which of these cards would you need to turn over to prove or disprove this rule?

Give it a whirl before reading on.

Many people turn over A and 2—but that's not quite right. While turning over A will tell you whether "one side" of the rule is true (*if* vowel, *then* even

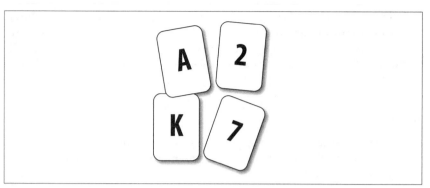

Figure 7-1. Each card has a letter on one side and a number on the reverse

number), turning over 2 won't tell you any more. It doesn't matter whether 2 has a K or an A on its reverse—the rules doesn't specify either being true. Along with A, the other card you need to turn over is 7. If 7 has an *A* on its reverse, then the rule is disproved no matter what the A has on its reverse. You *need* to turn over A and 7.

Very few people solve this riddle on the first try. It shows that humans do not possess an innate set of abstract logic rules. Yet somehow we manage to get by without those rules. Try this similar puzzle, in Figure 7-2.

Figure 7-2. Four people sit at a bar drinking beer or cola, the cards show age on one side and beverage on the other—who's breaking the rules?

Say there's a rule that you must be 21 or over to drink beer. Whose drinks and ages would you need to check to see if this bar is flouting the rules?

By simply swapping drinks and ages for cards A, K, 2, and 7, it's obvious this time around that there's no point checking what the 21 year old (think 2 card) is drinking—it wouldn't make any difference to the rule if she were drinking cola or beer, whereas the 16 year old's (think 7 card) drink is of much more interest.

How It Works

Why are logic problems so much easier when they're expressed as real-life situations rather than in abstract terms? One early hypothesis called *memory cuing* proposed that we solve logic problems by drawing on personal experience, without using any deductive reasoning. We've all experienced the problems of drinking ages enough times that we don't even have to think about who should be drinking what, unlike playing with letter and number cards.

Despite the substantial evidence behind memory cuing,[2,3] many scientists believe that in practice we use more than just experience—that there is in fact some thinking involved. Instead, researchers such as Cheng and Holyoak[4] think that, while we might not be so good at pure logic, we're excellent at the logic we need in real life—rules, permissions, and obligations. This type of logic—*deontic logic*—is what helps us solve everyday logic problems, by developing what they call "pragmatic reasoning schemas." Therefore, it shouldn't be surprising that our ability with logic is domain-specific, that is, limited to analyzing the complex web of permissions and obligations we encounter in life.

It's been suggested by Cosmides,[5] a leading light of evolutionary psychology (the study of how evolution may have shaped the way we think[6]), that the reason we seem to possess domain-specific logic is because it's been selected for by evolution over countless generations. Cosmides argues that the really important parts of Cheng and Holyoak's pragmatic reasoning schemas are those about people. In other words, we are all born with the mental logic required to understand the costs, benefits, and social contracts involved in dealing with other people. It's a compelling argument, since the ability to make beneficial deals is a valuable survival trait. However, Cosmides' theory can't be the whole story, since we have no problem in solving many logic problems that have nothing to do with costs, benefits, or indeed other people at all. For example, the rule "If you're going to clean up spilt blood, then you need to wear rubber gloves" is easily understood and applied even though it doesn't concern other people.

Before resigning yourself to a life without logic, it's worth remembering that along with the countless other skills that we aren't born with, we can understand logic the hard way—by learning it. Even if you don't, you can still console yourself with the knowledge that you're as good as any philosopher in the everyday logic that *really* matters.

End Notes

1. Syllogisms: some C are B, no A is B, therefore some C are not A. Deductive: reasoning in which the conclusion necessarily follows from true premises (e.g., if X, then Y). Inductive: the sort of reasoning that Sherlock Holmes might use, in which he draws a conclusion (which might be wrong) based on possibly incomplete or irrelevant information.

2. Johnson-Laird, P. N., Legrenzi, P., & Sonino-Legrenzi, M. (1972). Reasoning and a sense of reality. *British Journal of Psychology, 63*, 395–400.

3. Manktelow, R. I., & Evans, J. St. B. T. (1979). Facilitation of reasoning by realism: Effect or non-effect? *British Journal of Psychology, 70*, 477–488.

4. Cheng, P. W., & Holyoak, K. J. (1985). Pragmatic reasoning schemas. *Cognitive Psychology, 17*, 391–416.

5. Cosmides, L. (1989). The logic of social exchange: Has natural selection shaped how humans reason? Studies with the Wason Selection task. *Cognition, 31*, 187–276.

6. Evolutionary psychology is the study of how evolution may have shaped the way we think, and often controversial. "Evolutionary Psychology: a Primer" (*http://www.psych.ucsb.edu/research/cep/primer.html*), by Leda Cosmides and John Tooby, provides an introduction.

—Adrian Hon

H A C K #73   Fool Others into Feeling Better

Many of the unpleasant phenomena associated with injury and infection are in fact produced by the brain to protect the body. Medical assistance shifts the burden of protection from self to other, which allows the brain to reduce its self-imposed unpleasantness.

Injury or infection triggers a coordinated suite of physiological responses involving the brain, hormones, and immune system. The brain generates pain and fever, stress hormones mobilize energy from fat, and immune cells cause local swelling and redness. These processes are collectively known as the *acute phase response* because they occur rapidly and tend to subside after a few days. Medical assistance can help these unpleasant signs and symptoms to subside more quickly, even when that assistance is completely bogus—such as a witch doctor waving a rattle at you or a quack prescribing a sugar pill. This is known as the *placebo effect*.

In Action

It's hard to invent a placebo and try it on yourself, because the effect relies crucially on the sincerely held belief that it will work. Several experiments have shown that pure placebos such as fake ultrasound produce no pain relief when they are self-administered. So unless you can fool yourself that other people are caring for you when they are not, your experiments with placebos will have to involve other people.

Moreover, you will also probably have to lie. The placebo effect depends not just on other people, but also on the belief that those people are providing bona fide medical assistance. If you don't believe that the assistance provided by those around you is going to help you recover, you won't experience a placebo effect.

Sometimes a placebo effect seems to be triggered despite the absence of other people and the absence of deception. If you have ever felt better after taking a homeopathic remedy, for example, or after applying dock leaves to the pain caused by a stinging nettle, that was almost certainly a placebo effect, because it has been scientifically proven that such treatments are completely bogus. The essential factor, however, must still be present—a belief that this kind of treatment will help. Once you discover the truth about such bogus treatments, therefore, they cease to be capable of producing placebo effects.

Because it is hard (some might say impossible) to deceive yourself into believing something that you know to be false, deception is important for most placebo experiments. This plays a central role in many psychological experiments, and raises serious ethical problems. In universities and other research environments, an ethics committee must, quite rightly, approve experiments before they are allowed to proceed. It is therefore advisable to conduct the following experiment in the privacy of your own home, where ethics committees have no jurisdiction.

First, take an old medicine bottle and clean it thoroughly. Then fill it with a solution of tap water, sugar, and food coloring. The next time someone you know gets a headache or is stung by a stinging nettle, tell her that you have a special remedy that will help. If she asks what it is, tell her that it is a special solution of water and sugar and food coloring, and say that you have read somewhere (in this book) that this will help her feel better (that way, you won't even be lying!). Give her the colored water and ask her to drink a teaspoonful (if she has a headache) or to rub a small amount onto the affected area (if she has been stung by a nettle). See if it helps her feel better.

It will, if she believes it will—*and* if there's nothing really wrong with her (be careful here; don't delay medical treatment for someone who is hurt because you want to see if you can placebo-cure her).

Studies have shown that for some people in some situations the placebo effect can be as strong as morphine. In one particularly striking study,[1] patients who had undergone tooth extraction were treated with ultrasound to investigate whether this would reduce the postoperative pain. Unknown to both doctors and patients, however, the experimenters had fiddled with the machine, and half the patients never received the ultrasound. Since ultrasound consists of sound waves of very high frequency—so high, in fact, that they are inaudible to the human ear—there was no way for either the doctors or the patients to tell whether the machine was emitting sound waves; the test was truly double-blind. After their jaws were massaged with the ultrasound applicator, the patients were asked to indicate their level of pain on a line with one end labeled "no pain" and the other "unbearable pain." Compared with a group of patients who were untreated, all those treated with the ultrasound machine reported a significant reduction in pain. Surprisingly, however, it didn't seem to matter whether the machine had been switched on or not. Those who had been massaged with the machine while it was turned off showed the same level of pain reduction as those who had received the proper treatment. In fact, when the ultrasound machine was turned up high, it actually gave less pain relief than when it was switched off.

Other studies have shown that placebo medicines are more effective if delivered in person by doctors and that it helps more if the doctors are wearing white coats. Red pills give a bigger placebo effect than white pills, and placebo injections are more powerful still.

How It Works

Nobody knows for sure yet how the placebo effect works, but one theory is that the brain is very sensitive to the presence of social support during the process of recovery from injury and infection. The various components of the acute phase response are all designed to promote recovery and prevent further injury while recovery is taking place. Pain, for example, makes you guard the wounded area. But these measures also have costs; high levels of pain, for example, can actually lengthen the healing process. The brain makes a trade-off between the risks of further damage to the injured area and the delay to the healing process. The presence of social support during recovery shifts the balance between these competing risks because some of the burden of preventing further damage is transferred from the sick person to those around them. The sick person can therefore reduce his own costly self-protective measures, such as pain, and allow the healing process to progress more rapidly.

Another suggestion is that the placebo effect works by means of conditioning (see also "Make the Caffeine Habit Taste Good" [Hack #92]). Conditioning is a very general kind of learning process in which one stimulus is substituted for another. The classic example is Pavlov's dogs, which learned to salivate on hearing a bell after Pavlov had trained them to associate the sound of the bell with the arrival of food. In technical terms, an *unconditioned stimulus* (the sight of the meat), which leads naturally to a certain *unconditioned response* (salivating at the sight of the meat), is repeatedly paired with a *conditioned stimulus* (the sound of the bell). Eventually, the dogs learn the *conditioned response* of salivating at the sound of the bell. Pavlov's students showed that immune responses can also be conditioned, and others have gone on to suggest that this is what lies behind the placebo response. The unconditioned stimulus is a real drug or some other medical treatment that works even if you have never tried it before and don't believe in it. The unconditioned response is the improvement you feel after receiving the treatment. The conditioned stimuli are all the things that are repeatedly paired with the treatment—the size, shape, and color of the pill, for example. If you then take a pill that has the same size, shape, and color as the real one, but which lacks the active ingredient, you may still experience some improvement because your immune system has been conditioned to respond to such stimuli.

Placebos won't cure the vast majority of medical conditions. It is much easier and quicker to list the things that placebos *can* influence—pain, swelling, stomach ulcers, some skin conditions, low mood, and anxiety—than the things they don't. Everything else is probably not placebo-responsive. That said, placebos are able to help in the management of nearly all illnesses because nearly all illnesses involve pain, low mood, and/or anxiety.

End Note

1. Hashish I., Harvey, W., & Harris, M. (1986). Anti-inflammatory effects of ultrasound therapy: Evidence for a major placebo effect. *British Journal of Rheumatology 25*, 77–81.

See Also

- Evans, D. (2003). *Placebo: Mind over Matter in Modern Medicine*. London: HarperCollins.

—*Dylan Evans*

Maintain the Status Quo

#74   People don't like change. If you really want people to try something new, you should just coerce them into giving it a go and chuck the idea of persuading them straight off.

By default, people side with what already is and what happened last time. We're curious, as animals go, but even humans are innately conservative. Like the Dice Man, who delegates all decisions to chance in Luke Rhinehart's classic 1970s novel of the same name, was told: "It's the way a man chooses to limit himself that determines his character. A man without habits, consistency, redundancy—and hence boredom—is not human. He's insane."[1]

In this hack we're going to look at our preference for the way things are and where this tendency comes from. I'm not claiming that people don't change—obviously this happens all the time and is the most interesting part of life—but, in general, people are consistent and tend toward consistency. Statistically, if you want to predict what people will do in a familiar situation, the most useful thing you can measure is what they did last time. Past action correlates more strongly with their behavior than every other variable psychologists have tried to measure.[2] If you're interested in predicting who people will vote for, what they will buy, what kind of person they will sleep with, anything at all really, finding out what tendencies they've exhibited or what habits they've formed before is the most useful information at your disposal. You're not after what they *say* they will do—not what party, brand, or sexual allegiance they tick on a form—nor the choice they think they're feeling pressured into making. Check out what they actually did last time and base your prediction on that. You won't always be right, but you will be right more often by basing your guess upon habit than upon any other single variable.

This bias is the result of a number of factors, not least the fact that people's previous choice is often the best one or the one that best reflects their character. But also we have mental biases,[3] like the mental biases we have about numbers [Hack #70], which produce consistent habits and an innate conservatism.

Biases in reasoning are tendencies, not absolutes. They make up the mental forces that push your conclusions one way or the other. No single force ever rules completely, and in each case, several forces compete. We're mostly trying to be rational so we keep a look out for things that might have biased us so we can discount them. Even if we know we can't be rational, we mostly try to be at least consistent. This means that often you can't give the same person the same problem twice if it's designed to evoke different biases.

They'll spot the similarity between the two presentations and know their answers should be the same.

> I'm carelessly using the word "rational" here, in the same way that logicians and people with a faith in pure reason might. But the study of heuristics and biases should make us question what a psychological meaning of "rational" could be. In some of the very arbitrary situations contrived by psychologists, people can appear to be irrational, but often their behavior would be completely reasonable in most situations, and even rational considering the kind of uncertainties that normally accompany most choices in the everyday world.
>
> —T.S.

But some biases are so strong that you can feel them tugging on your reason even when the rational part of your mind knows they are misleading. These "cognitive illusions" work even when you present two differently biased versions of the choice side by side. The example we're going to see in action is one of these.

In Action

I'm going to tell you in advance that the two versions of the problem are logically identical, but I know—because your brain evolved in the same way mine did—that you'll feel as if you want to answer them differently despite knowing this. If your supreme powers of reason don't let you feel the tug induced by the superficial features of the problem (the bit that conveys the bias), take the two versions and present them to two different friends.

Here we go…

Version 1. A lethal disease is spreading through the city of which you are mayor. It is expected to kill 600 people. Your chief medical adviser tells you that there is a choice between two treatment plans. The first strategy will definitely save 200 people, whereas the second strategy has a one-third chance of saving 600 people and a two-thirds chance of saving no one. Which strategy do you choose?

Version 2. A lethal disease is spreading through the city of which you are mayor. It is expected to kill 600 people. Your chief medical adviser tells you that there is a choice between two treatment plans. The first strategy will definitely kill 400 people, whereas the second strategy has a one-third chance that nobody will die and a two-thirds chance that 600 people will die.

Do you feel it? The choices feel different, even though you know they are the same. What's going on?

How It Works

At least two things are going on here. The first is the effect of the way the choice is presented—the *framing effect*. Anyone who has ever tried to persuade someone of something knows the importance of this. It's not just what you say, but how you say it, that is important when presenting people with a choice or argument. The second thing is a bias we have against risking an already satisfactory situation—we're much more willing to take risks when we're in a losing position to begin with. In the examples, the first frame makes it look like you stand to gain without having to take a risk—the choice is between definitely saving 200 people versus an all-or-nothing gamble. The second frame makes it appear as though you start in a losing position (400 people down) and you can risk the all-or-nothing gamble to potentially improve your standing. In experimental studies of this dilemma, around 75% of people favor not gambling in the first frame, with the situation reversed in the second.[4]

So why do we gamble when we think we might lose out, but have a bias to avoid gambling on gains? I'm going to argue that this is part of a general bias we have toward the way things are. Let's call it the "status quo bias." This is probably built into our minds by evolution—nature's way of saying "If it ain't broke, don't fix it."

With habits, it is easy to see why the status quo bias is evolutionary adaptive. If you did it last time and it didn't kill you, why do it differently? Sure, you could try things differently, but why waste the effort, especially if there's any risk at all of things getting worse?

In Real Life

There's a way to hack this habit bias, and it's well-known to advertisers. If people generally stick with what they know, the most important thing you can do is get them to start off with your product in the first place (hence the value of kids as a target market). But you can make use of the bias: people choose based on what they did before, so it is more effective to advertise to influence what they choose rather than how they feel about that choice. Even if there's no good reason for someone using your product in the first place, the fact that they did once has established a strong bias for them doing so again. A computer user may prefer one browser, but if another one comes bundled with her new operating system, we can bet that's what she'll end up relying on. You may have no rational reason for choosing Brand A over Brand B when you buy jam, but if the manufacturers of Brand B can get you to try it (maybe by giving you a free sample or a special offer), they've overcome the major barrier that would have stopped you from buying it next time.

Status quo bias works for beliefs as well as behaviors. In many situations we are drawn to confirm what we already know, rather than test it in a way that might expose it to be false [Hack #72].

> It's an experience I've had a lot when debugging code. I do lots of things that prove to me that it must be the bug I first think it is, but when I fix that bug, my code still doesn't work.
> It's not just me, right?
>
> —T.S.

Another manifestation of our preference for the way things are is the so-called *endowment effect*,[5] whereby once we have something, however we acquired it, we give it more value than we would give up to obtain it. In one study, students were given a mug with their university emblem, worth $6. In a trading game they subsequently wanted an average of around $5 to give up their mug, whereas students without mugs were willing to offer an average of only around $2 to buy a mug. The mere sense of ownership that came with being given the mug was enough to create a difference between how the two groups valued the object. This is just one of the ways in which human behavior violates the rationality supposed by classical economic theory.

So we can see that if you want people to give something up, you shouldn't give it to them in the first place, and if you want to introduce something new, you should make people try it before trying to persuade them to accept it. If you can't do this, you should at least try and introduce the new change elements as part of the familiar experience.

End Notes

1. Rhinehart, L. (1971). *The Dice Man.*

2. Ajzen, I. (2002). Residual effects of past on later behavior: Habituation and reasoned action perspectives. *Personality and Social Psychology Review, 6,* 107–122. See also: Ouellette, J. A., & Wood, W. (1998). Habit and intention in everyday life: The multiple processes by which past behavior predicts future behavior. *Psychological Bulletin, 124,* 54–74.

3. The Wikipedia has an enjoyable, if unstructured, list of cognitive biases (*http://en.wikipedia.org/wiki/List_of_cognitive_biases*). A good introduction to cognitive biases and heuristics is Nicholls, N. (1999). Cognitive illusions, heuristics, and climate prediction. *Bulletin of the American Meteorological Society, 80*(7), 1385–1397 (*http://ams.allenpress.com/pdfserv/i1520-0477-080-07-1385.pdf*).

4. Tversky, A., & Kahneman, D. (1981). The framing of decisions and the psychology of choice. *Science*, 211, 453–458.

5. Kahneman, D., Knetch, J. L., & Thaler, R. H. (1991). Anomalies: The endowment effect, loss aversion, and status quo bias. *Journal of Economic Perspectives, 5*(1), 193–206. A reverse of the endowment effect is the windfall effect in which people value less highly money they didn't expect to come to them (like lottery wins and inheritance).

CHAPTER EIGHT

Togetherness
Hacks 75–80

What makes "this" a word, rather than being simply the adjacently written letters *t*, *h*, *i*, *s*? Or, to ask a similar question, why should we see a single dog running across a field rather than a collection of legs, ears, hair, and a wet nose flying over the grass? And why, when the dog knocks us over, do we know to blame the dog?

To put these questions another way: how do we group sensations into whole objects, and how do we decide that a certain set of perceptions constitutes cause and effect?

It's not a terribly easy problem to solve. The nature of causality isn't transmitted in an easy-to-sense form like color is in light. Rather than sense it directly, we have to guess. We have built-in heuristics to do just that, and these heuristics are based on various forms of togetherness. The word "this" hangs together well because the letters are in a straight line, for example, and they're closer to one another than the letters in the surrounding words. Those are both principles by which the brain performs grouping. To take the second question, we see the parts of the dog as a single animal because they move together. That's another heuristic.

This recognition acuity lets us see human forms from the tiniest of clues, but it also—as we'll see in "See a Person in Moving Lights" [Hack #77]—is not perfect and can be duped. We'll see how we can perceive animacy—the aliveness shown by living creatures—where none exists and how we can ignore the cause in cause and effect. Sometimes that's the best way to find out what our assumptions really are, to see when they don't quite match what's happening in the real world.

Grasp the Gestalt

HACK
#75   We group our visual perceptions together according to the gestalt grouping
principles. Knowing these can help your visual information design to sit well
with people's expectations.

It's a given that we see the world not as isolated parts, but as groups and single objects. Instead of seeing fingers and a palm, we see a hand. We see a wall as a unit rather than seeing the individual bricks. We naturally group things together, trying to make a coherent picture out of all the individual parts. A few fundamental grouping principles can be used to do most of the work, and knowing them will help you design well-organized, visual information yourself.

In Action

Automatic grouping is such second nature that we really notice only its absence. When the arrangement of parts doesn't sit well with the grouping principles the brain uses, cracks can be seen. Figure 8-1 shows some of these organizational rules coming into play.[1]

Figure 8-1. Two groups of triangles that point different ways and a middle triangle that can appear to point either way, depending on which group you see it being part of[2]

You don't see 17 triangles. Instead, you see two groups of eight and one triangle in the middle. Your similarity drive has formed the arrangement into rows and columns of the shapes and put them into two groups: one group points to the bottom left, the other points off to the right.

Each group belongs together partly because the triangles are arranged into a pattern (two long rows pointing in a direction) and partly because of proximity (shapes that are closer together are more likely to form a group). The triangle in the middle is a long way from both groups and doesn't fall into the same pattern as either. It's left alone by the brain's grouping principles.

You can, however, voluntarily group the lone triangle. By mentally putting it with the left-hand set, it appears to point down and left along with the other triangles. You can make it point right by choosing to see it with the other set.

How It Works

The rules by which the brain groups similar objects together are called *gestalt grouping principles* in psychology. Although there's no direct German-to-English translation, "gestalt" means (roughly) "whole." When we understand objects and the relationships between them in a single, coherent pattern rather than as disconnected items, we understand the group as a gestalt. We have a gestalt comprehension of each of the sets of triangles in Figure 8-1, for instance.

Four of the most commonly quoted grouping principles are proximity, similarity, closure, and continuation. An example of each is shown in Figure 8-2.

Figure 8-2. The four most quoted gestalt grouping principles

Proximity
> We preconsciously group items that are close together, so in the picture you see columns rather than rows or a grid. This principle is the cause of the triangles in the original diagram coming together into two sets and the reason the lone triangle didn't feel part of either of them.

Similarity
> We prefer to group together objects of the same kind. In the example, you see alternating rows of circles and squares rather than columns of mixed shapes.

Closure
> There's a tendency to complete patterns. There's no triangle in the example pattern, but we see one because the arrangement of the three Pac Man shapes would be completed if one were there.

Continuation
> Just as we like to see completed patterns, we like seeing shapes that continue along the same path, smoothly. We see two lines crossing in the example, rather than two arrowheads touching at their points or four lines meeting together.

When none of these principles apply, it's still possible to mentally group items together. When you put the middle triangle in Figure 8-1 with one group or the other, it picks up the orientation of the group as a whole. It's a voluntary grouping that modifies how you see.

Gestalt principles exist in visual processing not because they are always right, but because on average, they are useful. They're good rules of thumb for making sense of the world. It's not that similar things can't be separate; it's more that most of the time they aren't. Although random coincidences can happen, they are vastly outnumbered by meaningful coincidences.

The world isn't a mess of disconnected parts, and it's useful to see the connections—if you're hunting an animal, it makes sense to see it as a single gestalt rather than a paw here and a tail there.

End Notes

1. The gestalt grouping principles are interesting, but are they really useful? Good print or web page design involves easy comprehension, and knowing how the principles can conflict or mislead in your layout helps along the way. James Levin has applied the gestalt grouping principles to web design (*http://tepserver.ucsd.edu:16080/~jlevin/gp*).

2. Illustration inspired by Fred Attneave's demonstrations as used in "How the Mind Works" by Steven Pinker.

See Also

- Max Wertheimer was the first to identify the principles in his 1923 paper "Laws of Organization in Perceptual Forms" (*http://psy.ed.asu. edu/~classics/Wertheimer/Forms/forms.htm*).

- As well as the basic grouping principles, which work looking at static objects, others deduce grouping from behavior over time **[Hack #76]**.

To Be Noticed, Synchronize in Time

HACK
#76

We tend to group together things that happen at the same time or move in the same way. It's poor logic but a great hack for spotting patterns.

It's a confusing, noisy world out there. It's easier to understand the world if we perceive a set of objects rather than just a raw mass of sensations, and one way to do this is to group together perceptions that appear to have the same cause. The underlying assumptions involved manifest as the *gestalt grouping principles*, a set of heuristics used by the brain to lump things together (see "Grasp the Gestalt" **[Hack #75]** for the simplest of these, used for vision).

Perhaps the most powerful of these assumptions is termed *common fate*. We group together events that occur at the same time, change in the same way, or move in the same direction. Imagine if you saw, from far off, two points of light that looked a bit like eyes in the dark. You might think they were eyes or you could just put it down to a coincidence of two unrelated lights. But if the points of light moved at the same time, in the same direction, bounced with the characteristic bounce of a person walking, you'd *know* they were eyes. Using behavior over time allows you to stringently test spatial data for possible common cause. If the bouncing lights pass the common fate test, they're almost certainly a single object. Visual system tags this certainty by providing you with a correspondingly strong perceptual experience; if some things move together, it is almost impossible to see them as separate items instead of a coherent whole.

In Action

"Illusion—Motion Capture—Grouping" (*http://psy.ucsd.edu/chip/illu_mot_capt_grpng.html*; a Real video requiring Real Player) demonstrates just how completely your perception of a single item is altered by global context and common fate. Watch the video for at least 30 seconds. At first you see just a dot blinking on and off next to a square. But then other dots are added in the surrounding area, and as the first dot blinks off, they all shift right. Now your unavoidable impression is of the first dot moving behind the square. The appearance of the other dots, and their behavior, gives your visual system correlations that are just too strong to ignore. The single dot is still blinking on and off—you just can't see it like that any more.

"A Time Gestalt Principle Example: Common Fate" (*http://tepserver.ucsd.edu/~jlevin/gp/time-example-common-fate*; a Java applet),[1] shown in Figure 8-3, is an interactive demonstration of how your visual system deduces the shape of objects from movement, without any color or shading clues to help out.

You see a shape with a static-like texture moving across a similarly randomized background. Click anywhere in the image to start and stop the demo. Frozen, there is no pattern to see; you see just a random mess. This is the real force of common fate. The correlations exist only across time, in movement—it's only when the demo is moving that you can see an object among the noise.

How It Works

The gestalt grouping inferences are so preconscious and automatic that it's hard to imagine perceiving a world that the brain *hasn't* organized into objects. There's something very clever going on here; we are taking in very little information (only how the pattern changes over time), yet, in combination with an assumption that accidental correlations of visual patterns are

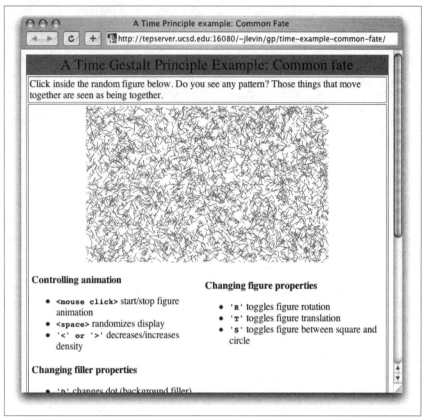

Figure 8-3. When the circle hidden in the pattern is moving, it's clearly seen; printed like this, it's invisible

unlikely, we construct a compelling perception of an object. In these demos, you just can't ignore the object. You are utterly unable to make yourself see a moving collection of dots instead of the shape in motion because the construction of the object is happening before the level of consciousness.

Common fate can lead to some sophisticated inferences. "Kinetic Depth" (*http://www.biols.susx.ac.uk/home/George_Mather/Motion/KDE.HTML*; a QuickTime video), just from a collection of moving lights, allows you to see an object with three-dimensional depth moving in a particular way. In this case, the pattern of dots causes you to see a sphere rotating on its axis.

What's really cute about this video is that there's an ambiguity in the visual information—you can see the sphere rotating in one of two ways. Your visual system makes a choice for you, and you see some of the dots moving behind some of the others, which move in the opposite direction. The set you see as "in front" determines the direction in which you see the sphere rotating. If you watch for a while, your perception will switch and you'll see it reverse. You don't need to make any effort to for this to happen; it occurs naturally, probably due to some kind of adaptation process. Since you see the sphere rotating in one particular direction, the neurons that represent that perception will be active. Over time, they actively tune down their response, and the neurons that code for the other apparent rotation can now dominate. This kind of gain control [Hack #26] plays a similar role in motion aftereffects [Hack #25], in which neurons that are active for particular directions of movement down-regulate after being consistently stimulated and neurons active for the opposing direction take over and dominate our perception when the consistent moving stimulus is removed.

All these demonstrations show just how effective correlations over time are in molding our perception. And not just perception—synchronizing stimuli can actually alter your body image, where your brain believes your hands are [Hack #64], for instance. The heart of the thing is similar—if two things correlate exactly, our perception treats them as part of the same object. For our brains, isolated inside the skull, perceived correlation is the only way we've ever had for deducing what sensations should be associated together as part of the same object.

Common fate can also draw inferences from points of light moving in much more complex ways than rotating spheres. For the case of biological motion [Hack #77], the visual system is specifically prepared to fit moving points into a schema based upon the human body to help perception of the human form. Alais et al. have suggested that the importance of common fate reflects a deeper principle of the brain's organization.[2] Neuroscientists talk about the *binding problem*, the question of how the brain correctly connects together all the information it is dealing with: all the things that are happening in different parts of the world, detected by different senses, whose component parts have properties represented in different cortical areas (such as color, contrast, sounds, and so on), all of which have to be knitted together into a coherent perception. The suggestion is that common fate reflects synchronization of neuron firing—and that is this same mechanism that may underlie the brain's solution to the binding problem.

End Notes

1. Part of Jim Levin's "Gestalt Principles & Web Design" (*http://tepserver. ucsd.edu:16080/~jlevin/gp*). Applet developed by Adam Doppelt.

2. Alais, D., Blake, R., & Lee, S. (1998). Visual features that vary together over time group together over space. *Nature Neuroscience. 1*(2), 160–164.

See a Person in Moving Lights

Lights on the joints of a walking person are enough to give a vivid impression of the person, carrying information on mood, gender, and other details—but only while the person keeps moving.

Visual perception has special routines for grouping things that move along together into single objects [Hack #76]. That's why we see cars as cars and not a collection of wheels, glass, and side-view mirrors just happening to travel along in the same direction. That's all well and good, but humans live not just in a world of objects like trees and cars, but a world full of *people*. Given how social we are, and how tricky other people can be, it's not surprising we also have specialized routines for grouping things that move like people together into single objects too. Looking at only a constellation of moving points of light attached to knees, elbows, and other parts of the body, we get a vivid perception of a person, a perception that doesn't exist at all when the points of light are still.

In Action

Open up your browser and point it at *http://www.lifesci.sussex.ac.uk/home/ George_Mather/Motion/BM.HTML*[1] or *http://www.at-bristol.org.uk/Optical/ DancingLights_main.htm* (both are QuickTime movies). What do you see?

Both are just points of light moving in two dimensions. Yet the first is clearly a person walking, and the second obviously two people dancing, fighting, and otherwise performing.

As with the common fate demos [Hack #76] of how we group objects by their behavior over time, you can remove the effect by pausing the movies. This information only makes sense when it is moving (shame we can't have animations in the book, really), which is why Figure 8-4 (a frame of the first movie) looks more like a random star constellation than a human figure.

The vivid impression of a walking human shows that we are able to integrate the correlations of the light points and match them to some kind of template we have developed for moving humans. It is orientation-specific, by the way. Watch the video upside down (it's easier if you have a laptop), and you won't see anything resembling human motion at all.

And we don't perceive just abstract form from the moving lights. The demo at *http://www.bml.psy.ruhr-uni-bochum.de/Demos/BMLwalker.html*, shown in Figure 8-5, allows you to vary the gender, direction, weight, mood, and energy levels of the walker using the sliders on the left.

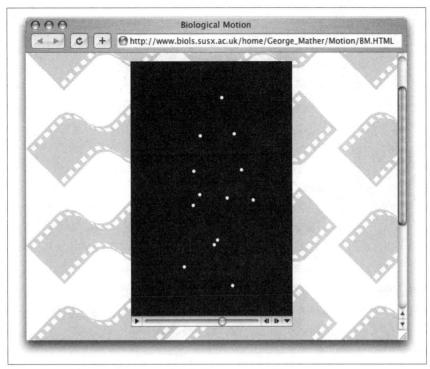

Figure 8-4. If this were moving, it'd look like a person walking

You can tell if the moving lights are from a heavyset man who's happy or if they are from a medium-build woman who is slightly afraid. All just from way the lights move.

How It Works

The effect is obvious. That we can perceive the human form—even mood and gender—just from moving lights demonstrates that we automatically extract underlying patterns from the normal human forms we see every day.

Through a combination of experience and specialized neural modules, we have learned the underlying commonalities of moving human forms—the relationships in time and space between the important features (the joints) of the human body. Our brain can then use this template to facilitate recognition of new examples of moving bodies. Being able to do this provides (for free) the ability to perceive a whole just from abstracted parts that move in the right way. A similar process underlies the perception of expressions in emoticons [Hack #93]. It's the reason cartoonists and caricaturists can make a

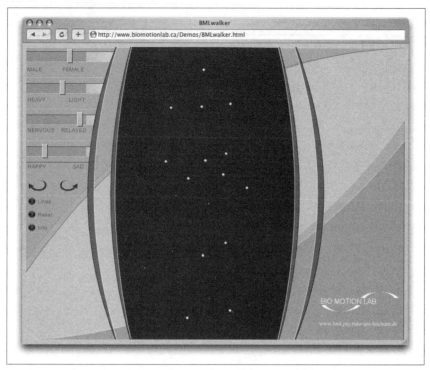

Figure 8-5. A happy heavyset man, as represented by points of light

living—showing just the essentials is as expressive, maybe even more expressive, than the full image with all its irrelevant details.

> Given our brains are so good at detecting human forms, it's surprising that emoticons are so common and stick people aren't. Perhaps it's because posture is secondary to facial expression, and anyway you'd need to articulate the limbs to get the full effect. Mind you, that's not to say you can't have dancing stick people in plain text online chat (*http://bash.org/?4281*).
>
> —T.S.

Perceiving biological motion from moving lights isn't something that falls out of other, normal, visual processes.[2] Brain imaging studies show that the process involves various brain regions, not only those normally involved with vision are brought to bear, but also those involved in object memory, spatial processing, and even motor processes.[3,4]

Even better, when the lights give the impression of a fearful person, the part of the brain (the amygdala) that normally responds to fearful expressions on faces is evoked.[5] Our specialized mechanisms for recognizing biological motion link direct to our emotions.

The algorithm for perceiving biological motion doesn't always get it right. A light-point walker can actually appear to move in two directions at once. True light-point walkers are based on real people, and you can tell which direction they're walking in. The "chimeric walker" QuickTime movies (*http://www.kyb.tuebingen.mpg.de/bu/demo/chimericwalker*) have been edited to superimpose two walkers moving in opposite directions, one to the left and one to the right. Your biological motion detection kicks in, and you see a person moving, as normal, but you're really looking at only one set of the superimposed dots—with a little effort you can see the person going the other way instead. With a little more effort you can flip between seeing the two walkers, voluntarily. The detection algorithm's been fooled; you would never see this particular moving dot configuration in the wild.[6]

In Real Life

If you are a cyclist, you can use our specialized adaptation to the perception of biological motion to your advantage. Fluorescent safety markings that are positioned to tap into this biological motion detection system, by being placed on the joints, have been shown to make you more conspicuous to motorists.[7]

End Notes

1. Movie on George Mather's Motion Perception tutorial pages (*http://www.lifesci.sussex.ac.uk/home/George_Mather/Motion/index.html*).

2. Neri, P., Morrone, C., & Burr, D. C. (1998). Seeing biological motion. *Nature, 395,* 865–866.

3. Pelphrey, K. A., Mitchell, T. V., McKeown, M. J., Goldstein, J., Allison, T., & McCarthy, G. (2003). Brain activity evoked by the perception of human walking: Controlling for meaningful coherent motion. *Journal of Neuroscience, 23*(17), 6819–6825.

4. Giese, M. A., & Poggio, T. (2003). Neural mechanisms for the recognition of biological movements. *Nature Reviews Neuroscience, 4,* 180–192.

5. Hadjikhani, N., & de Gelder, B. (2003). Seeing fearful body expressions activates the fusiform cortex and amygdala. *Current Biology, 13*(24), 2201–2205.

6. Thornton, I.M Vuong, Q.C., & Bulthoff, H.H. (2003). "Last But Not Least: a Chimeric Point Walker." *Perception, 32*, 377–383 (*http://www. perceptionweb.com/perc0303/p5010.pdf*).

7. Kwan, Irene, & Mapstone, James (2004). Visibility aids for pedestrians and cyclists: A systematic review of randomised controlled trials. *Accident Analysis and Prevention*, 36(3), 305–312.

HACK #78   Make Things Come Alive

Add a few tweaks to the way a thing moves, and you can make objects seem as if they have a life of their own.

Sometimes, when there isn't evidence of causation, your perceptual system detects self-causation and delivers up an impression of animacy—that quality of having active purpose that makes objects seem alive.

Animacy is simultaneously easy to see but hard to think about, and both for the same reason. We have evolved to live in a world of animals and objects. But living things are more difficult and more dangerous than objects, so our minds are biased in lots of ways to detect agency—things happening because someone or something wanted them to happen for a purpose (better to assume something happened for a reason than to ignore it completely, right?). This specialization for making sense of agency means we're disposed to detect it even if it isn't strictly there—it is natural for us to use the language of intentions to describe events when there are no intentions. If you say that water "wants" to find the quickest way down the mountain, people understand you far easier than if you start talking about energy minimization, even though the water doesn't strictly *"want"* anything. It's natural to feel as if your computer hates you, just as it is natural to feel that people are deliberately making things hard for you,[1] when the sad fact is that most people probably aren't spending too much time thinking about you at all, and your computer certainly isn't thinking about you.

We can take advantage of our disposition to detect agency in objects, making them appear to be alive by adding just a few simple characteristics to the way they move.

In Action

One way of showing that something is pretty psychologically fundamental is to show that children do it. As soon as children can see, they expect to find animate objects in their environment and prefer to watch them than simple moving objects.[2] So we'll show how fundamental it is to perceive animate objects by showing some movement to a young kid and seeing how he interprets it.

Of course, you'll need a young kid to try this on, the younger the better, as long as he can understand and answer your questions.

 If you can't get ahold of one, you can give this a whirl yourself, sitting yourself in front of the Internet, following the links provided in the next section "How It Works" and watching the movies yourself.

Get two objects: it doesn't really matter what they are as long as they definitely aren't alive and don't look remotely like anything alive—it will help if they are different sizes; two rocks or wooden building blocks will work rather nicely. Put the two objects on a table and ask the child to pay attention to what you're about to do. Move the bigger object slowly toward the smaller. When they're within 2 inches of each other, move the small object very quickly to another part of the table. Immediately, have the large object change direction and head toward the new location of the small object. The large object always moves slowly toward wherever the small object is; the small object always stays at least 2 inches away.

Now, ask the child "What's happening here?"

It should be obvious to you from reading this description, and it will be obvious to the child, that the large object is trying to catch the small object. Just from physical movements the child will infer a guiding purpose and attach it to some kind of inner belief that is a property of the objects ("the large rock wants to catch the small rock"). He could just as easily say "You are moving the rocks around in a funny way," but he probably won't. He prefers the explanation that involves the rocks having intentions.

How It Works

The first experiments with animation involved movies of three simple shapes, two triangles and a circle, moving around a large rectangle. You can see something similar in the moving squares and circles by Heider and Simmel (*http://research.yale.edu/perception/animacy/HS-Blocks-Flash.mov*; QuickTime), a frame of which is shown in Figure 8-6.[3]

Regardless of what they were told to pay attention to, people who watched the movie attributed personality traits and emotions to the geometric figures. The shapes act alive, and you can't avoid thinking about them in those terms.

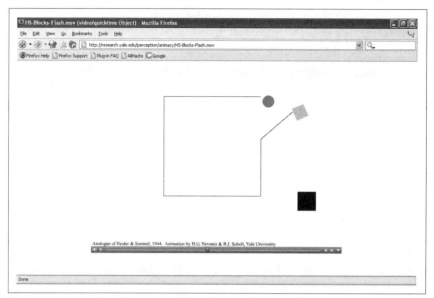

Figure 8-6. Notice how the static display offers no clues at all that the shapes are in any way animate

So what do simple objects have to do to look alive? The first, and most obvious, thing is to move on their own and to move in ways that seem self-caused. Changes in direction and velocity help.[4]

> My guess is that giving the object a rapid wobble or slow side-to-side roll while moving also helps give the impression that the thing is alive, although I haven't seen any studies confirming this. It mimics a walking, or feeling-the-way, motion and is something many people do spontaneously when pretending that an object is a living thing.
>
> —T.S.

If the shapes have an obvious "front" end to them and move along their main axis, that helps too. You can see this effect in a replication of the first movie, but with arrowheaded shapes at *http://research.yale.edu/perception/animacy/HS-Darts-Flash.mov*.

Shapes that follow goals and interact with their environment (pushing against things or swerving to avoid objects, for instance) also seem more alive. It isn't so important that the viewer can see the thing that is the goal of the object—merely acting to follow something is sufficient to create the impression of animacy. This last fact does make a kind of sense; one of the reasons our visual system has evolved to detect intention is not just to recognize it, but to predict what the purpose of someone or something's movement is. You may not know what a person is throwing rocks at, but the fact that you interpret their movements as "throwing rocks at something" means you will look for a target and that will increase your chance of finding out what it is.

End Notes

1. Hanlon's Razor: "Never attribute to malice that which can be adequately explained by stupidity" (*http://en.wikipedia.org/wiki/Hanlon's_Razor*).

2. Rochat, P., Morgan, R., & Carpenter, M. (1997). Young infants' sensitivity to movement information specifying social causality. *Cognitive Development, 12,* 537–561.

3. Heider, F., & Simmel, M., (1944). An experimental study of apparent behavior. *American Journal of Psychology, 57,* 243–259.

4. Tremoulet, P., & Feldman, J. (2000). Perception of animacy from the motion of a single object. *Perception, 29,* 943–951.

 ## HACK #79 Make Events Understandable as Cause and Effect

By following a couple of simple rules, you can show a clear pattern of cause and effect, and ensure your viewer is able to make the connection between separate things happening at the same time.

Research suggests that just as the visual system works to recover the physical structure of the world by inferring properties such as 3-D shape, so too does it work to recover the causal and social structure of the world by inferring properties such as causality and animacy.[1]

Perception is finding structure in sensations. Finding a structure to things lets you hold them in mind and store them in a memory-efficient way. If the structure corresponds to reality, it can also be used to provide predictions about the thing you're representing. So it's easier to think of several sections of cable on your desk as all being part of the same mouse lead, and once you've assumed that it's easy to find the mouse, you just follow the cable away from the stack.

We've already seen that the brain looks for structure in space [Hack #75] and structure in time [Hack #76] to organize perceptions. These principles apply to the basic perception of physical objects, as well as helping us understand how we make sense of our body images [Hack #64] and the bodies of other people [Hack #77].

But our visual system doesn't look for just static physical structures—it can also pick up on causal relationships between things. You don't see two things happening but rather one event: you don't stop to wonder why the plate smashed just at the same moment that it hit the floor.

This ability to detect causation and animacy [Hack #78] is a perceptual phenomenon, different from our slow deliberate reasoning about what causes what ("Hmm...why does my computer crash only after I have written at least 2000 words without saving?" is a different kind of nonperceptual, causal reasoning).

When our visual perception picks up on causes it does so quickly and without any conscious effort on our part. Like with many visual illusions, it happens without your consent and without any ability on your part to stop it, even if you wanted to and know that it is illusion.

In Action

Here's one way of seeing what I mean when I talk about the perception of causation. Make a pendulum, using whatever you have lying around and find something of similar size to whatever you use as a weight. It doesn't really matter what you use; I am using the cord from my camera with my keys as the weight. You'll also need another small object; I'm using a large red bottle lid from a drink bottle.

Hold the pendulum up in front of you and set it swinging left to right. Now take the other object in your free hand and wave it around at the side of the pendulum. It doesn't feel like anything special, does it? Now move the other object (in my case the bottle cap) in time with the pendulum, trying to keep it a fixed distance, say 5 inches, from the swinging weight. If you get the timing right, you should get the unmistakable impression that the object in your free hand is pulling the pendulum weight along and then pushing it back. This happens even though your body has direct evidence that the two events are causally unrelated: the pendulum moves itself and your own hand moves the unconnected object.

Notice that you don't just see the two things as moving together. You get a feeling, manufactured by your perceptual system and delivered direct into consciousness, that one thing causes another.

How It Works

The rules that govern the perception of causation are those you might expect. Events that happen in close succession and those that have a consistent relationship appear to be causally connected. But how close together in time and how consistent do things have to be to be perceived together?

One way of studying these questions is something called the launching paradigm (*http://www.carleton.ca/~warrent/210/michotte/michotte.html*), which was developed by Albert Michotte.

In the first demonstration (*http://www.carleton.ca/~warrent/210/michotte/michotte1.htm*; animated GIF), a red ball enters at the left of the screen and moves until it meets another red ball in the center of the screen. The first ball then stops, and the second ball moves off to the right. What you actually see however is more than that; you see a ball come along and knock into another one to start it moving, as in a game of pool.

If there is a pause between the two events, as in the second Michotte demonstration (*http://www.carleton.ca/~warrent/210/michotte/michotte2.htm*), you don't get the same impression of causality. How big does the pause have to be? Research has shown that if the pause is longer than 140 milliseconds, the feeling of one event causing the other is removed.[2]

I think this figure of 140 milliseconds might explain why, at a certain delay, using a gadget becomes annoying. If you press a key on your keyboard but the letter doesn't appear until a quarter of a second later, it removes the feeling that what you are doing with the computer is happening at the same time on the screen. The device stops being invisible in use and that stops you using it without thinking. It's annoying, in other words. I stop being able to type and have to start pressing the keys individually and waiting for the letters to appear on the screen before I press another one.

—T.S.

Spatial separation can also affect the perception of causality, although this isn't as critical as timing, as the pendulum test shows. A gap between the two balls in the launching paradigm removes causality, but this is a one-off causal relationship rather than a continuous one as simulated in the pendulum example. You can restore the feeling of causation by adding another ball between the two separated balls, so that you get a chain reaction from the first ball to launch the final one. Although the first and last balls are doing exactly the same thing as in the simple spatial separation example, making visible a causal relationship between restores the feeling of causality. Brian Scholl's movie at the Yale Perception and Cognition Laboratory[3] illustrates this (*http://research.yale.edu/perception/causality/toolEffect.mov*; QuickTime).

Scholl has also shown that visual events that don't normally create feelings of causal connection can be changed by the addition of other, related, simultaneous events that do create a perception of causality. This shows again that timing is the most important factor our visual system uses for inferring causality. (Incidentally, the reverse relationship also appears to be true. Events that we code as being causally related we perceive as being closer together in time than we would otherwise.[4])

So whether we perceive two events as causally connected is affected by what else is going on. When you hit a nail with a hammer, you feel as though you're the cause of the nail going in, even though your intention (the cause) and the strike (the effect) are separated in both time and space. The hammer, as a tool that provides a visual connection between the start and end events, ensures that a feeling of causality is present—one that wouldn't be if we saw the cause and effect events without it there.

Experiments have shown that delays of more than 2 seconds can prevent people learning that one event causes another[5]—although subsequent work has shown that something as simple as giving people a reason for the delay can double the maximum length of the cause-effect gap that can be coped with.[6]

The important message is that the brain doesn't really believe in coincidence, so if you can show what looks like it should be a causal effect, the brain will manufacture up a feeling of causation to go along with it. You can overcome a lack of direct contact between events by changing context, but you must get the timing right.

End Notes

1. Scholl, B. J., & Tremoulet, P. (2000). Perceptual causality and animacy. *Trends in Cognitive Sciences, 4*(8), 299–309.

2. Michotte, A. E. (1963). *The Perception of Causality* (T. R. Miles, trans.). London: Methuen & Co.

3. "Basic Causality & Animacy Demos" from Brian Scholl's pages at the Yale Perception and Cognition Laboratory (*http://pantheon.yale.edu/~bs265/demos/causality.html*).

4. Eagleman, D. M., & Holcombe, A. O. (2002). Causality and the perception of time. *Trends in Cognitive Sciences.* 6(8), 323–325

5. Shanks, D. R., Pearson, S. M., & Dickinson, A. (1989). Temporal contiguity and the judgment of causality by human subjects. *Quarterly Journal of Experimental Psychology, 41B*, 139–159.

6. Buehner, M. J., & May, J. (2004). Abolishing the effect of reinforcement delay on human causal learning. *Quarterly Journal of Experimental Psychology, 57B (2)*, 179–191.

See Also

- You have to pay attention to events to get the perceptual impression of causality: Choi, H., & Scholl, B. J. (in press). Effects of grouping and attention on the perception of causality. *Perception & Psychophysics*.

Act Without Knowing It

#80

How do we experience our actions as self-caused? It's not automatic; in fact, the feeling of consciousness may indeed have been added to our perception of our actions *after* our brains had already made the decision to act.

Place your hand on the table. Look at it as an object, not unlike just about anything else on the table. Now, raise one of your fingers. Why did you raise that one? Can you say? Was it a free choice? Or was the decision made somewhere else, somewhere in your brain you don't have access to? You experienced your finger being raised by *you*, but what was it in you that caused it?

If you record EEG readings [Hack #2] from the scalps of people just about to decide to raise their fingers and at the same time make them watch a timer and remember at what time they experienced deciding to raise their finger, they're found to report that the experience of deciding to raise their finger comes around 400 ms *after* the EEG shows that their brain began to prepare to raise their finger.[1] Stimulating particular parts of the brain using transcranial magnetic stimulation [Hack #5], you can influence which finger people choose to move,[2] yet they still experience their choice as somehow willed by them, somehow "theirs."

This is an example of how an action we feel we own may be influenced by things outside of our conscious deliberation. The feeling of conscious will isn't always a good indication that we consciously willed something. And the reverse can also be true. We can disown actions we are responsible for, doing things we don't feel are caused by our own will.

In Action

Draw a cross on a piece of paper. Next, make a pendulum out of something light: a button and a length of string is ideal. Now hold the pendulum over the cross and ask a question ("Is the button on this pendulum blue?" or "Is it lunchtime yet?" perhaps). Know that to indicate "yes" the pendulum will swing clockwise, and to answer "no" the pendulum will swing counterclockwise. Don't rest your arm or elbow on anything as it holds the pendulum. Just watch the pendulum as it begins to swing to answer to your question.

Odds are, the pendulum swung in the way that answered the question correctly.

How It Works

What you've just experienced is called the *ideomotor* effect.[3] It is the ideomotor effect that lies behind Ouija boards, dowsing wands, and facilitated communication (when helpers supposedly channel messages from the severely physically handicapped). There are no demons involved, except for the ordinary everyday human ones.

The movements produced in these cases are entirely self-caused (and, in the case of the Ouija board, self-caused *and shared* by a group of people)—but because we don't feel we've consciously caused the movement, we're able to disown the action and it appears to have an external cause, as if it has nothing to do with us. Spooky! We do (in case you were still worried) have everything to do with it. Muscle readings from people playing with Ouija boards show that self-generated signals move the marker; the marker does not move the people's hands attached to it. Ouija boards only provide answers that the participants already know—even if that knowledge is false. Some people have had conversations with "dead" people who have turned out to still be alive. Blindfolded participants for whom the board is rotated without their knowledge move the marker to the old, unrotated positions.

So when do we experience an action as self-caused? When don't we? Daniel Wegner of Harvard University[4] has suggested that "we experience conscious will when we interpret our own thought as the cause of the action." In other words, we infer our feeling of conscious will when we notice that our intention to act went hand in hand with whatever happened. That means that if we had no such intention, the feeling of conscious will doesn't occur and, conversely, that we can feel an event was self-caused even if it had nothing to do with us. It's similar to the feeling of causation [Hack #79], which we deduce from our perception of events—we have to, because it's impossible to perceive cause and effect directly. Our senses are all we have to work with.

Wegner suggests that the brain uses three basic principles in deciding whether to deliver an experience of conscious will: priority, consistency, and exclusivity. These are, respectively: that the thought precedes the action at an appropriate interval, that the thought is consistent with the action, and that the thought is the only candidate cause.

Now, in most situations, these conditions are met and we feel as if we properly own our actions. But in some situations, this isn't the case and we disown the action, like those of the pendulum. We make small muscle movements with the hand holding the pendulum, when thinking of the "yes" or "no" answer we expect to receive—muscle movements so small that we're barely aware that we're making them. Perhaps we would be aware of our muscles moving, except that the ultimate effect is so disproportionate: our hands move invisibly, but the pendulum swings obviously. The microthought versus the large swinging response violates the principle of consistency, and we can hardly believe that our own actions are a salient cause. That's why we don't experience self-cause and are willing to speculate about other, more proportionate, candidate causes: spirits from the afterlife and the like.

> Given this, it's easy to see how behaviors that happen without much conscious will or any effort manage to escape being labeled as self-caused, such as our "monkey see, monkey do" [Hack #98] response to other people's habits.

The fact that Wegner's principles are used to understand events external to the brain isn't too surprising. After all, we have no direct way of perceiving causation in external events other than by principles like priority, consistency, and exclusivity. What is even more interesting is that the brain uses the same principles for understanding internal events like conscious action. This suggests that there are serious limits to our conscious insight into the workings of our own brains. There are good computational reasons why this should be so. You'd be distracted if you were constantly being informed of just how all your decisions were being made by your brain. Most of the processing *has* to be below the surface for you to operate efficiently. The ideomotor effect and related phenomenon are evidence that when it came to conscious understanding of our own actions, our brain found it more convenient to evolve a secondary set of mechanisms to infer mental causation than open up our mental modules to give us direct, but time-consuming, insight.

End Notes

1. Kornhuber, H. H., & Deeke, L. (1965). Hirnpotentialänderungen bei Willkürbewegungen und passiven Bewegungen des Menschen: Bereitschaftspotential und reafferente Potentiale. *Pflügers Archiv, 284,* 1–17. Discussed in Wegner, D. M., & Wheatley, T. P. (1999). Apparent mental causation: Sources of the experience of will. *American Psychologist, 54,* 480–492.

2. Brasil-Neto, J. P., Pascual-Leone, A., Valls-Solé, J., Cohen, L. G., & Hallett, M. (1992). Focal transcranial magnetic stimulation and response bias in a forced-choice task. *Journal of Neurology, Neurosurgery and Psychiatry, 55,* 964–966.

3. Wikipedia entry for the ideomotor effect (*http://en.wikipedia.org/wiki/Ideomotor_effect*).

4. Daniel Wegner's home page (*http://www.wjh.harvard.edu/~wegner*) and his book on this topic. Wegner, D. M. (2002). *The Illusion of Conscious Will*. Cambridge, MA: MIT Press.

CHAPTER NINE

Remembering
Hacks 81–92

The idea of priming comes up more than once in this book. Given a single concept being activated in the brain, other associated concepts are quietly activated too, ready to impinge on consciousness or experience. Automatic associations lie behind the Stroop Effect [Hack #55], and the measurement of a type of priming is how we know that we unconsciously ready ourselves to make use of an object, just by laying eyes on it [Hack #67].

We dive into priming [Hack #81] in the first hack of this chapter, and from there, we'll see it manifested as subliminal perception [Hack #82] and implicated in the creation of false memory. For memory is the main topic here. We'll look at how false memories and familiarity come about [Hacks #83, #84 and #85], by using priming to activate concepts that have not been directly experienced.

We'll also look at how to build strong, true memories too, in the form of learning. Learning implicitly involves context, the situation you're in while you're doing the learning (that's another appearance of the associative nature of the mind). Exploiting this feature can help you learn better to begin with [Hack #86] and improve your recall skills in the future [Hack #87]. There's even a nifty trick on how to improve your memory using your built-in navigational skills too [Hack #89].

Along the way, we'll take in a grab bag of hacks on the reality of imagination. Such as how thinking about your muscles can make them stronger [Hack #88], or at least improve your control of them. Such as why you live your life from behind your eyes, but often remember it like a movie, in the third person [Hack #90]. And why you should fall asleep on the train to let your imagination run riot [Hack #91].

Last, but—particularly in the hacker crowd—certainly not least: caffeine. Why do people get so upset if you make their coffee the wrong way, and what's that got to do with learning anyway? Understand this, and make the caffeine habit taste good [Hack #92].

Bring Stuff to the Front of Your Mind

Just because you're not thinking of something doesn't mean it isn't there just waiting to pop into your mind. How recently you last thought of it, and whether you've thought of anything related to it, affects how close to the surface an idea is.

Things aren't just in your thoughts or out of them. It seems as if some things are nearer the surface while others are completely in the dark, tucked deep down in your mind.

The things near the surface jump out into the light without much prompting; they connect to other things you're thinking about, volunteer themselves for active duty in your cognitive processes, so to speak. This isn't always a good thing, as anyone who has tried to put an upcoming exam or interview out of mind will attest.

So what affects how deeply submerged mental items are? It probably wouldn't surprise you to hear that how recently something was last used is one of the key variables. Association is another factor: activating a mental item brings related items closer to the surface. Not always right to the surface, into conscious awareness, but closer at least, so that if you later reach for the general concept of the related item, the specific one will be more easily at hand. Psychologists use measures of the pre-preparedness of mental items to get a handle on the limitations of perception and on the associations between different concepts that your mind has absorbed.

In Action

We found this amusing when we were at school, so maybe you'll get the best results if you pick one of your more childish friends to try it out. For dramatic effect, claim beforehand—as we used to—that you can read your friend's mind. Then, ask her the following questions in quick succession:

1. What is 5 + 1?
2. What is 3 + 3?
3. What is 2 + 4?
4. What is 1 + 5?
5. What is 4 + 2?
6. What is the first vegetable you can think of?

Most people, most of the time, say "carrot."[1]

Here's something similar. Like the carrot game, it works best if you can get the person answering the question to hurry.

Tell her to say "milk" 20 times as quickly as she can, and then, just as she finishes, snap the question, "What do cows drink?" at her. If you've caught her off guard, she'll say "milk," even though the answer is truly "water."[2]

How It Works

Both of these examples take advantage of the principle that things—words, in this case—are not all equally accessible to consciousness. Some throw themselves into the limelight of awareness, while others are more reluctant to step forward.

Carrot is pretty much at the front of our minds when the topic is vegetables (especially after a bunch of arithmetic questions have flushed out other thoughts). With the cow question, saying "milk" 20 times puts that word right at the front of our mind, so much so that it gets out before we correctly parse the question.

This is all well and good if you want to know that a carrot is most people's prototypical vegetable or that they can be easily flustered if you get them to do something ridiculous like say "milk" 20 times.

But there is a valuable tool here for experimental psychologists as well. Encountering a word brings it forward in your mind. If you've heard a word a short while before, you are quicker to recognize it, quicker to make decisions about it, and more likely to volunteer it as an answer. You don't have to use just words—pictures and sounds too are more easily recognized after prior exposure.

The interesting thing is that these effects—called *priming*—persist after people have consciously forgotten that they have seen the item or even if they weren't aware of seeing the word at all [Hack #82]. The automatic nature of this effect allows cognitive psychologists to use it in a variety of tests to check whether people have been able to perceive material that they either weren't aware of at the time or have forgotten seeing. Psychologists call this kind of memory, which is revealed by performance rather than by explicit recall, implicit memory.

It has also become clear that things that are linked in your mind are primed by exposure to related things. So if you show someone the word "doctor," he finds it easier to subsequently detect the word "nurse" if the word appears covered by TV snow (the visual equivalent of white noise). Or if you show someone the word "red," he is more likely to complete a word stem like *gr___* with the word "green." If you show him the word "wine," he is more likely to complete with the word "grape." Both are valid answers, but the likelihood of one or the other being the first that comes to mind is affected by what other items have been primed in the mind.

We can think of all mental items being connected in a web of semantic units. When you see an item, it becomes activated, so that for a short while it is easier for it to reach a threshold of activity that pushes it into consciousness or allows you to recognize it. Activity can spread between related items in the web; sometimes this activity can influence your behavior in interesting ways **[Hack #100]**.

In Real Life

Primed concepts hover just below conscious thought, ready to pop out at a moment's notice. It is probably this priming that underlies the phenomenon in which, having learned a new word, you suddenly see it everywhere. The word is near the front of your mind and so all the times you would have otherwise ignored it become times when you now notice it. And when you're hungry, everything reminds you of food.

> My friend Jon used to play a trick on his girlfriend that uses priming and the fact that if you say something to a sleeping person she registers it without noticing that she has. He'd wait until she was asleep and then say a single word to her, like "kangaroo" or "tofu." A minute later, he'd wake her up and ask her what she was dreaming about. Often the word, or something related, would be incorporated into whatever she was dreaming about.
>
> —T.S.

Priming happens all the time; we're constantly noticing new things, bringing stuff to mind, and making associations. The interesting thing is that it is a two-way process, and one we underestimate. No one is surprised that the things we notice affect what we think of. Less often people account for the things we're thinking of affecting what we notice. More subtly, that which we noticed, even briefly and then forgot, influences both what we think *and* what we notice in the future. It feels like the same "you" who walks down the street every day, but what catches your eye and what occupies your mind are going to be different, in part, based on your TV viewing the night before, whether you're thinking about TV or not. It's not an intuitive thing to be able to account for, but it's part of the constant sifting and sorting of mental items that makes up our mental life.

End Notes

1. *New Scientist*'s "Last Word" column on "Carrot Brains" (*http://www. newscientist.com/lastword/article.jsp?id=lw613*).

2. Apart from baby cows, which might actually get milk, and cows in factory farms that probably drink some sort of antibiotically-enhanced nutrient-rich steroid-laden power juice.

Subliminal Messages Are Weak and Simple

Subliminal perception sneaks underneath the level of consciousness and can influence your preferences—but only a little.

Being exposed to a photograph for two-hundredth of a second can't really be called seeing, because you won't even be consciously aware of it. But having a photo flashed at you like this works it into your subliminal perception and means that next time you see it you'll—very slightly, mind—prefer it to one you've never been exposed to before.

In Action

Proving that mere exposure can change your preferences isn't easy to do at home, so it's best to look at the experiments. Robert Bornstein and Paul D'Agostino exposed a group of volunteers to images, either photographs or unfamiliar shapes, and then asked each person to rate the images according to how much he or she liked them.[1]

If you were one of those volunteers, you'd have spent 5–10 minutes at the beginning of the experiment being exposed to images for only 5 milliseconds each. That's a tiny amount of time for vision, only as long as a quarter of one frame of television. Exposed to a picture for that long, you're not even aware you've seen it. As a volunteer, you could be shown the picture later to look at, and it's as if you're seeing it for the first time.

When you're asked which images you prefer out of a larger selection, you'll rate images you were exposed to but can't recall seeing higher.

In Real Life

The rating exercise is a little like the game Hot or Not (*http://www.hotornot.com*) but with some of the photos flashed up at you faster than you can make them out beforehand. In Hot or Not, you see a photo of a person and rate it: 10 being Hot and 1 being Not. The web page then immediately reloads with another photo for you to rate, and you can also see how your score on the previous photo compared to what everyone else said.

All else being equal—all the photos being equally attractive—let's pretend you're rating all the photos 5 on average.

If you'd had the photo flashed up at you 20 times in that initial batch of image exposure, for only 5 ms each time (less than a tenth of a second in total!), you might rate that photo not a 5, but a 6.

> Given this works for mere exposure, below the level of awareness, the same effect should come about if the photo is presented in some other fashion that doesn't require your attention. Thinking of Hot or Not still, incorporating a photo into a banner ad (now we're all trained not to look at banners) for a few pages before you actually have to rate the photo should mean you like the photo more.
>
> —M.W.

How It Works

Two things are going on here. The first is subliminal perception. The visual system has just enough time to get the image presented into the brain, but not enough to process it fully to conscious awareness. In addition to subliminal perception, there is a priming [Hack #81] effect. Whenever some perception reaches the brain, the neurons that are involved in that representation persist in their activity for a while, and if you experience that thing again, your neurons respond more readily to it.

So when your perception of a particular face has been subliminally primed, when you see the photograph again, properly, your brain reports a very slight sense of familiarity. But because you can't actually recall seeing the photo before, you misinterpret this feeling as preference: you like the face in the photo more than you otherwise would have done.

Mere exposure is the phenomena behind the urban legend of subliminal perception, in which the words "Hungry? Eat popcorn" repeatedly flashed up (too fast to consciously see) during a movie is supposed to result in a colossal increase in popcorn consumption. It's correct inasmuch as repeated exposures lead to a stronger priming effect, and therefore a slightly stronger preference—but that's all.

The experiments that led to the "Hungry? Eat popcorn" legend were fabricated in the 1950s.[2] What mere exposure can do is slightly influence you if you're undecided about which goal to pursue. Being exposed to a picture of a particular chocolate bar could encourage you to pick out that bar if you're standing at a counter with a dozen different bars a few minutes later. What mere exposure *can't* do is give you an overpowering hunger to stand up, walk off, and find that chocolate, or even make you buy chocolate if you've already decided you want chips.

Nor can mere exposure influence you with complicated instructions. There's barely enough time for the image of the three words "Hungry? Eat popcorn" to bump through your visual production line, to make a representation in your brain, but certainly not enough for the words to be understood as a sentence. A photograph, a shape, or a single word is as far as it goes.

> To be honest, subliminal advertising doesn't seem worth the effort for such a small effect. Given that pretty, barely clothed people doing suggestive things on TV sell products so well, I don't see a shift to subsecond commercial breaks any time soon. Unless, of course, that's what the images are *telling* me to say.
>
> —M.W.

End Notes

1. Bornstein, B. F., & D'Agostino, P. R. (1992). Stimulus recognition and the mere exposure effect. *Journal of Personality and Social Psychology, 63*(4), 545–552.

2. The Snopes Urban Legends Reference page on subliminal advertising (*http://www.snopes.com/business/hidden/popcorn.asp*) gives more of the "eat popcorn" story. James Vicary, who made the claims in 1957, came clean some time later about the results of his experiments, but the concept of subliminal advertising has been doing the rounds since.

HACK #83 Fake Familiarity

Hack memory to make people feel they've seen something before.

The memory system is chockablock with hacks. The information that our environment constantly provides exceeds any viable storage capacity, so memory employs a variety of methods that allow it to be choosy. One memory experience we all know is the feeling of familiarity for previously seen things or people. The process beneath it is quick and feels automatic, with an almost perceptual flavor. As we will see, that is not too far from the truth. However, there are hidden layers that contribute to this process, and these can be revealed by the use of a memory illusion.

In Action

Try this teasing task, using stimuli from Whittlesea and Williams' 1998 study.[1] Or better yet find a volunteer to tax instead. Look at the words in

Table 9-1, one at a time (around 2–3 seconds a word), in both columns. Then take a breather for a minute or two.

Table 9-1. Study each word for 2 to 3 seconds each

MACHINE	ISOLATE
DAISY	FRAMBLE
FISSEL	SUBBEN
PNAFTED	STOFWUS
FAMILIAR	VASSIL
COELEPT	DETAIL
HADTACE	GERTPRIS
STATION	MEUNSTAH
PLENDON	HENSION

Now turn to the second list of words, Table 9-6, at the very end of this chapter. Go through the second list and check/tick with a pencil those that feel familiar (if you like, you can put a cross by those you definitely didn't see).

What did you experience? Most people find that while the real words were easy to identify one way or another, certain of the nonwords had a creeping feeling of familiarity. Possibly you checked/ticked some that, in fact, you hadn't seen. If so, your recognition memory has just been royally messed with.

How It Works

This test is a good way to bring out the heuristic, fast-and-loose nature of recognition memory. When we encounter something we have experienced before, familiarity can hit us extremely rapidly. This feeling need not be accompanied by extensive memory information, which shows it isn't due to deep memory retrieval. Instead, recognition memory seems to be piggybacking on the rapid incoming sensory information to flood us with this sense of "having seen." What qualities of perception might be useful? Well, as seen before, items that have been seen recently are processed faster and more easily [Hack #81]—we can call this *fluent processing*, or just *fluency*. The level of fluency you experience when you encounter something should be an ideal source of information for recognition memory; if you feel fluent in something, it's a good sign you've seen it before. But there's a problem.

Consider catching sight of your partner as you enter your home after work versus the situation in which you catch sight of a less familiar figure in an incongruous situation (say, your boss at a nightclub). The flash of familiarity comes in only the second situation, even though the first is far more common. So it turns out the fluency system is a little bit smarter. It needs to be, or we would spend our waking life overwhelmed by the familiarity of every experienced object in our environment. Other mechanisms are brought in to compensate for the high level of fluency associated with regularly encountered experiences. For example, words are processed extremely fluently, due to our dedicated language systems [Hack #49], and so the mind usually takes this extra fluency into account when presented with meaningful verbal items.

The complication in word lists like the ones in the tables is that there is no clear division between word things and certain of the nonwordlike things, the ones you felt you'd seen before. These nonwords are meaningless yet nonetheless have the structure of words and therefore feed into the mind as easily as they trip off the tongue, becoming more fluent than nonwords ought to be. This discrepancy—a "surprising fluency," as Whittlesea puts it—fools your brain into concluding you've seen the nonwords before. The effect extends to music, with famous tunes, well-structured (catchy) and ill-structured (less musical) novel tones. The brain takes a measure of its own speed of processing (fluency) and uses *that* to produce smart and fast information about the environment—in this case, whether the specific experience has been had before. Well-structured tunes get falsely tagged as already heard much more than the others, because they have more fluency.

> Not all false recognition research revolves around this internal measure of fluency. False familiarity can be produced by other means: for example, subjects can find the word "sleep" familiar when they have previously heard the word "snooze," because the two terms are associated, an effect known as priming [Hack #81]. The argument traditionally goes that the familiarity results not from fluency, but that, if you hear a word (and activate it in your brain), it passes on some of that activation to associated words. That's the principle behind the techniques in "Create False Memories" [Hack #85], although that's not to say that future research won't settle on an explanation based on a fluency mechanism for these false familiarity effects after all.

In Real Life

This kind of memory illusion serves advertisers well in their search for ways to get products in with the public: word-like product names are not only easier to repeat, but feel more familiar the first time around, as can musical jingles and catchphrases. Bearing in mind the slight, but real effect that mere exposure [Hack #82] can have, this makes fluency a design ambition. It could have more serious ramifications when it comes to the law, as the process of identifying criminals can involve amplification of ambiguous feelings, such as "I've seen you before—but where?" Such feelings could be produced by preexposure to a suspect among hundreds of mug shots before a lineup or a glimpse of the subject's face in a mug shot book before the ID session has officially begun.

But we must recognize that these highlighted errors reflect a fundamental process, one essential to our day-to-day behavior, as fluent processing flips us into familiarity mode only when something in the environment falls out of line with expectations. It's a handy hack, using "norms on the fly," as Whittlesea puts it.[1]

There is an ongoing debate about the localization of mechanisms upon which familiarity responses depend, with the parahippocampal gyrus (part of the limbic system [Hack #7], adjacent to the hippocampus in the temporal lobe) being touted as a candidate region. It is clear that, relative to the healthy brain, damage to temporal lobe regions impair both recognition and recall memory, but there is conflict over whether these amnesiac patients are more prone to these memory errors or actually less; this is becoming a topic of considerable interest in neuroscience.

Familiarity could be considered the cognitive equivalent of sensory pop-out (just like flat shapes that pop out into 3D using shading to emulate shadows [Hack #20]), but our brain makes sure these things pop out only when they tend to be useful, harnessing higher-level expectations and lower-level rules of thumb to home in on the interesting features of our environment.

End Note

1. Whittlesea, B. W. A., & Williams, L. D. (1998). Why do strangers feel familiar, but friends don't? A discrepancy-attribution account of feelings of familiarity. *Acta Psychologica, 98*, 141–165.

See Also

- "Social Psychology Principles Can Be Used to Facilitate Eyewitness Testimony" (*http://www.uplink.com.au/lawlibrary/Documents/Docs/Doc51. html*).

— *Alex Fradera*

Keep Your Sources Straight (if You Can)

HACK #84

When memory serves up information upon request, it seems to come packaged with its origin and sender. But these details are often produced ad hoc and may not fully match the true source.

Every memory has a source—or at least it ought to. That said, memories can often float loose from their moorings, making it some achievement that we manage to anchor mnemonic detail to their origins.

In Action

This test involves word stems, the idea being to complete the beginning of each stem in Table 9-2 with a word of your choice. So *ple___* (complete it with any number of letters) could be "please," or equally "pledge," "pleat," and so on. Complete the odd-numbered stems (the ones on the left) out loud; for the even-numbered ones (on the right), merely *imagine* saying the words. Use a different word for each stem (i.e., don't use "please" twice if you run across the *ple___* stem twice).

Table 9-2. Stem completion task. Think of a word to complete each stem. Speak the ones on the left out loud, but the ones on the right just in your head.

Complete out loud	Imagine completing out loud
1. BRE___	
	2. MON___
3. FLA___	
	4. TAR___
5. SAL___	
	6. FLA___
7. SPE___	
	8. BRE___
9. TAR___	
	10. SPE___
11. MON___	
	12. SAL___

Take a break! This is a memory test, so you need to pause for 1 or 2 minutes before reading on.

Now see if you remember your two *fla___* words (it should be fairly easy) and whether they were spoken or imagined. You've got a fair chance of being right, although you'd likely make a few slips across the whole list. Try the whole list if you like, giving both items and whether you said them out loud or in your head: *bre__*, *spe__*, *sal__*, *tar__*, *mon__*, and *fla__*. It's probable that you can remember what you said for most words, and usually whether it was spoken or imagined. But while this is not an impossible task, you are in no way guaranteed to get the source of a recalled item correct.

Now in the traditional view of the mind, the idea that memories could stray from their true context—that there is no master index putting all our memories in their place—is rather troublesome. On the other hand, consider what was done: when you come to look back, you have memories that are in most respects equivalent—for both spoken and imagined answers, you are left with a purely mental record of you saying the word. At the time, saying the word out loud was different from just imagining it, but now all that remains of both events is just an internal image of you saying the word. Yet, somehow, for the most part, we can distinguish the real event from the imaginary kind. That you've done it at all seems a testament to the memory system, as there are no obvious hooks to pull apart the problem.

Let's dig a bit deeper into this...

How It Works

If memories were items—whole events that were fed into memory from an ideal memory system—it would be odd for us to retrieve a detail stripped of context. In the previous task, this would be knowing a word but not knowing if it were really said; but other mistakes taken from research include confusing the gender of the voice that spoke a word, or whether information was presented in the lab, learned outside it, or given in an audio or visual modality. The fact that we can make these errors pushes us to accept that memories are not holistic (read: nicely packaged) entities. Given further consideration, it is hard to imagine how they could be so and still be useful.

Consider this: how could you (or your brain) objectively and instantly demarcate the boundaries of what constitutes a single event? An event is as long as a piece of string, just as an "item" is as many features as you need to make that item. Figuring out what an "event" or "item" is, is an implausible task. If the brain were to attempt it, we would be stuck halfway to nowhere.

Once we reject this view and, in so doing, are freed to look at memories as collections of features, we can again wonder how it is that we can reconnect a memory detail with its source. This is a property memory needs to function well, so it should come as no surprise that the brain has found a solution. This is the use of multiple processes (parallel processing is a common pattern [Hack #52]): one to allow quick automated categorization, coupled with a fact-checker to catch any major glitches and inconsistencies.

The quick system is a "heuristic" route, which relies on generalities about the mental world to make snap classifications. So, for example, there is usually a greater degree of perceptual and contextual information in *perceived* events relative to *imagined* events. Imagined images are probably sparser in content and richness of detail, so a memory that is full of detail and vividness can be quickly categorized as a good candidate for being a real memory. Even when the situations seem identical, there are subtle differences in memory quality that may be exploited; we can make comparisons in different modalities (audio/visual) to exploit different, but analogous, perceptual and contextual discrepancies.

> The second, a "systematic" route, steps through the event in question, using other knowledge bases to appraise whether this labeling is consistent with wider facts (despite my gut feeling, is it really likely I had a pillow fight with Viggo Mortensen last night?) and can step in and reverse decisions made by the quick route.
>
> —A.F.

In Real Life

Great examples of source confusion abound. The pioneer neurologist Charcot's patient LeLog was convinced his paralysis was due to his legs being crushed in a traffic accident, yet this injury had never occurred and, in fact, his paralysis had no physical basis. LeLog had mentally rehearsed this situation to the extent that it began to obtain the flavor of reality, leading Charcot to coin the notion that the mind may be parasitized by suggested ideas. A less extreme outcome of source confusion in the healthy mind is unconscious plagiarism.[1,2] This is the consequence of being presented with an idea, usually in a situation in which the ownership may not be explicit or emphasized (brainstorming in a group or hearing a ditty on the radio without any clear sense of the artist), and consequently believing the idea is genuinely your own. Often the individual will rehearse and revisit the idea, and this can demolish its association with an external source or speaker. These errors can lead to merry legal escapades, especially as the accused will be unwilling to back down even in the face of incontrovertible evidence, due to the certainty we have in our own memory. Even Mark Twain, that most individual and independent-minded writer, fell foul of this.[3] The same effect may lead to rather less costly squabbles, as evidenced by studies that show identical twins can dispute the possession of certain memories[4]; the degree of shared existence and confidences in these situations can lead to the real identity of memory protagonists being blurred.

When we turn to the abnormal functioning of the memory system, we are faced with a far more extreme example, that of patients who display confabulations.[5] These individuals will give fanciful, false responses to questions in totally good faith, mixing details from films, current affairs, or their distant past into statements about their current activities. These individuals can be otherwise functioning fairly normally, and rationally intact, even embarrassed by inconsistencies in the memories they express, but will insist that this is what their minds are offering them. Often information that has been recently presented will be regurgitated as distinctive personal experience, the source dislocated from the item itself.

The reason that we, unlike these patients, rarely produce phantoms of this magnitude is believed to be due to a stellar monitoring and assessment system distributed within the frontal lobes of the brain. It sifts through mental items and labels them correctly as fantasy, fact, or nonsense or warns us that we do not have enough certainty to say either way. We may occasionally forget whether we were intending to turn the oven off or actually did so, but it is rare indeed that we will find ourselves confusing an intention to complete an information-rich task (say, going to visit a relative) with actually having done so.

These systems seem to be at fault within these confabulators, which, in combination with deep memory deficits, allows the creative elements of the mind to weave stories out of piecemeal elements. Confabulations seem to require damage to the two systems together: a severe problem with memory coupled with the lifting of the monitoring systems that prevent flights of fancy and other intact but irrelevant memories being crowned with the status of authenticity.

 We should also note that, as with many memory dysfunctions, there are likely multiple kinds of confabulation. In particular, damage to the *posterior orbitofrontal cortex*, a structure in the anterior limbic system (the limbic system is implicated, in part, in memory. See "Get Acquainted with the Central Nervous System" **[Hack #7]** for more), is argued to cause insistent confabulation by a rather unusual route, namely damage to a motivational system.[6] The idea is that memories are normally given markers that signify whether the information "pertains to now," but damage to the brain region warps this mechanism so all memories are tagged this way. Any memory brought into consciousness is accompanied by a deep subjective feeling of relevance that is normally afforded to only truly relevant information.

End Notes

1. Stark, L. J., Perfect, T. J., & Newstead, S. (2004). When elaboration leads to appropriation: Unconscious plagiarism in a creative task. *Memory* (in press).

2. Applied info about plagiarism—has a cognitive bent but contains lots of practical tips for teachers—can be found at *http://www.psychologicalscience.org/teaching/tips/tips_0403.html*.

3. Mark Twain anecdote delivered at the dinner given by the publishers of *The Atlantic Monthly* to Oliver Wendell Holmes, in honor of his 70th birthday, August 29, 1879 (*http://www.search-engine-lists.com/marktwain/unconscious-plagiarism.html*).

4. Sheen, M., Kemp, S., & Rubin, D. (2001). Twins dispute memory ownership: a new false memory phenomenon. *Memory & Cognition, 29*(6), 779–788.

5. See "Soul In A Bucket," a chapter of Paul Broks' *Into the Silent Land* (London: Atlantic Books, 2003), which features a patient who confabulates and an eloquent summary of the features of the condition.

6. *Schnider, A.* (2003). Spontaneous confabulation and the adaptation of thought to ongoing reality. *Nature Reviews Neuroscience, 4*(8), 662–671.

—Alex Fradera

Create False Memories

Here is one way of creating memories of things that you haven't actually experienced.

We've seen how memory's way of orienting us to our surroundings has all the ingredients for a hack **[Hack #83]**—a fast-and-loose process that is expressed through gut sensation. Here we will see that even more measured and absolute experiences, like recalling an event or information, can also be fooled. The processes that sit behind familiarity, or word recall (in this example), use a whatever-works principle. They're ad hoc, not carefully designed filing systems that pack away memories and bring them out later for comparison or regurgitation. By seeing where these processes break down, here by constructing very simple false memories, we can shed light on how memory works.

In Action

Let's show false memory construction with a couple of word lists. First wrap your eyes around the words in Table 9-3, read them out loud once, then close the book and try to list all the words you saw.

Table 9-3. Read these words aloud straight off, and then close the book and write down all you can remember

THREAD	POINT	HURT
PIN	PRICK	INJECTION
EYE	THIMBLE	SYRINGE
SEWING	HAYSTACK	CLOTH
SHARP	THORN	KNITTING

Do the same with the next set listed in Table 9-4: read the words aloud, then close the book and make a list.

Table 9-4. As before, read these words aloud, and then write down all you can remember

BED	WAKE	SNORE
REST	SNOOZE	NAP
AWAKE	BLANKET	PEACE
TIRED	DOZE	YAWN
DREAM	SLUMBER	DROWSY

 Make your lists before reading ahead to get the most out of this hack.

Don't worry about the words you didn't get. But did your lists include either "needle" or "sleep"? If so, you should know that those two words were phantoms in your mind: They're not in either list! This is the *Deese/ Roediger/McDermott paradigm*, or DRM,[1] and highlights how the fallibility of memory is not limited to the absence of information but includes outright fabrications. Experts believe that this doesn't represent glitches in the system but an outcome of the healthy memory system—built as well as needs be.

One point ought to be noted: when this technique is used, subjects are asked not to guess and typically will afterward state that they reported the "critical lure" (the lure is one of the words we asked whether you'd seen just now, but which wasn't in either list, e.g., "needle") not because they had a hunch that it could be there, but because they actually remember seeing it.

In other words, there is a reported subjective experience of the word that wasn't there. This experience seems strong enough to produce better memory for the critical lures (which were never seen) than for the real items when retested two days later!

This technique can also be used to test recognition memory, but we are showcasing recall here due to the effect being so surprising, and recognition being already described [Hack #83].

How It Works

The exact causes of this phenomenon are still up for debate. Obviously, the similarity of the listed items to the critical lure is essential—in the parlance, these words are *associates of the lure*. A popular argument is that items are represented in the mind in a relational network, each neighbored by its closest associates: when an item is flagged, it sends activation to surrounding nodes, and with the DRM all the critical lure's neighbors are being flagged, setting it off as surely as you could burn down a building by setting fires all around it. Sure enough, the more associates you show, the more the phantom pops out.

> Interestingly enough, there have been some recent arguments that this might also be due to fluency [Hack #83], in that you actively pull the word "needle" out of memory to appraise whether it feels as if it were seen recently, and due to all the existing activation, it bubbles into consciousness quicker than it ought. The alternative view would be that when you are struggling to pick your brain for words, the ones that are selected are the most active. This may seem like a slender difference, but one is top-down—some specialist system is doing the choosing—and the other bottom-up.
>
> —A.F.

What is critical to understand is that an internal representation is being elicited, without the express intention of the subject, and later being confused with an external event. In this sense it is similar to, though distinct from, the memory error described in "Keep Your Sources Straight (if You Can)" [Hack #84].

In Real Life

It's clear that an idea can be lodged in our heads by using backdoor techniques. A thought can be created in our minds with just inference and association, rather than by being explicitly stated.

Indeed, explicitly making a claim or suggestion can provoke people to disagree. If you are trying to persuade people of something—such as your product being somehow better, brighter, or more healthy—it may be better to *imply an association* rather *than make a direct claim* that can be contested.

The DRM reveals how we may bypass rational channels and achieve this end directly in memory by exploiting the brain's tendency to elicit ideas and concepts as a consequence of exposure to its associates. It suggests that the words "injection," "thimble," and "thread" may spark a thought of "needle" due, not to a leap of logic, but to the dance of association within mental networks.

This hack also serves as a circumscribed example of truly false memory. As told in other hacks [Hacks #83 and #84], events can be falsely familiar, or wrongly identified as to their source—even to the extent of confusing imagination with true past events. Now we see that we can produce information that really wasn't there at all. In addition, studies show that totally false but plausible events can be inserted into people's diaries and then accepted as a true event.[2,3] We also know that people presented with a visual scene (such as a photograph) will often remember more of the scene than was actually presented; they fill in the scene with what makes sense to be there. It has been suggested that this phenomenon is a consequence of automatic activation of what is typically associated with this scene—very similar to the DRM situation about which we've been talking. So while we've suggested that memory may be somewhat constructed [Hack #83], these are examples in which memory is totally constructed, providing it fits into the scripts and representations we have of our lives.

Accurate memory is critical when it forms the basis of a criminal accusation. We discussed eyewitness memory [Hack #83] before, but we could also consider recovered memories, particularly those that involve alleged abuse.[2] Organizations have arisen to highlight how memory slips, such as filling in details that feel as though they could mesh with the situation or mistaking an imagined event for a real event, can lead to nonexperienced events seeming real. However, recent research demonstrates that we can direct ourselves to forget certain events, under the influence of frontally situated brain control systems (systems under voluntary control)—that is, given a list of words, you can say to yourself "forget these words" and find those words harder to recall in the future.[4] Given this, the idea that troubling events inevitably lead to strong and present memories isn't necessarily true, and it seems likely that recovered memories will need to be assessed on their individual basis and content.

The view of the memory system that brain and behavioral sciences have unlocked is one of distributed pattern completion. We ought to reject any notion of a *veridical* memory system (a memory system of statements corresponding exactly with a truthful reality). The brain doesn't favor discrete storage of information; there isn't a dusty file cabinet filled with DAT tapes stuffed with video and audio files and lists of facts.

Instead, memories are represented in the brain as networks of related features. Features that activate together cohere into a seamless, single, conscious memory. New memories are new associations in the same networks. The mechanisms that contribute to this coherence—the conscious experience of memory—are likely to be an exciting frontier in the years to come, and we hope to see neuroscientific advances combine with refinements of philosophical positions on the concepts of memory: from mental time travel (experiencing the past) to ways of knowing.

Memory may be constructed, but it works and indeed seems fairly optimal for many of our needs. It may be nonveridical—forget about any analogy of cameras rolling in our heads—but its fidelity is good enough that our past is maintained as a largely unbroken narrative, allowing us to be seated in an autobiographical identity.

Perhaps more important, the system is "good enough" to map the broad strokes of our realities: memory performs the functions we need it to. For example, our memory mechanisms mean we're particularly good at remembering the remarkable in our surroundings, and associated concepts come easily to mind. These are useful in real life. In general, it's handy that the concepts "bed" and "sheet" call the associated idea of "sleep" to mind—it's only in contrived list-learning situations, such as in the previous "In Action" section, in which we'd label that as a bad thing.

End Notes

1. Roedigger, H. L., & McDermott, K. B. (1995). Creating false memories: remembering words not presented in lists. *Journal of Experimental Psychology: Learning Memory and Cognition, 21*, 803–814.

2. Loftus, E. F., & Ketcham, K. (1994). *The Myth of Repressed Memory: False Memory and Allegations of Sexual Abuse.* New York: St Martins Press. See also *http://www.fmsfonline.org*, a group that campaigns against recovered memory movements.

3. Schacter, D. L., Norman, K. A., & Koutstaal, W. (1998). The cognitive neuroscience of constructive memory. *Annual Review of Psychology, 49*, 289–318.

4. Anderson, M. C., & Green, C. (2001). Suppressing unwanted memories by executive control. *Nature, 410*(6826), 366–369.

See Also

- Barclay, C. R., & Wellman, H. M. (1986). Accuracies and inaccuracies in autobiographical memories. *Journal of Memory and Language, 25,* 93–103.
- A good book on the whole issue: Schacter, D. L., Coyle, J. T., Fischbach, G. D., Mesulam, M. M., & Sullivan, L. E. (eds.) (1995). *Memory Distortion: How Minds, Brains, and Societies Reconstruct the Past.* Cambridge, MA: Harvard University Press.

—*Alex Fradera*

Change Context to Build Robust Memories

When you learn something, you tend to store context as well. Sometimes this is a good thing, but it can mean your memories don't lend themselves to being recalled in different circumstances.

This situation should sound familiar to almost all of you: you're trying to remember the name of the guy who wrote that book you read at some point in the not-too-distant past. You can't remember his name, but you can remember that he's a Canadian who moved to the United States and also writes about politics and has affairs with minor celebrities. You had a copy of the book about 5 years ago, the cover was reddish, and you packed it into a box when you moved and haven't seen it since then. You remember reading the book in the old café that they've since turned into a video rental store. You remember an amazing amount about the book and loads of information associated with it...just not the name of the guy who wrote it. What gives?

Often, you don't know in advance what details you need to remember for later recall. There aren't any clean boundaries between relevant and not relevant, and there are no tags reading "You will be tested on this later." So instead of remembering only what you choose to learn or are sure to need later, your brain files away many intricate details of context.

To you, this is just the context, but in your memory, it isn't necessarily sharply defined as such. Your memory is a set of interlinked and interleaved representations [Hack #87], so that in a fundamental sense the context can be part of the memory as much as the thing intended to be learned is part of the memory.

One consequence of this is that reinstating the original context helps you recall what you originally learned in that context. Another is that any consistent context associated with the learned item will become part of the memory for that item. Sometimes this can be a good thing, as is the case when you're trying to recall details you didn't know were going to be useful at the time or when you are trying to reproduce a skilled behavior in exactly the same circumstances in which you learned it. Other times it can hinder your recall of the memory in isolation—when you're out of that context.

In Action

Here's an example of how the automatic encoding of context affects learning—in this case, skill learning (skills are memories too). It's called the *contextual interference effect*, and it goes like this: practicing a collection of skills in a random order is better than practicing them in runs.

So, for example, if you are learning Japanese, writing each character of the hiragana (one of the three alphabets used in Japanese) is a separate motor skill. So it might be better to practice your hiragana by writing all of them out together, rather than copying out a hundred copies of one character, then a hundred copies of the next, and so on. You learn slower this way, but you remember better.

Ste-Marie et al. used this technique when teaching grade two students handwriting, practicing writing the letters *h*, *a*, and *y*.[1] After writing each letter only 24 times, the students who practiced the letters in a mixed-up fashion had better handwriting (i.e., better motor memories) than the students who practiced in blocks, as soon as the very next day. You can acquire new skills more effectively even after this short a time.

Even better, skills you have learned like this transfer better to new situations. If you learn by repeating the same skill again and again, you're going to learn it in the context of repetition rather than how to do it one-off. Practicing with a series of one-offs means you learn in many different contexts, and the memorized skill is more sharply defined. It's easier to recall and apply to a new context because it isn't interwoven as tightly with the learned context.

How It Works

Most of the research on the contextual interference effect has involved simple motor memories—these are skill memories, the kind you use in throwing Frisbees, juggling, or swinging a golf club.

The effect is generally found only for skills that require significantly different movements from each other. So, for example, you see a contextual interference effect if you mix practice of throwing underarm and overarm, but not if you mix practice of throwing a ball underarm exactly 2.7 meters and practice of throwing a ball underarm exactly 3.2 meters. The skills in the first example use the muscles in different combinations and with different relative timings. Separate motor memories are created for the movements. In the second example, the two skills are just parameter-adjusted versions of the same motor memory.

The contextual interference effect works only if you have some degree of experience in the skills you're practicing. To run into a contextual interference effect, the rough framework of the motor memory must already be established. For example, when you first start learning the Japanese alphabet, you don't even have a skill you can practice—you draw each character very deliberately (and badly!) and do it differently each time. Later, when you've learned the rough shape of the character and are beginning to produce it automatically, the rate at which you can improve the skill becomes open to the contextual interference effect.

One possible cause of the contextual interference effect is that interleaving the practicing of different skills requires concentration. It's certainly true that mixed practice is less boring, and we tend to remember less boring things more easily. But this also begs a question: interleaved learning may be better because it prevents boredom, but why does monotony bore us in the first place? Maybe boredom is the mechanism our brain uses to make us provide it a sufficient variety of input for optimal learning!

But the main cause of the effect is that random-order learning softens the brain's normal tendency to encode context along with the core memory. Usually this is a good thing—like when you are trying to recall where you first heard a song, met a person, or who wrote a book you once read—but it can prevent us forming sharp edges on our memories and reduce our ability to recall and use them in different situations.

End Note

1. Ste-Marie, D. M., Taylor, G., & Cumming, J. "The Effects of Contextual Interference on Handwriting Skill Acquisition" (*http://www.health. uottawa.ca/hkgrad/mllab/cieffe.html*).

See Also

- Magill, R. A. & Hall, K. G. (1990). A review of the contextual interference effect in motor skill acquisition. *Human Movement Science, 9,* 241–289.

- Ste-Marie, D. M., Clark, S. E., Findlay, L. C., & Latimer, A. E. (2004). High levels of contextual interferences enhance handwriting skill acquisition. *Journal of Motor Behaviour, 36,* 1, 115–126.

- Wright, D. L., Black, C. B., Immink, M. A., Brueckner, S., & Magnuson, C. (2004). Long-term motor programming improvements occur via concatenation of movement sequences during random but not during blocked trials. *Journal of Motor Behaviour, 36,* 1, 39–50.

HACK #87 Boost Memory Using Context

Your memories aren't stored discretely like objects in a filing cabinet; rather, they are interleaved with other things in memory. This explains why you're good with faces but not with names, why you should go back to your hometown to better remember your school days, and maybe even why you dream, too.

Human memory is not organized like a filing cabinet or a hard disk drive. In these storage systems, each memory is neatly indexed and stored so that it doesn't affect any other memory. The items in a computer memory don't affect processing unless they are explicitly retrieved, and to retrieve them, you have to consult an index to work out where they are. If you don't know where they are or if you don't have the right tag by which to access the files, you're out of luck—you're stuck with a brute force look through each file, one by one. The same holds for finding related items—you do it through some form of indexing system or again resort to a brute-force search. The system is content-blind.

But human memory is even further unlike any filing cabinet or computer memory system. This is the fundamental difference: *human memories are stored as changes in the connections between neurons, the self-same neurons that actually do the processing.*

So there are no passive storage locations: the processing-storage distinction fundamental to conventional computer architecture[1] doesn't hold. Instead, memories about things are stored by the same units that are responsible for processing them. As you look at a face, your brain doesn't need to send away for information on whether you've seen the face before, and it doesn't need to store or index that face so that it can be recognized later. The ease with which that face was processed by your neural units provides a signature that can be used to calculate familiarity [Hack #83]. If you see the face once, it makes it easier for the neurons that respond to that particular combination of features to respond together, effectively acting as a key for recognizing it later.

So it should be clear why recognizing faces is easier than recalling names. When recognizing faces, your brain is presented with some input (a face) and can tell if it is familiar just by checking whether the neurons for representing that face easily coactivate. (If all the neurons representing a face activate together easily, that means they've activated together in the past. That is, you've seen the face before.) For recalling the name, you have to recognize the face and then hope that the association with the word information you heard at the same time (the name) as you first met the face is strong enough to allow that to be activated. It's a different process (recall versus recognition) in a different modality (image versus words); no wonder it's so much harder.

Of course, if human memory *were* organized like computer memory, then recognizing faces would be an equivalent task to recalling names. Both would involve checking the input (the other person's face) against everything you've got stored. If you've got the face stored, bingo!—you recognize it. And the information you retrieve to recognize it would be automatically linked to the name, so recalling the name would be just as easy as recognizing the face. Unfortunately, on the flip side, recalling a face would be just as difficult as recalling a name.

—T.S.

The second important consequence of this fundamental difference is that memories are distributed between many neurons, all of which are involved in storing many other memories. This means that memories aren't stored independently of one another; so, learning something new can interfere with your memory of something old (and, of course, the things you already know affect what you remember about new material).

In Action

Forgetting something isn't just a matter of information falling out of your brain, as if your brain were a filing cabinet turned over. Traces remain of any information that is forgotten. This is why relearning things is easier than learning them for the first time. And because memories are fundamentally entangled with one another, remembering or relearning something brings related memories closer to the surface too.

One way of showing this is to relearn a subset of some set of knowledge that you have previously learned and forgotten. The effect of relearning should transfer to other memories in the same set,[2] benefiting all the associated memories, not just the ones you deliberately relearn.

The vocabulary of another language is a good example of something that you learn and use all together, and then forget. In my case, I've forgotten the French I learned at school. So, to demonstrate to myself that the entanglement of memories would produce a transfer effect I performed the following experiment: I took a list of 20 common *verbs* and tested myself to see how many I could remember the French for. It turned out I could remember the translation for 8 words. I then found out what the remaining 12 French words were. This was the relearning phase. If I wanted to be more thorough, I could have relearned some nouns and adverbs as well, but I didn't. Next, I tested myself on 20 common *adjectives*. This time I got 13 English-to-French translations right. After only a few minutes thinking about French again it was coming back to me—I was more than 50% better at the second set of words, despite being just as unpracticed at these as the first set. Retrieving one set of French vocabulary from my memory had strengthened the associations required for me to recall more and more.

How It Works

Think of the fundamental currency of memory as being associations, not items. This is core to the design of the whole system. It means that content can be accessed by anything associated with it, not just any single arbitrary tag. Human memory is content-addressable. This is unlike computer memory, where you access stuff only through the arbitrary tags you use to keep track of information and that you decide on at storage time (like filenames). The reason Google is so popular is that it gives us content-addressable memory for the Internet. You can type in pretty much anything you remember about the contents of a web page and it comes up in the results. And, also like the Internet, much of the meaning of memory is to be found in the connections and associations, which shift and recombine separately from the content.

A famous psychology experiment involved divers learning lists of words either on the docks or underwater and then being tested either on the docks or underwater.[3] Those who scored highest on the test were those who were tested in the same situation in which they learned the material (i.e., tested underwater if learned underwater, tested on the docks if learned on the docks). Those who scored lowest were those who switched contexts from learning to recall. This demonstrates the automatic encoding of context along with memories [Hack #86] and provides some justification for the advice I was given as a student that if you learned something when drunk you should go into the exam drunk. (It may well be true, but it might also be better not to have been drunk in the first place.) Being able to recall better in the original situation is one consequence of your context being automatically laid down in memory. Another consequence is the transfer effect, as shown in the preceding "In Action" section: memories are tangled up with other memories of the same type and themselves constitute a kind of memory context. Remembering one set of knowledge puts you in the right context, and the associated memories follow more easily.

The need to interleave many different memories in the connections between neurons may be one of the functions of sleep. It's vital to store new memories in the same networks of association as used by old memories, otherwise you'd have no way of moving between them. But at the same time, it's important not to overwrite old memories. There is evidence that the need for this process, called interleaving, may explain some features of our memory systems, and there's also evidence that it may occur during sleep as dreams or part of dreaming.[4]

End Notes

1. The Von Neumann architecture separates processing from data and code (*http://en.wikipedia.org/wiki/Von_Neumann_architecture*).

2. Stone, J. V., Hunkin, N. M., & Hornby, A. (2001). Predicting spontaneous recovery of memory. *Nature, 414,* 167–168.

3. Godden, D., & Baddeley, A. (1975). Context-dependent memory in two natural environments: On land and underwater. *British Journal of Psychology, 66*(3), 325–331.

4. McClelland, J. L., McNaughton, B. L., & O'Reilly, R. C. (1995). Why there are complementary learning systems in the hippocampus and neocortex: Insights from the success and failures of connectionist models of learning and memory. *Psychological Review, 102,* 419–457

 Think Yourself Strong

You can train your strength and skill with imagination alone, showing that there's a lot more to limb control than mere muscle size.

How your brain controls your muscles is something you don't notice until it goes wrong. When you drop a plate for no good reason, when disease or age rob you of the ability to will your muscles to move just like that, when you can't stop your legs trembling (even though that is possibly the least useful thing they could be doing in your situation), *then* you notice the gap between what you want to happen and what your muscles do. Normally the coordination of body movement happens so smoothly and (seemingly) instantaneously that it's hard to really believe there are any gaps in these processes. Hold your finger up in front of your face. Watch it carefully. And…ready…

curl it. Magic. How did that happen? It's impossible to truly introspect about the control system involved: our bodies appear to be the ultimate pieces of invisible technology.

But that doesn't mean there isn't a very complex system of control in place. It needs to be complex for the range of jobs done, at the speeds they're done. The standard *visuomotor feedback loop* (the delay between acting and getting visual information to update or correct that action) is 100–200 milli-seconds,[1] so much of this control has to happen without the aid of direct guidance from the senses. Movement must be controlled, at least in part, by processes that do not require immediate sensory feedback.

> There's that number again: 100–200 ms! It occurs all over this book, and I think this may be the root of it; the commonly found window for conscious experience [Hack #27] may be this size because of the uncertainty introduced by the delay between our senses and reactions. So this is the range over which our brain has developed the ability to predict, by simulation, the outcome of our actions.
>
> —T.S.

The thing is, movements are often so quick it doesn't feel as if feedback loops are intimately responsible. Rather, it often *does* feel as if you send a "go" signal to your hand to stretch a finger or catch a ball. So how can we show this is actually what's happening? One way is to work on developing the control system itself and see how that influences the resulting movement. If these systems do indeed exist, then developing them without simultaneously developing your muscles should still improve performance.

In Action

Using your imagination alone you can train the motor signals from your brain so that you are stronger, faster, and more skillful. This example takes 3 months to work, so you may want to just listen to how the experiment was done rather than doing it yourself. It's taken from a study led by Vinoth Ranganathan,[2] who was following up on a study done 12 years previously by Guang Yue in the Lerner Research Institute department of biomedical engineering.[3]

The study involved volunteers training, in two different ways, the muscle responsible for pushing outward the little finger. (To see what they were doing, put your hand palm downward on the table, fingers together, then imagine you're pushing a weight out by moving your little finger only to the side). They trained for 12 weeks, 15 minutes a day, 5 days a week. Some volunteers trained by actually tensing the muscle, but others were instructed to merely *imagine* doing so.

After 12 weeks, Ranganathan measured the force that the volunteers could exert with their little finger muscle. Both groups had become stronger, those actually tensing their muscles during training improving by 53%, those using imagination by 35%. That's not a large gap, especially if you consider that training just using your imagination is probably the harder task to do.

How It Works

The Ranganathan study used the little finger muscle because it is not used much. It is easier to see changes in strength here than in more primary muscles, such as those in the arms or legs.

 In the same study by Ranganathan et al., another group of volunteers showed they could increase the strength of a more important muscle—their elbow flexor—using just mental training too.

As well as measuring the force exerted by the volunteers before and after training, the researchers also measured the control signals sent by the brain to the muscle using EEG [Hack #2] and other measures. They were able to conclude that the main reason for the increase in strength was an increase in strength of the signal from the motor regions of the brain to the muscle, not an increase in the size and strength of the physical muscle.

This fits with other findings, including one that training muscles on one side of the body can increase the strength of the corresponding muscle on the untrained side.

The major part of any initial improvement in muscle control may be getting the signal right, rather than training the muscle. Correspondingly, the contextual interference effect—practicing skills in a random order is a better way to improve performance [Hack #86]—has been shown to work with mental practice too.[4]

Three Kinds of Motor Control

There are three classes of control system used to moderate movements while they occur, and these are used in situations from needing to move your arm more to catch a ball in a high wind to your legs changing their walking pattern onboard a ship.

Feedback

All neural systems include some noise [Hack #33], so even if your movements are planned correctly (you calculated the right amount of force to apply, etc.), your brain needs to check they are not going off course and reset them if they are. You are trying to catch a ball and realize your hand is out of place, so, while you're moving it toward the ball, you speed up your movement so it gets to the right place in time. An additional complication is learning movements across trials, when you know what you want to do (juggle three balls, for example) but you have to train your movements to successively improve each time you try.

Feedforward

A feedback system can work in isolation, detecting error and compensating for its effect. In comparison, feedforward systems use information from a component that may introduce error to anticipate the error itself. This component sends information ahead to whatever has to deal with the potential difficulty so it can be accommodated for. For example, the vestibular-ocular reflex [Hack #30] translates head velocity into compensatory eye velocities. Head movements introduce distortions into vision, so the feedforward mechanism notices the head motion and triggers eye movements to cancel out any motion blur before it even occurs.

Forward modeling

Some movements need correcting during their execution at a rate quicker than is possible with simple feedback. One way of doing this is to make a prediction of what the effect of a signal from your brain to your muscles will do (as described in "Why Can't You Tickle Yourself?" [Hack #65]). The prediction can then be used as pseudofeedback to control movements at a speed faster than would be possible with actual sensory feedback. Forward modeling allows batters to hit baseballs (or batsmen to hit cricket balls, depending on your preferred game) thrown at them at speeds faster than their simple sensory systems should allow them to deal with. This system also has advantages over feedback because of the difficulties that occur when a feedback signal is delayed. A late feedback signal means it's actually responding to a situation now past in which the error was larger, so the correction applied can cause an overshoot and lead to oscillations around the correct position rather than an iteration toward it (although introducing a damping factor—an automatic reduction of the delayed feedback signal—can compensate for this).

So movement control is more complex than it might at first seem. Making a muscle movement isn't as simple as sending it a simple "go" or "don't go" signal and letting ballistics (launch it, let it go) take care of the rest. Movements have to be controlled while they're in action, and the best control mechanism of the three in the list depends on the characteristics of the system: that is, how long it takes for information to influence action.

In Real Life

It isn't just strength that can be trained, but coordination as well. I once practiced with a very senior judo instructor who told me that an hour's worth of going through judo techniques in the imagination was as good as an hour's worth of actual training. I was skeptical at the time, but research seems to confirm his suggestion. For example, mental rehearsal of a piano sequence results in similar levels of improvement (and similar strengthening of cortical signals) as actual practice.[5]

So if you can't get to the gym, put aside some time for mental rehearsal of your exercises. You won't lose any weight, but you'll be better coordinated.

End Notes

1. Jordan, M. I. (1996). Computational aspects of motor control and motor learning. In H. Heuer & S. W. Keele (eds.), *Handbook of Perception and Action*. New York: Academic Press.

2. Ranganathan, V. K., Siemionow, V., Liu, J. Z., Sahgal, V., & Yue, G. H. (2004). From mental power to muscle power—gaining strength by using the mind. *Neuropsychologia, 42*, 944–956.

3. Yue, G. H., & Cole, K. J. (1992). Strength increases from the motor program: Comparison of training with maximal voluntary and imagined muscle contractions. *Journal of Neurophysiology, 67*, 1114–1123.

4. Gabriele, T. E., Hall, C. R., & Lee, T. O. (1989). Cognition in motor learning: Imagery effects on contextual interference. *Human Movement Science, 8*, 227–245.

5. Pascual-Leone, A. et al. (1995). Modulation of muscle responses evoked by transcranial magnetic stimulation during the acquisition of new fine motor skills. *Journal of Neurophysiology, 74*(3), 1037–1045.

Navigate Your Way Through Memory

#89   A 2,500-year-old memory trick shows how our memory for events may be based on our ability to remember routes to get to places.

Remembering where you are and what is currently happening are (as you might expect) both rather important. It turns out that orienting yourself in space may rely on some of the same brain areas as are used for remembering what has happened to you—areas that originally evolved to help animals find their way around, but now allow us to retain the episodes that make up our personal narratives.

The demonstration we'll use is a famous memory trick used to remember a list of arbitrary things, with the added bonus that the things are remembered in order. It's called the *method of loci* and involves remembering things according to where they are positioned along a route. Simply take your list of things to remember and place them along a familiar route, imagining each item (or something that will remind you of it) at key points on the route.

In Action

How many words do you think you could remember if given an arbitrary list and around 10 seconds per word in which to learn them? Knowing that my memory isn't all that good, I thought perhaps I could remember around 10. So I decided to use the method of loci to remember 20 words, twice that number. I didn't want to come up with my own list, because it would be easier for me to remember, so I used the 20 most common words appearing in the lyrics of the songwriter Tom Waits, as kindly provided by the excellent Tom Waits Supplement (*http://www.keeslau.com/TomWaitsSupplement/ Lyrics/common.htm*) and shown in Table 9-5.

Table 9-5. Imagine an item for each word at points along a route that is familiar to you. Rehearse for 4 minutes and then test yourself

1. NIGHT	8. HOME	15. DRINK
2. TIME	9. RAIN	16. STREET
3. LOVE	10. HEART	17. BLOOD
4. DAY	11. DEATH	18. RED
5. EYE	12. DOG	19. HAIR
6. DREAM	13. BLUE	20. GIRL
7. MOON	14. ROAD	

Perhaps you think 20 is too easy; feel free to use a longer list or give yourself less time, if you're so inclined. But 20 in 4 minutes seemed daunting enough for me. Starting with "night" (131 mentions across Tom Waits' entire discography) and finishing with "girl" (40 mentions), I imagined something to do with each item at each point of the journey from the front room of my house, where I was sitting, to my nearest subway station.

After mentally doing the journey and noting the items strewn along the way (a "love" letter at the foot of the stairs, a "drink" of coffee at the café on the corner, and so forth) and checking that I thought I'd remembered them all, my 4 minutes were up and I pulled out my notebook and got my pen ready to write down the list of items.

Normally with things like this my mind goes blank as soon as the thing I'm supposed to be remembering leaves my sight. But, using the method of loci, I was impressed with how quick and easy it was to remember all the words. (Yeah, yeah, I know I'm supposed to know that it works, but I still managed to impress myself.) I got every item right, and only two out of order.

Try it yourself. It doesn't have to be these words. It can be things, people, numbers—anything. This is one of the tricks professional memory artists use to remember lists of hundred, or even thousands, of things.

How It Works

There are several reasons this method works to help aid your memory, but the main one is the attaching of things to locations in space.

> The memory technique also benefits from something inherent in the dual structure of navigating: the landmarks and route mutually define each other, but each exists in its own right. The route allows you to chain from one memory item (or landmark) to the next. Because the landmarks exist apart from the route, even if you can't remember what is at a particular location, it doesn't have to stop your journey onto the next location or item.
>
> —T.S.

We know that the human brain has specialized mechanisms dedicated to remembering landmarks,[1] and that (interestingly) this region and those nearby seem to be responsible for giving humans and other animals a sense of where they are in space.[2] Brain imaging of people navigating through virtual environments has shown that even if we don't consciously recognize something as a landmark it still triggers a response in this specialized part of the brain.

This part of the brain, the *hippocampus* and nearby *nuclei*, is also known to be absolutely crucial for storing our memory for events. Psychologists call this kind of memory *episodic memory*, to distinguish it from memory for facts or memories of how to do things. People with hippocampal damage (like the hero of the film *Memento* (*http://www.imdb.com/title/tt0209144*), for example) aren't able to store new episodic memories, although they can retain memories for episodes that they stored before their injury and they can learn new facts (with lots of effort) and skills.

So we know that this same part of the brain, the hippocampus, seems to be crucial both for recording events and for helping us understand where we are in space. Evidence that this first function may have evolved from the second has recently been published.[3] It was found that the expectations and intentions an animal has affect how the hippocampus encodes memory for locations in the hippocampus. This encoding of context for locations at different times may have laid the foundations for the encoding of context in time for other memories. From this may have developed the memory for events, that ability to mentally time travel, which makes up what most of us think of as our memories.

In Real Life

You can see this landmark-specialized processing at work when we give and follow directions. If you are following directions and go past something that's an obvious landmark and your directions don't specify it, you know something's wrong. Interestingly there is also evidence from brain imaging that supports the well-known fact that men and women tend to navigate in a different manner; women tend to rely more on landmarks alone, whereas men rely more on absolute spatial position (the geometry of the situation) in combination with landmarks.[4] The information architect Christina Wodtke has observed that "On the Web, everyone's a woman," because there is no consistent spatial geometry; we are *all* forced to rely on landmarks.[5]

End Notes

1. Janzen, G., & van Turennout, M. (2004). Selective neural representation of objects relevant for navigation. *Nature Neuroscience, 7,* 673–677.

2. Burgess N., Maguire, E. A., & O'Keefe, J. (2002). The human hippocampus and spatial and episodic memory. *Neuron, 35,* 625–641.

3. Ferbinteanu, J., & Shapiro, M. L. (2003). Prospective and retrospective memory coding in the hippocampus. *Neuron, 40,* 1227–1239. Discussed in Jeffery, K. J. (2004). Remembrance of futures past. *Trends in Cognitive Sciences, 8,* 197–199.

4. Gron, G., Wunderlich, A. P., Spitzer, M., Tomczak, R., & Riepe, M. W. (2000). Brain activation during human navigation: Gender-different neural networks as substrate of performance. *Nature Neuroscience, 3,* 404–408.

5. Wodke, C. (2002). *Information Architecture: Blueprints for the Web*. Pearson. (See the sample chapter at *http://eleganthack.com/blueprint/sample.php* for the particular observation.)

Have an Out-of-Body Experience

Our regular experience of the world is first person, but in some situations, we see ourselves from an external perspective. These out-of-body experiences may even have a neurological basis.

We are used to experiencing the world from a first-person perspective, looking out through our eyes with our bodies at the center of our consciousness. This is sometimes known as the *Cartesian theater*.

Some people, however, claim to have out-of-body experiences, in which their consciousness seems separated from their body, sometimes to the extent that people feel as if they are looking down on themselves from a third-person perspective, rather than looking out from the inside. These claims are not common, but most people can experience similar out-of-body phenomena, in the form of memories of past events. Furthermore, research has identified certain specific brain areas that may be involved in producing the egocentric, "looking out of our eyes" perspective and found that out-of-body experiences can be induced by unusual activity there.

In Action

Remember back to when you were last lying down reading something: perhaps it was on holiday at the beach, in a local park, or just on the couch at home. Try and fix that image in your mind.

Now, notice where your "mind's eye" is. Are you looking at yourself from an external point of view—much like someone wandering by might have seen you—or are you remembering yourself looking out through your own eyes as you are while reading this book right now?

The majority of people remember a scene like this from a seemingly disembodied third-person perspective, despite originally having experienced it from a first-person point of view.

How It Works

The first study to explore this effect in detail was published in 1983 by Nigro and Neisser.[1] They made the link between the likelihood of recalling a memory as either a first-person or third-person image and emotions and discovered that asking someone to focus on their feelings at the time of the event was more likely to result in a first-person memory. The example in the preceding "In Action" section focused on a situation and was probably a fairly neutral emotional experience, so is likely to produce a third-person memory in most people.

Although this is a common experience when remembering the past, the majority of people do not have out-of-body experiences in the present. People who have recounted out-of-body experiences have sometimes been suspected of being overimaginative or worse, but such experiences are a well-known phenomenon in certain types of epilepsy and with specific forms of brain injury. This does not mean that people who experience out-of-body states necessarily have epilepsy or brain injury, but these sorts of conditions suggest that normal, but usually hidden, aspects of brain function may be involved in producing such experiences.

A study by Blanke and colleagues[2] examined five neurological patients who had frequent out-of-body experiences. On one occasion, a surgeon managed to reliably induce such an experience by electrically stimulating the cortex of a patient during brain surgery. When the surgeon stimulated the *tempero-parietal junction* (the area of the brain where the temporal and parietal lobes meet [Hack #8]), the patient reported that she felt an instantaneous sensation of floating near the ceiling and experienced the operating theater as if she were looking down on it, "seeing" the top of the doctors' heads and herself on the operating table. Ceasing the stimulation "returned" the patient to her body, and resuming it caused her to feel disembodied once more.

Brain imaging studies have shown that the tempero-parietal junction is activated in situations that involve calculating point of view from an egocentric perspective and mentally switching between views to understand a scene (for example, mentally working out a good place to stand to get the best view of a football game). With this in mind, it is perhaps not so surprising that unusual activity in this area might cause feelings of being detached from the body.

Although it is too early to say for sure, it seems likely that when we recall images that appear in the third-person perspective, the tempero-parietal junction is being recruited to help create this image. The previous exercise demonstrates that, in the context of memory, we all have the ability to experience the out-of-body state. It also suggests that there may be a sound neurological basis for such experiences and that healthy people who report out-of-body experiences are being less fanciful than some skeptics presume.

End Notes

1. Nigro, G., & Neisser, U. (1983). Point of view in personal memories. *Cognitive Psychology, 15,* 467–482.

2. Blanke, O., Landis, T., Spinelli, L., & Seeck, M. (2004). Out-of-body experience and autoscopy of neurological origin. *Brain, 127* (Pt. 2), 243–258.

—Vaughan Bell

H A C K #91 Enter the Twilight Zone: The Hypnagogic State

On the edge of sleep, you may enter hypnagogia, a state of freewheeling thoughts and sometimes hallucinations.

Hypnagogia, or the *hypnagogic state*, is a brief period of altered consciousness that occurs between wakefulness and sleep, typically as people "doze off" on their way to normal sleep. During this period, thoughts can become loosely associated, whimsical, and even bizarre. Hallucinations are very common and may take the form of flashes of lights or colors, sounds, voices (hearing your own name being called is quite common), faces, or fully formed pictures. Mental imagery may become particularly vivid and fantastical, and some people may experience *synaesthesia*, in which experiences in one sense are experienced in another—sounds, for example, may be experienced as visual phenomena.

It is a normal stage of sleep and most people experience it to some degree, although it may go unnoticed or be very brief or quite subdued in some people. It is possible, however, to be more aware of the hypnagogic state as it occurs and to experience the effects of the brain's transition into sleep more fully.

In Action

Although there is no guaranteed technique to extend or intensify the hypnagogic state, sometimes it can be enough to simply make a conscious effort to be aware of any changes in consciousness as you relax and drop off, if practiced regularly. Trying to visualize or imagine moving objects and scenes, or passively noting any visual phenomena during this period might allow you to notice any changes that take place. Extended periods of light sleep seem more likely to produce noticeable hypnagogia, so being very tired may mean you enter deep sleep too quickly. For this reason, afternoon dozing works well for some.

Some experimenters have tried to extend or induce hypnagogia by using light arousal techniques to prevent a quick transition into deep sleep. A microphone and speaker were used in one study to feed the sound of breathing back to the sleeper. Another method is the use of "repeat alarm clocks" (like the snooze function on many modern alarm clocks)—on entering sleep, subjects are required to try and maintain enough awareness to press a key every 5 minutes; otherwise, a soft alarm sounds and rouses them.

Try this yourself on public transport. Because of the low background noise and occasional external prompting, if you manage to fall asleep, dozing on buses and trains can often lead to striking hypnagogic states. In spite of this, this is not always the most practical technique, as you can sometimes end up having to explore more than your own consciousness if you miss your stop.

How It Works

Very little research has been done on brain function during the hypnagogic state, partly because conducting psychology experiments with semiconscious people is difficult at the best of times and partly because many of the neuroimaging technologies are not very soporific. fMRI [Hack #4] scanning tends to be noisy and PET scanning [Hack #3] often involves having a drip inserted into a vein to inject radioactive tracer into the bloodstream—hardly the most relaxing of experiences. As a result, most of the research has been done with EEG (electroencephalogram) readings [Hack #2] that involve using small scalp electrodes to read electrical activity from the brain.

Hideki Tanaka and colleagues[1] used EEG during sleep onset and discovered that the brain does not decrease its activity evenly across all areas when entering sleep. A form of alpha wave activity (electrical signals in the frequency range of 8–12 Hz that are linked to relaxed states) spreads from the front of the brain to the other areas before fading away. The frontal cortex is associated with attention (among other things), and it may be that the hypnagogic state results from the progressive defocusing of attention. This could cause a reduction in normal perception filtering, resulting in loosely connected thoughts and unusual experiences.

Electroencephalography (EEG) measures electrical activity from the brain, through small electrodes attached to the skull. The electrical signals are generated by neurons and the amount of synchronous neural activity results in characteristic EEG waveforms. Beta activity (above 14 Hz) is usually linked to high levels of mental effort and cortical activation, characteristic of the waking EEG. As mental activation decreases and sleepiness appears, both alpha (8–13 Hz) and theta (4–7 Hz) activity become more prominent. Delta activity (activity below 4 Hz) is associated with deep, "slow-wave" sleep.

Some scientists have argued that the hypnagogic state is not necessarily sleep-related and may be the result of a reduction in meaningful perceptual information, perhaps leading to defocused attention or other similar effects. A study published in 2002[2] aimed to test this by comparing hypnagogic states with a condition in which awake participants were fed unstructured sensory information in the form of white noise and diffuse white light. The researchers used EEG recordings and found that, although participants in both conditions reported unusual visual experiences, the pattern of brain activation were quite different, suggesting that hypnagogia is more than just the result of relaxation and lack of structured sensory input.

One problem with recording electrical activity from the scalp is that activity from structures that lie deep in the brain may not be detected. This means we could be missing important information when it comes to understanding what happens as we slip from consciousness into sleep, and even back again into wakefulness (known as the *hypnopompic state*)—particularly as deep structures (such as the brain stem, pons, thalamus, and hypothalamus) are known to be crucial in initiating and regulating sleep.

An ingenious study published in *Science* did manage to investigate the role of some of the deeper brain structures in hypnagogia,[3] specifically the medial temporal lobes, which are particularly linked to memory function. The researchers asked five patients who had suffered medial temporal lobe damage to play several hours of Tetris. Damage to this area of the brain often causes amnesia, and the patients in this study had little conscious memory for more than a few minutes at a time. On one evening, some hours after their last game, the players were woken up just as they started to doze and were asked for their experiences. Although they had no conscious memory of playing the game, all of the patients mentioned images of falling, rotating Tetris blocks. This has given us some strong evidence that the hypnagogic state may be due (at least in part) to unconscious memories appearing as unusual hypnagogic experiences.

In Real Life

Many authors and artists have been fascinated by this state and have tried to extend or use it to explore ideas or gain inspiration. To name a couple, Robert Louis Stevenson's *The Strange Case of Dr. Jekyll and Mr. Hyde* and many of Paul Klee's paintings were reportedly inspired by hypnagogic experiences.

End Notes

1. Tanaka, H., Hayashi, M., & Hori, T. (1997). Topographical characteristics and principal component structure of the hypnagogic EEG. *Sleep, 20*(7), 523–534.

2. Wackermann, J., Putz, P., Buchi, S., Strauch, I., & Lehmann, D. (2002). Brain electrical activity and subjective experience during altered states of consciousness: ganzfeld and hypnagogic states. *International Journal of Psychophysiology, 46*(2), 123–146.

3. Stickgold, R., Malia, A., Maguire, D., Roddenberry, D., & O'Connor, M. (2000). Replaying the game: Hypnagogic images in normals and amnesics. *Science, 290*(5490), 350–353.

See Also

- Although this is quite an old paper now, it is still one of the best reviews of the history, phenomena, and techniques associated with the hypnagogic state. Schacter, D. L. (1976). The hypnagogic state: A critical review of the literature. *Psychological Bulletin, 83*(3), 452–481.

—Vaughan Bell

Make the Caffeine Habit Taste Good

#92

Caffeine chemically hacks the brain's reward system, boosting the value we give not only to the morning cuppa, but also to everything associated with it.

I couldn't even begin to write this for you until I'd made myself a coffee. Some days I drink tea, but coffee is my normal stimulant of choice, and a cup of that ol' "creative lighter fluid" is just what I need to get started on my morning writing.

After you've drunk a cup of tea or coffee, the caffeine diffuses around your body, taking less than 20 minutes to reach every cell, every fluid (yes, *every* fluid[1]) of which you're made. Pretty soon the neurotransmitter messenger systems of the brain are affected too. We know for certain that caffeine's primary route of action is to increase the influence of the neurotransmitter dopamine, although exactly how it does this is less clear.[2] Upshifting the *dopaminergic* system is something caffeine has in common with the less socially acceptable stimulants cocaine and amphetamine, although it does so in a different way.[3]

> Neurons [Hack #9] use neurotransmitters to chemically send their signals from one neuron to the next, across the synapse (the gap between two neurons). There are many different neurotransmitters, and they tend to be used by neurons together in systems that cross the brain. The neurons that contain dopamine, the dopaminergic system, are found in systems dealing with memory, movement, attention, and motivation. The latter two are what concern us here.

Via the dopaminergic system, caffeine stimulates a region of the subcortex (the brain beneath the cerebral cortex [Hack #8]) called the *nucleus accumbens*, a part of the brain known to be heavily involved in feelings of pleasure and reward. Sex, food, all addictive drugs, and even jokes cause an increased neural response in this area of the brain. What happens with addictive drugs is that they chemically hack the brain's evolved circuitry for finding things rewarding—the ability to recognize the good things in life and learn to do more of them.

The jury is still out on whether most caffeine addicts are really benefiting from their compulsion to regularly consume a brown, socially acceptable, liquid stimulant. While some killjoys claim that most addicts are just avoiding the adverse effects of withdrawal, it is more likely that most people use caffeine more or less optimally to help them manage their lives. One study even went so far as to say "regular caffeine usage appears to be beneficial, with higher users having better mental functioning."[4] So it's not just pleasure-seeking, it's performance-enhancing.

Coffee is strongly associated with two things: keeping you awake and helping you do useful mental work. In fact, it can even be shown to help physical performance.[5] The association with creative mental work is legendary, although the cognitive mechanisms by which this works are not clear. As early as 1933, experiments had shown that a cup of coffee can help you solve chess problems,[6] but the need for experiments has been considered minimal given the massive anecdotal evidence. As the mathematician Paul Erdos said, "A mathematician is a device for turning coffee into theorems." Academics, designers, programmers, and creative professionals everywhere will surely empathize.

But this isn't a hack about the addictive effects of caffeine, or even about the mental stimulation it can provide. This is about how coffee can work its magic on me without passing my lips. It's having its effect while it's still brewing. I need to make a cup to get started, but I haven't begun drinking it yet.

In Action

Just knowing you have a caffeine hit coming tends to perk you up. We value more than just the chemicals here. To see this in action, find someone who is a certified caffeine addict. It doesn't matter if she is into tea or coffee, as long as she is *really* into it. I'd wager that she is also rather particular about how she takes it too. Does she have a favorite mug? Does she like the milk poured in before the tea? Is she picky about how the coffee beans should be ground?

Now, find something that doesn't affect the taste of the drink, but that she always does—it doesn't really matter what. Stop her from doing it. Give her coffee to her in a glass. Put the milk in after the tea. Do the opposite of the way she likes something done.

She'll freak. Or at the very least she *really* won't like it.

The more she's into caffeine, the more particular she'll be about the drink being made and delivered in just a particular way. Weird, eh? She's addicted to a complex molecule; the delivery of it into her system, in any form, is enough to create the positive effects of the drug and remove any associated withdrawal symptoms. But she insists on the precise method of delivery. How come?

How It Works

By chemically hacking the reward circuitry of the brain, caffeine gives us a stark view of a couple of the basic animal learning mechanisms. These are called *classical conditioning* and *operant conditioning* and are associated with the scientific school called *behaviorism*, which dominated modern psychology until the 1970s.

You've probably heard of Pavlov, the Russian scientist whose experiments with dogs established the basic principles of classical conditioning. This basically says that, if something happens at the same time as something rewarding, it comes to be associated with the response to—and can eventually substitute for—the rewarding stimulus. In this case, the caffeine is the intrinsically rewarding stimulus (because it hacks your reward circuitry) and everything else (the smell, the taste, the cup, the time of day) comes to be associated with the reward. This is why decaf can actually work wonders (particularly if your subject doesn't know it is decaf, thanks to the Placebo Effect [Hack #73]) and why just making a cup of coffee makes me feel more alert, even without drinking it. When I used to write essays late at night at college, just the sound of the kettle reaching the boil would make me feel more alert. The response (perking up) becomes associated with the things

that normally accompany the actual cause (the caffeine)–the smell of coffee, the sound of the kettle boiling, and so on.

The other major kind of conditioning, *operant conditioning*, states that
rewards reinforce the actions that precede them. While this sounds pretty
obvious, you can get a very long way just by looking at the world through
the lens of "What actions are rewarded? Which are punished?" In the case of
our caffeine experimentation, everything leading up to the consumption of
the caffeine is rewarded. No wonder we develop superstitions about how the
caffeine should be prepared. In fact all drugs are associated with prepara-
tion rituals: from the Japanese tea ceremony, to clinking glasses of beer, and
up to the harder drugs and things like the shooting rituals of heroin users.

These learning mechanisms are intrinsic and are found in all complex animals. They are deeply programmed into our brain and can operate without
conscious effort or memory. Decades of work have explored how the time
scales, constraints, and interactions of these forms of learning combine with
different stimulus and response pairings and different combinations of
reward and punishment. For example, we know that rewards are often better motivators than punishments, partly because they are more precise; you
can simply reward the behavior you want, whereas with punishment you
tend to punish getting caught, rather than accurately punishing the behavior you don't want.

This associative form of learning is basic to human nature, and its effects are
widespread. If you reward your child by giving in after 20 minutes of nag-
ging, is it surprising that this habit becomes common? If your manager pun-
ishes people who make mistakes, is it any wonder that people at work cover
up their errors rather than admitting them? And if I've drunk a cup of coffee
on a thousand previous occasions just before starting work, is it any wonder
I feel a sense of contentment when sitting down to write with a steaming
mug of the black stuff beside me and feel distress when I'm deprived of it? It
may be arbitrary which mug I started drinking my coffee in, but now it has
been wired into my brain via the reinforcing effects of caffeine. The coffee
really does taste better when drunk from my favorite mug.

End Notes

1. Two thoughts for you: (1) plants probably evolved caffeine as an insecti-
   cide, and (2) caffeine is used in animal artificial insemination to make
   sperm swim faster.

2. Caffeine probably blockades a messenger chemical that competes with
   dopamine (adenosine), so this in turn causes an increase in the effect of

dopamine. The "inhibition of inhibition" pattern is standard for many connections and chemicals in the brain.

3. Some indication of the levels of obsession invoked by caffeine can be seen at *http://coffeegeek.com*.

4. Discussed and referenced in Stafford, T. (2003). Psychology in the coffee shop. *The Psychologist, 16*(7), 358-359. Available online from *http://www.bps.org.uk*.

5. "Caffeine and Exercise Performance" (*http://www.elitetrack.com/caffeine.pdf*).

6. Holck, H. (1933). Effect of caffeine upon chess problem solving. *Journal of Comparative Psychology, 15*, 301–311.

Fake Familiarity word game part 2. See "Fake Familiarity" [Hack #83].

Table 9-6. Which of these have you seen before?

BASEMENT	MEUNSTAH
CADPECHT	MESTIC
BLENTIRP	FASHION
DETAIL	TUMMEL
NOTIRGIN	SUBBEN
GARDER	FISSEL
GERTPRIS	COELEPT
FRAMBLE	FAMILIAR
CRIPPLE	ISOLATE

CHAPTER TEN

Other People
Hacks 93–100

We don't live in a lifeless world—we live in a world of other people. It's other people, not rocks or trees, that have minds of their own, minds just as capable as ours. It's other people with whom we gang together to fight off threats, build knowledge, build cities, and sustain life. It's other people we need to fit in with.

A good deal of this book has been about the patterns of the world as they're reflected in our minds, as assumptions and expectations. Assumptions like the direction of sunlight, as comes through in our specialized routines for processing shadows on objects [Hack #20]. And, to pick another example, our observation and subsequent assumption that cause and effect tend to sit together in both time and space [Hack #79], which we use as a heuristic to make sense out of the universe. These are good assumptions to make. It's their very robustness that has lodged them in the functioning of the brain itself.

So how do our assumptions about other people, as constituents of our universe, manifest themselves in the deep operations of the mind? We'll look at how we have a dedicated module for processing faces [Hack #93] and how eye gaze tugs at our reaching response [Hack #97] just like any physical location Simon Effect task [Hack #56].

We'll look at how we signal emotion, how emotion is induced, and how we use it to develop common feeling in a group [Hacks #94 and #95].

And, speaking of fitting in, we'll finish by seeing how exposure to photographs of faces and the written word triggers our drive to imitate [Hacks #98 #99, and #100], from mirroring gestures to automatic mimicry of social stereotypes.

Understand What Makes Faces Special

#93 We have dedicated neural machinery for recognizing faces from just a few basic features arranged in the right configuration.

It's an important evolutionary skill to be able to quickly and efficiently recognize faces that are important to us. This allowed our ancestors to conform to the social hierarchies of the groups in which they lived, to keep checks on who was stronger and who was weaker than they were, and to track potential mates.

While faces are very important things to recognize, they are also all remarkably similar. Eyes, noses, and mouths—and it is these features that we rely on most when we discriminate between faces—all look pretty much alike, and the ratios of the spacing between them do not leave too much scope for differing widely either. Nevertheless, it is remarkably easy for us to distinguish between faces.

In Action

Take a look at the two pictures in Figure 10-1.

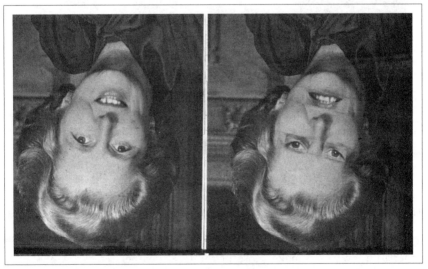

Figure 10-1. Two upside-down faces, but you should have no problem recognizing who it is[1]

While you might detect some sort of difference between them, the odds are that both will look like pretty normal upside-down pictures of a face (and you might well be able to identify who it is, too). Now turn the book upside down. The face on the right is a grotesque: its eyes and mouth have been inverted. But you probably didn't notice this (and it certainly is not as striking as when the faces are the right way up). This is a neat demonstration of the fact that faces are normally processed *holistically*. When they are the right way up, we "understand" faces as a whole based on their internal components; turning them upside down disrupts this ability. We then have to rely on componential encoding instead and judge the face simply in terms of the individual items that make it up. This makes it much harder to detect that something is "wrong" than when we are able to use holistic processing. While, of course, we rely on differences in hairstyle and color and other factors when identifying people in the real world, experiments have shown that we rely most on the central features of faces.

Another example of the way in which we are "primed" for the ability to recognize faces is how difficult it feels to look at the face shown in Figure 10-2.

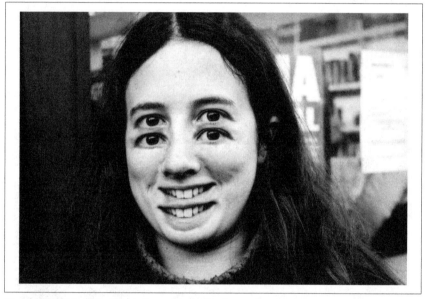

Figure 10-2. It's difficult to look at this double face

This is because the two sets of internal features are competing with each other to allow us to make sense of the face. Neither set can win, so our visual system can't settle on the stimuli and make sense of it the way it would with a normal face.

How It Works

So how does the brain recognize faces? It turns out that there is a section of the brain that is specialized for recognizing facelike stimuli. In imaging studies,[2] it has been shown that a section of the *fusiform gyrus*, which borders the temporal and occipital lobes, is more active when participants view images of faces than when they view other pictures. This area is now termed the *fusiform facial area*. It is specialized for viewing faces in an upright orientation, suggesting that faces as they are normally seen are treated as a specialized type of object by the brain. It is easy to recognize partial or degraded images, though, such as with low-quality CCTV images.[3] Again, this would make sense in allowing us to identify people in low lighting or among other objects such as trees.

When looking at faces, our eyes dart most around the mouth and eyes [Hack #15], the two features that are absolutely essential to depict a face in a cartoon. Although other features—particularly hair—are used to recognize individuals, it is the mouth and eyes that define a face. Experiments with subliminal stimuli have shown that faces, especially emotional faces, can be processed by the brain at exposures too quick for conscious appreciation. Even a face shown to you too fast to be consciously seen influences your feeling of familiarity with it; mere exposure [Hack #82] is good enough. This is another sign of specialized neural networks for face processing in the brain.

In Real Life

There is some debate concerning whether this "face recognition" system is actually specialized for this purpose or is a general categorization system, with categorizing faces just one ability we've picked up through experience. For example, people who are expert at recognizing species of birds or types of cars show activation of the fusiform facial area when shown pictures of their specialist subjects.[4] Another type of evidence comes from studies of people who have developed *prosopagnosia*, an inability to discriminate faces, even though the ability to discriminate other types of objects seems intact. Interestingly, some people who are experts with some category of object—sheep, for instance—have been known to retain the ability to discriminate between the specialty objects even when they lose the ability with faces.[5]

Whether or not the fusiform facial area is specialized for faces, it is clear that we are very good at identifying faces. Most researchers agree that by 3 or 4 months of age babies are skilled at facial discrimination.[6]

We are so good at identifying faces that our brains are primed to see them everywhere. We see them in clouds (where they aren't) and in smileys (where they are). Our ability to perceive faces so readily from a relatively small amount of information in the smileys or emoticons used in text and online messaging—the fact that we can readily understand that :-) is intended to represent a happy face and ;-) a wink—is a legacy of how important face recognition has been to us evolutionarily.

End Notes

1. Thompson, P. (1980). Margaret Thatcher: A new illusion. *Perception, 9*, 483–484. Reprinted with permission from Pion Limited, London. Many thanks to Peter Thompson for supplying the image.

2. Kanwisher, N., McDermott, J., & Chun, M. (1997). The fusiform face area: A module in human extrastriate cortex specialized for face perception. *The Journal of Neuroscience, 17*(11), 4302–4111.

3. Burton, A., Wilson, S., Cowan, M., & Bruce, V. (1999). Face recognition in poor-quality video: Evidence from security surveillance. *Psychological Science, 10*(3), 243–248.

4. Gauthier, I., Skudlarski, P., Gore, J.C., & Anderson, A. W. (2000). Expertise of cars and birds recruits brain areas involved in face recognition. *Nature Neuroscience, 3*, 191–197.

5. McNeil, J., & Warrington, E. (1993). Prosopagnosia—a face specific disorder. *Quarterly Journal of Experimental Psychology Section A: Human Experimental Psychology, 46*(1), 1–10.

6. Nelson, C. (2001). The development and neural bases of face recognition. *Infant and Child Development, 10*, 3–18.

—*Andrew Brown*

 ## Signal Emotion

#94   Emotions are powerful on the inside but often displayed in subtle ways on the outside. Are these displays culturally dependent or universal?

We find our emotional lives impossible to untangle from ourselves and examine critically. They're a core part of who we are. If you could imagine it, a life without feelings would be far more alien than any Mr. Spock. Emotions prepare us for situations both physiologically and cognitively too, and emerge from multiple dedicated systems that interact below the level of consciousness. Advances in psychology and neuroscience unveil these systems, and reveal how we signal our emotional states to others and decode even subtle emotional expressions.

In Action

Take a stroll down an imaginary lane in a distant, foreign land. You've no knowledge of the language spoken and no idea of the local customs and practices. Before you is a fork in the road with no clear sign of which direction leads to where. Thankfully, you spy a local working the land. Hungry for information to guide you, you point to the first path. His mouth broadens until his teeth are visible. After taking this in, you point to the second.

His brow furrows as his mouth becomes small and tight. Lo and behold, despite any language and cultural barriers, you most likely have enough information to know that the first is probably a better bet.

Try it yourself. Consider the photo in Figure 10-3.

Figure 10-3. What emotion is this face signaling?[1]

I'm sure there is no doubt in your mind what is being expressed here. At the very least, it's a very different face from that shown in Figure 10-4.

Figure 10-4. What emotion is this second face signaling?[2]

It's clear that the first face is happy and the second is in a less than positive mood.

Obvious, you say?

It might feel so, but before you dismiss this disambiguation out of hand, you should know that many of the cues are fairly subtle and there's a lot more going on behind the scenes than you might realize. In fact, these cues can slip by brain-damaged patients entirely, even those whose perception is otherwise fairly good. Let's dig a little deeper.

How It Works

We may take it for granted, but the existence of a universal emotion expression system is an impressive feat. Masses of evidence show that our brains are wired to distinguish and respond to expressions of a number of emotional states. The *basic emotions*, a concept born of lauded psychologist Sylvan Tomkins, are anger, fear, disgust, sadness, surprise, and happiness. We can be confident that these are really universal thanks to the cross-cultural work of Paul Ekman, the leading proponent of basic emotion theory, whose work with tribes in New Guinea confirm what our example asserts: despite some cultural nuances, a smile is a smile worldwide.

Furthermore, it turns out that this capacity is not only universal, but also innate. The ubiquity of our expressions is not purely a consequence of convergence by imitation, as they are present to some extent even when there is no input.[3] German ethologist Irenäus Eibl-Eibesfeldt conducted research in the 1960s that showed that congenitally blind children still produced emotional expressions via the face, even those who were also severely cognitively-impaired. This preserved ability of the sensory impaired has been noted often, including Charles Darwin's comment that blind children can "blush with shame."

Basic emotions are distinct categories, and each appears to be distinctly localized within the brain, as evidenced by both imaging studies [Hack #4] and observation of brain-damaged patients. While the amygdala, a part of the limbic system [Hack #7], is traditionally considered the emotion area, it is tied most closely to fear. Meanwhile, disgust appears to be instantiated in the basal ganglia and insula and quite unrelated to the amygdala. Other emotions also show distinct neural patterns of activation [Hack #9]. This may imply that the emotions arose for distinct functional needs, arguably independently. Many see fear as essentially a response to external threat. Disgust has been characterized as a complementary system that deals with internal threat—an eject response that seeks to rid the body of toxins. The disgust face itself is really just an extension of the gagging reflex. Stories can be told (although with less confidence) for the other emotions.

The *limbic system* is a fairly deep, old part of the brain, beneath the cortex [Hack #8] (the outer layer of the brain), and the *amygdala* falls just under the surface of the more anterior and medial part of the temporal lobe, making it bulge into what is called the uncus. The *basal ganglia* are a collection of structures that reside close by. The *insula* is a gyrus (or fold) of the temporal lobe, on its surface but somewhat hidden by the way the cortex overlaps just there. All structures are found twice, once in each hemisphere and all broadly in the same neighborhood—just under (or on, in the case of the insula) the temporal lobe.

The basic emotions produce expressions that are hard to fake given the genuine physiological changes that accompany them. There are subtle cues, such as a flush or tightening of muscles. These are handy for others to spot—as a source of useful information—but they can also benefit the one expressing the emotion, as when an angry face says "Don't try and take this from me; I'm willing to die to protect it." Discriminating the real Mr. Angry from a faker is therefore highly important, so we evolved to detect ever more subtle signs and distinguish real emotion from mere pantomime.

For a social animal such as humans, it pays to be adept at deciphering genuine and subtle signs—as well as at giving them out—in order to quickly communicate within a group and coordinate emotions (group communication is discussed in "Make Yourself Happy" [Hack #95]). Coordinated emotions are essential for cooperative responses to situations, and recent work has been looking at how coordination can occur over longer distances—after all, using facial expression as a group communication tool is limited to face-to-face interaction. Voice is one possibility, and there has been investigation into whether vocal behaviors, such as crying and laughing, accompany certain emotions in the same way that facial expressions do. Maybe research into the vocal component of emotion will resolve the mystery of why only one of the six basic emotions is positive. As Ekman has suggested, there may be many more, but expressed via the voice rather than the face.

In Real Life

Because emotional expressions are the automatic outcomes of emotion, they are hard to totally suppress; likewise, they are hard to fake. What this means is that practice and attention to the features of expressions on others' faces can allow us to divine the true intentions and feelings of those around us. While we're all pretty good at this sort of "mind reading," some take this ability further; just think how important these cues are to police detectives, security operatives, psychologists, and high-stakes gamblers.

End Notes

1. Photo of James Cronin by Matt Locke (*http://www.test.org.uk*).

2. Photo by Anita B. Patterson, provided by MorgueFile (*http://www. morguefile.com*).

3. This is Noam Chomsky's "Argument from Poverty of the Stimulus," which concluded innateness if a skill is developed without sufficient stimulus. It is reviewed in Geoffrey Pullum's "Learnability, Hyperlearning, and the Povery of the Stimulus" (*http://www.ecs.soton.ac.uk/ ~harnad/Papers/Py104/pullum.learn.html*).

See Also

- Paul Ekman's web site (*http://www.emotionsrevealed.com*) has essays, training CDs, and the original photo sets of the basic emotions and offers emotion recognition workshops.

- "Emotions Revealed: Recognising Facial Expressions" (*http://www. studentbmj.com/back_issues/0404/education/140.html*) is a good, simple article by Ekman summarizing the basic emotion research.

- "Neuropsychosocial Factors in Emotion Recognition: Facial Expressions" (*http://www.neuropsychologycentral.com/interface/content/ resources/page_material/resources_general_materials_pages/resources_ document_pages/neuropsychosocial_factors_in_emotion_recognition.pdf*) discusses in more depth how emotions are signaled. The article is in the Resources section of Neuropsychology Central (*http://www. neuropsychologycentral.com*).

- Scott, S. K., Young, A. W., Calder, A. J., & Hellawell, D. J. (1997). Impaired auditory recognition of fear and anger following bilateral amygdala lesions. *Nature, 385*(6613), 254–257.

- Eibl-Eibesfeldt, I. (1973). The expressive behaviour of the deaf-and-blind-born. In M. von Cranach & I. Vine (eds.), *Social Communication and Movement*, 163–194. London: Academic Press.

- Malcolm Gladwell's article "The Naked Face" (*http://www.gladwell. com/2002/2002_08_05_a_face.htm*) looks at Paul Ekman, the emotions, and facial expression and asks how much of our thoughts we give away on our faces.

—Alex Fradera and Disa Sauter

Make Yourself Happy

#95 Turn on your affective system by tweaking your face muscles—or getting an eyeful of someone else doing the same.

Find yourself a pen, preferably a nontoxic, nonleaky one. We're going to use this little item to improve your quality of life and give you a little pleasure.

In Action

Put the pen between your teeth, in far enough so that it's stretching the edges of your mouth back without being uncomfortable. Feeling weird? Just hold it there for a little, and appraise your level of mood. You should find that you end up feeling just a little happier.

If you want to go for the reverse effect, remove the pen (maybe give it a wipe), then trap it between your upper lip and nose like a mustache. If you're feeling anything, it's likely to be a touch of gloom, particularly in contrast to when you had the pen in your mouth.

Alternatively, if you're pen-averse, refer to the pictures in "Signal Emotion" [Hack #94] and scrutinize the smiling face for a while. You should find yourself perked up—while the unhappy photo will likely send you downhill if you stare at it a little.

How It Works

Emotional expressions are much more than just by-products of our *affective system*, the system that deals with emotions. Expressions serve as agents that transmit emotions to other individuals and are crucial in creating and maintaining our own emotional experience. And while aspects of this may be conscious and deliberate—my girlfriend may throw me a grin to let me know she's not mad that I've been glued to the computer all evening, and that reassurance will make me happy—there is a deeply automatic component. This is termed *primitive contagion* and is characterized as a three-stage process: it begins with perception, which triggers mimicry, which itself produces emotion. "Signal Emotion" [Hack #94] deals with how we perceive emotions, so here we'll unpack the other two stages: mimicry and resulting emotion.

Mimicry. An array of experiments shows that, when emotional faces are presented, subjects produce corresponding facial expressions. For example, subjects can tell from recordings of their faces which emotions they must have been looking at originally. Additionally, facial EMG changes occur after only a few hundred milliseconds: the *zygomatic muscles* (in the cheeks) used for smiling show more activity after seeing a happy face, while the *corrugator* muscles (between the eyes, at the top of the nose) used for frowning are more active after viewing anger.

> *Electromyogram* (EMG) is a measure of small electrical currents muscles produce when they're active. Thus, EMG changes in a particular place indicate that a muscle there is being used.

It seems this is something we just can't help. Show emotional faces (photographs in newspapers usually fit the bill) to a friend and look for the flicker of mimicry his face invariably betrays. The stronger the expression portrayed in the picture, the stronger your subject's emotional response. The phenomenon can even be found when a face is shown subliminally [Hacks #82 and #99] and the viewer is unaware of seeing any kind of expressive face; the facial muscles betray the effect.

Resulting emotion. The act of making an emotional expression has an effect on our emotional state. This has been shown experimentally, most convincingly when the experience is divorced as much as possible from labels like "smiling" (as in the case of pushing back on your lip): simply activating critical muscles produces the effect. This deep coupling to the motor system (a fundamental and ancient function of the brain) underlines the primitive nature of emotions. Direct and automatic feedback means muscular changes make you happier in general without having to invoke concepts of "happy" or a "smile": a joke really is funnier with the pen in your mouth.

These steps—observation, facial mimicry, and finally acquisition of the observed emotion—are an effective way of unifying a group of people under one emotion and therefore of marshaling social units to act together. You can see the benefits of having a whole group being scared—aroused and ready for rapid action—if the situation warrants it, rather than some of the group not taking the threat seriously and everyone else trying to convince them. Lengthy persuasion can be avoided given that emotional communication is often automatic. Emotions act as orienting systems, and the adaptive benefit is clear when you consider the importance of rapid mobilization of individuals in a group under certain circumstances: confrontation, escape, or rejection of poisonous food.

In Real Life

Stand-up comics could learn a thing or two from our example—perhaps comedy clubs should have a pen-in-mouth policy. The broader point is that, for any communicator, direct visual or aural contact is extremely useful as a means of emotionally orienting an audience. If you want them to be angry, CAPS LOCK WON'T CUT IT relative to a tremor in the voice or a scowl. Similarly, smiles and laughter are contagious. Remote communication can reduce the availability of these cues, although the advent of videoconferencing and other technologies is changing this. Emoticons are a simple attempt to hack into this system, although it remains for the cunning designer to find ever more effective ways of simulating truly contagious emotions. We may also note that women are more facially expressive in response to emotional stimuli, although it is uncertain whether they are also more emotionally affected; one could consider how gender differences could affect social dynamics.

See Also

- "Left Brain Right Brain" (*http://www.abc.net.au/catalyst/stories/s1139554.htm*) includes a further experiment you can perform, exploring the relationship between mouth muscles and emotion.
- Ulf Dimberg, U., Thunberg, M., & Elmehed, K. (2000). Unconscious facial reactions to emotional facial expressions. *Psychological Science 11*(1), 86–89.
- Wild, B., Erb, M., & Bartels, M. (2001). Are emotions contagious? Evoked emotions while viewing emotionally expressive faces: Quality, quantity, time course and gender differences. *Psychiatry Research, 102*, 109–124.
- Levenson, R. W., Ekman, P., & Friesen, W. V. (1990). Voluntary facial action generates emotion-specific autonomic nervous system activity. *Psychophysiology, 27*(4), 363–384.

—Alex Fradera & Disa Sauter

Reminisce Hot and Cold

#96
Find the fire that's cooking your memory systems.

Our emotional system contributes not just to how we respond to the world at a given moment, but how we store representations of what has happened in the past. The makeup of our memories is not decided dispassionately by an impartial documentary reel in our brain, but by passionate, loaded mechanisms that draw out the aspects with the most juice.

In Action

Read the following two tales.[1] There will be a quiz at the end of class.

Tale 1. "A mother and her son are leaving home in the morning. She is taking him to visit his father's workplace. The father is a laboratory technician at Victory Memorial Hospital. While walking along, the boy sees some wrecked cars in a junkyard, which he finds interesting.

"At the hospital, the staff are preparing for a practice disaster drill, which the boy will watch. Makeup artists were able to create realistic-looking injuries on actors for the drill.

"After the drill, while the father watched the boy, the mother left to phone her other child's preschool. Running a little late, she phones the preschool to tell them she will soon pick up her child. Heading to pick up her child, she hails a taxi at the number 9 bus stop."

Tale 2. "A mother and her son are leaving home in the morning. She is taking him to visit his father's workplace. The father is a laboratory technician at Victory Memorial Hospital.

"While crossing the road, the boy is caught in a terrible accident, which critically injures him. At the hospital, the staff prepares the emergency room, to which the boy is rushed. Specialized surgeons were able to reattach the boy's severed feet.

"After the surgery, while the father stayed with the boy, the mother left to phone her other child's preschool. Feeling distraught, she phones the preschool to tell them she will soon pick up her child. Heading to pick up her child, she hails a taxi at the number 9 bus stop."

OK, it's a very easy quiz: which tale stands out more for you? It's likely to be Tale 2.

Cahill and McGaugh's study[1] used extended versions of these tales, in order to investigate our current hack: the special status of emotional events in memory. It's generally the second story that is more memorable, particularly the central section—this is peculiar because other memory studies indicate that we're typically better at remember events at the beginning and at the end of a story like this. This, along with evidence coming from similar studies, suggests that we have a specialized memory response to emotional stimuli.

The central section of the story isn't more memorable because it contains an unusual emotional event (we remember unusual events better), it's more memorable because of the physical effect emotion has on you. If you did this test while on propranolol, a drug that prevents physiological arousal by blocking beta-adrenergic receptors (preventing increase in heart rate and release of adrenaline), you would find the emotional parts of the story no more memorable than the dull parts. On the flip side, if you were given yohimbine, a drug that increases arousal by stimulating the activity of the adrenaline product norepireprine and so causing a more rapid heart rate, the memory for these sections would be even greater. We don't find it emotional because it is objectively memorable, but it becomes memorable because we are allowed (in the absence of drugs like propanonol) to find it emotional.

How It Works

It's indisputably very useful for the memory system to give special status to events that set off our affective, emotional system. Fearful stimuli, disgusting food sources, kith who have angered you—all are elements worth remembering. However, a memory system totally preoccupied with emotional content would constantly disregard the worthy in favor of the frivolous, never retaining any information about currently neutral stimuli (such as food when one is not hungry) when there are more emotional stimuli present. The current best guess is that we resolve this by possessing two memory systems—a "hot" system for dealing with emotional information and a "cool" one for handling neutral content. Increasingly, the evidence suggests that this is instantiated in the brain through a primary memory system built around the hippocampus [Hack #89] for cool content, while hot content is handled in the amygdala, the limbic structure involved in various aspects of emotion processing.

There is evidence to implicate the amygdala in memory.[2] Lesions in the amygdala disrupt learning—a type of memory that has a motivational, and hence emotional, component—and imaging studies show that greater amygdala activation during the study of emotional information (but not neutral information) is associated with better memory for it. (Interestingly, the lateralization seems to be gender-determined, with different parts of the amygdala—left and right—being used by women and men, respectively.) Epinephrine (adrenaline) enhances memory performance, but only if the amygdala is intact. Finally, patients with amygdalic lesions (the amygdala is damaged) are more poorly conditioned to aversive stimuli; that is, they don't learn to cease behavior that causes them pain.

As the names imply, the hot system is impulsive and quick, producing rapid physical responses (such as a flush of shame) in comparison to the more reflective, contemplative cool system. Current models suggest that that information flows through the hot system in order to reach the cool system, and as a consequence, all input gets cooked: emotional components are amplified and accentuated, potentially at the expense of other details.

The idea that the amygdala is involved in hot, emotional memory is supported by the discovery that the memory boost associated with emotional words doesn't occur if the *stria terminalis*—this is the connective junction that links the amygdala to the rest of the brain—is no longer intact. For example, if this junction is removed, norepinephrine (which is associated with arousal) ceases to produce memory benefits. Similarly, glucocorticoid, a stress hormone, enhances learning if it is plugged into the hippocampus, unless the amygdala is damaged or chemically blocked. So it is clear the amygdala and hippocampus memory systems are not working in isolation.

The evidence that there are two systems at all comes from the differential effects of stress on the two types of memory: increasing arousal always enhances memory for emotional features, but memory for the neutral features (such as context and detail) starts to suffer under high conditions. Seeing one change (an increase of arousal) have two different effects is good evidence for multiple systems.

In Real Life

Apart from our own observations that emotionally charged events will be memorable (to the point where it is difficult to imagine how it could be otherwise), the most powerful example of the preoccupation with emotion designed into our memory systems is post-traumatic stress disorder (PTSD).[3] Individuals suffering from PTSD experience flashbacks, the intrusion of imagery and memories from or related to the traumatic events that typically produced the condition. The worse the trauma, the more likely that PTSD will result, and sufferers have consistently higher resting heart rate and blood pressure, relative to a comparable group.

It is established that PTSD patients have smaller hippocampal volumes, although it is not clear whether the traumatic stress reduces the hippocampus or whether smaller hippocampi are a risk factor for PTSD. These individuals show poorer general memory performance, and while the flashbacks themselves are full of vivid detail, they are often gappy and the patients show inability to actively recall any other details besides those that impose themselves upon them. This would fit with the two-systems theory: the flashbacks themselves have well-coded (or "hyperencoded") emotional content, but the stress precluded the recording of further detail. While the emotional content comes easily to mind, their general high level of stress, possibly coupled with suboptimal transfer from the hot to cool systems, produces poorer memory for the cold, neutral information.

End Notes

1. Reprinted and abridged from *Consciousness and Cognition*, Vol 4, No 4, Cahill, L., & McGaugh, J., "A Novel Demonstration of Enhanced Memory Associated with Emotional Arousal," pages 410–421, Copyright (1995), with permission from Elsevier.

2. A good book to get a full picture of amygdala, learning, and memory: LeDoux, J. (1996) *The Emotional Brain: The Mysterious Underpinnings of Emotional Life*. New York: Simon & Schuster.

3. The Post-Traumatic Stress Disorder Alliance (*http://www.ptsdalliance. org/home2.html*) hosts educational resources on this condition.

See Also

- "How Brain Gives Special Resonance to Emotional Memories" (*http:// www.sciencedaily.com/releases/2004/06/040610081107.htm*).

—Alex Fradera & Disa Sauter

HACK #97 Look Where I'm Looking

We are innately programmed to follow other people's eye gaze to see what they are looking at. It's so deeply ingrained that even cartoon eyes can interfere with our mental processing of direction.

Eyes are special. They're part of a two-way sense. Wherever I look, you can tell what I'm looking at. You can tell if I'm paying attention to you or not, as well as hazarding a good guess as to what I'm really thinking about. Following gaze isn't a learned behavior. As far as the brain's concerned, gaze direction is a first-class citizen of the real world, as important as location. In the case of location, the Simon Effect [Hack #56] demonstrates that we have a tendency to react to a prompt in the same direction as that stimulus. This hack shows that we interpret gaze direction in much the same way as location: a cartoon pair of eyes looking in one direction has the same effect.

In Action

A team at the University of Padua in Italy constructed an experiment to see the effect of gaze.[1] They drew a pair of cartoon eyes—just two ovals with a colored oval (the iris) within each, as shown in Figure 10-5. The irises were colored either blue or green, and the cartoon could be looking either straight ahead or to one of the sides.

People taking part in the experiment had to report the color of the irises, hitting a button on the left for blue and on the right for green. The apparent

Figure 10-5. Cartoon eyes similar to the ones used in the experiment: show this page to someone and watch what her eyes do—see if you can catch her just flicking off to the right as the cartoon eyes trigger her automatic gaze-following routine

gaze direction wasn't important at all. Despite that, it was faster to hit the button for green on the right when the eyes were looking the same way (to the right) and slower when they were looking the other way. The same held true for blue and the eyes looking left.

Thinking this might be nothing to do with the ovals looking like eyes, to investigate further, the team put together another task. Instead of ovals, the cartoon "eyes" were squares, with square "irises" in each, and looked much less like eyes (as shown in Figure 10-6). And sure enough, the significant reaction time difference (between gaze pointing in the same direction as the response key and in the opposite direction) went away.

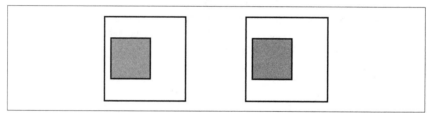

Figure 10-6. Square "eyes" similar to the ones used in the experiment: we don't follow the gaze of robot eyes

> It's possible this is why the X Windows toy "xeyes," which puts a pair of eyes on your computer desktop that follow your mouse cursor around, is so uncannily handy for avoiding losing your pointer.[2]
>
> —R.D.

How It Works

Essentially, this experiment shares a mechanism with the Simon Effect [Hack #56]. Given that the brain translates gaze direction into location, the same effect gets triggered: if attention has already been directed to the left because of the stimulus, it takes a very short time more to make a response on the right.

It makes sense that we treat gaze with such respect. If someone's looking at us, it usually means that some kind of interaction, for good or ill, is in motion. And if there are a few people looking at the same place, they've probably spotted something you should know about. Gaze is physically so tiny, but figures large in our social world. Just think how it feels to make eye contact with a stranger (sometimes good, sometimes embarrassing) or how difficult it is to have a conversation with someone looking elsewhere. If you doubt this, try repeatedly glancing over somebody's shoulder while you're talking with him, and see how long it takes him to crossly ask you what you're up to or glance over his shoulder to see what you're looking at.

> I've a suspicion that this is why arrows work so well as symbols. Given we can look at cartoons of eyes and still follow gaze, how reduced can that cartoon get and still work? OK, it doesn't work with square eyes, but the salient features of eyes are that they're long and pupils go into the corner and pick up an arrowhead shape when they're looking off to the side. Just like an arrow, in fact—which leaves me wondering whether arrows (in print, in signage, and everywhere) are very good learned symbols or whether they tap into something deeper.
>
> —M.W.

This deep gaze perception is also sometimes referred to as shared, or joint, attention. The use of two people paying attention to the same object is most obvious for infants. When infants are learning, they need to be able to make associations between objects, words, actions, and so on. If there were no way to point or direct an infant's attention, it'd be next to impossible to teach her anything. At about 12–18 months, children follow eye gaze: they can observe your eyes, tell what you're looking at, and look over *there* instead. It's this automatic mechanism of joint attention that is used in making a shared understanding of the world.[3]

> Pointing performs much the same function as gaze, indicating where to pay attention. Of course, this doesn't work for dogs, as is well-known by anyone who's tried pointing as a way to get a dog to look somewhere—only to have the animal stare at the end of the pointing finger. The only way to teach association for dogs, who don't understand such abstract symbols as pointing, is to wait until they're paying attention to whatever you want to teach them about anyway and then do whatever you were going to do. It could be argued that our real defining characteristic, as humans, is the ability to understand the symbol "that." Without it, we wouldn't be able to talk about objects that aren't present, and wouldn't be able to learn from other people's mistakes.
>
> (Some dog lovers may disagree, but then this is what makes them dog lovers, isn't it?)
>
> —M.W.

Shared attention is one thing that infants use as a springboard to develop an understanding of other minds, not just the world of objects. Children with autism—individuals with an impaired understanding of other people's intentions—don't follow gaze automatically as other children do.

In Real Life

The effortless, rapid, almost unconscious encoding of gaze direction makes it an ideal social signal, which, of course, leaves it open for abuse. Spot how many advertisements have a large face with eyes directed exactly at what they want you to read.

End Notes

1. Zorzi, M., Mapelli, D., Rusconi, E., & Umlità, C. (2003). Automatic spatial coding of perceived gaze direction is revealed by the Simon Effect. *Psychonomic Bulletin & Review, 10*(2), 423–429.

2. Lowcoders have written a Mac OS X clone of xeyes, called iEyes (*http://www.lowcoders.net*).

3. Driver, J., Davis, G., Ricciardelli, P., Kidd, P., Maxwell, E., & Baron-Cohen, S. (1999). Gaze perception triggers reflexive visuospatial orienting. *Visual Cognition, 6*(5), 509–540.

Monkey See, Monkey Do

We mimic accents, gestures, and mannerisms without even noticing, and it
seems it's the mere act of perception that triggers it.

We're born imitators, even without knowing we're doing it. I have a British
accent, but whenever I spend a couple of weeks in North America, I start to
pick up the local pronunciation. It's the same with hanging around certain
groups of friends and ending up using words common in that group without realizing I'm picking them up.

Imitation doesn't require immersion in a culture. You can start mirroring
people's movements without realizing it in moments.

In Action

I find a lot of psychology experiments a little mean, because they often
involve telling the participants the experiment is about one thing, when
actually it's about something else entirely. Tanya Chartrand and John
Bargh's experiments on what they dub the Chameleon Effect fall into this
category of keeping the participants in the dark (but are harmless enough
not to be mean).[1]

Chartrand and Bargh had volunteers take part in a dummy task of describing photographs while sitting in pairs, taking turns looking at each photo
and speaking outloud their free associations. What the volunteers didn't
know was that describing the photographs wasn't the point of the experiment and that their partner wasn't a volunteer but a confederate in league
with the experiment organizers. The confederate exhibited some subtle
behavior, either rubbing his face or shaking his foot for the 10-minute duration of the experiment.

What the experimenters were actually watching was how often a subject
would rub her own face or shake her own foot—ultimately, how much a
person could have her behavior influenced by the confederate, a person she
hadn't met before and had no requirement to be friends with. The answer:
behavior is influenced a lot.

Sitting with a face-rubbing confederate, a volunteer would rub her own face
once every 100 seconds, on average. Normally, away from exposure to face-
rubbing, she'd have about 30 seconds longer between touches.

The results are similar and more dramatic for foot shaking—a doubling of
shaking from just over once every 3 minutes to once every 80 seconds, just
while sitting for about 10 minutes with someone who is shaking his foot
every so often.

Given that this works, you've a chance to be rather mean. Next time you're in a café with friends, or at dinner, try scratching or touching your face and see what happens. Triggering a very particular response like a nose scratch may be rarer, but you can definitely get whoever you're with to do a bit of face touching.

You can be quite subtle too. In the experiments, the subjects were asked whether they'd noticed any standout behavior from the confederates: they hadn't. So it's not a matter of deliberate mimicry.

How It Works

Nonconscious imitation isn't limited to gestures. We adopt the same tone of voice and even the same sentence structure as conversational partners, and so in this way couples who have been married for a long time really do come to resemble each other.[2]

> There's a great example of how—nonconsciously—we mimic facial expressions, found when O'Toole and Dubin[3] watched mothers feeding their children. The mother would usually open her mouth, ostensibly as a signal for the kid to open his mouth too. But it turned out that, 80% of the time, the mother opened her mouth *after* the child did so. The child was opening his mouth just because food was on the way; the mother was mimicking without knowing it, just following her child's lead.

So why imitate? That's still an open question. It may simply be part of the mechanism we use to perceive other people. Anything we perceive has to have some kind of representation in the brain—otherwise it wouldn't be a perception—and so there are representations of straight edges, faces, colors, and so on. There are also single neurons that activate when a very specific action takes place: grasping and pushing with your hand activate two different neurons. What's remarkable is that these same neurons activate when you simply *see* somebody else doing the same movement, even if you're not doing it yourself.[4]

Mirror neurons, found in the frontal cortex, are therefore not just what the brain is doing to tell your hand to grasp or push, they're actually the internal representation of that movement, whether you're perceiving it in yourself or in somebody else. They're the very idea of "grasp," divorced from implementation detail.

Now, we know that if you hear a word, the representation of it in your brain causes associated words to be primed [Hack #81]. Hearing the word "water" will mean you're more likely to shout out "river" (which has therefore been primed) than "money" when somebody asks you to free-associate from the word "bank." You don't even need to have had conscious awareness of the word that has primed you [Hack #82]—all that matters is the representation of the word being constructed in your brain somehow, not that it makes it through the filter of attention.

> The same may be true for perceiving gestures and movements of other people. Even though you're not concentrating on their movements, other people do have some kind of representation in your brain, and the way you understand them is in terms of your own mirror neurons. In turn, the mirror neuron for "scratch" is activated and primes that activity next time your hand is idle. Seeing someone scratch, in this model, would make it more probable for you to scratch yourself.
>
> I find that even reading about it has the same effect. Are you a little itchy right now?
>
> —M.W.

In Real Life

Whatever the mechanism, the result of two people mirroring each other is clear: mirroring is part of building rapport. If you're a fan of people watching, you can often tell how well two people are getting along by watching very small movements and how shared they are—do the pair you're watching lean back at the same time or synchronize laughing? Try looking round a table and see whether good friends mirror each other more than randomly chosen pairs. It can stand out a lot, when you're looking for it.

> One big question is why mirroring is such a strong part of rapport. I think the question of why we mirror is a simple answer of learning from the society we're born in. We don't have all the knowledge we need for the world hardwired in our brains from birth; we have to acquire it from those around us, and mirroring is just the tiniest manifestation of that picking up of behavior.
>
> —T.S.

End Notes

1. Chartrand, T. L., & Bargh, J. A. (1999). The chameleon effect: The perception-behavior link and social interaction. *Journal of Personality and Social Psychology, 76*(6), 893–910. This, and other papers by Tanya

Chartrand, can be found on the publications page of her web site: *http://faculty.fuqua.duke.edu/~tlc10/bio/pdf_articles/article_index.htm.*

2. Dijksterhuis, A., & Bargh, J. A. (2001). The perception-behavior expressway: Automatic effects of social perception on social behavior. In M. P. Zanna (ed.). *Advances in Experimental Social Psychology*, 33, 1–40. New York: Academic Press. (Highly recommended as a broad and comprehensive review.)

3. O'Toole, R., & Dubin, R. (1968). Baby feeding and body swap: An experiment in George Herberts Mead's "Taking the role of the other." *Journal of Personality and Social Psychology*, 10, 59-65. Cited in Dijksterhuis & Bargh (2001).[2]

4. V. S. Ramachandran, "Mirror Neurons and Imitation Learning as the Driving Force Behind 'the Great Leap Forward' in Human Evolution" (*http://www.edge.org/3rd_culture/ramachandran/ramachandran_p1.html*).

HACK #99 Spread a Bad Mood Around

Have you ever found yourself in a confrontational mood for no reason? It could come down to what you've been reading.

We know our moods are affected by the world around us. It's easy to come home from a day at work when everything's gone wrong and stay grumpy for the rest of the evening. Then there are days when your mood is good or bad for no apparent reason at all. I've had miserable-mood days because I've finished a really great, but sad, novel in the morning and not even connected my mood with the book until that night. Thinking about mood like this, the regular way, makes us consider moods as long-timescale phenomena that we just have to live with, like the weather. Like the weather, moods in this frame seem impenetrable to understanding. Instead, it's good to take a different approach: how do moods begin? What's the smallest thing we can do that has an effect on our mood?

That's what this hack is about, showing that the words we encounter can make us ruder people in a matter of minutes—and not words that are meant to elicit a strong emotional response or ones that are taken to heart, but ones in the context of an innocuous word puzzle.

In Action

Puzzles are an excellent way to get people to keep words in mind for a substantial time. One such puzzle is the scrambled sentence test. Given a scrambled sentence of five words, such as "he it hides finds instantly," you have to make as many four-word sentences as you can, as fast as you can.

John Bargh, Mark Chen, and Lara Burrows used this test style[1] and incorporated 15 words to do with impolite behavior: "aggressively," "intrude," "brazen," and so on. They also had polite and neutral versions of the test. The subjects were unaware there were different forms of the test at this time and also unaware of the real point of the experiment.

Each subject spent about 5 minutes doing the puzzle, but that (of course) wasn't the point of the experiment. The critical point came when a subject stepped out of the room to say he'd finished, only to see the person running the experiment engaged in conversation. The question was: would he interrupt? Only just over 15% of those who'd been puzzling over polite words interrupted within 10 minutes, while of those who'd been using words like "obnoxious," more than 60%—*four times as many*—interrupted in that same 10-minute period.

Participants who did interrupt also did so faster if they'd been using the words about impoliteness: they took an average of $5\frac{1}{2}$ minutes to intrude versus more than 9 minutes for everyone else, even when you discounted the 85% of the politely primed group who didn't interrupt at all.

You can try a more subjective version of this procedure by using a technique called the Velten Procedure[2] to automatically induce moods in groups of people, then see if you can spot the difference. This technique uses, as developed by Velten in the 1960s, sheets of paper full of either positive or negative statements. So make a bunch of copies of two sets of statements (there are some samples online at *http://www.dur.ac.uk/m.j.eacott/cogmem3.txt*). The positive page should say things like "I am a worthwhile person," "I feel good about myself," and "People like me." The negative one should have phrases like "Nothing I do ever turns out right," "People feel contempt for me," and "I am a bad person."

Choose a sheet and read it to yourself for 5 minutes. By the time you finish, you really will feel happier or glummer. It's amazing how strong the effect is.

The effect is stronger still with a roomful of people. So, find such a room, and leave everybody with a positive Velten and tell them to read it to themselves for 5 minutes. When you come back, everyone should be jubilant. But try leaving another group the negative Velten. The atmosphere will be distinctly cold on your return. It goes to show the importance of social feedback in creating and amplifying mood.

> In my final year of college, I made myself a "study Velten" to take to the library: "I like revising," "My concentration is in top form today," "Nothing will distract me from work today."
>
> —T.S.

How It Works

The experiment goes to show that only 5 minutes of manipulating words—just words, not personal commentary or difficult situations—has a noticeable effect on behavior. It's a variety of concept priming [Hack #81], in which reading words associated with a particular concept subtly brings that concept to mind, from where it enters your thoughts at some point in the future.

What's true for words bringing word concepts to mind is also true for face rubbing or foot jiggling [Hack #98]. Merely perceiving someone else performing the action activates the concept of that action in your brain, and it becomes more likely.

Bargh et al., with the scrambled sentence test influencing politeness, and the Velten Procedure, both show that there's a crossover between words and behavior. There's a commonality between how the meaning of impoliteness, written down, is represented in the brain, and the representation of the *behavior* of being impolite. Precisely how this works, we don't know, only that the effect can be observed.

Something to be aware of is that negative emotions are contagious (we already know that emotions are picked up just from observation [Hack #95]), so a whole bad-tempered exchange can be triggered subliminally by something quite irrelevant.

Chen and Bargh[3] did another experiment involving pairs of people playing a guessing game together. One of the pair had been subliminally shown pictures that would put her in a hostile mood.

In carefully controlled circumstances, tapes of the guessing game interaction were listened to, and the participants' behavior rated. Three things were discovered: people who had been subliminally activated as hostile (using pictures they couldn't consciously see) were indeed judged to be more hostile. The partners in the guessing game, encountering this hostility, themselves became more hostile. And finally, both participants judged the other as more hostile than they would have done if the subliminal exposure had not taken place.

All of this happens more or less automatically. Our moods are governed by what we encounter; if we're not looking out for it, we don't even get a say on whether to accept the influence or not.

In Real Life

Let's say you have a meeting scheduled at which you know you're going to have to put your foot down. There's no reason you shouldn't have a Make Me Angry application to subliminally flash angry faces on your monitor for 5 minutes beforehand, if you really want to step into that encounter in a bad mood. Is this any different from talking yourself up before a big meeting or game?

One specific detail of Chen and Bargh's experiment on contagious hostility should give us serious pause. To invoke the hostile mood, the experimenters used faces that activated a racial stereotype in the participants. Given we walk slower having considered the stereotype of the elderly [Hack #100], the fact that a stereotype can affect us deeply isn't a surprise, but that it's a racial stereotype is saddening. Chen and Bargh performed this experiment to show that this kind of racial stereotyping is a self-fulfilling prophecy. If you anticipate someone is going to be hostile, you become so yourself, and you infect the other person with that mood. Your stereotype is thus reinforced, without having any necessary basis in truth to begin with. It's alarmingly easy to push people into roles without realizing it and to find our own prejudices confirmed.

End Notes

1. Bargh, J. A., Chen, M., & Burrows, L. (1996). Automaticity of social behavior: Direct effects of trait construct and stereotype activation on action. *Journal of Personality and Social Psychology, 71*(2), 230–244.

2. Velten, E. (1968). A laboratory task for induction of mood states. *Behavior Research and Therapy, 6*, 473–482.

3. Chen, M., & Bargh, J. A. (1997). Nonconscious behavioral confirmation processes: The self-fulfilling consequences of automatic stereotype activation. *Journal of Experimental Social Psychology, 33*, 541–560.

You Are What You Think

100

Thinking about how certain stereotypes behave can make you walk slower or get a higher score in a general knowledge quiz.

The concept of priming [Hack #93] runs all the way through explanations of how perception influences behavior. Subliminal perception of photographs can prime you to prefer those photos in the future [Hack #82], and simply spending time with someone who is, say, rubbing his face can infect you with his mannerism [Hack #98]. It's not necessary to consciously perceive the photographs or the gestures for them to automatically alter our behavior.

Nowhere is this truer than in *exemplar activation*: being exposed to ideas of stereotypes of people (the exemplars), not even the people themselves, will prime the characteristic traits of those people, and you'll begin to act in that way. It's very odd, and very cool.

In Action

Here's what John Bargh, Mark Chen, and Lara Burrows did[1]: they gave 30 psychology undergraduates word puzzles to do (undergraduates are the raw material for most psychology studies). In half of the experiments, the puzzles included words associated with the elderly, like "careful," "wise," "ancient," and "retired." In the other half, all the puzzle words were neutral and not deliberately associated with any single concept. Immediately after individual students had completed the puzzle, they were free to go.

Bargh and team timed, using a hidden stopwatch, how long it took each undergraduate to walk down the corridor to the elevator. Students who had been given the puzzle featuring elderly related words took, on average, a whole second longer to make the walk—an increase from 7.3 to 8.3 seconds. They had picked up one of the perceived traits of the elderly: slower walking speed.

How It Works

The specifics of how exemplar activation works is still an open question, but the basic mechanism is the same as how we pick up mannerisms [Hack #98]. It's a feature of the brain that perceiving something requires activating some kind of physical representation of the thing being perceived: simply making that representation primes that behavior, making us more likely to do what we see. Exemplar activation takes this a little further than we're used to, because it's the reading of words—in an apparently unrelated task to walking along the corridor—that primes the concept of "the elderly," which then goes on to influence behavior. But the principle is the same.

Slow walking is only the half the story, though. Ap Dijskerhuis and Ad van Knippenberg[2] performed similar experiments. Instead of influencing their subjects with an "elderly" stereotype, they set up an experiment in which participants had to spend 5 minutes describing either professors or secretaries. (The subjects, again, were undergraduates.)

This time the experiment measured general knowledge, so the next stage of the experiment had the subjects answering Trivial Pursuit questions. They weren't aware the two stages were connected.

What happened is almost unbelievable: subjects who had previously described professors—known for their perceived intelligence—attained, on average, 60% correct answers, against 46% for the people who had to describe secretaries.

It could be that people who have been considering the professor stereotype are more likely to trust their own judgment; the particular attribute of this stereotype that is causing the response isn't really known. The people exposed to the secretary stereotype didn't do any worse than they should have done: compared to people who hadn't been primed at all, they got about the same number of questions correct and worked their way through the questionnaire in only 6 minutes (compared to an 8-minute average). So in this case it turns out that both stereotypes have good qualities going for them. Secretaries are efficient. But it isn't always the case that stereotypes are positive.

People who identify with groups commonly stereotyped to be poor at math tend to do worse at math tests when their membership in that group is made relevant immediately before the test, as with a checkbox at the top of the test that asks them to indicate their ethnic identity or gender.[3]

Fortunately, it is possible to counteract this kind of exemplar activation. If you were in this situation, the activation can be overridden by reasserting yourself against the stereotype. Women who have been explicitly told that the math test they are about to do shows no gender bias *don't* underperform—it's the subtle, nonconscious stereotyping that has a real effect (like having to tick a box at the top of the page), causing people who identify with a commonly stereotyped group to take on the stereotype assumption, even if incorrect. Once thinking about the stereotype and the effects it might have is made conscious, the bias disappears.

These exemplar activation experiments are as challenging as any you'll find in psychology. Word puzzles about the elderly slow your walking speed (and actually your reaction time too); just focusing on the stereotype of a professor for 5 minutes makes you better at general knowledge. But it also reinforces the stereotype: people who already hold that identity are pushed into their pigeonholes. Our need to conform runs deep, even when it's against our best interests. But in those cases, concentrating on your individuality is all you need to push back.

End Notes

1. Bargh J. A., Chen, M., & Burrows, L. (1996). Automaticity of social behavior: Direct effects of trait construct and stereotype activation on action. *Journal of Personality and Social Psychology, 71*(2), 230–244.

2. Dijksterhuis, A., & van Knippenberg, A. (1998). The relation between perception and behavior, or how to win a game of trivial pursuit. *Journal of Personality and Social Psychology, 74*(4), 865–877.

3. Dijksterhuis, A., & Bargh, J. A. (2001). The perception-behavior expressway: Automatic effects of social perception on social behavior. In M. P. Zanna (ed.), *Advances in Experimental Social Psychology*, 33, 1–40. New York: Academic Press.

Index

We'd like to hear your suggestions for improving our indexes. Send email to *index@oreilly.com*.

blindness
  change, 51, 134–136
  daily, 32
  inattention, 137–139, 141
  TMS and, 8
blinking, startle response and, 106, 107
blood
  brain and, 10
  cognitive function and, 22–24
  magnetic features of, 7
  measuring flow of, 22
  retina and, 49
body schema, 207–210, 257
BOLD (blood oxygen level dependent)
    fMRI, 7
Bornstein, Robert, 277
brain
  as association machine, 163
  common labels, 15
  how it works, 2–4
  split-brain patients, 226
  unused potential, 9–12
  (see also neuropsychology)
brain cells (see neurons)
brain imaging research
  action-relevant objects and, 220
  basic emotions and, 322
  landmarks and, 304
  movement and location, 80
  on hemispheres, 228
  perceiving biological motion
      and, 260
  tempero-parietal junction and, 307
  10% myth and, 10
brainstem
  defined, 13
  locating sounds and, 151
  sleep and, 310
branding techniques, 164
brightness
  defined, 74
  inhibition of return and, 127
  luminancy differences, 72–76
  Pulfrich Effect and, 76–79
  (see also light)
Broca, Paul, 10
Broca's area, 10, 224
broken escalator
      phenomenon, 200–203
Brown, Andrew, 9–12, 317–320

Bunday, Karen, 221–225
Burrows, Lara, 339, 340, 342

C

caffeine habit, 311–315
Calisham, Tara, 3
candela, 74
carotid pulse, 22, 24
Carruthers, Peter, 195, 197
Cartesian theater, 306
categorical perception, 192
categorization, 284, 319
cause and effect, 251, 265–269
central nervous system
  dura mater, 34
  overview, 13–16
  tour of, 2
cerebellum
  action-relevant objects and, 220
  defined, 13
  as old brain, 14
  self-generated touch and, 212
cerebral blood flow, 22–24
cerebral cortex, 14, 17, 18
cerebral lobes, 17
      (see also frontal lobe; occipital lobe;
          parietal lobe; temporal lobe)
cerebrum
  defined, 14
  inferior temporal lobe and, 36
  overview, 16–19
  striate and, 35
Chabris, Christopher, 137
Chameleon Effect, 335
change
  blindness to, 51, 134–136
  resisting, 246–250
channel decorrelation, 84
Chartrand, Tanya, 335
cheaters, detecting, 239–242
checker shadow illusion, 72–76
Chen, Mark, 339, 340, 342
Cheshire Cat experiment, 49
Choudhury, Suparna, 210–215
classical conditioning, 313
classification, 285, 319
closure grouping principle, 253
cochlea, 149, 155
cocking head, 153

enzymes, neurotransmitters and, 21
epilepsy
    electrical activity and, 5
    out-of-body experience and, 307
    split-brain patients and, 226
epinephrine (adrenaline), 329
episodic memory, 304
Erdos number, 238
Erdos, Paul, 236, 238, 312
escalators, broken, 200–203
ESP, 159
estimating
    low-frequency events and, 235
    numbers, 232–234
Evans, Dylan, 242–245
events
    demarcating boundaries of, 284
    emotional stimuli, 328
    estimating low-frequency, 235
    false memory of, 290
    memory of, 330
    perception of, 285
evolutionary psychology, 241, 242
evolutionary theory, 10
exclusivity, 270, 271
executive system, 23
exemplar activation, 342–344
experimental psychology (see cognitive
        psychology)
extelligence, 155
eyes
    hearing with, 190–192
    hemispheres and, 227
    moving, 43
    tracking movement of, 43
    variant eye chart, 38, 40
Eyetrack III project, 43

F

faces
    analyzing parts of, 230
    fixation and, 44, 46
    hypnagogic state and, 308
    mimicry and, 336
    noticing, 129
    object recognition and, 37
    priming, 278

    processing, 317–320
    recognizing, 126, 295, 296
    shadows and, 60
    tweaking muscles, 325–327
fake familiarity, 279–282, 315
false memories, 209, 286, 287–292
familiarity
    fake, 279–282, 315
    false memory and, 287
    priming and, 278
fear, 322
feedback, motor control and, 301, 326
feedforward, motor control and, 301
filter
    attention as, 137–139
    marginal sounds and, 158
firing up, 20, 81
fixation
    defined, 43
    gap effect and, 55–56
    looking at a face, 44, 46
    peripheral vision and, 44
    reading example, 45
fixational movements, 96, 99
flashbacks, PSTD and, 330
flash-lag effect, 90–93
FlashWare, 130
flickering, 148
flinching, 33, 106–107
fluent processing (fluency), 280–282,
        289
fMRI (functional magnetic resonance
        imaging)
    basic emotions and, 322
    hypnagogic state and, 309
    overview, 7, 8
    oxygenated blood and, 22
    purpose of, 2
    visual feedback and, 210
focus
    depth cues and, 67
    on details, 112–115
    grabbing attention, 123, 124
    negative priming and, 142
    random drift in, 96
    voluntary, 111
force prediction, 214
forebrain, 13

hippocampus
    emotional system and, 329
    glucocorticoid and, 330
    limbic system and, 14
    memory storage and, 304
    PSTD and, 330
    purpose of, 305
    temporal lobe and, 17
hiragana, 293
Hon, Adrian, 239–242
horizon of simultaneity, 187
hostility, contagious, 340
"hot" system, 327–331
hydrocephalus, 11
hypercolumns, 36
hypnagogic state, 308–311
hypnopompic state, 310
hypothalamus, 14, 310

I

ideomotor effect, 270
imagination
    activating, 274
    change blindness and, 134–136
    detecting sounds and, 158
    hypnagogic state and, 308
    mental space, 101–106
    out-of-body experiences, 306–308
    perceived events, 285
    PSTD and, 330
    strength training and, 298–302
imitation (see mimicry)
inattention blindness, 137–139, 141
inductive reasoning, 242
inferior temporal cortex, 36, 215
inhibition of return, 126–129, 141
insula, 322, 323
integration
    attention across locations, 176–178
    color identification, 179–182
    combining modalities, 186–188
    cortex and, 19
    feeling more, 188–190
    location responses, 182–186
    McGurk Effect, 190–192
    sound and vision, 173–176
    talking to self and, 195–199
    thrown voices, 193–195
intensity, object, 67–70

interaural level difference, 150
interaural time difference, 150–153
interleaved learning, 292–298
intuition, 226

J

James, William, 111
Jarrett, Christian, 52–54, 200–203, 215–218
Jeffress Model, 151
joint attention, 333, 334
Jones, Myles, 6, 8, 9

K

Kare, Susan, 60
Katnelson, Alla, 197
Kitaoka, Akiyoshi, 95, 99, 100
Kitazawa, Shigeru, 205
Klee, Paul, 311
Kleffner, D. A., 57, 60
Klein, Raymond, 128
known size, 70–72
Köhler, Wolfgang, 163

L

landmarks, 304, 305
language
    brain processing, 160
    cortex and, 37
    ease of relearning, 297
    frontal lobe and, 17
    hemispheres and, 228
    as mental process, 2
    overview, 162–165
    phonemes and, 161
    phrases and, 165
    as recombinant, 166
    right hemisphere and, 228
    simultaneous processing and, 170
    talking to self and, 195–199
    temporal lobe and, 17
    thought and, 195
    Wada test and, 223
lateral geniculate nucleus (LGN), 34
lateral occipital complex (LOC), 36
lateral thinking, 159
lateralisation, 226–230
launching paradigm, 267

music, 228, 281
myelin/myelination, 17, 147

N

names, recalling, 296
naming consultants, 164
negative priming, 121, 127, 139–142
nerve cells (see neurons)
nerves
    corpus callosum and, 17
    optic, 34
    photoreceptors and, 46
    signals and, 13
    spinal cord and, 13
neural noise, 108–110
neuroimaging
    mental rotation and, 104
    on analyzing faces, 230
    purpose of, 2
    tickling machine and, 212
neurons
    actions and, 336
    adaptation and, 83, 85
    atrophy of, 11
    auditory timing and, 149
    binary nature of, 20
    coincidence-detector, 151
    decision-making and, 2
    defined, 19–22
    deoxygenated blood and, 7
    EEG and, 5
    electrical impulses and, 8, 13, 19,
        310
    glial cells and, 11
    as gray matter, 17
    hypercolumns and, 36
    information encoding and, 20
    looming objects and, 107
    memory and, 295, 296
    mirror, 336, 337
    motion aftereffect and, 257
    motion and, 79
    neurotransmitters and, 312
    PET and, 6
    polysensory, 189
    prevalence of, 22
    priming and, 278
    Pulfrich Effect and, 78
    representational maps and, 30

stimuli and, 84
synchronization of firing, 257
timing information and, 187
visual cortex and, 169
neuropsychology
    overview, 9–12
    purpose of, 1, 2
    testing executive system, 23
neuroscience
    binding problem, 257
    defined, xxii
    fMRI and, 7
    habituation experiment, 83
    on hemispheres, 228
    signaling emotions and, 320
neurotransmitters
    caffeine and, 311
    defined, 19
    electrical impulses and, 20
    enzymes and, 21
Nicholls, Neville, 237
noise
    localizing, 153
    marginal sounds and, 158
    neural, 108–110
    variability in people and, 3
norepinephrine, 330
noticing, act of, 129
noun phrases, 165, 167
nuclei, 304
nucleus accumbens, 312
numbers, estimating, 232–234

O

object files, 122
objects
    agency in, 262
    animacy of, 262–265
    attention and, 113
    common fate, 255
    endowment effect, 249
    grouping, 252–254, 258–262
    known size and, 70–72
    looming, 107
    mental imagery of, 101–106
    motion and, 62–66
    multiple object tracking, 118–123
    occlusion-based cues and, 67
    perspective-based cues and, 66

S

saccades
  defined, 43
  gaps in vision and, 50–52, 55
  tutorial on, 45
  (see also movement)
saccadic suppression, 51, 54
sadness, 322
sampling, visual process and, 43
Sauter, Disa, 320–331
Schoemaker, Paul, 233
Scholl, Brian, 267
search engines, 3, 297
seeing (see vision)
Sejnowski, Terrence, 91
self-causation, objects and, 262–265
self-perception theory, 4
sensation
  grouping as objects, 251
  keeping up-to-date, 203–207
  perception and, 265
  phantom limb and, 209
  self-generated, 210–215
  vision and, 188–190
sensory cortex, 27, 28, 30
sensory homunculus, 18, 27–31
sensory systems
  adaptation of, 83
  binding problem and, 257
  channel decorrelation, 84
  combining modalities, 186–188
  conflicting feedback, 207, 209
  detection and, 173–176
  feedback delays, 200–203
  (see also specific senses)
sentences
  defined, 160
  grammar and, 167
  left hemisphere and, 228
  memory buffer overrun and, 165
  mimicry of, 336
  parsing into phrases, 167
  rearranged letters and, 170
  treelike structure of, 167
Serendip web site, 47
shading, 57–61
shadowing, 177, 197
shadows
  checker shadow illusion, 72–76
    motion and, 62–66

Pulfrich Effect and, 78
  rotating snakes illusion, 95–101
  3D shapes and, 57–62
Sham, Ladan, 174
Shannon, Bob, 160
shape(s)
  continuation and, 253
  from shading, 57–61
  negative priming for, 141
  object animacy and, 264
shared attention, 333, 334
Shepard, Robert, 103
signals
  action potential and, 20
  alpha wave, 309
  balancing and, 157
  EEG and, 5
  of emotion, 320–324
  hearing and, 149
  LGN pathways, 35
  multisensory integration and, 187
  myelin and, 17
  neural noise, 108–110
  neurons and, 8, 13, 19, 310
  processing, 124
  retina and, 34
  saccadic suppression and, 51
  strength training and, 300
  up-to-date sensations and, 203
similarity grouping principle, 253
Simon Effect, 182–186, 331–334
Simon, J. Richard, 182
Simonotto, Enrico, 108, 109
Simons, Daniel, 136, 137, 138
simultaneity, horizon of, 187
sine-wave speech (SWS), 162
size gradient, 70–72
skin, sensation and, 203–207
sleep
  electrical activity and, 5
  function of, 298
  hypnagogic state and, 308–311
smell, forebrain and, 14
software, speech recognition, 161
somatosensory cortex
  mapping, 28
  tickling and, 212
  touch sensations and, 27, 189
somatotopic map, 30

V

V1 (visual cortex), 35
V2 (visual cortex), 36
V3 (visual cortex), 36
van Knippenberg, Ad, 343
velocity
    feedforward and, 301
    object animacy and, 264
    Pulfrich Effect and, 76–79
    vestibular system and, 157
Velten Procedure, 339, 340
ventral stream, 36
ventriloquism, 173, 174
verb phrases, 165, 167
verbal fluency, 23
veridical memory system, 291
vertigo, 157
vestibular system, 156, 157
vestibular-ocular reflex, 96, 301
vibration
    crossed hands and, 204
    fundamental of sound wave and, 154
    sound and, 150, 154, 186
video games, 117, 143–146
vision
    body schema and, 207–210
    constraints in, 32
    dominance of, 174
    feeling more and, 188–190
    gaps in, 50–52, 55–56, 134
    hearing with eyes, 190–192
    hemispheres and, 17, 227
    location and, 149
    location information and, 173–176
    neuron atrophy and, 11
    as postdictive, 92
    processing, 171
    proprioceptive information and, 204
    thrown voices and, 193–195
    touch and, 187, 205
    visual processing, 1
    (see also peripheral vision; visual
        processing; visual system)
visual cortex
    hemispheres and, 226
    motion and depth, 79
    movement and, 93
    neuron speed in, 169
    occipital lobe and, 17

optic chiasm and, 34
optic lobe and, 124
parvocellular pathway, 93
processing and, 171
retina and, 18
signals and, 124
touch and, 187
visual processing and, 35, 36
visual processing
    dizziness and, 157
    dual-stream theory of, 217
    gestalt principles and, 254
    grabbing attention and, 123–126
    object tracking, 116
    overview, 32–42
    right hemisphere and, 228
    seeing people, 258–262
    shadows and, 57
    sound and, 147
    tricking the mind, 215–218
    (see also vision; visual system)
visual selective attention, 113
visual short-term memory (VSTM), 138
visual system
    causal relationships and, 266, 267
    illusionary depth and, 76
    inferring motion, 62
    overview, 33–36
    saccadic suppression and, 51
    subliminal perception and, 278
visuomotor feedback loop, 299
voluntary behavior, 123–126
voluntary focus, 111
vos Savant, Marilyn, 235
VSTM (visual short-term memory), 138

W

Wada test, 223
Waits, Tom, 303
weather forecasts, 237
Wegner, Daniel, 270, 271
Wernicke, Carl, 10
Wernicke's area, 10
wheels, movement of, 88
white matter, 17
withdrawal reflex, 13
Wodtke, Christina, 305

women
    directions and, 305
    exemplar activation and, 343
    expressiveness of, 326
    strokes and, 160
words
    behavior and, 340, 342
    critical lure, 288
    fluency and, 280
    forgetting, 290
    left hemisphere and, 228
    meaning and, 163
    memory of, 284
    method of loci and, 303
    moods and, 338, 340
    morphemes and, 160
    onomatopoeic, 164
    phrases and, 165
    priming and, 336
    recalling names and, 296
    stria terminalis and, 330
writing, 293

Y

Yarrow, Keilan, 53
yohimbine, 329
Yue, Guang, 299

Z

zygomatic muscles, 325

Colophon

Our look is the result of reader comments, our own experimentation, and feedback from distribution channels. Distinctive covers complement our distinctive approach to technical topics, breathing personality and life into potentially dry subjects.

The tool on the cover of *Mind Hacks* is an incandescent light bulb. While many assume that Thomas Alva Edison invented the light bulb in 1879, Edison's actual achievement was to advance the design of the light bulb from a patent he purchased in 1875 from Canadian inventors Henry Woodward and Matthew Evans. Edison's improvement was to place a carbon filament in a vacuum bulb, which then burned for 40 hours. An English chemist, Humphrey Davy, invented the first electric light—an arc lamp—by connecting two wires to a battery and attaching a strip of charcoal in the middle of the circuit. Other inventors continued to make various incremental improvements in such areas as the filaments and the process for creating a vacuum in the bulb, but in 1879, Edison developed a triple threat: a carbon filament, lower voltage, and an improved vacuum in the bulb.

In 1882, Pearl Street Station, in New York City, was the first central electricity-generating station constructed to support the light bulb invention. Although the alternating-current method of generating electricity proposed by Nikola Tesla proved to be the superior technical solution, Edison was engaged in a battle for control of America's electric infrastructure. Edison declared that his direct current system was safe and that alternating current was a deadly menace, which he publicly demonstrated for years by using alternating current to electrocute dogs and cats.

But in 1893, when alternating current was used at the Chicago World's Fair to light 100,000 incandescent lightbulbs, the nearly 27 million people who attended the Columbian Exposition saw the safe and impressive demonstration of that technology. The event signaled the demise of direct current systems in the United States.

Sarah Sherman was the production editor and proofreader for *Mind Hacks*, and Norma Emory was the copyeditor. Meghan Lydon provided production assistance. Mary Anne Weeks Mayo and Emily Quill provided quality control. Lucie Haskins wrote the index.

Hanna Dyer designed the cover of this book, based on a series design by Edie Freedman. The cover image is an original photograph. Clay Fernald produced the cover layout with QuarkXPress 4.1 using Adobe's Helvetica Neue and ITC Garamond fonts.

David Futato designed the interior layout. This book was converted by Julie Hawks to FrameMaker 5.5.6 with a format conversion tool created by Erik Ray, Jason McIntosh, Neil Walls, and Mike Sierra that uses Perl and XML technologies. The text font is Linotype Birka; the heading font is Adobe Helvetica Neue Condensed; and the code font is LucasFont's TheSans Mono Condensed. The illustrations that appear in the book were produced by Robert Romano and Jessamyn Read using Macromedia FreeHand MX and Adobe Photoshop CS. This colophon was written by Reg Aubry.

Better than e-books

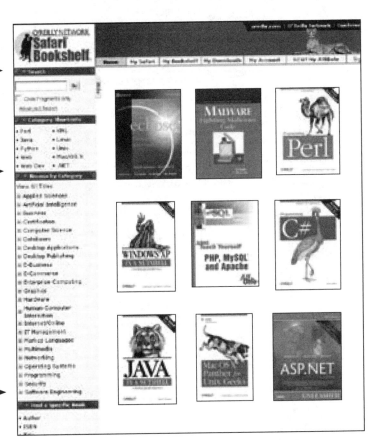

Search

inside electronic versions
of thousands of books

Browse

books by category.
With Safari researching
any topic is a snap

Find

answers in an instant

Read books from cover
to cover. Or, simply click
to the page you need.

**Search Safari! The premier electronic reference
library for programmers and IT professionals**

O'REILLY NETWORK
Safari Bookshelf

Addison Wesley · Sun microsystems · ALPHA · Java · Microsoft Press · Peachpit Press · O'REILLY · que · New Riders · Cisco Press · macromedia PRESS · PRENTICE HALL PTR · Adobe Press · SAMS

Related Titles Available from O'Reilly

Hacks

Amazon Hacks

BSD Hacks

Digital Photography Hacks

eBay Hacks

Excel hacks

Flash Hacks

Gaming Hacks

Google Hacks

Harware Hacking Projects for Geeks

Home Theater Hacks

iPod & iTunes Hacks

Knoppix Hacks

Linux Desktop Hacks

Linux Server Hacks

Mac OS X Hacks

Mac OS X Panther Hacks

Network Security Hacks

PayPal Hacks

PDF Hacks

PC Hacks

Smart Home Hacks

Spidering Hacks

TiVo Hacks

Windows Server Hacks

Windows XP Hacks

Wireless Hacks

Word Hacks

O'REILLY®

Our books are available at most retail and online bookstores.
To order direct: 1-800-998-9938 • *order@oreilly.com* • *www.oreilly.com*
Online editions of most O'Reilly titles are available by subscription at *safari.oreilly.com*

Keep in touch with O'Reilly

1. Download examples from our books

To find example files for a book, go to:
www.oreilly.com/catalog
select the book, and follow the "Examples" link.

2. Register your O'Reilly books

Register your book at *register.oreilly.com*

Why register your books? Once you've registered your O'Reilly books you can:

- Win O'Reilly books, T-shirts or discount coupons in our monthly drawing.
- Get special offers available only to registered O'Reilly customers.
- Get catalogs announcing new books (US and UK only).
- Get email notification of new editions of the O'Reilly books you own.

3. Join our email lists

Sign up to get topic-specific email announcements of new books and conferences, special offers, and O'Reilly Network technology newsletters at:

elists.oreilly.com

It's easy to customize your free elists subscription so you'll get exactly the O'Reilly news you want.

4. Get the latest news, tips, and tools

http://www.oreilly.com

- "Top 100 Sites on the Web"—PC Magazine
- CIO Magazine's Web Business 50 Awards

Our web site contains a library of comprehensive product information (including book excerpts and tables of contents), downloadable software, background articles, interviews with technology leaders, links to relevant sites, book cover art, and more.

5. Work for O'Reilly

Check out our web site for current employment opportunities:

jobs.oreilly.com

6. Contact us

O'Reilly & Associates
1005 Gravenstein Hwy North
Sebastopol, CA 95472 USA

TEL: 707-827-7000 or 800-998-9938
(6am to 5pm PST)

FAX: 707-829-0104

order@oreilly.com
For answers to problems regarding your order or our products.
To place a book order online, visit:
www.oreilly.com/order_new

catalog@oreilly.com
To request a copy of our latest catalog.

booktech@oreilly.com
For book content technical questions or corrections.

corporate@oreilly.com
For educational, library, government, and corporate sales.

proposals@oreilly.com
To submit new book proposals to our editors and product managers.

international@oreilly.com
For information about our international distributors or translation queries. For a list of our distributors outside of North America check out:
international.oreilly.com/distributors.html

adoption@oreilly.com
For information about academic use of O'Reilly books, visit:
academic.oreilly.com

O'REILLY®

Our books are available at most retail and online bookstores.
To order direct: 1-800-998-9938 • *order@oreilly.com* • *www.oreilly.com*
Online editions of most O'Reilly titles are available by subscription at *safari.oreilly.com*